STREET
WITHOUT JOY

Praise for *Street Without Joy*

"Mr. Fall's book is a dramatic treatment of a historic event.
It is recommended reading."
—*The New York Times Book Review*

"A poignant, angry, articulate book."
—*Newsweek*

"Military history at its best."
—*Chicago Sunday Tribune*
Magazine of Books

"Definitive military history of the Indochina conflict . . ."
—*The New Republic*

STREET WITHOUT JOY

The French Debacle in Indochina

Bernard B. Fall

Introduction by George C. Herring

STACKPOLE
BOOKS

Published in paperback in 2005 by
STACKPOLE BOOKS
5067 Ritter Road
Mechanicsburg, PA 17055

Printed in the United States of America

10 9 8 7 6 5 4 3 2 1

Originally published in 1961 by The Stackpole Company

Art by Dorothy Fall

Maps by Bernard B. Fall

ISBN 0-8117-3236-3 (paperback)
ISBN 978-0-8117-3236-9

The Library of Congress has cataloged the hardcover edition as follows:

Fall, Bernard B., 1926–1967.
    Street without joy / Bernard B. Fall ; introduction by George C. Herring.
       p.   cm.
    Originally published: Harrisburg, PA : Stackpole Co., 1961.
    ISBN 0-8117-1700-3
    1. Indochinese War, 1946–1954. I. Title.
DS553.1.F35   1994
959.803'5—dc20   93-34825
                                            CIP

TO THOSE WHO DIED THERE

"Be men. If you are Communists, go and join the Viet-Minh. There are people there who fight well for a bad cause."

—Marshal de Lattre de Tassigny,
Commander-in-Chief in Indochina,
in an address to Vietnamese high
school graduates, July 11, 1951.

"Anti-Communism will remain a useless tool in our hands as long as the problem of nationalism remains unsolved."

—Marshal Philippe de Hautecloque "Leclerc,"
Commander-in-Chief in Indochina, 1945-47.

"The People's army is the instrument of the [Communist] Party and of the revolutionary State for the accomplishment, in armed form, of the tasks of the revolution."

—Vo Nguyên Giap,
Viet-Minh Commander-in-Chief,
in *People's War—People's Army*,
Hanoi, 1961.

MAPS AND ILLUSTRATIONS

Page

CONTENTS

Introduction

Bernard B. Fall's *Street Without Joy* is one of a handful of truly classic accounts of the wars in Indochina. Originally published in 1961, just as the Kennedy administration was escalating the war in Vietnam, it attracted little initial notice in the United States. By 1967, however, when the United States was engaged in full-scale war and Fall himself had been killed reporting combat in the very area he had written about, it had become standard reading for the U.S. officer corps in Vietnam. It remains today perhaps the best English account of France's frustrating and ultimately unsuccessful effort to subdue the Vietminh insurgency.

Bernard Fall came naturally by his chosen profession as a student of war. He grew up in France against the backdrop of World War II, lost both parents in that conflict, and by his own recollection experienced his "first whiff of war" at age twelve. As a teenager, he joined the resistance, and he fought with the Allies in the liberation of France and the drive toward Berlin.

He later conceded that he became a specialist on Indochina by "sheer accident." While he was studying for his doctorate at Syracuse University, one of his professors suggested that he might focus on the area because French was his native language and because no one else was doing it. He thus went to Indochina in 1953 at his own expense to research a doctoral dissertation on the Vietminh revolutionaries (later published as *The Vietminh Regime*). While there, he often accompanied French troops on operations in the field, and his letters to his wife recounting his experiences provided the basis for *Street Without Joy*.

Thus began what he would call his "bad love affair" with Indochina, an obsession that would earn him the reputation as one of the world's foremost authorities on the area. He would return there numerous times. Other books followed *Street Without Joy,* including, most importantly, *The Two Vietnams: A Political and Military Analysis* (1963) and his epic account of the dramatic battle of Dienbienphu, *Hell in a Very Small Place* (1966).

Fall brought to his work enormous energy and a powerful intellect. A brash and flamboyant individual, well built and of medium height, he cut a dashing figure in his chosen role as a war correspondent in Vietnam. He aspired to be a great writer, and he had a rare talent for languages. His zest for digging out facts through research in the field made him contemptuous of those who wrote about wars from the comfort and safety of their studies. Intense and hard-working, he became "like one possessed," according to his wife, after he was diagnosed with a rare, incurable disease. He returned to Vietnam in 1967 certain that his days were numbered. While accompanying U.S. Marines on a mission in what he called "my area," the "street without joy" north of Hue, he was killed by a land mine.

Fall prided himself on being an independent scholar. Although he was a major contributor to the bitter debate on Vietnam that wracked the United States in the 1960s, he usually stood above it. Highly critical of what he regarded as America's abandonment of France in the First Indochina War, he was sometimes dismissed as an apologist for his native country. Yet he harshly criticized French colonialism and French strategy and tactics. An admirer of Ho Chi Minh and the Vietminh, he was firmly anti-Communist. Neither hawk nor dove, Fall rejected both escalation and an American withdrawal as inadequate responses to the complex situation wrought by French and American intervention in Vietnam. He was, however, sharply critical of an American policy that, he believed, was based on abstractions divorced from the realities of Vietnamese history and compromised by chronic and usually unwarranted optimism. He developed a deep and abiding empathy for the victims of the wars in Vietnam, especially for the common soldiers who fought on all sides. He remained a French citizen, but he felt great affection for his adopted countries, Vietnam and the United States. Although a critic of U.S. policy in an era when criticism was not welcomed and thus, in his own words, the "unwelcome bearer of ill tidings," he became a person of considerable influence, his works avidly read by both those Americans who fought in the war and those who protested against it.

Street Without Joy does not pretend to provide a comprehensive account of the First Indochina War. It focuses almost entirely on the period after 1950 when Chinese and American intervention had both enlarged and internationalized the conflict. It is episodic, singling out for special attention a series of major French operations between 1951 and 1954, Operation Lorraine in the Red River Delta, Operation Camargue, a 1953 effort to clean up the Vietminh-infested area known by French soldiers as the "street without joy," the disaster that befell Groupement Mobile No. 100 in the Central Highlands of Annam, and the battle of Dienbienphu.

Published more than thirty years ago, the book appears in some small respects dated. Fall worked without access to top-level documents, and his observations — often quite critical — about U.S. support for France and the possibility of U.S. intervention at Dienbienphu do not hold up under the close scrutiny that is possible today. The language at times is that of the period; frequent references to the "Reds" stamp his work as vintage 1950s. His refusal to concede that the Vietminh were "genuine" nationalists dates to that era when all communists were assumed to be subservient to Moscow.

These minor flaws aside, *Street Without Joy* has much to commend it. Fall brilliantly conveys the peculiar ambience of a war that if not unique was certainly extraordinary: a war without fronts where, as he emphasizes and reemphasizes, terrain and people triumphed over technology. He describes the land and people in words and phrases that verge on the poetic. He portrays the sights, sounds, and indeed smells in such graphic terms that the reader has the sense of being there and actually experiencing the mud, the heat, the leeches, the pain. He includes hundreds of small vignettes that tell much about the war, such as the Vietminh's initial reaction to the horrific effects of napalm and the suffering of French soldiers from primitive Vietminh poison darts. He portrays with particular deftness the agony of Groupement Mobile 100 and particularly of the 1st Korea Battalion, a unit that had survived two years combat in that earlier war only to be wiped out in the much different, and from Fall's standpoint, much more deadly environment of Vietnam.

The people, however, are his main focus. Fall is ahead of his time in detailing the role of women, a subject more often than not omitted from traditional military history. He singles out the contributions of female reporters, soldiers, nurses, and, of course, the notorious *Bordel Mobile de Campagne,* or mobile field brothel. His chapter on prisoners of war anticipates, in important ways for the United States, the agony over POW-MIA issues that persists to this day. Most of all, he writes about the common soldier. Regrettably, because of the lack of access, he is unable to chronicle except in the most elementary way the war as fought by the Vietminh. He concentrates on the French soldier, who might be from any of numerous nationalities but who endured the harsh land and the brutal combat for the glories of the French Union.

Fall's primary theme is the uniqueness of the war and the inability of the French to understand and adapt to it. Armed, equipped, and trained for conventional, European-style war, the French Union forces set off in search of the classic set-piece battle in which they could use their superior firepower to defeat the more lightly armed rebels. But in this war without fronts, this "war of vast empty spaces," in every instance save two they failed to get what they sought, and their armor and firepower became a burden in rugged terrain against highly mobile enemy forces. In the one instance, they succeeded when Vietnamese General Vo Nguyen Giap abandoned his usual caution and prematurely committed his regular forces. In the other, ironically, at Dienbienphu, they got their set-piece battle but in circumstances singularly disadvantageous to them. *Vietnamese* firepower and human wave assaults besieged and ultimately overwhelmed the French. Dienbienphu was not typical of the war, Fall concludes, but it epitomized French mistakes in fighting it, particularly their stubborn overestimation of their own ability and their repeated underestimation of the enemy.

In a chapter added to the 1964 edition, Fall foresees, sometimes with uncanny accuracy, American repetition of French mistakes. Analyzing the course of the Second Indochina War to 1964, he errs badly (like many U.S. policymakers) in underestimating North Vietnam's willingness to risk its industrial base to American bombing by escalating the conflict. Otherwise Fall is on the mark. He highlights the National Liberation Front's skill in integrating political

and military actions, and he criticizes the Diem regime's unwillingness to enact the political reforms necessary to make the strategic
hamlet program effective. Agreeing with dissident American journalists like Neil Sheehan and David Halberstam, he contrasts the
optimistic statements from U.S. military leaders with the reality of
repeated South Vietnamese defeat. Fall especially criticizes the
Americans for ignoring or forgetting the "bloody lessons" of the
French war by attempting to use conventional warfare and technology to defeat guerrillas. "The West is still battling an ideology with
technology," he concludes with remarkable prescience, "and the successful end of that Revolutionary War is neither near nor is its
outcome certain."

In a final chapter, Fall stresses the importance of what he calls
"revolutionary war." Defining it as the "application of irregular
warfare methods to the propagation of an ideology or political
system," he carefully distinguishes revolutionary war from guerrilla
or partisan war. Because of its political dimension, Fall insists,
revolutionary war cannot be dealt with by military means alone. He
criticizes the Americans for following the French in trying to use
technology to compensate for "the woeful lack of popular support
and political savvy" of the regimes they tried to prop up. Quoting
approvingly a slogan posted on barracks walls in the First Indochina War—"Remember—the enemy is *not* fighting this war as per
French Army regulations"—he warns that revolutionary war will
continue to pose a challenge and that dealing with it cannot be left
to "happy improvisation." The West must understand it and learn
how to fight it.

Have Fall's arguments stood the test of time? Were they validated
or discredited by the Second Indochina War? The debate on these
issues remains as heated today as in Fall's time. Some analysts of
the war stress that the United States, by accident or design, had
thwarted the enemy's revolutionary war strategy by 1968, particularly as a result of the disastrous Communist Tet Offensive. Ultimately, they contend, the United States and South Vietnam were
defeated by conventional North Vietnamese armies that were supplied by the Soviet Union with conventional weapons and overwhelmed their South Vietnamese counterparts in the most conventional of operations.[1]

Nevertheless, many scholars still subscribe to arguments much like Fall's. In words reminiscent of *Street Without Joy,* John Gates contends that "revisionist" interpretations advanced in recent years neatly fit the conventional thinking that has typified the U.S. military throughout the twentieth century. They err, as those Fall criticized, by equating revolutionary war with guerrilla war. In fact, Gates contends, in the period after Tet, the enemy continued to carefully integrate and skillfully employ all aspects of warfare. It used protracted warfare to undermine the position of the United States. It used guerrillas in coordination with conventional operations for intelligence and logistics, in combat, and for political agitation to undermine the South Vietnamese government. Thus, he concludes, "the 1975 attack was the *coup de grace* of a successful peoples' war rather than the *coup de main* depicted in many recent American accounts." Like Fall, Gates notes that the United States has learned nothing from its failure in Vietnam because it has refused to recognize the true nature of the war that was fought there.[2]

Street Without Joy thus remains not only a splendid account of a conflict often forgotten in the aftermath of America's war in Vietnam, but it also speaks directly to a debate that continues to rage among military experts on the nature of the two wars in Indochina and the proper ways to fight them.

GEORGE C. HERRING

Lexington, Kentucky
June 1993

---

[1]See for example Harry G. Summers, Jr., *On Strategy: A Critical Analysis of the Vietnam War* (New York, 1984) and Timothy J. Lomperis, *The War Everyone Lost — and Won* (Baton Rouge, 1984).

[2]John M. Gates, "People's War in Vietnam," *Parameters* 54 (July 1990), 325–44.

Foreword

Georges Clemenceau is reputed to have said (and perhaps he did) that war was too important to be left to soldiers. Nobody seems to have come forward with the obvious corollary, which is that peace is too precious to be left to politicians.

Such aphorisms, while they may delight those who like their thinking supplied for them in tasty capsules, wholly over-simplify the complex problem with which they deal. They can be true, certainly, but at the same time they are nonsense.

For war is itself a political act. Politics cannot be separated from war, nor war from politics. Political considerations do not cease abruptly with the onset of war, and military considerations can never be far from the politician's mind, even in times of peace.

The threat of war, particularly in this day of air-delivered nuclear weapons, must inevitably temper political decisions. Conversely, war conducted in a political vacuum is not war at all but pointless slaughter. In the end, war becomes the last resort of the politician, who must turn over its conduct, though not its ultimate objectives, to soldiers.

Since World War II, war has assumed a new dimension. It is still the final expression of politics in the Clausewitzian sense, but it has become more than that. War is now an *interim* instrument of politics, to be applied at will and withdrawn at will. This modern use of military force has come to be known as "limited war," although wars of limited objectives with limited means are nothing new in the somber history of human conflict.

What is new is twofold: the emergence of what Dr. Fall has defined as "active sanctuary," and the fearful shadow of the mushroom cloud that rose from the ruins of Hiroshima. Equally

9

important with the application of limited war is the vexing problem of keeping it limited. It is this last consideration that has persistently enfeebled the resolution of the Western powers in meeting the recurrent military adventures that have kept the postwar world in turmoil.

To add further to all these complications, the political and military conflict which has plagued the world since 1945 is shot through with ideological overtones. The fragmentation of organized society into a host of small nations, mostly former colonies, without political experience and with little or no hope of ever attaining economic viability, but fiercely nationalistic nevertheless, has provided rich ground for the seeds of an ideology which promises an easy and profitable retreat from the cul-de-sac of political ineptitude and economic stagnation.

The great powers which preach this ideological road to salvation have not been backward in taking advantage of the opportunities offered them by the political and economic jumble which was the heritage of the last war. They have managed to swallow some nations whole and to chew up others piecemeal. Resistance to this process has brought the Western world into military contact with them or their satellites, but always in such a manner that it has had to operate in the propaganda fog of "colonialism" or "imperialism."

It is just such an operation that Dr. Fall deals with here. He is peculiarly well equipped for the task he has undertaken. A member of the French Resistance while still a boy, he became a subaltern in a Moroccan division during the liberation of France. Returned to civil life after the war, he adopted the remarkable course of going to Indochina in 1953 to gather first-hand material for his doctoral thesis. He was there again in 1957, and in 1959 spent several months in Southeast Asia on a special research assignment on Communist infiltration.

Thus he was a witness of much of what he has put into his fine and revealing book. Much of what he could not see for himself he was able to derive from French official papers made available to him by the Ministry of Defense in Paris. He not only saw the valiant and generally futile efforts of the French Union Forces to cope with a new kind of war, but he brought to his evaluation of what he saw a firm basis of military knowledge and experience.

The picture he draws is not a pleasant one. He presents for critical inspection two widely divergent military philosophies, one built on the mobility of the individual soldier, the other resting on the mobility of armies. In the sort of terrain where the fighting took place there could be no question of which philosophy eventually would be proved correct, a truth which the French were unable to see through the doctrinal cloud which enfolded them.

There was no lack of equipment for modern war in the hands of the French Union Forces (FUF), nor was there any lack of individual gallantry where gallantry was called for, whether the troops involved were French, African or Asian. But this very plentitude of heavy equipment proved a handicap in the test of battle. Not only did it tie the FUF to what few roads there were, but both the equipment itself and the doctrine it imposed led FUF commands time after time into easily contrived ambushes. The French contended against the jungle while the Viet-Minh made use of it.

As the war develops in Dr. Fall's narrative, its two general phases come clearly to light. At first the French attempted to hold the fortress barrier they had constructed in North Viet-Nam, an attempt which failed because the enemy controlled the surrounding jungle and took full advantage of it for maneuver and surprise.

In the second phase, the French attempted to match Viet-Minh mobility on foot with the mechanical mobility so essential to warfare against forces equally mechanized. Again the Viet-Minh made use of the jungle to nullify French mechanized mobility and power. Even when the French took the offensive, the initiative remained with the Viet-Minh, who could attack at will from the jungle, choosing their targets, and, at will, retire into the jungle again. All this presented a problem the French never managed to solve, burdened as they were with the doctrine saddled on them by their mechanization plus the "lessons" derived from World War II and Korea.

They did approach a solution in the formation, equipment

and tactical employment of their *Dinassaut*. These heavily armed and armored flotillas, making use of the water courses which are the principal highways in much of Indochina, were almost uniformly successful. But even they could not solve the most pressing problem of all: deep penetration and consequent control of the jungle.

Nor was one of the basic problems ever mastered or even remotely approached. That was the always pressing one of logistics. The appetites of armored vehicles mounting automatic weapons are gargantuan and insistent. The comparison between the supply of a squad mounted in a half-track and that of a squad trotting through the jungle, each man with a four-day ration of rice in a bag slung about his neck, would be ridiculous had it not proved so tragic.

There is a lesson in this book for the United States. The sort of war fought by the French in Indochina may well be a model for those to which U.S. forces already have been committed and to which they likely will be committed to an ever greater extent in the future. It is begging the question to argue that a few atomic bombs dropped in the right places would remove the necessity for the brutal kind of infighting the French consistently met in Indochina.

In the first place, United States or United Nations troops most probably would be committed at the invitation of a government threatened by aggression. The physical consequences to a country of modern conventional war fought over it are clearly demonstrated by what happened to Korea. It would not be unreasonable to suppose, in view of that experience, that compromise with the enemy might appear a less costly solution than war. And surely no people could be blamed too much for preferring slavery masquerading as freedom to obliteration in the process of atomic liberation.

From the practical standpoint, atomic weapons demand for optimum efficiency that their targets be clearly defined and of a magnitude comparable with the effects of the bomb. That is to say, concentrations of troops or dumps or transport constitute atomic targets, not a handful of soldiers lurking in the jungle (even if they could be seen from the air), a rice paddy ready for the harvest, or a single elephant plodding along with 1½ tons on its back. Nor would there be profitable "strategic" targets; there would be little point in immolating Hanoi, for instance, in the name of liberating North Viet-Nam from the aggressor.

There seems to be small room for doubt that the French experience in Indochina points the way for the future, even though it is a signpost which reads, "Success in Opposite Direction." Equipment of local forces to the point that they resemble U.S. units in all important particulars may stimulate local pride and conform to doctrinaire military thought. But it will not prepare them for the sort of warfare they most probably would face should some new military application of ideological pressures suddenly appear in some far corner of the earth.

The same considerations must apply to the equipment and training of our own forces. It is all very well to equip U.S. troops with nuclear loaded missiles, to organize them into divisions designed to minimize the effects of nuclear blasts, to put wheels under every soldier and to base doctrine on the assumption that the only future war will be a continental war with nuclear weapons. But what of the inescapable reality that the enemy may choose to apply pressure where its effects will do him the least harm? These pressures have been applied many times in many parts of the world. The American response to some of them is described in the three new chapters at the end of Dr. Fall's book. How right or wrong it may be, time will tell us—but will it tell us in time?

The United States Army was no more indoctrinated and trained for that sort of war than were the French in Indochina. What it calls for is individual stamina and fortitude, for the understanding and acceptance of battlefield conditions almost unimaginable in their demands on human endurance, for recognition in doctrine that these requirements exist and that they may very well have to be met.

It is true enough that the U.S. Army is training specialists in counter-insurgency warfare to pass on their skills to indigenous forces. But along with this effort goes a great and perhaps mistaken dependence on the newer tools of mechanized battle. Could it be that one American, indoctrinated in the political aspects of insurgency, would outweigh on the scales of war, a platoon of fighting men flying blindly into the jungle?

This nation is foremost in providing its troops with the mechanical means of war. What is needed now, in the light of France's failure in Indochina, is a search for stout legs, stout hearts, fertile brains, and an understanding of the new relation of big politics to little wars.

MARSHALL ANDREWS

Haywood
Chantilly, Virginia

Author's Preface

This is not a history of the two "Indochina Wars"—that fought by the French from 1946 to 1954 with their Vietnamese allies, and that fought by the South Vietnamese and *their* American allies since 1957—but a historical sketch of certain key developments in both wars, and of the men who fought on both sides. As a battlefield, Indochina is unlike any other fought over by Western forces previously, for warfare there assumes the aspect of what the French called *"la guerre sans fronts"*—a war without fronts—and, therefore, without secure rear areas. The term "Indochina" is used advisedly, for the war again involves all of Viet-Nam and Laos and the border areas of Cambodia; and the outcome of combat operations in South Viet-Nam will, of course, affect the whole of the Indochinese peninsula, Thailand included.

No Western combat operations in recent decades quite resemble those fought for eight years from the Tonking highlands to the swamps of Camau. They are, in any case, wholly out of the range of American past experience. In sheer size alone, Indochina, with its 285,000 square miles, is larger than New Guinea, Burma, or the puny 85,000 square miles of Korea. In contrast to the treeless spaces of Korea, Indochina is covered to the extent of *eighty-six* percent with dense spontaneous growth and to the extent of at least *forty-seven* percent with outright jungle.

While New Guinea or Burma, or the smaller Pacific Islands, offered similar terrain features to American troops during World War II, the whole tactical situation was so different as to make any valid comparison quite difficult. In the case of the Pacific Islands, the Japanese defenders used—as long as they could—the same weapons as the American forces and (making allowance for their greater frugality) were subject to the same logistical burdens. As American air and naval superiority became firmly established, the Japanese generally began the land battle cut off

15

from their own rear supply lines, a situation which was never achieved in Indochina, or in Korea, for that matter.

The Burmese theater never involved large bodies of American ground troops, and the only United States unit of regimental size which was involved in direct ground fighting, the 5307th Composite Unit (Provisional), better known as "Merrill's Marauders," remained in combat only from February until August 3, 1944, having suffered a fate which closely resembled that of many French units in Indochina later on.

Another vital feature separates the Indochina war from other comparable situations in the Far East: the Japanese were as alien to the combat environment and, particularly, to its civilian population, as the Allies were. In fact—and this was true particularly during the last two years of World War II—the sympathies of the population were often with the Allies and against the Japanese. Allied-led guerrilla forces could operate with a fair chance of success in many areas occupied by the Japanese without being betrayed to them. In the case of the Indochina war, the French were definitely the "aliens" and the Communist-led Viet-Minh forces could count on the instinctive support of the native population. Where such outright support did not exist, as was true in certain heavily Catholic areas, well-applied terror could insure at least the neutrality of the population in the struggle. As will be seen later, almost nowhere did the French succeed in creating viable anti-guerrilla guerrilla forces, and French tactical intelligence was often faulty because of this Communist-created isolation of the French forces from the population in which it operated.

In the case of two equally alien forces—the Japanese and Allies in Burma and the Pacific, the United Nations and the Chinese Communists in Korea—the force which will treat the native population with greater understanding and kindness will eventually gain its loyalty or at least its benevolent neutrality. In the case where only one side is alien, even his kindest acts can be used against him by the native adversary's psychological warfare—and the psychological warfare of the Viet-Minh was one of the most effective of its kind.

To this must be added the hard fact that, at the outset at least, the Indochina war was one of colonial re-conquest. As such, it suffered from a psychological handicap which hurt the French even with their own allies until the whole operation became "sanctified" when the Communist conquest of the Chinese mainland and the subsequent attack on Korea made Indochina an important pawn of cold war strategy in the Far East. This, of course, changed neither the psychological nor the terrain factors, and the belated influx of large amounts of American equipment— equipment that was largely unsuited to the kind of war being fought there—could, of necessity, affect very little the eventual outcome of that war.

The Indochina war became deadlocked politically in 1948, when French political hesitations failed to make the Vietnamese nationalists an effective counter-force in the psychological struggle. It became strategically hopeless when the Chinese Reds arrived on Indochina's borders late in 1949 and China thus became a "sanctuary" where Viet-Minh forces could be trained and refitted. And it was lost militarily as of 1953 when the cease-fire in Korea allowed the concentration of the whole Asian Communist war effort on the Indochinese theater.

The dénouement of the Indochina war was, therefore, about as foreordained as that of a Greek tragedy. Yet, the French Union Forces fought well to the last; Frenchmen as well as Foreign Legionnaires, Vietnamese, Cambodians and Laotians as well as Algerians, Moroccans and Senegalese. Close to 95,000 men, including four generals and 1,300 lieutenants, died on the battlefield or behind the barbed wire of Communist prison camps.

A book including factual accounts of a war can hardly be anything else but a collective enterprise. Many books have been written in France on various aspects of the Indochina war, most of which I have been able to consult in the course of my work. They are listed in the bibliography (appendix III) at the end of this book. In addition, the French Army in Indochina published two weekly magazines which, like *Yank* and the *Stars and Stripes* in the United States forces during World War II, left veritable gold mines of detailed information on various aspects of the war. Those publications, *Caravelle* and *Nouvelles du Nord-Viet-Nam*, not only brought official communiqués and views, but also stories contributed by unit reporters, biographies of various commanders, and a rather unique "Help Wanted" column: in it, soldiers or noncommissioned officers advertised in order to find men of similar rank and job who wanted to switch positions with them. It was not at all unusual to read the following:

> Sgt., Inf. Regt. South Viet-Nam, seeks exchange jobs with sgt., Mobile Group, North Viet-Nam. For details, write Box 709, *Caravelle*.

Very often, the number and direction (from the southern to the northern theater, or to Laos) of the proposed exchanges (they were called "permutations") was a good indicator of which way the war was going.

In addition to those official magazines, a French group in Indochina produced a monthly magazine whose color photos, slickness and presentation stood in no way behind those of *Life* magazine. Each of its issues not only contained some excellent articles on Asian art or history—that is, on the larger cultural context in which the conflict was fought—but also some superb first-hand reports on combat operations written by local journalists of important overseas newspapers, or by Frenchmen in Indochina. Published by Robert ("Bob") Aeschelmann, now the editor of *Paris-Jour, Indochine—Sud-Est Asiatique* constitutes perhaps the best first-hand record available on that tragic period of Indochina's history. It often contained some extremely valuable articles on our Communist enemy, which I found out later came directly from French Intelligence and were one means of briefing the soldiers and officers on an important subject which they might otherwise not have read about. *Indochine* folded at the end of the war, in August 1954.

The most valuable documentary source of them all is, however, the French Army's historical records, where all the unit diaries and operation plans and reports are stored as the various commands make them available. In the case of the Indochina war, the complete closing-out of French forces in the Far East brought the almost totality of those files to the *Service Historique de l'Armée* behind the massive walls of the Fort de Vincennes at the outskirts of Paris.

I shall be forever grateful to Monsieur Pierre Guillaumat, French Minister of the Armed Forces in the cabinet of President Charles de Gaulle until 1960, for giving me access to those files.

Brigadier General de Cossé-Brissac, a survivor of Flossenburg concentration camp and a scholar in his own right, Director of the *Service Historique de l'Armée* since 1953, should be thanked here for his kind cooperation during my research in his services. Lt. Col. Jouin, head of the Overseas Section of the Historical Service, was unfailing in his patience and kindness in tracking down for me, in the maze of crates and shelves filled with files yet to be cataloged, the documents which I wanted to see. At no time was I asked to submit my notes or remarks to them for approval or censorship.

However, even the best documents cannot replace the direct experience of field research. As a candidate for a doctorate degree, I was able to be in Indochina during the crucial year of 1953, and as a Frenchman who had formerly served with a Moroccan division I was given the courtesy by many units of accompanying them into their areas of operation. Since my whole first trip to Indochina was entirely financed out of my own savings and not from the liberal donations of various foundations, I doubly appreciated that hospitality.

Living with the men who were doing the fighting, I came to know and respect many of them throughout Indochina. Not being a journalist, I was not given the special attentions to which the press was subject and thus escaped the various operations specially staged for it at times. This made me miss many of the contacts with the great or near-great who, from time to time, came to the area. On the other hand, I met many a soldier, French or Asian, who could tell me in his own terms what it was like to be out along the defense perimeter, wet and afraid; and learned how it felt to pry off a few leeches or to struggle with dysentery, for I had had to do it several times myself and hadn't liked it. But after a while it knocked the intellectual superciliousness out of me.

The upshot of my personal experiences and interviews which I could not use for my research went into a diary in the form of letters to the American girl who is now my wife. In those I tried to render the feeling of the atmosphere in which we were living and in which this war was being fought. Sometimes, there were touches of gaiety to the grimness, and sometimes there was pathos, because that is the way a human being behaves, no matter what. I feel that it has a place in a book on any war as long as wars are not entirely fought by button-pushing automatons.

Rather than run the risk of forgetting anyone in particular from among the many people who were so kind to me during my wartime stay in Indochina, I would like to remember here the units themselves with whom I was associated during that time: the 1st *Chasseurs Blindés* (Armored Cavalry) and Airborne Group No. 1 based in Hanoi; the Autonomous Zone North-West (ZANO)—the official name for the ill-fated Lai-Chau airhead behind Communist lines; the 1st Vietnamese Mobile Group, then in Hung-Yen; the 3d Foreign Legion Regiment in Bac-Ninh; the Quang-Yen training center for Vietnamese commando forces; the 5th *Cuirassiers* (Armor) at Thu Dau Mot; and the Liaison-Pacification Offices for North and South Viet-Nam. Lastly, I wish to thank the pilots of the late General Claire L. Chennault's "Flying Tigers" whose free-riding passenger I often was during their airlift operations in North Viet-Nam and Laos.

During my stay in Laos in the summer of 1959 on a research project of the Southeast Asia Treaty Organization (SEATO), I was able to add some more pieces to the overall puzzle of the Indochina war, thanks to the faithful friendship of acquaintances from previous trips and the unflagging hospitality and support of the Royal Laotian authorities, civilian as well as military. While I was in Samneua Province, Brigadier General Amkha Soukhavong, commander of the Laotian Army's northern zone, enabled me to visit directly most of the outposts in his command thanks to the acrobatics of Captain Catry, a French civilian pilot with the "Air Laos" civilian airline. Farther to the north, Major Tiao (Prince) Sibolavong Sisaleumsak, the commander of the Namtha sector facing Red China, also proved a perfect host during my stay with the 13th Volunteer Battalion.

A research grant by the Rockefeller Foundation and some additional teaching at the Royal Institute of Administration in Cambodia permitted me in 1961-62 to do further research for the present edition of this book. Consultation of new documents in Paris in 1963-64, thanks to the authorization of Monsieur Pierre Messmer, the successor of M. Guillaumat as France's Minister of

Defense, allowed me to improve and flesh out events described in previous editions, particularly those dealing with air and naval operations. Renewed field investigations, notably in usually inaccessible North Viet-Nam, as well as the many letters which I have received from interested readers, both French and American; added further incentive to include in this book new information about what can in all fairness be called the "Second Indochina War." The first round of it ended in the defeat of the pro-Western forces in Laos in 1962. Its second round in Viet-Nam is, at the time of this writing, in deep jeopardy.

This book would have never been undertaken without the friendly advice and encouragement of Colonel Rodger R. Bankson, U.S. Army, former Editor-in-Chief of the *Military Review* of the U.S. Army Command and General Staff College at Fort Leavenworth; and would have never become an acceptable manuscript without the patience and friendly interest of Marshall Andrews, author of *Disaster Through Air Power,* and a military analyst with the Research Analysis Corporation in Washington, who sacrificed long hours he could have devoted to his own writing to help me with mine, and who kindly consented to author the Foreword.

The persons and events presented in this book are in all cases true and authentic to the best of my knowledge and belief. Only in a very few cases did I change the name of persons involved in order to spare additional grief to their surviving family members or embarrassment to themselves.

A letter which accompanied a Certificate of Appreciation which I received from the Department of Defense in 1961 referred in part to my "tireless efforts to secure the facts and data as they are, and not as one wishes them to be." This has been my guiding principle in all my research work, no matter how painful the process is at times to national pride or to widely held prejudices. I am therefore happy to claim sole responsibility for all views and opinions expressed in this book.

Howard University, Washington, D. C.   B. B. F.
September 1964

How War Came

W AR came to Indochina in the wake of the crumbling of the European colonial empires in Asia during World War II. When France lost the first round of that war in June 1940, Japan found the moment ripe to take over additional real estate in Asia in preparation for her own further conquests. Indochina, then held by a force of about 70,000 French troops equipped with completely obsolete material—there were 15 modern fighter planes and one operational tank company in the whole country—found itself faced with the territorial appetites of both Japan and her sole ally and satellite in Asia, Thailand. In true Axis fashion, Thailand signed a non-aggression pact with France on June 12, 1940.

Open warfare between French Indochina and Thailand began on January 9, 1941. The French at first lost some ground, but began to counterattack as reinforcements arrived along the Thai border. On the seas, one old French cruiser sank one-third of the whole Thai fleet in a naval engagement off the island of Koh-Chang on January 17, and Japan, seeing that the war was turning against its pupil and ally, imposed its "mediation" between the two parties. A cease-fire began on January 28, followed on March 11, 1941, by an agreement in which the French were forced to surrender to Thailand three provinces in Cambodia and two provinces in Laos.

However, and this is a well-ignored fact in the United States, the French already had fought a short but bloody war with the Japanese in September 1940—more than one year before Pearl Harbor. On June 19, 1940, a few days before France signed an armistice with the Axis in Europe, the Japanese government

22

asked the French to let Imperial troops pass through North
Viet-Nam in order to attack the Chinese Nationalists through
their "back-door" in Yunnan. This move was also designed to
cut off the flow of American supplies for General Chiang Kai-
shek's forces through the port of Haiphong. The British, under
similar Japanese pressures, were to close the port of Singapore to
such shipments as of June 27, and to close for a time the Burma
Road, a few months later.

Even before the Japanese ultimatum, General Catroux, then
Governor-General of Indochina, had sent a purchasing mission
to the United States in order to acquire 120 modern fighter planes
as well as modern antiaircraft guns, already fully paid for by
France under contracts passed earlier. But on June 30, the French
ambassador in Washington wired Catroux that his request had
been turned down by Under Secretary of State Sumner Welles,
because,

> . . . considering the general situation, the Government of the United
> States did not believe that it could enter into conflict with Japan and
> that, *should the latter attack Indochina, the United States would not*
> oppose such an action.*

Secretary of State Cordell Hull, in his memoirs, confirms the
fact, adding that, "with Japan in control of key points in Indochina, we were reluctant to sell any additional equipment to
Indochina," hoping that Indochina would "delay and parlay
and hold out to the last minute against Japanese demands," since,
in Hull's view, "Japan would not dare make a military attack at
this time."**

Unfortunately, all the American assumptions then made proved
wrong within a few weeks. When the French had asked for U.S.
equipment, Indochina was not yet occupied by Japan, and the
equipment might have helped them to "delay and parlay" from a
better position of strength. And the Japanese did "dare make a
military attack" when the French, poorly armed as they were,
refused to give in under pressure.

Abandoned by both their allies and their own government in

*Telegram cited in full in Gen. Catroux' book *Deux actes du drame indo-
chinois*, Paris: Plon, 1959, p. 55. Italics in original text.
**Hull's *Memoirs*, New York: Macmillan, 1948, Vol. I, pp. 906-907.

France which, under German pressure, had begun to negotiate
an accord with the Japanese, the French troops in Indochina were
quite alone. While the negotiations were going on, Japanese
troops, on September 22, 1940, at midnight, crossed the North
Vietnamese border at Lang-Son and Dong-Dang and began to
attack the French border forts on a front of 45 kilometers. Fierce
fighting began around the forts, which held out until they ran
out of ammunition. Two days later, Japanese aircraft bombed
the port of Haiphong and on the evening of September 24, a
Japanese naval landing force began to unload troops at Haiphong for a march on Hanoi. A total of eight hundred Frenchmen
were killed in the two days of fighting but the situation was hopeless. Marshal Pétain's government in France, prodded by events
in Indochina, signed the agreement permitting the Japanese to
station troops in the area, and General Nishihara, the Japanese
officer negotiating with the French, termed the attack a "dreadful
mistake." But the deed was done, and Indochina was lost to the
Japanese.

As the whole Pacific was engulfed in the war fifteen months
later, the desperate French fight was soon forgotten, and all that
remained of it in the memory of Allied statesmen was that the
French had signed an agreement with the Japanese and thus had
"collaborated." Soon, this ban on dealing with the French in
Indochina was even extended to those who were fighting the
Japanese in the resistance movements. As Secretary of State
Cordell Hull noted in his memoirs, the President instructed him
on October 13, 1944, that "nothing" was to be done "in regard
to resistance groups or in any other way in relation to Indochina."

Thus, when the Japanese, in a surprise attack on March 9,
1945, destroyed and captured whatever French troops and administrators remained in Indochina, this order apparently was
executed to the letter, in spite of the desperate pleas for help by
the succumbing French garrisons. In the words of General Claire
L. Chennault, the famous commander of the "Flying Tigers" and,
in 1945, of the 14th Air Force,

> . . . orders arrived from Theater headquarters stating that no arms
> and ammunition would be provided to French troops under any
> circumstances . . . I carried out my orders to the letter but I did

not relish the idea of leaving Frenchmen to be slaughtered in the jungle while I was forced officially to ignore their plight.*

The northern garrisons, which had hidden some of their heavy weapons in secret caches and were on a permanent alert status, fought to the death; at Lang-Son, the Japanese in a blind rage beheaded French General Lemonnier and the civilian administrator, Governor Auphelle, under the eyes of the defenders when both refused to call upon Lang-Son's garrison to surrender. A small body of troops under General Alessandri fought its way out to Yunnan, only to be interned by the Chinese Nationalists as if they were unfriendly aliens instead of allies.

On March 11, 1945, the Japanese forced the Emperor of Annam to proclaim the end of the French protectorate and the "independence" of his country under Japanese "protection." The spell of French overlordship in Indochina was broken forever.

In the meantime, native guerrilla groups had begun operations late in 1944 in the remotest areas of North Viet-Nam and in the neighboring Chinese provinces of Yunnan and Kwang-Si. They were led by two able Communist leaders, Ho Chi Minh and Vo Nguyên Giap. Ho, under various aliases, had been a Communist since 1920; and Giap, the military "brains" of the group, also had been a Communist since the earliest beginnings of the movement in Indochina. Lung Yun, the local Chinese war lord who supported them (and who died in 1962 in Red China), knew this, but it apparently was unknown in Chungking, wartime headquarters of the Chinese Nationalists.

Soon, posing as "nationalist guerrillas" only interested in evicting both the Japanese and French imperialists from their native country, these "Viet-Minh" acquired a reputation far in excess of their military accomplishments. Those, according to Allied sources, were limited to the attack of a small Japanese gendarmerie post at the Tam-Dao mountain resort. But the fact remains that,

---

*Chennault, C. D., *Way of a Fighter*, G. P. Putnam's Sons, New York, 1949, p. 342. Through research in the archives of the U.S. Air Force, carried out in 1963, I am now able to state that General Chennault at least partly disregarded the orders received from Washington: fighters of the 51st Fighter Group and transport aircraft of the 27th Troop Carrier Squadron, did indeed fly support missions in behalf of the retreating French forces. I am not able to state to what extent that disobedience contributed to Chennault's subsequent removal from command.

after the collapse of the French, the Viet-Minh* were the only pro-Allied movement of any consequence in the country. American O.S.S. missions and some weapons were parachuted to them.

When V-J Day dawned, the Viet-Minh were the only group of any size in Viet-Nam to exploit the power vacuum existing in the area. Their Communist training gave them an unbeatable head-start over the small idealistic nationalist groups which now began to squabble over details while the Communists were taking over the country under their very noses. A small book published by Truong Chinh, then the secretary general of the Indochinese Communist Party (ICP), which is completely unknown in the West, shows clearly how the Viet-Minh took over the country *and* the anti-colonial revolution. On August 13, 1945, the ICP met at the village of Tan Trao, in the hill province of Tuyen-Quang. According to Truong Chinh,

> . . . the ICP met in a National Congress, decreed the general uprising, and put into place the Vietnamese democratic republican regime . . . The National Congress began at the very moment when the order of general insurrection had been given. Thus, its session was rapidly closed . . .
>
> In the course of this history-making Congress, the ICP proposed a clear-cut program: guide the rebels so as to disarm the Japanese *before the arrival of the Allies in Indochina;* to take over the power that was in the hands of the Japanese and their puppets; and to receive, *as the authority in control of the country,* the Allied forces coming to demobilize the Japanese.**

The passage is self-explanatory. The worst of it is that the program was carried out to the last detail by the Viet-Minh; the fact that the troops which came to northern Indochina were Nationalist Chinese (those in the South were British) further aggravated the situation. Not only did the Chinese not retrieve from the Viet-Minh the many excellent Japanese weapons which they had had the time to acquire and hide—for it took the Chinese about three months to come down from Yunnan on foot—but in

---

*"Viet-Minh" is a Vietnamese abbreviation for "League for the Revolution and Independence of Viet-Nam." The movement was abolished in 1951, but the name has stuck to the Communist North Vietnamese regime ever since. The term "Viet-Cong" is a deprecating South Vietnamese word for "Vietnamese Communists."

**Truong Chinh, *La revolution d'août*, Hanoi 1946, p. 7. Emphasis added.

addition, they sold large amounts of their own brand-new American lend-lease weapons to the Communist revolutionaries.

A French expeditionary force of less than two divisions was allowed to re-enter North Viet-Nam in February 1946 under the terms of an agreement negotiated by the French with the Viet-Minh (which, in the meantime, had proclaimed a republic on September 2, 1945) and the Chinese Nationalists. But the Viet-Minh had had about ten months in which to establish their administration, train their forces with Japanese and American weapons (and Japanese and Chinese instructors), and kill or terrorize into submission the genuine Vietnamese nationalists who wanted a Viet-Nam independent from France but equally free of Communist rule. The first round of the war for Indochina already had been lost for the West before it had even begun.

The French managed to lose the second round—that of political negotiations—through their own stubbornness and their unwillingness to see the situation as it was: they had been defeated, through their own fault and that of their allies; and they did not have the overwhelming military force needed to make a military test of strength between themselves and the Viet-Minh which would be so obviously hopeless for the latter that they would not attempt it. And France, in 1946, seemed a likely bet for Communist domination herself. The French forces sent to Indochina were too strong for France to resist the temptation of using them; yet not strong enough to keep the Viet-Minh from trying to solve the whole political problem by throwing the French into the sea.

The outbreak of the Indochina war can be traced back to that single, tragic erroneous estimate—which, in some ways, resembles the Communist gamble in Korea, and, in the long run yielded equivalent results: the partition of Viet-Nam in one case, and the continuance of partition in the case of Korea.

Once full-scale hostilities had broken out, the French, for budgetary and political reasons, could not immediately make the large-scale effort necessary to contain the rebellion within the confines of small-scale warfare. During the first phase of active operations, that is, between December 1946 and November 1949, the French simply sought to take the whole Viet-Minh force into a series of ever-widening classical "pincers." Particularly during the autumn of 1947, a fairly ambitious undertaking, dubbed "Operation Lea" and combining daring paratroop drops with deep armored stabs, sought to wipe out the revolution by capturing its top leaders.

"Lea" would have been a hazardous undertaking under any circumstances. In the Indochina of 1947, it was, furthermore, a wild gamble at finishing the whole war in one single master stroke. There were two reasons for this: at home, the French legislature was beginning to balk (as parliaments are always prone to when faced with military operations in peacetime) at the cost of the Indochina war and the French government had promised it to reduce the French forces there from 115,000 to 90,000 men; and also, a small rebellion had broken out in the Texas-sized island of Madagascar off the east coast of Africa and 15,000 French troops were urgently needed there. Thus, the French High Command felt compelled to use all its available reserves before they would be withdrawn altogether. On the French side, twenty battalions and support units totaling 15,000 men were thrown into the fight to "crack" Ho Chi Minh's main redoubt. On the Communist side, more than 40,000 well-armed men defended a 100-by-100 mile triangle of Tonkin's most inaccessible jungles and mountain crags.

The French plan provided for a concentric attack by three columns: the Airborne Half-Brigade under Lieutenant Colonel Sauvagnac (known after the initial of its leader as "Groupment S"); a main force of three armored, three infantry and three artillery battalions, reinforced by an engineering and a transport battalion, under Colonel Beauffre ("Groupment B"); and a shipborne three-battalion force under Lieutenant Colonel Communal ("Groupment C"). The whole 4th Fighter Group, equipped with "Spitfire"-IX's, was thrown into the battle, along with German-built "Junkers-52" trimotors and American-built C-47's as transports, and French Morane liaison aircraft. Ancient American-made "Catalina" flying boats assured long-range reconnaissance missions.

Airborne Groupment "S" jumped off at dawn on October 7, 1947, with 1,137 paratroopers landing directly over the rebels' headquarters area at Bac-Kan, Cho Moi and Cho Don with so little warning that they still found Ho Chi Minh's mail, ready for signature, on his worktable and captured one of his ministers,

along with Japanese and Nazi German instructors*. At the same
time, important depots fell into French hands, along with two
hundred French and Vietnamese hostages, taken along by the
Communists when they had left Hanoi in December 1946. But
the main prizes, Ho Chi Minh and the other senior leaders—
particularly General Giap—had flown the coop and never came
close to capture again.

In the meantime, Groupment "B" had left the border fort of
Lang-Son for a difficult stab along Road 4 and the northermost
key town of Cao-Bang in the hope of sealing off all of northeastern Viet-Nam from the neighboring Chinese "sanctuary." The
remaining airborne troops were now thrown into the battle to
hold the road bridges northwest of Cao-Bang until the Beauffre
Task Force had broken through. It did so on October 12 and
immediately pushed part of the motorized Moroccan Colonial
Infantry Regiment (R.I.C.M.) southward to join with Sauvagnac's hard-pressed paratroopers who were still on their own in
the midst of the enemy's best troops. At Phu Thong Hoa, north
of Bac-Kan, the enemy decided to stand and fight, in the hope of
holding off the Moroccans long enough to destroy the paratroops
piecemeal; but after three days of bitter fighting, the R.I.C.M.
joined hands with Sauvagnac's men, who had held out on their
own for nine days.

The river-borne stab of Groupment "C" began on October 9,
as its two infantry battalions, reinforced by commando units, began to move up the Red and Clear Rivers aboard French Navy
LCT's (Landing Craft, Tanks). Running into trouble with sand
banks, the task force landed one battalion at Tuyên-Quang and
pushed on northward against the resistance of Viet-Minh forces
which began to feel the pressure of the second French pincer
closing around them. But the French were not to be stopped: this
was "war" in the conventional sense to them and theirs was a
professional army who knew how to use its tanks, artillery, paratroops and fighter-bombers. Another armored column from Groupment "B" began to claw its way through the jungle and over

---

*Those Germans had been part of Nazi missions operating with the Japanese,
who preferred (like their Japanese partners) to co-operate with the Viet-Minh
rather than to fall into Allied hands and risk being tried as war criminals.

the enemy-sabotaged bridges—the real heroes in this struggle were, as in Burma a few years earlier, the combat engineers—via Nguyen-Binh down river in the direction of Chiem-Hoa, where the river force of Group "C" was having trouble. On October 19, 1947, they met at Chiem-Hoa, a full 120 miles inside rebel territory. The main Communist redoubt in Indochina had become a vast pocket—except for the fact that, in that kind of war and that kind of terrain, the term "encirclement" was of course totally meaningless. Between the towns and key points the French now garrisoned along the triangle there were vast stretches where whole Viet-Minh regiments could slip through, and did. On November 8, one month after it had begun, "Lea" was called off.

It was followed on November 20 by another month-long operation, significantly called *Ceinture* ("Belt"), designed to crush enemy forces in a quadrangle northwest of Hanoi and abutting on Thai Nguyen and Tuyên Quang. Again eighteen battalions, eighteen Navy landing craft and paratroops were committed to crush some of the Viet-Minh's best regular units: Regiment 112, the "Capital Regiment" (later on the core of the 304th "People's Army" Division), and Brigade *Doc-Lap* (Independence, later on part of Division 308). But as was to be the case later many times for almost twenty years, the enemy slipped through the conventional battle lines and armored stabs; yielded weapons and depots if he had to, but lived to fight another day. On the other hand, a much more modest operation, led by two T'ai mountaineer battalions on their own home grounds, cleared the Viet-Minh for almost five years from the T'ai Highlands between the Black and Red Rivers—a lesson that, unfortunately, was forgotten in the roar of tank engines and "Spitfire" fighters with which the French regulars preferred to fight their offensives.

To be sure, the enemy had suffered heavily: his main headquarters and depots had been in part lost and he had suffered 9,500 casualties (but were they really *all* combatants?); and the French had gained a vast acreage of jungle real estate, whose patrolling proved costly in manpower and supplies. On December 22, 1947, the French pulled back to the lowlands with the exception of the string of border forts which were left hanging, as it

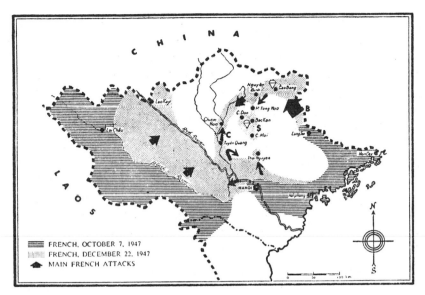

The "Pincers" Fail, 1947.

were, in "mid-air" but preserved at the least the illusion of French control along the confines of China.

For the French, the search for the big set-piece battle in which they could outmaneuver and outgun the enemy, began then. It was to end seven years later, when they found the set-piece battle in a small mountain valley whose English name would be "Seat of the Border County Administration." Its Vietnamese name was Dien Bien Phu.

2

Set-Piece Battle--I

From the Red River Delta to the Hoa-Binh Salient

THE arrival of the Chinese Communists on the borders of North Viet-Nam in November 1949 closed the first chapter of the Indochina war and doomed all French chances of full victory. From then on, the Viet-Minh possessed, like the Reds in Korea, a "sanctuary" where they could refit and retrain their troops with full impunity in Chinese Communist training camps at Nanning and the artillery firing ranges of Ching-Hsi. Soon, Viet-Minh battalions began to appear in full field formations, equipped with heavy mortars and pack howitzers, followed shortly thereafter by complete artillery battalions using American-made recoilless rifles and 105mm howitzers. After nearly a year of relentless training, Vo Nguyên Giap, the Communist commander, felt that his newly-forged tool was ready for the first direct showdown with the French.

Beginning on October 1, 1950, Giap attacked one by one the string of French forts along the Chinese border with fourteen battalions of regular infantry and three artillery battalions. Separated from the French main line of resistance by 300 miles of Communist-held jungle, the dispersed French posts, though numbering close to 10,000 troops, never had a chance. By October 17, all of the garrisons along the border, including three paratroop battalions dropped in during the battle in the forlorn hope of reopening the main road to the key fort of Lang-Son, had been completely destroyed. Lang-Son itself, which could perhaps have been defended for a certain time, was abandoned in an almost-panic with 1,300 tons of ammunition, food, equipment and artillery still intact.

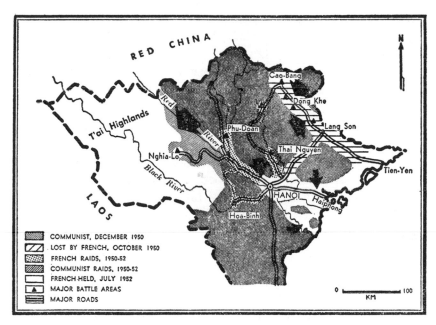

Operations in North Viet-Nam, 1950-52.

When the smoke cleared, the French had suffered their greatest colonial defeat since Montcalm had died at Quebec. They had lost 6,000 troops, 13 artillery pieces and 125 mortars, 450 trucks and three armored platoons, 940 machine guns, 1200 sub-machine-guns and more than 8,000 rifles. Their abandoned stocks alone sufficed for the equipment of a whole additional Viet-Minh division.*

By January 1, 1951, the French had lost control of all of North Viet-Nam to the north of the Red River and were now desperately digging in to hold on to the key pawn of the whole Indochina war—the Red River delta. On the Communist side, General Giap pressed on. The guerrilla groups of 1946-1949 had transformed themselves into battalions, then into regiments, and now began to take their final shape as 10,000-man divisions.

---

*It should be remembered here that at the same time, exactly on October 24, 1950, the Chinese "People's Volunteers" made their appearance in North Korea and inflicted upon the American forces near the Yalu losses in men and equipment which made the subsequent retreat from North Korea the most expensive American defeat since Corregidor.

The first series of five divisions—the Divisions 304, 308, 312, 316, and 320—was created in 1950, soon to be followed by a so-called "351st Heavy Division" of the Soviet artillery division type and composed of two artillery regiments and one combat engineer regiment. The Viet-Minh felt ready to throw the French into the sea.

It was late in 1950 that Giap elaborated his final plan to defeat the French armies in Indochina. In a remarkable staff study presented by him before the political commissars of the 316th Infantry Division, Giap outlined the Indochina war as consisting of three stages. First was that of the initial retreat of the Viet-Minh forces until they had time to re-train and consolidate. The second phase would begin when the French, failing to destroy the Viet-Minh guerrilla forces, would allow them to re-equip themselves and with the help of the Chinese Communists, to eliminate slowly but surely most of the small French posts in the Viet-Minh base area. The third stage was to be the total destruction of the French troops. In Giap's own words:

> The enemy will pass slowly from the offensive to the defensive. The *blitzkrieg* will transform itself into a war of long duration. Thus, the enemy will be caught in a dilemma: he has to drag out the war in order to win it and does not possess, on the other hand, the psychological and political means to fight a long drawn-out war.

Giap was no fool. A French-trained history professor and a member of the Indochinese Communist Party since 1930, he probably was in a better position to evaluate his enemy's potential than anyone else. Being perfectly informed as to the situation of French morale at home and fully aware of American hesitation to commit United States troops in a "colonial" war, Giap felt it important to liquidate the French as a military threat before the arrival of massive American material aid. Giap stated further:

> Our strategy early in the course of the third stage is that of a general counter-offensive. We shall attack without cease until final victory, until we have swept the enemy forces from Indochina. During the first and second stage, we have gnawed away at the enemy forces; now we must destroy them. All military activities of the third stage must tend to the same simple aim—the total destruction of French forces.

Ho Chi Minh.

We shall go on to the general counter-offensive when the following conditions will have been fulfilled: (1) superiority of our forces over those of the enemy; (2) the international situation is in our favor; (3) the military situation is in our favor. We will have to receive aid from abroad in order to be able to carry out the counter-offensive, but to count solely upon it without taking into account our own capabilities is to show proof of subjectivism and of lack of political conscience. But on the other hand we cannot deny the importance of such aid.

When we shall have reached the third stage, the following tactical principles will be applied: mobile warfare will become the principal activity, positional warfare and guerrilla warfare will become secondary.

By the 10th of January, 1951, the bulk of Giap's troops—81 battalions including 12 heavy weapons battalions and 8 engineer battalions—were ready for the general counter-offensive, the big push on to Hanoi itself. In fact, within Hanoi and the whole delta area, Communist propagandists had begun to post leaflets with the inscription "Ho Chi Minh in Hanoi for the *Têt.*" (*Têt* is the Chinese lunar new year which usually falls in the middle of February.) French intelligence had identified the approximate whereabouts of the enemy's concentration and the enemy had given its target date and main target.

For the first time since the beginning of the Indochina war, the French were going to have the opportunity of fighting a set-piece battle.

On the French side, the arrival of Marshal de Lattre de Tassigny as the new Commander-in-Chief had given sagging French morale a badly needed shot in the arm. De Lattre had assumed command of the Indochina theater on December 17, 1950 and had undertaken several measures which none of his predecessors had dared to undertake; he mobilized the French civilians living in Indochina for additional guard duties, thus liberating garrison troops for active combat; and sent back to France the ships which had arrived to evacuate the French women and children living in Indochina. As de Lattre said, "As long as the women and children are here, the men won't *dare* to let go."

From what was known of the enemy's intentions, the major thrust would come from the Tam-Dao Massif in direction of Vinh-Yen. On the French side, two mobile groups,* the North African Mobile Group under Colonel Edon and Mobile Group No. 3 under Colonel Vanuxem defended the approaches to Vinh-Yen, anchoring the resistance around a series of low hills emerging above the alluvial plains.

On January 13, the Communist attack began. As usual, the first movement of Giap consisted in attempting to divide the French forces by a diversionary attack which almost succeeded. A major portion of Communist Division 308 attacked Bao-Chuc, a small post held by about 50 Senegalese and Vietnamese who fought to the last man and succumbed after executing two bayonet counterattacks in the attempt to clear the defenses from their assailants. Colonel Vanuxem's whole mobile group barreled north to come to the help of the post and fell into an extensive ambush near Dao-Tu, losing in the process nearly a whole Senegalese battalion and a large part of the 8th Algerian Spahis. It was only through the providential help of Vinh-Yen's artillery and the presence of French fighter-bombers that the remainder of Vanuxem's mobile group fought its way back to Vinh-Yen. By January 14, the Viet-Minh had achieved its first objective. The French were now blocked with their back against a marshy lake formed by a dead branch of the Red River, leaving the area east of Vinh-Yen with a gap of three miles which was practically undefended.

*Mobile Groups (abbreviated G.M. in French) were composite units resembling the United States regimental combat team.

It looked as if Giap would be able to make good his promise. Morale was low in Hanoi, and the newspapers in Paris, always willing to play up the "uselessness" of the Indochina war, carried big headlines announcing the soon-to-be-expected fall of Hanoi.

It was then that de Lattre decided to take personal charge of the battle. On the 14th of January in the afternoon he personally flew into Vinh-Yen with his small liaison plane, and from Vinh-Yen he ordered the beginning of a thousand-kilometer airlift of reserve battalions from South Indochina into the North. At the same time he ordered Mobile Group No. 1, composed of three battalions of crack North African troops, to break through immediately in the direction of Vinh-Yen with reserve ammunition for battered Mobile Group No. 3. By the afternoon of the 15th of January, Mobile Group No. 1 took Hill 157 which overlooks the road to Vinh-Yen, thus carrying out the first part of its mission. Both mobile groups were instructed to reoccupy the hill line to the north of Vinh-Yen on the following day.

Once more, the bulk of the enemy forces seemed to have evaporated into thin air; at 1500 on January 16, Hills 101 and 210 were reoccupied by the French against light enemy opposition. But all of a sudden, at 1700, with the sun already setting behind the mountains, the French saw small groups of men emerging from the forest-covered hills of the Tam Dao—the whole 308th Division had gone over to the attack and the battle for Hanoi had begun. Dragging with them their heavy mortars and heavy machine guns as a mobile base of fire, the Communists first attacked Hill 47, then Hill 101 and later again 47 and Hill 210. For the first time in the Indochina war, the French faced the unsettling experience of "human sea" attacks: waves upon waves of Viet-Minh infantry threw themselves against the hastily dug defenses of the hill line. De Lattre, who had returned for a second time to Vinh-Yen, recognized the gravity of the situation. All available fighter-bombers in Indochina and transport planes capable of dumping bomb canisters were marshaled into what became the most massive aerial bombardment of the Indochina war.

Waves of fighter-bombers threw up a curtain of roaring napalm between the attacking Communists and the exhausted French defenders, literally roasting thousands of the enemy, but to little

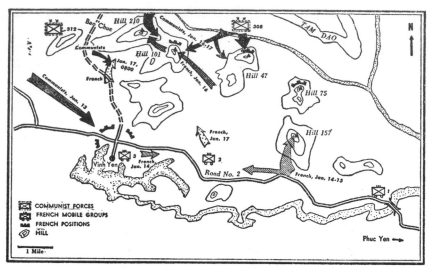

The Battle of Vinh-Yen.

avail. At 1400 on the 17th of January, after merciless hand-to-hand combat with hand grenades and tommyguns, the last survivors of Hill 101, having spent their ammunition, fell back into the plain. With 101 in Communist hands, Hill 47 became untenable and at 0400 Colonel Edon ordered its evacuation. Of the whole hill line to the north of Vinh-Yen, only its two anchors, Hill 210 in the north and 157 in the south, were still in French hands.

Now, de Lattre threw in his last reserves, the newly-constituted Mobile Group No. 2 composed of two Moroccan battalions and one paratroop battalion. On the morning of the 17th, Mobile Group No. 2 was inserted in the front to the southwest of Vinh-Yen and in the early dawn of January 17th, Colonel Vanuxem's Mobile Group No. 3 attempted one last desperate counter attack in order to re-establish contact with Hill 210. One of its battalions again got badly mauled by a suicide attack of Division 312, but once more, the napalm of the fighter-bombers did its deadly job and by noon of January 17, Giap's troops began to disappear in the woods of the Tam Dao. The French looked around themselves with disbelief: the enemy had been defeated and the French remained masters of the battlefield. The battle of Vinh-

Yen had cost the Communists 6,000 dead and 500 prisoners.

To the Viet-Minh, their defeat in the open field must have been cruelly frustrating. It was obvious that Giap's troops were not yet ready for the general counter-offensive. Disappointment found itself clearly expressed in the diary of a Viet-Minh officer, which contained the following revealing passage:

> Our division has been on the attack ever since this morning. We are forming a group of about 10 elite battalions who should be able to take Viet-Tri* before tomorrow.
>
> The French troops react in terrible fashion. We're waiting here all morning. Here and there one can see the battle develop, but my company, unfortunately, has nothing to do. Yes, we would certainly like to participate in the battle which will decide the fate of Hanoi. It is already January 13th and *Têt* will be here in a few weeks, in a month and a half. We want to be in Hanoi for the *Têt!* To the south we can hear the guns rumble like drums. French shells are getting closer and closer and we already have seen some of our wounded leaving the line and coming back to where we are.
>
> The platoon commanders come over to me bringing resolutions and petitions from their men. It is always a great comfort to me, before every assault or particularly dangerous action, to feel the unity of the men and the cadres, and with it, that of the whole People's Army.
>
> I accept all the petitions. Each platoon requests the honor of being assigned the most difficult or the most dangerous mission.
>
> All of a sudden a sound can be heard in the sky and strange birds appear, getting larger and larger. Airplanes. I order my men to take cover from the bombs and machine-gun bullets. But the planes dived upon us without firing their guns. However, all of a sudden, hell opens in front of my eyes. Hell comes in the form of large, egg-shaped containers, dropping from the first plane, followed by other eggs from the second and third plane. Immense sheets of flames, extending over hundreds of meters, it seems, strike terror in the ranks of my soldiers. This is *napalm*, the fire which falls from the skies.
>
> Another plane swoops down behind us and again drops a napalm bomb. The bomb falls closely behind us and I feel its fiery breath touching my whole body. The men are now fleeing in all directions and I cannot hold them back. There is no way of holding out under this torrent of fire which flows in all directions and burns everything on its passage. On all sides, flames surround us now. In addition, French artillery and mortars now have our range and transform into a fiery tomb what had been, ten minutes ago, a quiet part of the forest.

---

* 10 miles to the west of Vinh-Yen.

We flee through the bamboo hedges towards the west and I cry, "Assemble in the woods behind the hill!" But who listens to me and who can hear me?

Behind us, French infantry now attacks; we can hear their screams. We are now passing through the platoon which had remained in reserve. I stop at the platoon commander.

"Try to delay the French as much as possible. I'll try to regroup my men behind the hill!"

His eyes were wide with terror. "What is this? The atomic bomb?"

"No, it is napalm."

The men continue to flee in all directions and I see a political commissar, pistol in hand, trying desperately to regroup them.

We can now hear clearly the yells of the enemy who is pursuing us . . .*

There was no doubt that Giap had suffered a severe defeat in the battle of Vinh-Yen and in a remarkable post-mortem of January 23, 1951, he openly admitted some of his errors. Of course he sought to spread the blame around, accusing some of his troops for their lack of aggressiveness, and even of "cowardice"—which was certainly not justified—for having lacked determination in pushing direct infantry attacks against the well-entrenched French artillery positions and armored combat teams. However, he paid a significant homage to the civilian porters, who had worked two *million* man-days and brought to the battle area 5,000 tons of rice, ammunition and weapons.

The hard fact remained, however, that the Communist troops were not yet ready for the general counter-offensive which was to sweep the French into the sea. On the other hand, the French lacked the necessary cross-country mobility and, for that matter, necessary manpower or airpower to exploit such an unexpected victory as that of Vinh-Yen. Even under the leadership of such an inspired commander as Marshal de Lattre, the French could do little else at the end of the battle of Vinh-Yen but to consolidate their position on the hill line and settle down to await the next Communist attack.

---

*Cited by Captain Despuech, in his translation of Ngo Van Chieu, *Journal d'un combattant Viet-Minh*, Paris 1954: Éditions du Seuil.

The author was able to visit the Vinh-Yen battlefield in what is now Communist North Viet-Nam in July 1962. The scars of war can still be seen on Hill 157, and small French and Viet-Minh war cemeteries dot the countryside. The French cemeteries, though showing lack of care, are undefaced. Viet-Tri, then a mound of ruins, is now a bustling industrial town.

Undeterred by his unsuccessful attack against Vinh-Yen, Giap now shifted his battle force farther towards the hill range of the Dong Trieu. This was a particularly sensitive area to the French defense of the Red River delta, because it controlled not only the approaches to the important coal mines of North Viet-Nam, but also because a determined thrust of less than 20 kilometers could endanger the vital port of Haiphong, thus destroying all French hopes of holding out in North Viet-Nam. Leaving the 304th and 320th Infantry Divisions on the northwestern edge of the delta to attract the French reserves into the opposite direction, Giap shifted the 308th, 312th and 316th Infantry Divisions in the direction of Mao Khé. The attack began in the night of March 23 to 24. By March 26th, the whole first line of posts had fallen into Communist hands, but the deep bay of the Da Bach River permitted the intervention of three French destroyers and two landing ships whose concentrated fire broke up the enemy's attempt at penetrating into Mao Khé itself.

As often in war, a small post finds itself unexpectedly in the center of a vast action. This was now the case of Mao Khé. Originally the post had been designed to cover the mine area and was composed of three positions: a small garrison at the mine itself composed of 95 guerrillas of the Thô tribe from Lang-Son and three French noncommissioned officers under the command of a Vietnamese, Lieutenant Nghiem-Xuan-Toan. An armored car platoon of the Moroccan Colonial Infantry Regiment (RICM) defended the village of Mao Khé situated astride Road 18 about 1,000 meters to the south of the Mao Khé mine, while the Catholic church of Mao Khé, located about 100 meters to the east of the village and south of Road 18, was defended by a weak company of the 30th Composite Battalion of Senegalese infantry and Tho partisans. It was those 400 men who were to support the initial shock of a Communist attack by three divisions. At 0400 of March 27, Mao Khé mine was hit by a barrage of 75mm and 57mm shells. Within the first few minutes of combat, the lieutenant commanding the post was wounded and two of the French NCO's were killed, but the first two mass attacks broke under the fire of the defenders. At 0515, a tremendous explosion shook the whole complex: Viet-Minh "Volunteers of

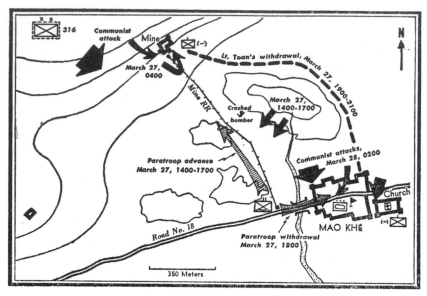

The Defense of Mao Khé.

Death" (the Communist version of the Japanese *Kamikaze*) had infiltrated the position and blown a breach into the outer wall through which now poured Viet-Minh infantry. In the early dawn, under the command of the last French NCO, himself seriously wounded, the Thô partisans repelled the Viet-Minh assault in hand-to-hand combat and again consolidated their position. When daylight broke the Communist pressure relented somewhat since French B-26's and Hellcats began to bomb the open plain around the post with napalm and fragmentation bombs.

At 1400, the 6th Colonial Parachute Battalion attempted to break through to Mao Khé mine from Road 18 but was bogged down by the concentrated enemy artillery and machine-gun fire, in spite of French artillery and air support. One Hellcat dive-bomber, caught in Communist antiaircraft fire, smashed into no-man's-land. But even the painfully slow progress of the para-troopers gave the battered defenders of Mao Khé the last desper-ate chance to make a get-away. At 1900, Toan started the evacu-ation of Mao Khé mine. Detouring the Communist position be-tween Mao Khé mine and Mao Khé, the survivors of the previous night's battle made their way to Mao Khé village, taking with them all their wounded and a long column of the wives and children of the Tho partisans who had lived with their husbands in the post. Their break-out took the Communists completely by surprise and they reached Mao Khé village without being attacked.

This was but a meager respite, because the village, in turn, became the major target of the Communist attack. At 0200 of March 28, a Communist barrage was laid down on Mao Khé village and Mao Khé church. Screaming waves of Viet-Minh infantry slashed both into the village defenses and into the defenses of the church. Two of the bunkers of Mao Khé church, destroyed by shaped charges, fell into enemy hands, and in the village, two of the watch towers, severely hit by bazookas, crumbled, burying all their defenders and the machine guns. The three armored cars of the RICM were soon buried under the collapsing houses of Mao Khé and their crews formed an infantry platoon in support of the 6th Paratroop Battalion now fighting for every house in the fiercely burning village. As French artillery from Dong-Trieu began laying down pre-arranged fires almost on top of the position, and the Communists began firing into every house with bazooka shells or incendiary grenades, the whole village soon became one blazing inferno. But when the morning dawned, the paratroopers, Thô partisans, Senegalese, and Moroccan armored cavalry had held on to their position and 400 dead Communists were lying in and about the ruins of the village. On their side the French had lost more than 40 dead and 150 wounded. Once more Giap had failed to breach the French defensive front around the delta.

Giap was to try yet for a third time to smash the French delta position, this time from the south, in a classical maneuver which combined the frontal attack by his regular divisions with an attack from *inside* the delta directed against the front by two regular Viet-Minh infantry regiments which had been previously infiltrated into the delta.*

---

*The device of supporting a frontal attack by troops infiltrated behind the enemy's main line is one which the Russians used regularly against the Germans in World War II. A known instance where such a maneuver was used with great success by the United States Army in World War II is that of the infiltration of the 142d and 143d U.S. Infantry Regiments of the 36th Division behind German lines in Italy, south of Rome.

The 64th Infantry Regiment of the 320th Division was in-filtrated 30 kilometers deep behind the French lines near Thai Binh where it joined forces with Independent Infantry Regiment No. 42, a crack Viet-Minh outfit which was permanently sta-tioned behind French lines and which survived all French efforts at annihilating it until the end of the war.

The terrain lent itself ideally to a surprise attack. The western bank of the Day River rose steeply over the French-held eastern bank, and the alluvial dish-pan flat plain of the Red River delta was studded in this area by steep limestone cliffs covered with dense vegetation and pierced by innumerable caves and holes which offered perfect bomb-proof concealment to enemy forces. The only advantage which played in favor of the French was that the river itself was navigable enough to permit the support of the French garrisons by one of the famous *"Dinas-saut,"** the Naval Assault Divisions, whose creation may well have been one of the few worthwhile contributions of the Indo-china war to military knowledge. This concentration of mobile riverborne firepower permitted fairly effective attacks on the enemy's supply lines which, of necessity, had to cross the Day River.

The enemy's plan was quite simple. While concentrated attacks

---

*As will be seen in chapter 3, the *Dinassaut* were rivercraft units constituted by the French Navy for the specific purpose of supporting landborne units along the many Indochinese rivers. They were composed of locally-modified American landing craft of various types which had been provided with armor plates and with tank gun turrets as artillery. The average *Dinassaut* had about twelve ships, including an armored LSSL (Landing Ship Support, Large) as flagship, two LCM (Landing Craft, Material) of the armored "Monitor" version as fire base, and about six other LCM carrying 81mm mortar batteries, cargo and one or two company-size Marine commandos. Some *Dinassauts* (French abbreviation: DNA) such as DNA No. 3 in the Red River delta, would grow as large as twenty and more craft and would include their own reconnaissance aircraft and LCT (Landing Craft, Tank)-borne armored vehicles.

As I was to find out through subsequent research, *Dinassaut* No. 1 played an important role in the defense of Mao-Khé both through artillery support and through the successful beaching of the 6th Paratroop Battalion prior to the big Communist attack of March 28, 1951. DNA No. 3 played a decisive role in holding the Day River line. Its Marine Commando, 80 strong, held on through-out the night of May 28-29, 1951, inside Ninh Binh church, losing all but 19 men. On June 6, a second *Dinassaut,* hastily formed with some landing craft found in Haiphong and named *Dinassaut* "A," was thrown into the battle. It was the concentrated gunfire of its flagship, LSSL No. 6, which finally saved the key position of Yen Cu Ha.

of Division 304 against Phu Ly and Division 308 against Ninh-Binh, the anchors of the French position, were to pin down French reserves, the 320th Division, by rapid thrusts to the east and south, would wipe out the line of weak French posts between Ninh-Binh and the sea and would reoccupy the Catholic bishopric of Phat-Diem, thus partially dismantling the French positions in the southern part of the Red River delta as well as dealing a severe psychological blow to the anti-Communist Vietnamese Catholics. At the same time, Regiments 42 and 64 attacked French concentrations and supply lines in the rear areas, isolating through their actions the whole battlefield and preventing French reinforcements and supplies from reaching the hard-pressed defenders of the Day River Line.

The initial Viet-Minh attack, which began on May 29, benefited, as was almost always the case, from the effect of total surprise. As dawn broke, the bulk of the 308th Infantry Division overran the French positions in and around Ninh-Binh, penetrating into the town and pinning down the remaining French survivors in the church. During that chaotic first night of the battle, a battalion of hastily-gathered Vietnamese reinforcements from nearby Nam-Dinh was thrown into the battle. One of its companies, headed by the French commander-in-chief's only child, Lieutenant Bernard de Lattre, was ordered to hold at all costs a French fort situated on a crag overlooking Ninh-Binh. In spite of intense mortar shelling, de Lattre's company held on, but when dawn came, young de Lattre and two of his senior NCO's lay dead on the crag. (Before the Indochina war was over, twenty more sons of French marshals and generals were to die in it as officers; another twenty-two died in Algeria later.) At the same time an ambush mounted with bazookas and recoilless cannon on both sides of the Day River severely disabled several of the unarmored craft of the *Dinassaut* which had steamed up the river to come to the help of Ninh-Binh; while a diversionary attack of the 308th to the south of Ninh-Binh succeeded in crossing the Day River and annihilating a string of small French posts. The French High Command reacted swiftly at the news. Within 48 hours three mobile groups, four artillery groups, one armored group and the 7th Colonial Paratroop Battalion were thrown

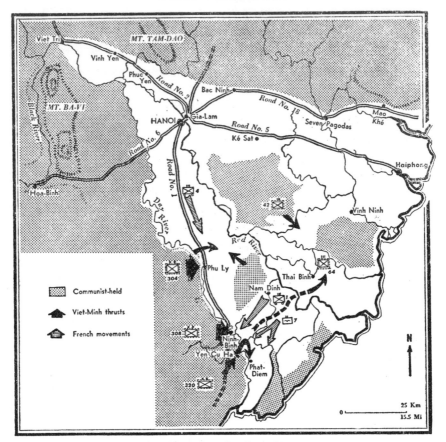

The Battle on the Day River.

into the battle. The climax of the battle was reached during the
night of June 4-5 with the key post of Yen Cu Ha changing
hands several times. But the bulk of the enemy troops, now
hampered by the ravages of the French river craft and aircraft
among the hundreds of small junks and sampans which constituted the enemy's supply line across the Day River, began to
fall back to the limestone hills. On June 18, 1951, the third
battle for the delta had ended.

All the battles had been less than conclusive victories for the
French, but had given the Viet-Minh an ample opportunity to
measure their own limitations and to find out the major weak-

nesses of the French. Vo Nguyên Giap was never again to forget the lessons for which his troops had paid so dearly.

While the last battles were raging around the Red River delta, the 312th Infantry Division of the Viet-Minh already had begun to wade across the upper Red River into the T'ai area. The first thrust, begun on April 2, ended around April 25 and was meant to be nothing else but a strong reconnaissance for further large-scale operations. The intervening rainy season which begins in northern Indochina around that date, interrupted the Communist campaign which was resumed at the end of the rainy season on September 22, 1951. This time the whole 312th Division crossed the Red River valley at Yen-Bay in order to crack open the first French center in the T'ai territory, Nghia-Lô. The battle for the Indochinese highlands had begun in earnest.

Once more luck and great mobility played in the favor of the French. De Lattre committed three of his precious reserve of nine paratroop battalions in and around Nghia-Lô in a desperate effort to hold on to the northern mountain areas he felt were decisive if he wanted to cover northern Laos or keep the enemy from concentrating all his strength on the heavily-infiltrated Red River delta. On October 5, after repeated assaults against Nghia-Lô and other posts, the enemy was stopped once more—and for the last time—from penetrating into the T'ai country.

But de Lattre realized that this temporary retreat was nothing but a brief respite given him by Giap and his Chinese advisers before new tactics could be devised to cope with the new offensive spirit instilled into the French forces by de Lattre after the disastrous border campaign of 1950, and by the ever-mounting influx of American equipment. In order to take advantage of this temporary stalemate this time, de Lattre decided to strike first and in an unexpected direction: instead of aiming at the enemy's main centers of resistance in the northeast, he struck out across the bend of the Black River and captured the city of Hoa-Binh.

What was to become the "meat-grinder" battle of Hoa-Binh,* lasting from November 14, 1951 to February 24, 1952, had at

---

* Its French code name was "Lotus."

its outset several practical and political considerations: on the tactical side Hoa-Binh constituted the major road link between the northeastern Communist strongholds which received Communist aid and equipment, and the central Vietnamese stronghold around Thanh-Hoa, where the 320th Communist Division had operated until now in almost total isolation. The road leading from the northeast to Thanh-Hoa via Hoa-Binh constituted a vital communications artery; to sever it certainly would not completely destroy the flow of Communist supplies to the rebel forces in central and southern Viet-Nam (since they were mostly not subject to road transport anyway) but it certainly might prevent or at least hamper for a certain length of time the influx of such enemy equipment as artillery, trucks, and machines used for the production of ammunition. Another important consideration was that of maintaining the allegiance of the Muong mountaineers whose members had so far remained fiercely loyal to the French. Two Muong battalions were fighting on the French side and thousands of Muong tribesmen had taken refuge in the delta. Hoa-Binh was the capital of the Muong tribe and thus constituted a psychological point of attraction of no mean importance.

Furthermore, the French National Assembly was about to debate the Indochina budget for 1952-53 and the French government was badly in need of a victory in order to pass that difficult internal hurdle. And finally, the French were in the process of asking a greatly increased American participation in sharing the cost of the Indochina war. Thus, a French victory in Indochina—contrasting with the completely stalemated situation in Korea—would make such an increased outlay of funds attractive to American Congressmen.

At dawn of November 14, 1951, three French paratroop battalions* descended slowly upon Hoa-Binh, occupying the city

---

*This was the last operation in which the French used tri-motor Junkers-52's for their parachute and resupply operations. After Hoa-Binh, massive arrivals of American C-47's permitted the elimination of those planes, whose prototypes were then about 25 years old. The C-47 prototype, has, of course, now reached about the same age limit. Only in 1953 did the French receive some of the new S.O. "Bretagne" transports, twin-engine planes with auxiliary wing-tip jet engines for short-terrain takeoffs; and American-made C-119 "Flying Boxcars."

against almost no resistance. At the same time, a total of fifteen infantry battalions, seven artillery battalions, two armored groups, reinforced by two *Dinassauts* and adequate engineering forces to repair the sabotaged road and bridges; began to churn their way into the narrow Black River valley. The next afternoon, all major objectives were in French hands with a minimum of losses and almost no enemy resistance. Faithful to his own methods, Giap had refused combat as soon as he saw that his troops had neither the required numerical superiority nor an adequate route of withdrawal to justify such a stand. The French had stabbed with all their might—and had encountered empty space.

For General Giap, this French invasion of the wooded hill areas appeared as an excellent opportunity to repeat the successes obtained on Road No. 4 in 1950. With amazing rapidity (and this time without offering suitable targets to the French Air Force) Giap ordered nearly all his regulars to the battle for Hoa-Binh: the 304th, 308th and 312th Infantry Divisions with artillery, anti-aircraft and engineering troops; and the Regional Troops (semi-regular forces) stationed to the west of the Red River Delta. Finally, the 316th and 320th Infantry Divisions, the former being stationed on the northern flank of the delta and the latter being partially infiltrated along the Day River front, were given the order to penetrate deeply into the French lowland positions and to disorganize French supply lines feeding the Hoa-Binh pocket.

Two major avenues of approach were open to the French to maintain their "hedgehog" around Hoa-Binh. One was Road No. 6 leading via Xuan-Mai and Xom-Phéo to Hoa-Binh. Road No. 6 had been fully sabotaged by the Communists in 1946 and equally thoroughly plowed under by the French Air Force since, and not maintained in any state of repair since 1940. In other words, it was barely more than an unimproved path which French engineering troops and bulldozers were now preparing frantically to provide Hoa-Binh with an overland approach. However, French combat engineers, until almost the end of the battle, never had the time to clear away the underbrush on both sides of the road which offered ideal hideouts to Viet-Minh commandos. Along most of its length, the road was further controlled by cliffs, hills,

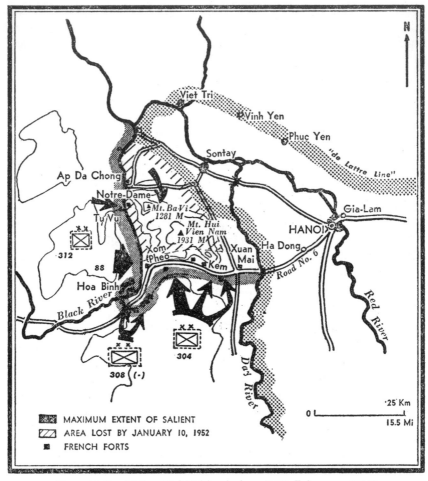

The "Hell of Hoa-Binh," November 1951-February 1952.

and mountains which the French could neither occupy nor control at all times. As it turned out, the battle for Hoa-Binh was to become first and foremost a battle for the communications leading to it.

Communications with Hoa-Binh via the Black River were almost three times as long as via Road No. 6, but the river offered the advantage of allowing heavy bulk transportation by landing craft and at most places provided wider fields of fire than the road. But here also, the fact remained that landing craft, with their thin, unarmored flat sides riding high in the water, offered excellent targets to Communist recoilless cannon and bazookas. Thus, in the case of the river route as well as that of Road No. 6, the French had developed a system of forts and strong points strung out on both sides of the communications artery which was costly both in manpower and equipment. And as the battle for Hoa-Binh wore on, the problem of resupplying the string of posts covering the approaches became almost as difficult (sometimes even more so) as that of supplying the pocket of Hoa-Binh itself. To retain control of Tu Vu, Notre-Dame Rock or Ap Da Chong —each of which became the subject of a costly battle in the attempt to maintain open the communication lines with Hoa-Binh— soon over-shadowed the principal objective of the whole operation.

In fact, it can be said that soon enough both sides had lost sight of the reasons for which Hoa-Binh had become important in the scheme of things as the French High Command wrestled with the problem of how to extricate its troops from the whole operation without losing too many of them, too much face, and all the political benefits it expected to reap from the situation. Yet, in the first days of heady optimism, the Western press had hailed the Hoa-Binh operation as "a pistol pointed at the heart of the enemy." But among the men in Indochina who had to face the battle and who survived to tell about it, it was better remembered as "the hell of Road No. 6" or "the hell of Hoa-Binh."

By December 9, 1951, two regiments of the Viet-Minh 312th Division and one regiment of the 308th were in position to attack Tu-Vu, anchor of the Black River line. The French, sensing that such an operation was under preparation, sought to head off the attack by one of their own. At dawn the 10th, three French infantry battalions supported by artillery, tanks and the French Air Force and led by the 1st Colonial Paratroop Battalion, made contact with about five enemy battalions, but could not prevent the major enemy movement against Tu-Vu which was attacked as of 2100 on the same day.

The attack on Tu-Vu was a portent of things to come in its intensity and brutality. Defended by two Moroccan rifle companies and a tank platoon and organized into two separate strongpoints, it could be expected to resist a reasonable amount of Communist pressure. It was furthermore covered by an outpost line which precluded a surprise general attack on the strong points themselves. The position, however, was endowed with two fatal weaknesses: it was cut in two in the middle by the Ngoi Lat, a small tributary of the Black River, which allowed communications between the two strongpoints only via a flimsy foot bridge; and the position as a whole constituted a beachhead on the west bank of the Black River which meant that any help in case of a severe attack would have to involve a night-time river crossing operation under enemy fire—a hazardous enterprise at best.

The attack came after an intensive preparation fired by the enemy's heavy mortars. Since the mortars were firing from a defiladed position, they were, of course, impervious to the counter-battery fire of the French artillery and out of range of the French mortars on the other side of the river. After a preparation of about 40 minutes, enemy fire concentrated on the southern strong-point and at about 2210, shrill screams of *"Tiên-lên!"* ("For-ward!") were heard as enemy infantry threw itself across the barbed wire and the minefields without regard to losses, which, under the concentrated fire of the French automatic weapons, were murderous. One "human-wave" attack after another was smashed by French defensive fires, supplemented by the artillery batteries from the east bank of the river now firing directly into the barbed wire of the French positions. By 2340, it was obvious that the southern strongpoint could no longer be held; the barbed wire entanglements, now covered with a carpet of enemy bodies, had become totally useless as a hindrance; most of the emplace-ments for automatic weapons had been blasted to bits by enemy mortars and the surviving Moroccans were rapidly running out of ammunition. At 0115, the commander of Tu-Vu ordered the last survivors of the southern strongpoint to cross the bridge to the northern position.

But the northern strongpoint was to be given no respite. At 0300, five battalions threw themselves against the 200-odd men of Tu-Vu. The tanks of the armored platoon, guns depressed to minimum elevation, fired into the screaming human clusters crawling over the parapets into the position, their heavy treads

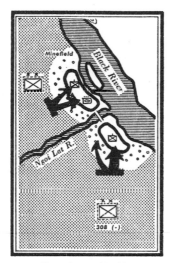

Death at Tu-Vu.

crushing heads, limbs, and chests by the dozens as they slowly moved like chained elephants in the little open space left in the post. But soon they, too, were submerged by the seemingly never-ending human wave, with scores of hands clawing at their turret hatches trying to pry them open; stuffing incendiary hand grenades into their cannon, firing tommygun bursts into their driving slits; finally destroying them with pointblank bazooka bursts which lit up their hulls with the sizzling of white-hot metal. The sweetish smell of searing flesh rose in the air. All the five tank crews died to the last man, roasted alive in their vehicles.

But time had also run out for the rest of the garrison of Tu-Vu. With their backs to the Black River, many of the survivors rolled down the steep embankment into the water and then waded or swam towards a small island in the river for a last stand. But the Communists appeared satisfied with their victory. As the morning came, heavy silence reigned over Tu-Vu, and Moroccan patrols slipped off the island back into the post. They found it deserted of enemy fighters and stripped of all weapons. But the enemy also had left behind more than 400 bodies.

The see-saw battle for the control of the Black River line was to continue throughout the rest of the month of December, with varying degrees of success. The French now threw into the battle

Mobile Groups No. 1, 4, and 7 and the 1st Airborne Group, reinforced by armor; but once more the enemy was to refuse combat on any terms but his own. He vanished in caves of the limestone hills only to appear again at the beginning of January around the pocket of Hoa-Binh. This time, the main action of his effort was the overland route to the pocket. Along the Black River line, Giap's forces now reverted to the dreaded pattern of *pourrissement,* of the slow but careful erosion of the French posts covering the approaches to the river. To be sure, as at Tu-Vu, the French were always capable of re-occupying the post that had just been submerged but there was a point of rapidly diminishing returns in this sort of exercise, past which the French High Command had to accept the total evacuation of the sector as preferable to the ever-rising blood-letting its permanent occupation demanded; the occupation of Hoa-Binh was in fact rapidly becoming an "Operation Meat Grinder" in reverse.

This situation led, between the 6th and 10th of January 1952, to the progressive evacuation of the mountain massif around Mount Ba-Vi and the withdrawal of all posts on the west bank of the Black River with the exception of one important bridge-head seated at its point of confluence with the Red River. This gave the Viet-Minh one whole river bank from which to prepare ambushes on the river convoys which now had to be escorted by heavily armed improvised river warships. Made up of American landing craft of various types equipped with tank turrets, twin-mounted or quadruple-mounted heavy machine guns and float-ing mortar batteries, often carrying their own complement of shipborne Marine commandos and even a few light tanks or armored cars, the *Dinassauts* were to render invaluable services to the hard-pressed defenders of the Hoa-Binh pocket. Probably the bloodiest river battles since the American Civil War were fought out between the French and the Viet-Minh in the re-stricted confines of the Black River around Notre-Dame Rock and later on the various tributaries of the Red River in the delta area, with ships being attacked and sunk by gun fire, mines, and even frogmen. The French Admiral in Far Eastern Waters was re-sponsible for the tactical direction and administration of naval units from aircraft carriers and heavy cruisers to small self-contained "fleets" fighting on their own 250 miles inland on streams and rivers for which there did not even exist naval charts and for which their craft had never been designed. And neither, for the past 150 years, had the French Naval Academy taught any kind of tactics even remotely applicable to that situation.

Throughout the month of December, the little naval craft had maintained the Black River open as a communication line with Hoa-Binh, at the price of ever increased shellings and losses. Then, on January 12th, the Viet-Minh ambushed one whole river convoy south of Notre-Dame Rock. Undeterred by the murderously accurate fire, the little patrol boats did their best to cover the lumbering landing craft hauling the supplies. Heading straight for the enemy river bank, they sprayed the enemy gun positions with mortar and automatic gun fire, but to little avail. Most of the ships of the convoy were severely damaged and forced to turn back; and of the escorts, four patrol boats and one heavily armed LSSL were sunk in the river. The first jaw of the pincers around Hoa-Binh had closed. The French no longer attempted to push through river convoys to Hoa-Binh. The stage was now set for the battle of Road No. 6.

In fact, the battle for the road already had begun while the agony of the Black River line was still going on. The enemy had now occupied the commanding heights around Hoa-Binh itself and possessed an intermittent view of Hoa-Binh airfield which was now and then under enemy fire. Increasingly accurate Communist antiaircraft artillery, along with the shelling of the airfield, already had cost the French a half dozen aircraft either destroyed on the strip itself or on the pre-set flight path approaching the airfield. Hoa-Binh itself was defended by five infantry battalions and one artillery battalion while Road No. 6 was held by ten strongpoints with a total of one infantry battalion, one artillery battalion, two armored battalions and an engineer group. Against this meager force, the Communists threw the whole 304th Division and Regiment 88 of the 308th Division, all now fully re-equipped with brand-new Red Chinese equipment and equally new American equipment captured by the Chinese Reds in Korea and transferred by them to the Indochinese theater.*

The tactics used by Giap against the forts along Road No. 6 were monotonously identical to those used by him in 1950 against the French border positions, and in December 1951 against the Black River line. On January 8th, 1952, the whole 88th Viet-Minh Infantry Regiment attacked the vital hill position of Xom-Phéo, defended by the 2d Battalion of the Foreign Legion's crack 13th Half-Brigade.

The hill was held by two of the 2d's four companies, with the remaining two companies holding positions directly astride Road No. 6. With the carefulness and deliberateness which is the trademark of the Foreign Legionnaire, the whole hill had been fortified with deep trenches, earth bunkers, and well-prepared barbed wire and minefields. Atop the hill, the men had dug four-man bunkers, with one squad in each platoon constantly manning the parapets.

Active day-and-night patrolling had been routine procedure and early on January 8, an ice-cold night particularly well lit by the moon, two patrols of 5th Company had remained in ambush in the no-man's land more than one kilometer away from Xom-Phéo until 0100. At 0110, the first patrol carefully wound its way through the corridor in the mine field and the barbed wire entanglements back to home base, followed at a five-minute interval by the second patrol. In the course of their patrol, neither of the two squads had encountered any contact with the enemy. Now, with the second patrol hardly inside the forward trench, a series of shadows rose behind them. Without the slightest hesitation, Corporal Felipez, of 1st Platoon, raised his tommy

---

*This was to be the case throughout almost the whole latter part of the Indochina war. The Communists had standardized their equipment in Korea along Russian lines, while it was always easy for the Viet-Minh in Indochina to capture American ammunition or spare parts from the French to fit their own American-made equipment.

In fact, it happened quite often that the French would capture from the Communists American equipment produced in 1950 or 1951, while French equipment of similar American manufacture dated from the earlier parts of World War II. In 1952, for example, the Communists in Indochina had a decided superiority in heavy 75mm recoilless rifles captured from the Americans in Korea, while the French Army still had to make do with the underpowered 57's.

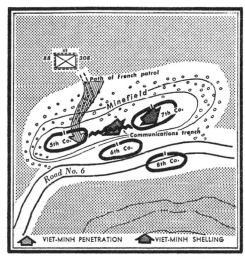

Failure at Xom-Phéo.

gun and began to fire. Almost simultaneously, the first salvo of
enemy mortar shells slammed into 5th Company's position: the
Viet-Minh had simply followed the patrols back to Xom-Phéo
using them as guides through the mine field!

Within seconds, the carefully prepared positions of 1st and 2d
Platoons were overrun, with the 1st Platoon being practically
submerged in its own bunkers before it had a chance to react.
At the same time well-prepared mortar fire pinned down 7th
Company in its position, preventing it from using the communications trenches to 5th Company. A few seconds later, 4th Platoon was also attacked, thus leaving only 3d Platoon in position
to act as a reserve. With incredible speed, indicating that the
whole operation had been carefully rehearsed not only on the
map and at the sand table but also through individual visual reconnaissance, Viet-Minh assault troops began to mop up the bunkers
one by one with concentrated charges of TNT and bangalore torpedoes. By 0145, the positions of 1st and 2d Platoons had
become untenable and the survivors had fallen back on 3d Platoon.
Fourth Platoon was still holding out. By 0230, the Foreign Legionnaires of 5th Company began to hear extremely close blasts of
recoilless rifles and mortars which could only have come from
weapons which the Communist troops had dragged with them

in the hope of being able to use them immediately against 6th Company and 8th Company down on the Road, a procedure that was as unorthodox as it was efficient.

But 5th Company, though badly mauled, refused to cave in. At 0400, with most of their officers and senior NCO's dead or wounded and half the position overrun, the Foreign Legionnaires counterattacked with fixed bayonets and hand grenades. In the savage hand-to-hand combat which ensued, no quarter was given and as dawn rose, the Viet-Minh who had penetrated into the position were being slowly hacked to pieces. They, too, were crack troops, and not a single Viet-Minh withdrew from the position. As one of the survivors of 3d Platoon was to say later on:

> "Finally one last surviving Viet-Minh broke and ran. He jumped the barbed wire in one single leap, began to zig-zag down the ravine, hoping to get away. We literally cut him to shreds. It probably isn't a nice thing to say, but I think I must have emptied a whole clip into him. He had fallen down but he was still rolling down the ravine. Then Sgt. Thomas, one of the few survivors of the 1st Platoon, touched my shoulder and, motioning me to cease firing, raised his carbine; a single shot rang out and the body now remained motionless. It was 1st Platoon's revenge."

Viet-Minh losses had been extremely heavy. On the following morning, 5th Company counted more than 700 dead around Xom-Phéo. Its own losses had also been severe; 1st Platoon had been nearly wiped out and 2d Platoon was in hardly better shape. To be sure, the enemy stab at Xom-Phéo had failed, but it in no way loosened the grip of the 304th Division on Road No. 6. In fact, on the following day, January 9, it occupied the hills overlooking Kem Pass and nearly destroyed the whole mobile battalion of the road's covering force which passed through, unaware that part of the road was under enemy control. The second jaw of the Communist pincers around Hoa-Binh had closed.

A weak attempt at breaking through to Hoa-Binh made later by three infantry battalions and one artillery battalion, bogged down on the Viet-Minh blocking position at Kem Pass. The French, now re-examining the whole situation, resorted to a procedure which, though painfully slow, should perhaps have been employed at the outset. They began to use hundreds of men and locally-recruited laborers to clear away the underbrush from both sides of Road No. 6 in order to create clear fields of fire for the weapons of their convoys and to eliminate further occurrences of "zero-distance" ambushes which already had cost them close to one hundred vehicles along the twenty-five miles of road between the Red River delta and Hoa-Binh.

Even so, and in spite of considerable reinforcements, the airborne task force under Colonel (later General) Gilles made only painfully slow headway against ever-increasing enemy resistance along Road No. 6. In fact, the whole twenty-five mile stretch had now become one vast Calvary, finally absorbing twelve battalions of infantry and three artillery groups (not to speak of hundreds of fighter-bomber and aerial supply missions) to resupply five infantry battalions locked up in a pocket without the slightest offensive value.

It took the Gilles task force from January 18 to January 29—eleven full days!—to cover the twenty-five miles between the Day River and Hoa-Binh, and each mile had been dearly paid for in French lives. It had now become apparent that far from drawing the enemy into a "meat-grinder" operation, the French had been compelled to draw nearly one-third of all their mobile forces available in the Red River delta into an area where those forces became unable to contribute to the mopping-up of enemy guerrillas now infiltrating the vital Red River plain on an increasingly massive scale. While Marshal de Lattre was dying in Paris from cancer in January 1952, the decision was made in Indochina by his successor, General Salan, to evacuate the whole Hoa-Binh salient, thus making available vitally needed troops for the forthcoming battle in the delta and in the T'ai highlands.

But to execute now the withdrawal from Hoa-Binh in the face of direct pressure by three Communist divisions proved to be a great deal more complicated than the initial occupation of Hoa-Binh by surprise. As one senior French officer remarked wryly; "I guess Marshal de Lattre died just in time in order not to be saddled with a retreat."

The evacuation of Hoa-Binh was given the code name of "Operation Amaranth" and involved a three-leap withdrawal along Road No. 6 as well as a temporary re-opening of the Black River all the way to Hoa-Binh itself. The actual operation began on

February 22, 1952 at 1900, with landing craft of all sorts ferrying across the Black River more than 200 trucks loaded with ammunition, equipment and food; more than 600 porters carrying supply loads for the combat troops; and close to a thousand Muong civilians. At 0600 on the following morning, the combat troops themselves began to cross the river and fall back to Xom-Phéo under a constant umbrella of artillery and fighter-bombers. More than 30,000 shells were fired in support of the salient between February 22 and 24. Apparently, the enemy had been taken by surprise, for its first reaction occurred only at 0800. From then on the whole retreat became one continous battle as French units held on to each post to the last minute to allow troops behind them to funnel through to the next post.

At the Black River, the battle had begun once more for the small ships fighting their way north and east out of the trap. Vietnamese, French, Moroccans, and Foreign Legionnaires fought with the strength of despair to break out of the encirclement. Finally, on February 24, 1952, the last elements of the 13th Foreign Legion Half-Brigade—which was to be totally destroyed two years later at Dien Bien Phu—crossed the fortified delta line at Xuan-Mai.

On a piecemeal basis—one company annihilated here, one battalion mauled there, a truck convoy lost in an ambush elsewhere— the battle of Hoa-Binh had been in fact almost as expensive for the French as the loss of the border forts in 1950 or the later siege of Dien Bien Phu. The enemy's losses certainly had been heavy. The repeated use of "human-wave" attacks no doubt had cost him an important measure of his immediate combat potential. Seen from a long-range viewpoint, however, the French once more had been the heavier losers, for while the Viet-Minh used the battle for the Black River salient as a sort of dress rehearsal for a future show-down battle, the French apparently failed to consider the operation as either a dress rehearsal or as a portent of things to come.

Ironically enough, the name "Hoa-Binh," in Vietnamese, means "Peace."

3

Set-Piece Battle--II

The Northwest and "Operation Lorraine"

THE concentration of the bulk of the French mobile reserves around the Hoa-Binh salient led, on the French side, to a progressive neglect of the other theaters of operations. This had been considered by the French High Command to be an acceptable risk as long as the battle for Hoa-Binh promised to pay the expected heavy dividends in destroyed enemy regular units, and the gamble seemed to pay off in South Viet-Nam and Cambodia, where the slowing down of French operations did not seriously impair the local situation. In fact, the energetic anti-terrorist operations carried out by Vietnamese government authorities soon led to an end to urban bomb-throwing and sabotage. It may be considered as remarkable that not one single major incident of terrorism took place in Saigon from late 1952 until the end of the Indochina war.

In the key Red River delta, however, the situation had deteriorated at an alarming rate. Profiting from the focusing of French attentions upon Hoa-Binh, General Giap had once more thrown into the battle the 316th and 320th Divisions, soon reinforced by elements of the 304th withdrawn from Hoa-Binh and Independent Regiments 42 and 48 infiltrated into the delta. By March 1952, the French were mounting combined operations involving several mobile groups *behind* their own lines in order to keep their communications open.

More and more the solidity of the whole French position in the Red River Delta rested on the shoulders of a small group of young energetic colonels whom de Lattre had nicknamed *Maréchaux d'Empire*—Marshals of the Empire—in remembrance of the group of daring French military leaders whose fast-moving armies held Napoleon's empire together. This was exactly the case with

61

the half-dozen regimental and airborne combat teams commanded by such men as Colonels Vanuxem, de Castries, Kergaravat, Blanckaert, Gilles, and Langlais, who soon became famous for the drive and energy with which they led their mobile groups into battle.

It took a special kind of guts and dash to command the ever-moving microcosm of an army which constituted a mobile group in Indochina. There were some which were composed mainly of North Africans and Senegalese, such as Mobile Group 1; another, such as Vanuxem's Mobile Group 3, included Muong mountaineer battalions which he himself had organized; in Cambodia, Mobile Group 51 would again be composed of North Africans, while the ill-fated Mobile Group 100 included a majority of Frenchmen from the battalion that served in Korea. Each mobile group, of course, would also include a large helping of Vietnamese troops and 1953 finally saw the creation of an entirely Vietnamese mobile group in the center of the Red River delta, at Hung-Yen.

The background of the commanders would be as diverse as the troops themselves. Vanuxem, for example, though a regular soldier, was also an *agrégé de philosophie,* which means that he had passed the extremely stiff examination which permits one to become a university professor of philosophy in France. With his reddish beard, his huge frame, and his dark green beret adorned with the five-pointed silver star of the Muong, he certainly was an amazing figure of a military leader. But even Vanuxem was hardly more amazing than the northern theater commander appointed in 1953, Major General Cogny. A regular army officer, Cogny had fought in the underground against the Germans, had been captured and tortured by the Gestapo and ended the war as a "walking skeleton" at the infamous Mauthausen concentration camp. His encounters with the Gestapo had left him with a severe limp. A six-foot-three giant, Cogny, too, had a remarkable academic background: an LL.D. and a diploma (equivalent to a Master's Degree) from the French Institute of Political Science.

Then there were men such as Bigeard, a paratroop major who was to become a lieutenant colonel at Dien Bien Phu. He began World War II as a master sergeant, was taken prisoner by the Germans in 1940, escaped from Germany all the way to French

West Africa, parachuted into France in 1944 to help create guerrilla units, and commanded the 6th Colonial Parachute Battalion in Indochina. And there were the others: de Kergaravat, commander of Mobile Group 4, with his horn-rimmed glasses, his droop-brim campaign hat and long jaw, looking very much like an English country squire; and de Castries, with the bright red field cap of the Spahis, his eternal silk scarf and his reputation as a great ladies' man.

These were the men and the troops who were to carry the burden of the battle until the end of the Indochina war, constantly shunted about in a clanking and roar of hundreds of truck and tank engines, wrapped in clouds of dust during the dry season and covered with mud during the monsoon; hardly ever at rest, doing their repairs and maintenance during brief periods of lull, stretching the endurance of matériel and troops to the breaking point. Those were the troops which, with barely a breathing spell between the battle of Hoa-Binh and the mop-up operations in the delta, now had to face a renewed Viet-Minh offensive from an entirely different direction.

The Viet-Minh, having seen the possibilities and limitations of French heavy equipment during the battles around the periphery of the Red River delta, now had decided on the final course which was to bring it eventual victory—an attack across the top of the Indochinese peninsula. The French would find it almost impossible to use heavy equipment; their Air Force would be fighting at maximum range against troops hidden under a thick canopy of trees; and the Viet-Minh could make fullest use of its inherent quality of fast cross-country movement, rapid concentration from dispersed points of departure, and hit-and-run ambushing of troops unfamiliar with jungle fighting. As early as October 1952 the Communist High Command had decided upon a military strategy from which no French initiative and no amount of American military aid were going to cause it to deviate until the end of the war.

The battle for the T'ai hill country began on October 11, 1952, with three Communist divisions—the 308th, 312th, and 316th—advancing in three columns across the Red River on a 40-mile front. The 308th and 316th divisions had left one regiment each, Infantry Regiment 176 and Infantry Regiment 36, in general reserve around the vital passages of the Red River; to the north of the three divisions, Independent Regiment 148 stabbed westward on its own in a wide arc of circle. The intervening year between the first Viet-Minh thrust and the present attack had in no way changed the basic relationship of forces in the area. The French line of posts immediately to the west of the Red River still remained as weak and tenuous as ever and the city of Nghia-Lô, though somewhat better fortified and now defended by about 700 men, still was no match for a determined Communist attack led by a 10,000-man division equipped with recoilless cannon and 120mm heavy mortars.

In less than six days after the first crossing of the Red River, the 308th Division had swept ahead of itself all the small French outposts and had appeared across 40 miles of jungle in front of and around Nghia-Lô. Here again, the Communist penetration had followed the usual pattern. A few days before the beginning of the actual attack, the villages surrounding Nghia-Lô began to be deserted, by the adolescents and men first and women and children later. Then, the usual French "contacts," local tribesmen serving as agents for French Intelligence, would cease to report in, sending their wives instead to plead that their husbands were "away on a hunt" or sick, or far away at the marriage of a distant relative. To the experienced French officer, these symptoms were clear enough—a Viet-Minh attack was in the process of being built up.

The local French commander responded by increased patrolling in the area, by French counter-ambushes on the usual paths of approach, and by requesting increased air reconnaissance throughout the whole area. This is exactly what had happened around Nghia-Lô between October 11th and October 17th, and without the slightest effect. In fact, on the very day preceding the arrival of the 308th Division, two French companies had made a sweeping probe around the camp, visiting villages and searching out likely places of hiding but had found nothing. Likewise, French air reconnaissance, scanning without pause all the known assembly areas, could find no indication whatever of large-scale Communist movements. Here and there, a small group of men advancing single file through the high grass was caught in the open by a French reconnaissance plane, but by the time the plane made a second sweep the enemy would have disappeared from the path and blended into the surrounding countryside.

In view of the French mastery of the air, the Viet-Minh troops had made a veritable fetish out of camouflage. The greatest pains would be taken even in safe rear areas to camouflage anything which could offer the French a suitable target. This constant emphasis on perfect camouflage, carried out relentlessly even when at rest, made the Communist soldier as well as the civilian population unbeatable masters at the game. The palm-leaf helmet of the Communist soldier with its constantly-worn camouflage net on it was the major trade-mark of the regular. In addition, every regular Viet-Minh soldier on the march carried a large wiremesh disk on his back and head, adorned with the foliage of the terrain through which he was passing. As soon as the terrain changed, it was the responsibility of each soldier to change the camouflage of the man ahead of him as the surroundings changed. Rarely would a Communist unit be in too much of a hurry not to take the time to change camouflage when it left a dark green forest to enter a lighter green grassland area or the marshy brown of a rice field about to be harvested.

"I just *know* the little bastards are somewhere around here" was the standard complaint of the French reconnaissance pilots, "But go and find them in that mess."

Once more Communist camouflage had been perfect. The first inkling the French had that they were about to be attacked—save for the general feeling that something was afoot—was when, on October 17 at 1700, an intense mortar barrage fell with extreme accuracy and ferocity on Nghia-Lô Hill, smashing the barbed wire, ploughing passages through the mine fields, and knocking out French gun crews. At 1730, the dreaded cry of "Tiên-lên!" was heard and Viet-Minh infantry appeared on top of the battered defenses. In less than one hour, all of Nghia-Lô Hill had fallen into enemy hands. French air support, alerted a few minutes after the beginning of the battle, came just in time from the Red River delta to witness the departure of the prisoners, with their hands raised, between a double column of Viet-Minh guards. The French position at Nghia-Lô village still kept on fighting and held out until morning, but when the first supply plane came in at dawn for a dropping of badly needed ammunition and blood plasma, the French tricolor had ceased to fly over the charred ruins of Nghia-Lô. The French main anchor in the T'ai hills had been lost inside of twenty-four hours and now it was obvious that all the French posts to the north and west of Nghia-Lô would be crushed without hope of succor if the Viet-Minh were to reach the Black River before the garrisons were able to complete their withdrawal.

Once more the ghost of the border disaster of 1950 rose in front of the French High Command: the choice that was finally made consisted in throwing to the enemy as a sacrificial lamb one paratroop battalion which, by a determined rear-guard action, would draw upon itself the main effort of the enemy and would give time to the slower and larger units to fall back on the Black River. There was not the slightest illusion as to the chances of survival of the paratroop battalion; if it lived long enough to accomplish its mission, its expenditure would have been well worth it. The decision was made in Hanoi and the battalion chosen for the mission of sacrifice in the T'ai country was the 6th Colonial Parachute Battalion of Major Bigeard.

On October 15, the unit was placed on alert status and that evening, the commander of the Airborne Forces, Colonel Gilles, asked Father Jeandel, the paratroop chaplain, to be ready for a combat operation the next morning at 0530. "How long will the operation last, Sir?" said Jeandel.

"I don't know exactly," said Gilles. "In any case take your portable altar along and everything that is necessary to say Mass. If the operation will take longer than expected, we'll have Mass wine and hosts parachuted to you. Good luck."

On October 16, 1952 at 1120, the first wave of fifteen C-47's took off from Hanoi in the direction of Tu-Lê, twenty miles to the northwest of Nghia-Lô. The first wave was to be followed by a second wave at 1430. Bigeard himself, as usual, was in the lead plane. The faces of the men were taut; the usual cracks and jokes were missing. They knew now where they were going, what they were going to do, and that only a few of them would live to tell

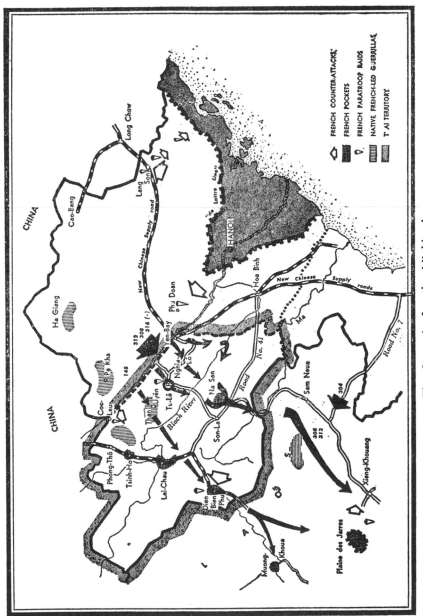

The Struggle for the Highlands.

about it. Father Jeandel, in the camouflaged uniform of the para-troops—with a black crucifix adorned with a small silver figure of Christ hanging around his neck above the belly parachute and the small package of the portable altar cradled on top of his combat pack—had found a seat not far away from Major Bigeard. The chaplain jumped as a member of the Headquarters "stick." And there was Tu-Lê: a few small elongated hillocks sur-rounded by jungle-covered hills.

The post itself, located in the center of the small plain, was hardly more than a reinforced medieval-looking belfry surrounded by ten strands of barbed wire and a few open communication trenches connecting five machine gun emplacements. The post commander, who had a taste for orderliness, had laid out the name of the post on a hillock in six-foot tall letters made of flagstones. The whole plain was about four miles long and a muddy path connected the post with the nearby Meo tribal village. From any viewpoint, the place was as uninviting a trap as could be found in which to make a last stand.

The first paratroop wave landed at 1300, followed by the rest of the battalion at 1600. They immediately began to dig in around the post of Tu-Lê in preparation for the battle to come; these were elite soldiers, Vietnamese as well as French, and they in-tended to sell their skin dearly. October 17, the first patrol of the 6th Parachute Battalion reported contact with three elements of the 312th Division at about 8 kilometers from Tu-Lê. That same night, the men of the 6th Parachute Battalion at Tu-Lê were silent and distant witnesses to the agony of Nghia-Lô. The rumble of gunfire and the flash of explosions could be heard and seen twenty miles to the southeast.

At 1800 on the following day, the first enemy elements reached the crests around Tu-Lê from both the south and the east; the 1st T'ai Mountaineer Battalion had pulled out during the preced-ing day and moved north and west; the 17th Moroccan *Tabor* (battalion) and the 3d Battalion of the 1st Moroccan Rifle Regiment were pulling out in the direction of the Black River. Fifteen miles to the southeast of Tu-Lê, however, at Gia-Hoi, a lone rifle company still was frantically trying to extricate itself from enemy ambushes in order to fall back to Tu-Lê. It will never be known whether Bigeard's decision to wait for the company from Gia-Hoi was responsible for the encirclement of the 6th Paratroop Battalion at Tu-Lê, but the fact remains that on October 19, at 2100, when he received Hanoi's orders to pull out of Tu-Lê in the direction of the Black River, Bigeard decided to give the garrison of Gia-Hoi until morning to make its junction with his forces. (In any event, to attempt a break-out from the valley in the middle of a pitch black night probably would have resulted in total dispersion of the battalion within a short time).

The 19th of October was a gloomy day at Tu-Lê. As is often the case in the upper region of Tonking, the sky was covered with a dense layer of clouds which prevented the French fighter-bombers and reconnaissance planes from operating over the T'ai hills. Still, by sheer luck, a roving fighter-bomber did intercept a column of about 600 Viet-Minh soldiers moving in the direction of Tu-Lê, but the losses which it suffered from the ensuing strafing were but a drop in the bucket in comparison to the masses of manpower which now surrounded the paratroopers at Tu-Lê.

At about 0300 on October 20, the enemy attack on Tu-Lê began with its usual heavy barrage of mortar fire, and the paratroopers dug in for their last stand. Two enemy charges were beaten off; at dawn, Bigeard's men were still holding their own behind the barbed wire and the belfry of Tu-Lê. Again, the weather was unkind to the French; the sky above the high mountain valleys was tightly packed with cumulus clouds which canceled all chances of air support. The 6th Colonial Paratroops was strictly on its own.

It was now obvious that any further attempts at holding out at Tu-Lê were useless; not only would they mean certain doom for the battalion, but it was certain that the enemy would soon simply by-pass the hedgehog, blocking it by a few battalions of its own and would resume its march forward without bothering about the post, leaving it to wither on the vine as it had done with many other French posts before and would do with many thereafter.

But there was the problem of the wounded. It was an axiom among the airborne forces that no wounded were ever left behind for the enemy. The paratroops, as an elite force, were an object of particular hatred to the Viet-Minh who would often submit them to grisly torture before killing them.

The battalion already had five severely wounded stretcher cases and the French made preparations to carry them along on the trek to the Black River. Each stretcher was assigned four two-men teams for portage and protection. The dense tropical heat, coupled with the famous Meo paths which lead straight up on one side of a hill and straight down the other, exhausts two stretcher bearers with their 200-pound load in less than fifteen minutes. The same held, of course, for the crew-served weapons (mortars and machineguns) and for the radio sets and ammunition, which had to be handcarried. Nearly every paratrooper, including the officers, carried an additional burden beyond his regular field pack.

The trek began with unexpected easiness. The Viet-Minh for some reason had withdrawn from contact with the pocket and the paratroopers succeeded in clearing the first line of hills without being intercepted. An advance detachment which had preceded the battalion to the Tu-Lê pass the day before, radioed back that it too, had had no contact with enemy forces. Apparently luck had been with the French at least this once. But the Viet-Minh had merely bided its time; rather than lose a large number of men in mass attacks at the outset of a campaign, the 312th Division preferred to let the French battalion withdraw from its fixed position, where its guns were able to inflict heavy damage on the assailants, to let it string itself out along a jungle path where it could be hacked to pieces at leisure. Thus the whole 6th Parachute Battalion walked into a vast trap laid between Tu-Lê Pass and the first hill line. The density of the automatic fire which now greeted the French was unheard of in the Indochina war; according to Lieutenant Trapp, leader of the rear guard platoon who became a prisoner at that battle and could see enemy equipment from close up, the 312th Division carried one light machine gun for every ten men, one automatic rifle for every five, and a great number of sub-machineguns. The battle was soon over for the two rear guard companies; they were wiped out but their sacrifice saved the remainder of the battalion, including Major

Bigeard. Almost constantly harassed by the enemy, several times in danger of being submerged, Bigeard and his men grimly fought on in their race to the Black River. They reached it on October 22, having covered more than forty miles of jungle paths in less than two days at the cost of more than three-fifths of the battalion. They were exhausted, begrimed, suffering from malaria and leech bites, but they were still a fighting unit. And they had carried with them all their wounded who had not been taken prisoner at Tu-Lê Pass.

In the meantime, the battlefield around Tu-Lê was littered with more than a hundred French wounded. Father Jeandel had remained with them in the hope of being able to help them, but for most of them any help would have come too late. The Viet-Minh simply had done nothing for them. They had been merely assembled and laid side-by-side in the mud, their wounds exposed to the open air, their horrible mutilations left unattended. They were moaning softly, begging for water or an early death.

One of the French officers who had been taken prisoner during the battle and who passed near the post several days later came away, ashen-faced, as if he had seen hell itself:

"You know, this was worse than anything I'd ever seen. The whole place looked like something straight out of Dante's Inferno or one of the drawings of Goya. The wounded were still lying there just like on the first day, intermingled with men who had died several days ago and who were beginning to rot. They were lying there unattended, in the tropical sun, being eaten alive by the rats and the vultures. If only they had all been dead! But imagine, there were still some of them who were able to moan."

Of the 110 lightly wounded or unwounded paratroopers who had been taken prisoner at Tu-Lê and at the pass on October 20, 1952, only four, including Father Jeandel, survived their ordeal in Viet-Minh prison camps to see the day of their liberation in August 1954.

The mauling received by the paratroopers at Tu-Lê made it necessary to give them an additional head start on the pursuing Reds. Another small post would have to make a final sacrifice to give Bigeard's men the precious few hours they needed to make their break and to give the other garrisons a fighting chance of reaching the Black River alive. The choice fell upon tiny Muong-Chen, 33 kilometers to the northwest of Nghia-Lô, held by 80 T'ai irregulars of the 284th Local Suppletive Company under the command of French Master Sergeant Peyrol and three other French NCO's.

On the evening of October 20, Bigeard's column reached Muong-Chen, a hill post overlooking the path leading to the Black River, composed of one bunker made of tree logs, two small barracks and one other unfinished bunker. Peyrol and his men had been working at the fortifications of their post, supplementing the lack of barbed wire by bristling bamboo fences, but the post was never meant to be more than a fortified police station rather than a strongpoint designed to stop a determined enemy attack. But this was precisely the mission Bigeard was going to assign it.

"Look here, Peyrol," said Bigeard. "I've got five hundred men with me, paratroops. We've got one mission—to hold out long enough in the mountain areas until reinforcements can be made available for the Black River line. The Viets are about one hour behind us and we need an additional three hours. You're going to give us those additional three hours. It's your two platoons against our battalion and the other garrisons in the T'ai country."

"You've got to last three hours at least, and we can make it."

Peyrol, 34, gulped hard. His eighty men against the bulk of the 312th Division—they wouldn't have a ghost of a chance. And back home, in Verdun, this was his little girl's birthday. He had even kept a bottle of champagne—it was lukewarm, of course, but nevertheless champagne—for the occasion. Well, he'd drink it another time, if there was another time.

"Bien, mon Commandant," said Peyrol.

"Thank you," said Bigeard, "I knew you fellows wouldn't fail me."

Both men stepped back into the dusk, where the paratroopers were lying on the ground along the path, resting on their packs which they hadn't even bothered to unstrap. They knew that they had to march on in a few minutes with their rations and heavy ammunition clips and their wounded on the stretchers.

At about 1815, the last paratrooper in his mottled battle dress had disappeared to the west and Master Sergeant Peyrol and Sergeant Cheyron set about the business of gaining three hours for Bigeard. The T'ai partisans were digging in silence new firing emplacements for the automatic rifles, deepening a few communications trenches, and refilling some of the sandbags which had flattened out during the recent rains. Although they had not been told about the forthcoming mission, they knew, in the mysterious way in which news travels in countries where nearly everybody is illiterate, that huge enemy forces were coming; and as good hunters who had stalked prey ever since they were able to walk, they had estimated their own chances of survival just as accurately as had the French major.

Within less than an hour after the departure of the paratroopers, the first Viet mortar shells began to rain down on Muong-Chen. Again, the enemy had succeeded in establishing himself within firing distance without being detected by any of the patrols which the besieged garrison had established on the likely paths of approach. Viet-Minh intelligence or previous reconnaissance had been, once more, perfect. The main thrust of the attack was directed against the southern bunker, where a small fold of the terrain provided shelter from the French automatic weapons. This was followed by a direct assault against the unfinished blockhouse, which was taken by successive waves of grenadiers, Communist troops armed only with hand grenades. They first blew up the wire and bamboo obstacles and then killed the BAR (automatic rifle) teams. Scores of the grenadiers died or were wounded in the attempt, but the following waves jumped into the position over the bodies of their dead or dying comrades.

But Muong-Chen, battered and smoking, still held three hours later. However, at 2200, the situation had become hopeless; all the heavy weapons had either run out of ammunition or had been destroyed and the garrison was about to be crushed simply by the sheer weight of enemy bodies falling on top of the men in the trenches and gun emplacements. Their death or capture in Muong-Chen would in no way delay the Viet-Minh any longer. Peyrol decided to attempt a break-out. Having booby-trapped the remaining bunker and reserve ammunition, firing all their weapons at top speed, the men made a break for a path which they had recently hacked out of the jungle and which, for that reason, was perhaps unknown to the enemy. Peyrol's long shot paid off; in the pitch-black night, they knew their way better than the Viets and soon were mercifully swallowed up by the jungle.

When the survivors counted themselves as dawn broke, there remained three Frenchmen and about forty T'ai tribesmen. And now began a deadly game of hide-and-seek, for the enemy had sent two companies in their pursuit. The chase was to last 12 days and cover more than 200 kilometers of treacherous jungle, involving river crossings (made more difficult by the fact that Sergeant Cheyron could not swim) and the scaling of mountain chains 8,000 feet high. Private Destaminil soon had to walk barefoot since his feet, bleeding and swollen, no longer fitted into his boots.

On the second day, the providential intervention of a roving fighter-bomber saved them from being annihilated in a trap which, nevertheless, cost them ten men. On the third day, they ran out of food, but the jungle-wise T'ai were able to find some meager corn cobs and manioc roots which provided some sustenance. At every halt, Peyrol vainly attempted to contact a French post on the SCR-300 radio which was, miraculously enough, still in working order. Whatever French posts there were left in the northwest were beyond the range of their transmitter.

Still, one evening, a seemingly French voice replied and indicated the map coordinates to a drop zone to the north of their present march route. A hot debate ensued: did the message come from one of the French long-range commando groups (GCMA) permanently operating behind Communist lines, which often had hacked out a small secret airfield in the jungle through which they could fly out wounded and receive supplies; or was the message a trap set up by the Viet-Minh, which they used to lure French aircraft within the range of a Communist *flak* battery or to induce French supply aircraft to parachute to them supplies destined for commando groups or for stragglers such as they were? Peyrol finally made the decision—unpopular at the time—not to respond to the call and not to identify his own party.

It turned out later that he had been right. The transmitter had been a Communist trap.

Near Bat-Chien, barely one mountain range away from the Black River, they nearly fell on top of a Viet-Minh platoon bivouacking along the path. They remained for five hours frozen in their tracks, watching the enemy breaking camp, before resuming their own march. By now, undermined by hunger, thirst, and dysentery, even the native T'ai were barely more than ragged shadows staggering along, held together by nothing else but the grim determination to reach the Black River.

On November 5, 1952, the last crest was climbed, the blue sky became brighter as the tree canopy thinned out and then, the T'ai lead scout stopped in his tracks, pointing ahead: *"La Rivière Noire,"* said he.

And there it was, reddish-brown, swift, and treacherous—but safety lay on the other side. There still was the steep descent to the river bank; and steep descents, in the jungle, are more harrowing than steep climbs. The dead-tired men fell more often than they walked but by 1600, they had reached the valley bottom. Once more Providence appeared, this time in the form of a T'ai tribesman from a nearby village.

"You cannot pass during the daytime. You must go back into the trees; there are many Viet-Minh patrols all along the river but your men are on the other side. You stay here 'till nightfall. I will come back with rice for you and guide you."

Can he be trusted? The T'ai themselves did not know: the Viets pay high premiums for French stragglers, particularly for their weapons and most of all for their radio sets. The prizes for the men would make the tribesman a rich man for life. But Peyrol and his men were too weak to care.

By nightfall, the T'ai was back with a basket of gluey rice, the standard food staple of the mountaineers. The men wolfed down the rice, drinking the muddy water of the river. The tribesman, however, warned Peyrol against attempting the crossing that night.

"The French are no longer close to the river and there are Viet-Minh patrols on the other side also. But tomorrow I will know where to cross. I will find you rafts to cross over. You cannot swim the river. It is too swift."

The men nearly cried with frustration; to be so close to safety and yet to be unable to reach it was almost more than they could bear. But they had no choice. Once more they bedded down on the cold and moist jungle floor. On the following day, a little Morane reconnaissance plane circled the river. Unable to contain themselves, Peyrol and his men walked out into the open, shouting and waving the tricolor from Muong-Chen which they had carried with them. The plane swooped down low and dropped a message canister: "Saw you. Put away that flag and stay out of sight. Will notify buddies opposite you. *Bonne chance.*"

On the evening of that day, Peyrol and his men crossed over in makeshift rafts made of a native hut which they had found near the river bank, thanks to the faithful T'ai tribesman. Still dragging their weapons and radio set, they made the crossing without incident. Peyrol lost his field glasses and Cheyron his shoes in the process, as a sort of propitiatory gift to the river gods.

Dark shadows stepped out of the forest near the point where they landed. One last pang of insane fear, a grabbing for tommy guns and hand grenades—then the familiar French voices reached them; they were a rescue column from the nearby post of Muong-Bu which had been alerted to their presence by the Morane.

But now the pent-up emotions of the past two weeks, the nervous and physical exhaustion of the hell which they had just survived, caught up with them. Peyrol and his men collapsed on the spot, crying like children, unable to walk another step. They had been given up for dead long ago by everyone and Bigeard had requested posthumous citations for their brave rear guard fight at Muong-Chen.

Of the eighty-four men who had defended Muong-Chen, sixteen reached the Black River. And Master Sergeant Peyrol still carried his champagne bottle.

The sacrifice of the 6th Colonial Parachute Battalion had merely delayed, but in no way altered, the fate of the northwestern highlands of Viet-Nam. Two airheads were hastily organized, Lai-Chau and Na-San; but they soon became little else than tiny friendly islands in a Communist sea which now began to overlap into northern Laos. By the beginning of November, 1952, the enemy had reached the Black River along almost all its length and hardly two weeks later it had reached the hill line between the Black River and the Nam-Ma (Ma River) where the French had organized the strong point of Na-San which had been rapidly fortified by four infantry battalions, one artillery group, and engineering forces airlifted in around the clock in less than four days. Here again, when a series of heavy probing attacks showed that Na-San was going to be an expensive assault without further strategic results, the Viet-Minh High Command simply by-passed the fortified zone, while pinning down the French forces with a small covering force, and continued its victorious and almost unchecked sweep across the wide empty spaces of the mountainous north. The small post and airfield of Dien Bien Phu, then defended by a weak Laotian infantry unit, fell on November 30, 1952. In view of the rapidly deteriorating situation, the French High Command decided to gamble once more upon a deep stab into the enemy's communication lines and supply system along the Red River, in the hope that this would lead the enemy commander to withdraw a large part of his assault divisions in the northwest to the defense of his own rear areas. This was the strategic assumption that gave rise, on the French side, to the mounting of "Operation Lorraine."

"Operation Lorraine" was to consist of four specific stages. During the first stage, lasting from October 29 to November 8, 1952, the attacking forces were to open a bridgehead across the Red River in direction of Phu-Tho. During the second stage, the Phu-Tho bridgehead was to be enlarged so as to link up with a task force heading north directly from Viet-Tri along Road No. 2. The two forces would then progress together along Road No. 2 in direction of Phu-Doan where Airborne Group No. 1 would be dropped in exactly on time to meet with the column progressing overland. Both groups would then be joined by a *Dinassaut* (Naval Assault Division), which would prevent the escape of any enemy forces by water. During the third stage, the French forces would destroy the numerous enemy equipment and matériel depots known to be located in the Phu-Doan area. This threat to the enemy's main depots should, according to the experts, bring about a rapid withdrawal of the bulk of the Communist forces from the northern hill area in order to save their depots from total destruction. Further exploitation of the break-through, either by permanent occupation of that part of the Red River valley or by further and deeper stabs into Communist-held territory, would depend upon the general military situation in the Red River delta and upon the value of the objectives reached during the earlier three stages. The forces allotted by the French High Command to "Operation Lorraine" were perhaps the largest ever assembled in Indochina for any single operation: four complete mobile groups, one airborne group with three parachute battalions, two infantry battalions and five commando units; two armored sub-groups and two tank destroyer and reconnaissance squadrons; two *Dinassauts,* as well as two artillery battalions and important engineering forces: a total of more than 30,000 men.

On the Communist side, the problem was fairly simple. Since the approximate strength of the French thrust was well known, as well as its direction, the Communist High Command had to take a calculated risk in estimating that the French thrust would run out of steam before it could reach the really important supply centers at Yên Bay and Thai-Nguyên*. General Giap decided, therefore, to proceed with his offensive into the T'ai country, but amputated one regiment from each of two of his assault divisions to cover his rear communication lines in the Red River Valley. Both units, Infantry Regiment No. 36 of the

---

*It must be understood that practically all French troop movements in Indochina took place in a "fishbowl." Since practically no troop movements could take place at night for fear of costly ambushes, even the smallest movement of troops, tanks or aircraft was immediately noticed by the population and brought to the attention of Viet-Minh agents. Thus, the only effect of tactical surprise which could be achieved was that of speed in executing a movement, rather than in the concealment of the movement itself. The Communist High Command, therefore, nearly always had a fairly accurate idea of French forces in any given sector and knew how many of those troops could be made available for mobile operations. Since the number of troops required to protect a given number of miles of communication lines also was a known constant, it was almost mathematically possible to calculate the maximum depth of the French penetration and its duration. On the French side, the dilemma of the choice between a deep penetration for a short time or a shallow penetration for a long time was never satisfactorily resolved. "Operation Lorraine" is a clear example of this dilemma.

308th Viet-Minh Infantry Division and Regiment 176 of the 316th Division, were stationed in North Viet-Nam's "Little Mesopotamia," the low-lying, water-logged plain between the Red and the Clear Rivers. Both regimental commanders were given strict orders to stop the French offensive at all costs before it reached Yên Bay and Thai-Nguyên, but were given full operational freedom as to how to achieve this objective. In any case, they were told not to expect any additional forces.

This ruthless procedure of letting each unit carry its own responsibilities to the utmost was one of the hallmarks of Viet-Minh command practice and always worked to their fullest advantage. On two other occasions when the French High Command hit hard one Viet-Minh unit in the hope of drawing off other Communist units from their initial objectives, the French found to their dismay that the enemy commander never used fresh reserves merely to cover the withdrawal of already expended troops. This was also going to be the case in "Operation Lorraine."

On the French side, the very size and heaviness of the units involved in the offensive made the restoration of roads and bridges an overriding condition of movement and slowed down the whole operation to a crawl. Three full battalions of combat engineers, reinforced by the bulk of the engineering forces at the disposal of the northern theater headquarters, worked frantically day and night throwing unwieldy pontoon bridges across the many streams and filling the deep gaps torn into roads and dikes by Viet-Minh saboteurs. (It should be noted in passing that the whole Indochinese war theater did not possess one single tank-dozer; all such work had to be done with commercial-type bull-dozers with the drivers fully exposed to enemy sniper fire.)

In view of the fact that the enemy had flooded the area and destroyed the road immediately north of Viet-Tri, the French High Command decided to gain at least a small measure of surprise by pushing due west across the mouth of the Black River in the direction of Hung-Hoa where the terrain, higher than "Little Mesopotamia," was more favorable to the movement of tanks and trucks. Once in Hung-Hoa, the French planned to push north into the peninsula formed by the bend of the Red River and to outflank Communist defenses by crossing the Red River once more and creating beach heads on the other bank.

In the late hours of October 29, 1952, the first French assault boats, their engines running at low speeds so as to reduce the noise, left the right bank of the Red River opposite Trung-Ha and secured a beachhead without encountering enemy opposition. Silently, the men left the boats and began to scale the top of the dike while a liaison team of combat engineers busied itself with the ruins of what had been the peacetime ferry ramp. A few minutes later, the first pontoon ferry with a light tank aboard left Trung-Ha and soon thereafter rumbled into the new bridge-

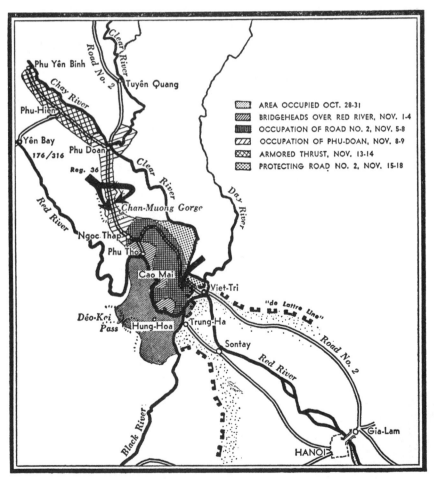

AREA OCCUPIED OCT. 28-31
BRIDGEHEADS OVER RED RIVER, NOV. 1-4
OCCUPATION OF ROAD NO. 2, NOV. 5-8
OCCUPATION OF PHU-DOAN, NOV. 8-9
ARMORED THRUST, NOV. 13-14
PROTECTING ROAD NO. 2, NOV. 15-18

"Operation Lorraine"—the Offensive.

" . . . *conditions almost unimaginable in their demands on human endurance* . . . " (p. 13)
Vietnamese paratroops counterattack at Dien Bien Phu.

Along bay in North Viet-Nam, one of the most scenic spots in Asia.

*" . . . the little patrol boats did their best to cover
the lumbering landing craft . . . " (p. 55)*

" . . . This is napalm, the fire which falls from the skies . . . " (p. 39)
A village is bombed in the Red River Delta.

" . . . the new Russian equipment
the Viets are getting . . . " (p. 94)

". . . The two fighters swooped down in turn
and raked the area with machine guns . . . " (p. 111)

(Note French fighter in center.)

" . . . Wallowing in the water of the paddies isn't *as*
bad as lying in half-dried mud . . . " (p. 112)

Field Marshal Juin (r.) and General de Linares (third from r.) inspect
the fort of Ninh-Binh and a Vietnamese Dinassaut unit. (p. 45) Young
Lt. de Lattre died on the crag.

"... paratroops dropped ... in the forlorn hope of opening the
main road ... " (p. 32) Airborne raid on Lang-Son.

"... The Crabs (front) and Alligators (rear) were French nicknames
for American-built amphibious vehicles ... " (p. 148)

" . . . to find a Viet-Minh hideout . . . would be a matter of sheer luck . . . " (p. 114)

Guerrilla with camouflage

" . . . three beachheads had been secured on the east bank of the Red River . . . " (p. 89)

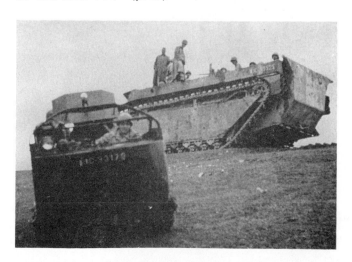

" . . . The commandos and the Amphibious Group hit the beach almost without stopping . . . " (p. 151)

" . . . the huge 155mm "Long Toms" of one of the artillery strongpoints which covered most of the Delta . . . " (p. 178)

head. Within the next two days the hold was secured and anchored
to the south on the Déo-Kei Pass. To be sure, Viet-Minh snipers
had here and there taken a few pot shots at the advancing troops,
but so far the whole operation had been on schedule and had
not met any real enemy opposition.

By November 4, three beachheads had been secured on the
east bank of the Red River and two full mobile groups—Mobile
Group No. 1 under the command of Lieutenant Colonel Bastiani
and Mobile Group No. 4 under the command of Colonel de
Kergaravat—began their race across the swamps and rice paddies
in direction of Road No. 2. One day later, with emergency repairs completed along the road, the remaining French forces, under
the command of Colonel Bonichon, broke out of the bridgehead
of Viet-Tri in the direction of Ngoc Thap. In the face of such
overwhelming French strength, the two battalions of the 176th
Viet-Minh Infantry Regiment, caught between the two French
columns, simply melted away and filtered back to their own lines.
By November 7, the French forces had occupied close to 500
square miles of enemy territory without having encountered a
single Communist unit of any size.

By the evening of November 7, both French columns met at
Ngoc Thap; Colonel Dodelier, senior officer present, assumed
command of the combined push north. Spirits were high among
the troops now assembled, a bit awed by their own show of
strength and also a bit nervous at the apparent absence of enemy
reaction. Too many men remembered that most operations in
Indochina began with an initial slow reaction on the part of the
enemy who, marching on foot, took a great deal longer to concentrate forces for a counter-push. "But," the old Indochina hands
were heard to say, "once the Viet gets going, he sure gets going
and the later he reacts the worse it is."

The part of the operation which followed now was the most
delicate, for it required almost split-second precision on the
part of three different forces subordinated to three different
services:

1. A task force under the direct command of Colonel Dodelier
and composed of Mobile Groups No. 1 and 4, reinforced by parts
of Armored Sub-Groups 1 and 2 under Lieutenant Colonel de

Boisredon and Major Spangenberger, was to cover the 25 miles between Ngoc Thap and Phu-Doan in less than seven hours regardless of enemy opposition and losses sustained in smashing it.

2. Its arrival at Phu-Doan was to coincide with the dropping of Airborne Group No. 1 under the command of Lieutenant Colonel Ducourneau on a drop zone near Dong-Trai on the Clear River opposite Phu-Doan.

3. The Navy's *Dinassaut* No. 3 was to reach the drop zone a short while later to take aboard all the parachutes, help ferry the paratroops across to Phu-Doan, pick up the wounded, and help beat down any enemy opposition which might possibly make itself felt from the other river bank.

A combined operation of this type is never an easy command problem. Carried out with units of different national origins and with as variegated a training background as can be imagined and which did not have any time at all to rehearse the movement now undertaken, it presented more than the usual handicaps. The fact remains that Dodelier's ground troops, the paratroopers and the Navy met exactly at the rendezvous at the appointed time.

Here again, Communist resistance was perfunctory at first. Having saddled up early in the morning of the 9th at Ngoc Thap, Dodelier's armor smashed head-on into a Communist road block near the village of Thai-Binh at the southern entrance to an almost canyon-like four-kilometer-long depression, the valley of Chan Muong. But again, Communist Regiment 36 apparently was not yet in the mood for a knock-down, drag-out fight. Within a short while the tanks' guns had cleared the road block; and the infantry, which was traveling with the tanks, temporarily occupied the commanding heights on both sides of the road. The way was clear for an unimpeded dash on Phu-Doan.

Ducourneau's airborne group, in the meantime, had embarked in lumbering C-47's in the Red River delta. Since there never were enough transport aircraft in Indochina, all the available civilian airline craft and pilots had been requisitioned for days in advance to reinforce the two transport groups of the French Air Force available in the north. For days before the raid, the civilian aircraft had been seen circling around the delta in patrols of three which was something airline pilots were unaccustomed to. This practice—it was in fact further extended as the war went along, to the point that civilian pilots and aircraft were finally flying daring commando supply missions behind enemy lines and maintaining the night time light-flare vigil over embattled Dien Bien Phu—made it further impossible to maintain operational secrecy, since the airlines had to be told by Army High Command the exact dates at which the airplanes were needed, how many airplanes were needed, and for how long they would be needed.

On this morning of November 9, the aircraft had taken off slowly from the various airports around Haiphong and Hanoi, had assembled north of Hanoi by flights of five, and then had headed northwest in neat little inverted V's like so many flock of geese. On their way north, they had seen the long lines of tanks and vehicles crawling north along Road No. 2, towards their meeting point. Air-ground contact had been maintained constantly, and the paratroop commanders knew that opposition, thus far, had been light.

Spirits were high in the aircraft as the men hooked in their static lines. At about 1030, the target hove in sight—a wide open green plain, covered with fairly dry rice paddies; about as near ideal a landing ground as you could find for paratroops in Indochina. The first man out the plane door was, as usual, what the French call *"le Sikki,"* a dummy made up to look like a paratrooper and weighted down with the proper weight of a man. This dummy, thrown out first with a parachute on, permits the gauging of air speeds on the ground and also, if lucky, may draw enemy fire first and thus reveal some of the enemy guns near the drop zone. In this particular case, both *"le Sikki"* and the paratroopers who followed him were lucky. There apparently was no enemy opposition anywhere near the drop zone, and the whole drop went on as methodically as a training jump. By 1500, Ducourneau's three airborne battalions had assembled, the first naval craft had beached near the drop zone to collect the parachutes and the few light jump casualties, and had begun ferrying the paratroopers across to Phu-Doan. In Phu-Doan itself, it was obvious that the enemy had underestimated the speed with which the French would arrive.

The population had, as almost always when opportunity per-

mitted, taken to the hills and the town was deserted. But as the
French infantry now fanned out into the houses and huts in and
around the town, it became obvious that Phu-Doan had indeed
been, as French intelligence reports had indicated, a fairly important forward matériel depot. House after house yielded its share
of ammunition, rifles, bazookas and mortars. But the prize was
yet to come.

As Mobile Groups 1 and 4 consolidated their hold on the
city, a tank company of Mobile Group 1 pushed farther north
toward Phu Hien, to establish an outpost line against a possible
enemy counter attack. In the lead tank Lieutenant Marion, seated
on the edge of his turret, kept a careful watch over the countryside. With his fair complexion and crew cut, Marion looked more
like a young West Pointer than a graduate from Saint-Cyr, and
well he might have been, for he was a direct descendant of
Lieutenant Colonel Francis ("the Swamp Fox") Marion, the
Revolutionary War hero from South Carolina whose guerrilla
tactics had been so successful against the British in 1780.

As young Marion looked out over the plain around himself, his
eye suddenly caught a minute detail along a side road: fresh tire
tracks. Under usual circumstances, such a find would have been
of no importance, but in the battle against the Viet-Minh in
1952, this still constituted an element of concern. To be sure,
the Communists had inherited from the French and Japanese an
odd assortment of ancient vehicles which they had laboriously
transformed to operating on charcoal or rice alcohol; but these
were generally light panel trucks and their tires, hand-vulcanized
with odd bits of rubber, were most of the time in worse shape
than their engines. And this was exactly why the new tire marks
off the Phu-Doan—Yên Bay highway had caught Marion's attention; they belonged to heavy, broad-wheeled trucks with brand-
new, military-type tires. Now that *was* unusual, thought Marion,
for though the Viets had captured hundreds of American-built
French trucks, they had been able to repair few of them and, in
any case, had not used them so close to the Red River delta.

After a brief radio consultation with the company commander, Marion took his platoon off the main road.*

A bare 500 yards off the highway, hurriedly covered with bamboo fronds as they had been pushed off the road, was Marion's answer: two deserted army trucks painted in dark green color, their bodies covered with a makeshift roof of corrugated sheet metal.

"What do you know," said Corporal Chauvin, one of the tank drivers, "American GMC's and in good shape, too."

The trucks, at first glance, did look like American GMC's, with their rounded cabs and their open windshields, though they seemed somewhat shorter, as well as higher on their wheels. As the tanks passed them by and their crews now had a good look at their front grills and fenders, it became obvious that the two trucks were not of any American type they had ever seen: the grill was higher and the fenders, far from the squarish aspect of the American military vehicles, were almost round and directly attached to the front bumper by a neat "fender skirt." The tires, also, were not of the standard straight-cleat American type, but showed deep V's like those seen usually on agricultural tractors. With its short wheelbase, its high construction, open windshields and tractor tires, this vehicle was exactly built for tropical warfare and cross-country movement. Whoever had designed the vehicle and given it to the Viets obviously knew his business.

Within a few minutes, after circumspect probing had disposed of the always-present danger of booby traps, the Frenchmen were crawling all over the two trucks.

"It certainly doesn't look American," said one tank mechanic. "Look, the speedometer is calibrated in kilometers."

"Look at the trademark!" said Chauvin; "looks like 'Monotoba' or something."

Marion jumped off his vehicle and had a look for himself: "That isn't Latin lettering! It's Russian and the name is МОЛО-

---

* In a letter addressed to me on December 11, 1962, Captain Marion points out that I erred in attributing to him the discovery of the Molotovas ("discovered by comrades from the neighboring Armored Group"), but that the above incident led him to the discovery of the important Communist arms dumps. My error occurred when I interviewed both Marion and his colleague from the Armored Group in 1953. It does not affect the events described here.

TOBA. These are the famous 'Molotovas' we've heard about, the new Russian equipment the Viets are getting."

Here was finally proof positive that the Soviet bloc had joined the war in earnest, supplemented almost at once by the find of Russian automatic weapons in Phu-Doan itself by the men of Mobile Group 4. And this was only the beginning; by the end of the Indochina war, close to 800 Molotovas had been delivered to the Viet-Minh and had become a vital link in the supply chain which fed the battles in the Northwest. Better adapted to the terrain and warfare that was fought here than were the American vehicles given the French, they further reduced the technological gap between the French and the Viets. When excellent new Soviet antiaircraft guns and 120mm heavy mortars were delivered to the Viets in 1953 along with Chinese fire control personnel and artillerymen, the Communists began to have an actual edge in ground firepower, regardless of American aid deliveries to the French.*

As the French now began to comb through Phu-Doan and its surroundings in a methodical manner, the haul of captured equipment began to assume respectable proportions. In addition to the two Molotovas, an American jeep was found, as well as 150 tons of ammunition, 500 rifles, 100 tommy guns, 22 machine guns, 30 BAR's, 40 light mortars, 14 medium mortars and two Soviet heavy 120mm mortars, 23 bazookas and three recoilless cannon.**

"Considering that they knew we were coming and that they

---

*According to one French officer, Captain Jacques Despuech, author of *Le Trafic des Piastres,* the table of equipment for a French battalion in Indochina provided for 624 rifles, 133 submachineguns, 41 BAR's, 4 81mm mortars and 8 60mm mortars, while the corresponding battalion of the 304th Viet-Minh Division counted 500 rifles, 200 submachineguns, 20 BAR's, 8 81mm mortars, 3 recoilless cannon and 3 bazookas.

Yet a high South Vietnamese (i.e. anti-Communist) official stated, in the presence of State Department and U.S. military officials in New York on October 24, 1959, that "powerful modern French armies" in Indochina had been defeated by "poorly armed Vietnamese fighters who . . . *never were helped by Russian or Chinese troops.*" See *News from Viet-Nam,* Washington, November 2, 1959. Of such doctrinaire blindness Western defeats are made.

** According to Capt. Marion (*op.cit.*), a total of 1,400 rifles, 80 mortars, 3 recoilless cannon, 23 bazookas, and a total of 100 automatic weapons, along with 200 tons of ammunition, constituted the total haul. Perhaps the somewhat smaller figures cited apply to weapons of specifically Soviet origin only.

must have used the whole population to haul away everything that was movable," Colonel Dodelier wrote later in his personal report of the operation, "it can readily be imagined how important this secondary depot must have been, and how large the Viet-Minh main depots in Yên Bay and Thai-Nguyên must be. This certainly sheds a new light on the enemy's future offensive intentions."

With Phu-Doan solidly in French hands, and the two mobile groups reinforced by the 1st Airborne Group, the French High Command decided to push on farther in the hopes of drawing off troops from the Communist main thrust into the T'ai hill country, which had been the main purpose of "Operation Lorraine." One after another, the tank platoons, with infantry saddled up behind the turrets and bunching tightly together for better protection against the biting cold of the upland dawn, rumbled north in the direction of Phu-Hien. The surrounding mountains were shrouded in the low-lying *crachin*—the morning "spittle" of the dry season—and the countryside was deserted; small villages lying off the road were empty of any life, like so many ghost towns. Here and there, a shot would ring out and a rifleman in a truck or in the back of the armor would crumple and his body would be transferred to one of the rapidly emptying gasoline or ration trucks.

But the tanks continued to roll to the north, racing through Phu-Hien as deserted as the other towns, by-passing Yên Bay which lay about ten miles to the west of their route, and finally reaching Phu-Yen-Binh, 40 miles to the northwest of Phu-Doan and almost 100 miles north of the de Lattre Line, in the afternoon of November 14. By then, it had become obvious that the strategic purpose of the raid no longer was valid since the Viet-Minh had reached the Black River and was about to engulf the rest of northwestern Tonking, and the commitment of so many troops in an area far off from the main centers of the battle— the Red River delta and the Northwest—completely deprived the High Command of a mobile reserve. Furthermore, the logistical support of more than 30,000 men over such a distance mortgaged practically all the air transport (about 100 C-47's) then available in Indochina; and the other war theaters, particularly the new islands of resistance in the T'ai hills, were clamoring for airlift. On November 14 in the afternoon, General Salan ordered the beginning of the withdrawal phase of "Operation Lorraine." The last deep French penetration into Communist territory had ended.

The withdrawal was an even more delicate operation (as withdrawals usually are) than the advance had been, for the enemy was now fully alert. The French could only rely on their greater speed to carry out the movement without being trapped by the Viet-Minh in the midst of folding their tents. By November 15, Mobile Groups 1 and 4, reinforced by Armored Sub-Groups 1 and 2, had returned to Phu-Doan, from which the paratroops had pulled out the day before. The next leap was to be from Phu-Doan to Ngoc-Thap, about 18 miles to the south along Road No. 2 past the canyon of Chan-Muong.

At dawn of November 17, the heavy convoy began its movement out of Phu-Doan, with Colonel de Kergaravat's Mobile Group No. 4 in the lead and Lieutenant Colonel Bastiani's Mobile Group No. 1 forming the rear guard. Both groups included their own artillery, plus that of Mobile Group No. 3 and one battery of 155mm medium howitzers. In addition, Mobile Group No. 4 included a tank platoon of the Moroccan Colonial Infantry Regi-

Chan-Muong.

ment (RICM), and Mobile Group No. 1 had retained Armored Sub-Group 1. The three infantry battalions which had remained with the groups were among the best in Indochina: the *Bataillon de Marche Indochinois* (BMI), a composite unit made up of Europeans, Cambodians, and tough Vietnamese mountaineers, led off followed by the 2d Battalion of the 2d Foreign Legion Infantry Regiment* with the 4th Battalion, 7th Algerian Rifles, closing the march.

At 0700, two companies of the Algerians, under the personal command of the battalion commander, began the methodical sweep of the road ahead of the convoy through the village of Chan-Muong before it was to enter the valley of the same name. About four kilometers long and surrounded by hills entirely covered by thick, matted jungle, the valley bottom covered with high growths of manioc, Chan-Muong offered the ideal spot for an ambush. About midway through the valley, its bottom narrows to less than 150 yards between two steep cliffs before it broadens again as it reaches the village of Thai-Binh. In the southwestern corner of the hill complex surrounding the Chan-Muong valley, Hill 222, with its old Chinese fort, dominates the area.

The first sweep brought the Algerians almost to the entrance of the valley south of the village of Chan-Muong without incident. But at about 0800, the Algerians began to find freshly-dug holes in the road, probably Communist attempts at mining the road which had been disturbed by the patrols of the Algerian infantry. By now it was obvious that an enemy ambush was likely to occur and the Algerian riflemen redoubled their attention. As the leading 2d Platoon wound its way around the road bend to the south of Chan-Muong, the platoon's lead scout, Private Abderrahman, stopped dead in his tracks, pointing straight ahead: the road was barred by large boulders and tree trunks hastily thrown across it. The enemy had been preparing the ambush all night; there was nothing left for the French to do but fight their way through it.

Warily, the Algerians now fanned out on both sides of the road and approached the barricade. At 0820, enemy small-arms

---

*The Foreign Legion has its own armor, paratroop, and amphibious units, in addition to infantry, just as, in the United States, the Marines have their own aviation and armor.

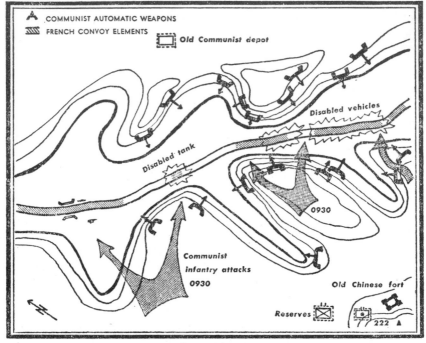

Ambush at Chan-Muong.

fire began to hail down from the cliffs on the two rifle companies which immediately opened fire in return. A few minutes after the fire fight began, the Algerians requested the support of an armored platoon of Mobile Group 4, followed at 0830 by the whole 2d Battalion of the 2d Foreign Legion Regiment. By 0900, the infantry and the tank platoon had cleared the barricade and the approaches to the valley of Chan-Muong, re-established communications with the French troops stationed at Thai-Binh on the southern end of the canyon, and the lumbering column of "soft" (that is, unarmored) vehicles, more than two miles long, began to enter the valley.

In the bleak light filtering through a thick layer of clouds, with the ragged limestone hills completely smothered under a black-green layer of vegetation, Chan-Muong looked less inviting than ever. In spite of the moist heat, the slight breeze which blew through the narrows sent chills down the spines of the men huddled in the trucks. The tanks which were interspersed with various elements of the truck convoys had buttoned up their turret hatches and raised their guns from the traveling to the firing position. Most of the infantry, prevented from fanning out into the valley bottom by the densely planted manioc fields, walked single file on each side of the trucks. At 0930 the lead elements of Mobile Group No. 4 reached the French outpost at Thai-Binh without incident. The central element of the convoy—vehicles of the headquarters column, the reserve ammunition of the artillery batteries, and the cumbersome engineering equipment—had reached the center of the valley; and the rear guard of Mobile Group No. 1 had begun to cross the bridge at the northern mouth of the canyon, 1500 yards south of the village of Chan-Muong.

It was at this precise moment that all hell broke loose in the valley. Communist artillery and mortars opened fire on all elements of the convoy from both sides of the road, the sound of the shots echoing back and forth in the narrow valley. Some of the enemy pieces were as close as 50 yards from their targets; at such distances, they could not miss. Within a few minutes one of the tanks of the RICM blew up in a blinding flash of exploding ammunition and gasoline, effectively blocking nearly all Mobile Group No. 1 behind it.* Having eliminated from the site the hardest hitting part of the whole convoy and pinning down the infantry elements of Mobile Group No. 4 at the southern end of the canyon, the enemy now set methodically about destroying the soft parts of the convoy caught in the middle.

The Communist infantry—its battle cries almost drowned out by the artillery barrage—was on top of the vehicles even before the shelling stopped. These were not part-time guerrillas, but two battalions of regulars of Regiment 36 in camouflaged pith helmets and short-sleeved cotton quilted olive-green jackets. In the ensuing melée, no quarter was given on either side; while the Communist troops finished off the drivers and headquarters troops with burp guns, hand grenades, and daggers, specialized Communist saboteurs blew up the vehicles one by one. Within a few minutes the French convoy had been engulfed along a front of

---

*It should be remembered again that the French in Indochina did not possess a single armored bulldozer (tank-dozer) and only a very few armored tank retrievers, so that any disabled tank which blocked a road had to be removed by a highly vulnerable open bulldozer or retriever.

800 yards, with the northern and the southern ends of the convoy fighting by themselves.

Fortunately for the French, the two mobile group commanders were not caught in the trap but were with the lead and rear-guard elements. At 1015, Colonel de Kergaravat, who was near Thai-Binh with the bulk of Mobile Group No. 4, passed command of all elements to the north of the canyon to Lieutenant Colonel Bastiani, the commander of Mobile Group No. 1. The change of command became effective at 1025. At the same time, de Kergaravat began to call for air support and ordered the artillery elements which had remained with him to open fire on hastily designated targets along the presumed line of departure of the Communist infantry attack.

In the valley itself, the fight around the vehicles had degenerated into a veritable massacre, with the Viet-Minh methodically killing all of the French wounded lying on the ground around the convoy. Fortunately, the intervention of the French Air Force at about 1200 against the enemy rear area, notably the Communist regimental CP and rear artillery positions near the old Chinese fort close to Hill 222, somewhat eased the pressure around the convoy itself.*

It became obvious to Bastiani that the problem for the rear part of the convoy not only lay in reopening the road, but in clearing the surrounding hill areas from the deadly enemy artillery and mortar fire before a reasonable attempt could be made at resuming the withdrawal. Remarkably enough, communications between the battalions on the road had not broken down and Bastiani had been able to maintain contact not only with de Kergaravat but also with the infantry commanders whose units were fighting for their lives around the vehicles burning fiercely in the middle of the trap. By 1500, the battle plan had been worked out; while the remainder of the Algerian Rifle Battalion would cover the convoy itself, the *Bataillon de Marche Indochinois* (BMI) would attack and secure the enemy gun positions along

---

*During a visit to the Museum of the Revolution in Hanoi in July 1962, it turned out that my guide, a captain in the VPA, had been a member of Regiment 36 during the Chan-Muong ambush. He said to me: "From where I was I could clearly distinguish the rank insignia of the French colonel [i.e., Bastiani] who was down there, giving his orders to the officers of his staff."

the eastern flank of the road, while the one-and-a-half companies of the Foreign Legion Battalion caught in the trap would attack three enemy hill positions in direction of the old Chinese fort. At the same time, de Kergaravat's infantry would counterattack in the direction of the convoy while the third company of the BMI would attack directly southward along the road, clearing it of all obstacles as it went along until it had re-established communications with de Kergaravat's Mobile Group No. 4.

By a near-miracle of disciplined will power, the company commanders of the BMI and the Foreign Legion got their units disentangled from the hand-to-hand combat around the vehicles for the counterattack into the hills. At about 1530, under the covering fire of the tank guns and the heavy machine guns, French infantrymen—less than 500 strong—began to claw their way into the hills. As soon as French intentions became clear to the enemy, the Viets in turn recalled their infantry from the road in order to gain free fields of fire for their heavy machine guns and mortars in their well-camouflaged hill emplacements. (As the later mopup of the French infantry was to show, almost none of the enemy's guns had been destroyed by French air action or counter-battery fire but were only silenced when they were overrun by the infantry itself.)

Again the murderous hammering began against the waves of advancing French infantry. While the Foreign Legionnaires, who had to cover a shorter distance between the valley bottom and the hill line, soon made rapid progress on their side of the valley and secured the commanding hill positions within an hour, the men of the BMI were pinned down three times by the enemy barrage. Then, at 1630, the valley suddenly resounded with the strident notes of a French bugle calling for something that had almost disappeared from the Western military vocabulary—a bayonet charge.

With their last ounce of strength, the survivors of the *Bataillon de Marche* rose out of the bushes and charged forward. This time, the Viet-Minh had had enough; all of a sudden, the enemy fire ceased as if cut off by a curtain and Regiment 36 again melted away into the jungle. The valley of Chan-Muong returned to its normal silence. Save for the smoldering remains of the French

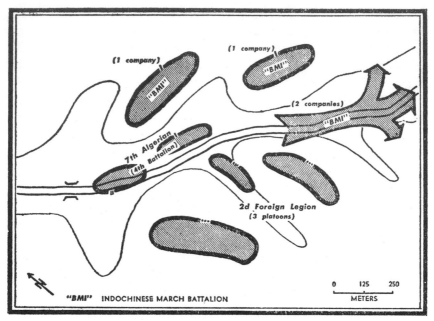

Counterattack at Chan-Muong.

vehicles and the ghastly heaps of dead and wounded around them, there scarcely was any evidence that an enemy attack had taken place here. Slowly, with their guns swung to the rear, two tanks pushed the carcass of their destroyed brother into the ditch. The able-bodied men also helped in clearing the road of the other disabled vehicles and by 1715, the rest of the convoy, this time with Armored Sub-Group 1 in the rear guard, filtered through the canyon toward Thai-Binh. The exhausted infantry—it had been fighting constantly for ten hours since 0700—fell back onto the road and made its exit under cover of the rear-guard tanks.

But this was not to be the last enemy attack of the day. At 1830, Regiment 36 again stabbed at the rear guard armor with "Molotov cocktails" and bazookas, damaging several vehicles but being beaten off by the concentrated fire of the French artillery of the convoy now established in a hedgehog position at Thai-Binh. But Thai-Binh itself was a decidedly unhealthy place for a bivouac and de Kergaravat decided to push on in spite of the darkness, feeling it was better to risk a night ride than to be caught in yet another trap which the exhausted infantry would surely not be able to pry open. The convoy finally made camp at Ngoc-Thap at 2230, having continuously marched and fought for about eighteen hours. The ambush at Chan-Muong had cost the French a dozen vehicles, including one tank and six half-tracks, as well as 56 dead, 125 wounded and 133 missing. Many of the latter were killed on the spot by the Viet-Minh.

Wearily, the French continued their struggle along Road No. 2 to the Viet-Tri bridgehead. The salient on the right bank of the Red River was evacuated on November 17 and 18, and by November 23, "Operation Lorraine" had shrunk to the size of a narrow bridgehead about five miles deep around Viet-Tri, anchored on the two posts of Phu-Duc and Co-Tich. Here again, the enemy had had time to catch up with the French withdrawal and on November 24 at 0200, one battalion of Regiment 36, probably reinforced by elements of Regiment 176, mounted a typical Viet-Minh two-punch attack. While Communist mortars laid down a heavy barrage on Co-Tich, the bulk of enemy infantry attacked the CP of the 1st Muong Battalion near Phu-Duc.

With their uncanny tactical sense, the Viets had soon found one company-size strongpoint which, imperfectly covered by interlocking artillery fire, would provide an easy victim. Without relaxing their mortar fire on Co-Tich and their infantry pressure on Phu-Duc, the French strongpoint covering Road No. 2 was overwhelmed by the Viets in two hours of fierce hand-to-hand combat. A French armored counterattack at 0500 came just in time to save the wounded from being burned to death by the exploding ammunition of the destroyed post. The attack had cost the French 12 dead (including one officer) 40 wounded (including two officers), and 41 missing (including two officers).

By December 1, 1952, the French had blown up all permanent installations to the north of the Viet-Tri bridgehead, had removed all pontoon bridges and heavy equipment still remaining north of the Red River, and had returned to the relative safety of the de Lattre Line. "Operation Lorraine" had cost almost a whole battalion in casualties; it had immobilized a considerable part of the mobile forces available in the northern theater of

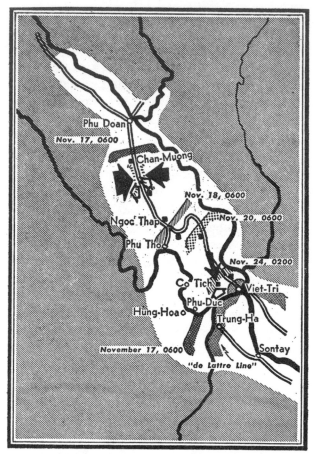

"Operation Lorraine"—the Withdrawal.

operations; and had put a considerable strain on French air transport at a moment when it had become crucial in the defense of
the northwestern mountain area.

No doubt, the enemy depots which had fallen into the hands
of the French at Phu-Doan were of some importance; but in that
case, the extension of the raid in direction of the vital depots of
nearby Yên Bay should have been included if the operation was
to have a lasting tactical effect.

But this is, of course, "Monday-morning-quarterbacking." As it
was—and the subsequent deadly ambush of the withdrawing
French at Chan-Muong proved it—the French already had over-

extended themselves a great deal by attempting "Operation Lorraine" at all. It must also be remembered that the depots, while an important objective of the French thrust, were nevertheless a secondary target in comparison to the major objective which the French had been pursuing for close to two years: that of being able to maneuver the enemy's hard-core regular divisions into a situation where they could be destroyed in one great battle, a minor-key Stalingrad where French fire power, mobility, and air power could come into full play.

This desperate search for the set-piece battle became an obsession of the successive French commanders-in-chief in Indochina until the end of the war. But Giap, the Communist commander, had made his mistake once, in 1951, against de Lattre, and he was not going to repeat it. In dozens of different engagements involving units from single regiments to more than two divisions, Giap preferred to sacrifice those parts of his units which were hopelessly trapped rather than let himself be "sucked" into the type of meat-grinder operation which the Americans could carry out so effectively against the "human wave" attacks of North Korean and Chinese Communists in Korea.

The set-piece battle had, in fact, become the credo of not only the French who were fighting the Indochina war but of the United States which, after 1952, had become more and more directly involved in its financial and often in its strategic aspects. The now-famous "Navarre Plan," named after the unlucky French commander-in-chief in Indochina in 1953-54, provided, according to as authoritative a source as the late Secretary of State John Foster Dulles, that the French forces were to break "the organized body of Communist aggression by the end of the 1955 fighting season," leaving the task of mopping up the remaining (presumably disorganized) guerrilla groups to the progressively stronger national armies of Cambodia, Laos, and Viet-Nam.

The Communists were to give the French one last opportunity to meet them face to face. When it occurred in March, 1954 at Dien Bien Phu, it took place in the same hazardous tactical situation and terrain as the costly battle for the pocket of Hoa-Binh, with the sole difference that the French air supply handicap had been lengthened by 200 miles and the enemy's

firepower had increased by 300 percent. The result of that encounter was not unexpected for anyone who could read the signs.

As the Communist commander-in-chief, Vo Nguyên Giap,
was to explain later on to a French visitor, "The [French] Expeditionary Corps was strategically surprised because it did not
believe that we would attack—and we attacked; and it was tactic-
ally surprised because we had succeeded in solving the problems
of concentrating our troops, our artillery and our supplies.

"This way of reasoning [on the part of the French] was logical,
but of a too-formalistic logic. We did construct our supply roads;
our soldiers knew well the art of camouflage, and we succeeded
in getting our supplies through."

And that, basically, was what counted in that kind of war.

4

Diary: Milk Run

MAY 31ST. It all began with Dave Saylor, the U.S. Air Force liaison officer in Hanoi, asking me casually how I'd like to take an airplane ride today, and me saying that this would be a splendid idea for Sunday morning. Up at 5:30, catching a breakfast *"à la Française,"* that is, a pot of coffee, bread, butter and jam; into a French Air Force jeep across Doumer Bridge to Gia-Lam Air Force base. The place looked slightly upset—the counter-push was on in Laos and a forward element was cut off in Ban-Ban short of howitzer ammunition and gasoline. No airfield anywhere near it, so the load was rigged for parachuting. On the airfield apron a group of "Flying Boxcars" stand side by side with their tail gates wide open. To put it more exactly they have no tail gates; the French found that the tail gates were only a bother and their absence makes unloading easier in case of bulky loads. Of course, in flight it feels like sitting in an open-door garage in the middle of the sky. That makes for one hell of a draft, but in this climate nobody minds anyway.

The pilots are American, from Chennault's "CAT." My pilot's name is Kusak, from Rochester, New York. The loading itself is done by French paratroopers from one of the Airborne Re-supply Companies. Fascinating as the dickens to see them lash down the heavy loads on the floor of the plane. In fact, in typical French fashion the load isn't even completely lashed down as the plane begins to roll off the apron onto the runway.

No time to waste, there is a long line of Flying Boxcars waiting their turn; several other forward bases are due for re-supply today. Clothing is very informal: everybody in shorts and not even wearing a light shirt. Even at 8,000 feet the temperature is about 65°.

Likewise nobody wears a parachute—except me. They strapped one on me in order to follow regulations; not that it would do me any good in case of a mishap. There isn't a single airfield for hundreds of miles around which could take our plane in case of engine trouble, and parachuting without adequate preparation hundreds of miles behind hostile lines in the jungle was hardly a valid alternative to riding down the plane. And, loaded as we are with high explosives, there wouldn't be much left of us in case of a direct hit by enemy antiaircraft fire. Well, anyway, regulations were observed and I crawled about in the airplane, feeling silly with my parachute on my back.

Squeezed in with the pilots and the French navigator, I could look about the countryside. It's really too beautiful for words; the lacework of the little dikes with their rice paddies, the dark green patches of fields hidden behind bamboo clusters and trees; then the jagged limestone cliffs rising steeply out of the dishpan flat plain and, suddenly, like a carpet of blue-green velvet—the jungle. This whole change of scenery takes place in less than ten minutes.

With the last rice paddy behind us the whole landscape sort of turns silent. No trace of human activity, no foot-paths, draft animals, roads. "Viet territory," says the navigator over the intercom. Kusak leans to the left, looks down over the countryside, nods and says something to the co-pilot, which I can't hear over my intercom set. Nothing else to do but get comfortable. The course is set at about due west for one hour. The navigator switches his receiver on a broadcast wave band and fiddles with the controls. All of a sudden, loud and clear, we can hear a British voice reciting a Sunday morning sermon. Something about loving one's fellow man, I think. The navigator grins.

"Radio Singapore."

Clouds come out now as we cross the first mountain ranges. The plane begins to rock, both pilots check the controls and the navigator goes from one side of the cockpit to the other, trying to get a visual bearing. Up here, particularly in the rainy season, anything else is quite worthless and practically no airfield has navigation aids anyway. I crawled out of the cockpit into the cargo hold where the French riggers have been quite busy. They apparently still are, but this time it's a process in reverse. They are getting the loads ready for the drop. A strong buzzer sounds all of a sudden; this means we are five minutes off target.

We're still 4,000 feet above ground when two riggers go all the way to the edge of the cargo hold to start unfastening the chains which hold the load to the bottom of the plane. Of course, they have no parachutes on. With true logic, the commander of the airborne resupply unit felt that parachutes would be quite useless for the riggers because, should the plane sway at the time of the unfastening of the safety chains and the two men fall out, the six tons of ammunition that would fall out right after them would obviously crush them to death. So why waste two good parachutes?

This is the tricky part of the whole thing: the load has to be unlashed as the plane goes down into its final approach run, but should it hit air turbulence at this precise moment much of the load might fall out prematurely. On the other hand, a steady approach run, of course, gives the enemy a good chance to zero in whatever antiaircraft guns he may have in the area. But apparently there is no choice, particularly when you have as narrow a DZ (Drop Zone) as Ban-Ban. Here we go. The plane goes into a shallow dive and, as we hit the Drop Zone, sharply noses upward. The two riggers, warned by buzzer, jump up on the sides of the plane as the whole load in a roar of clanking metal and whooshing static lines leaves the plane in a few seconds. All of a sudden, the picture of the sky through the tail gate is replaced by that of lush vegetation, by what seems to be a small city and a few huge white and yellow flowers which seem to blossom out under us: the cargo chutes are opening.

For the riggers the job wasn't over yet. All four of them now jumped forward to haul in the static lines flailing madly in the slipstream. The sky now reappears at the end of the Boxcar but in the left-hand corner of it, as the pilot puts the plane on one wing to "peel" it out of the way of the falling load. Another steep turn and I can feel the gravity pushing me smack back against the wall of the cargo hold. I climb back into the cockpit where there is a better view. One can see now the white cargo chutes on the grass surrounded by little ants coming out of the yellowish

Bombing a Village.

zigzag of trenches dug around the village. A glistening white "T" in the middle of the position marks the center of the drop zone. Kusak's done an excellent job—everything fell within our own lines.

Then it happens: A slight tremor on our left wing and some holes appear in it, seemingly out of nowhere. Communist flak. It's an odd feeling for I'd never been in an airplane in a combat zone and feel so damn' naked. The Boxcar, lightened of all its load, again turns on its wing and again climbs steeply. Kusak reaches back, taps my shoulder and points his thumb downward. I look out the window but see nothing. He yells: "Fighters." Sure enough there were two French fighters, way below us, looking tiny like toys against the backdrop of the jungle. They had been on a covering mission, and our navigator had informed them of the ack-ack. Their conversations came through clearly on the intercom, since our navigator had switched to the fighter channel.

"Now, how do you like that? Get that ass of yours out of the way. I want to make a pass at the village."

"Can't see a darn' thing. Do you see anything?"

"Can't see anything either, but let's give it to them just for good measure."

Another swoop by the two little birds and all of a sudden a big black billow behind them. It was napalm—jellied gasoline, one of the nicer horrors developed in World War II. It beats the conventional incendiaries by the fact that it sticks so much better to everything it touches.

"Ah, see the bastards run now?"

Now the village was burning furiously. The two fighters swooped down in turn and raked the area with machine guns. As we veered off, the black cloud just reached our height. Scratch one Lao village—and we don't even know whether the village was pro-Communist or not.

The way back is uneventful. Jokes are passed around, Kusak is congratulated for the perfect drop—some of the stuff actually hit the "T"—and then the navigator switched to the Voice of America in Manila for its Sunday jam session. Back in Hanoi just in time for a late lunch at the Air Force Officers Mess: red wine at will, cold cuts, sirloin steak with French-fried potatoes, green salad, cake and coffee; thirty-five cents. Oh, yes, debriefing. A French Air Intelligence Officer with an American "civilian" from "CAT." "How was it, Al?"

"Oh, just the routine crap, some pretty accurate machinegun fire. They're getting better, you know?"

"Got to make one more trip today, Al."

"Geez, man, let me at least have my lunch. I'm pooped."

So we did, and later on Al went back with a new crew of French paratroop riggers for one more round of the "routine stuff."

Kusak and "CAT" stayed with the French to the bitter end. One particularly fondly-remembered type was Earl McGovern, a giant with a huge beard and so large that they had to build him a special pilot's chair in his plane. Affectionately referred to as "Earthquake McGoon," he flew wing to wing with Kusak into the hell of Dien Bien Phu in April, 1954, when his plane—loaded with ammunition—was hit by Communist flak fire. Perhaps McGovern could have jumped and saved his skin, at the risk of see-

ing his plane crash in the center of the French position with the
effect of a blockbuster.

Kusak heard over the intercom the voice of "Earthquake Mc-
Goon" saying, "I'm riding her in." With the plane ablaze and
with the last power remaining in the engines, McGovern crashed
his "Boxcar" into the enemy lines. The plane exploded on impact.

"Mop-Up"

June 2. Back from an operation in the rice paddies—one of
the *ratissages* (mop-ups). Like most mop-ups, this one was a flop.
Spent the whole day crawling in the blazing sun across rice fields
and dikes, trying to "box in" a village presumed to be the headquarters of a Communist guerrilla battalion. All the stenches of
nature seemed to be on the loose. There are layers of odors, slices
of odors, packages of odors, odors for my nose and for everyone else's in the world. Too bad that there isn't yet a standard
system to translate odors into colors. If one could translate those
stenches into colors Picasso's wildest abstractions would look like
a painting by Grandma Moses. Wallowing in the water of the
paddies isn't as bad as lying in half-dried mud. At least as long
as there is water on top of the mud there's a certain feeling of
coolness even if the water has a temperature of 85°.

Of course, the Communists had been informed of the operation, as they usually are, either by the cumbersomeness of our
preparations or by spies infiltrating among the Vietnamese cooks
and shoe-shine boys and girl friends and other paraphernalia
with which the French units in Indochina are always bogged
down. Like clockwork, each such mop-up operation begins by
an aerial reconnaissance, which only puts the Commies on notice
that something is afoot; then this is followed up by long columns
of trucks carrying the troops necessary for the operation. And,
as if all this weren't sufficient to wake up the whole neighborhood, there generally come along a few tanks to provide for artillery support, I suppose, whose clanking can be heard five miles
around.

This reminds me of the kettle drums and cymbals which the
Vietnamese traditionally take along on tiger hunts. As they say,
the drums and cymbals may not help to catch tigers, but at least

they scare. And to them this is the purpose of the whole thing. They feel that a tiger scared is as good as a tiger dead. I'm afraid that to scare the Viet-Minh is not good enough.

Finally by four o'clock we were close enough to the village to see what was going on. The village is perfectly quiet in the brooding summer heat. Not a soul around, not even dogs were to be seen. Yet the men were supposed to be in the fields working! But the fields seem equally empty. The men around me exchanged knowing looks: another dud. The Communists had been warned.

Merely to appease their professional conscience and so as not to make the operation a total waste, the men crawled on and finally rose on top of the last dike. At one end of the line, the captain commanding the company raised and lowered his arm. Bayonets fixed, everyone began a weary dog trot. Apparently the same thing was true with the other companies forming the ring around the village. The village entrances are reached and all of a sudden the population pours out of the houses as if by signal. Mostly old women and children led by the village mayor and his notables, recognizable by their tightly wrapped black turbans. We are now near the *dinh*, the community house, on the village square. The French intelligence officer, speaking perfect Vietnamese apparently, interrogates the village chief with an air of weary exasperation.

His answers are voluble but obviously negative. No, he has not seen any Communist guerrillas in a long time. No, their village has not made any contributions to the Communist rice tax; no, all their men and youngsters were accounted for and if they are not here now it is because they are working out in the fields (we, of course, hadn't seen anybody working out in the fields). And on it went.

There were some shrieks in the background as some of the soldiers searched the houses for hidden entrances and arms caches. Some of these are extremely ingenious. The entrance may well be under the fire of the open hearth, then a long tunnel would connect it with the village pond, with the actual hideout being under the pond itself. Or the entrance would be in the pond through a siphon, with the result that the hideout would be foolproof even to bloodhounds or mine detectors. In other words, to find a Viet-

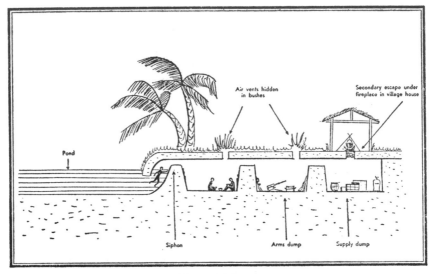

Village Hideout.

Minh depot or hideout in such a village would be a matter of sheer luck or torture, for very seldom does Intelligence succeed in getting direct information on the existence of such a hideout in a Communist-controlled village.

In this particular case torture proved unnecessary. One of the few young men in the village apparently lost his nerve and started running. A wild fusillade ensued. The men had to give vent to their pent-up animosity after that endless approach crawl of the afternoon. The cries of the intelligence officer to get the fellow alive came too late. There wasn't much left of the fellow when we got to him. To be sure he had some leaflets on him and, naturally, everybody immediately swore that they had never seen him before, that they didn't know a thing about him, that he had just arrived in the village and that they had been too afraid of the nasty Viet-Minh to tell anything to the nice French, etc.

It was 1800 and no time was to be lost if we wanted to get back to the main road before dark settled. The platoon commanders' whistles called the men back out of the houses where some of them were in the process of grabbing ducks and chickens.

The march back was uneventful and the truck trip back jerked the last bit of strength out of us. Arrived at Hai-Duong caked in mud from head to foot, sunburnt through my shirt and with one or two leeches on my legs, black and fat ones. They are no problem. All you do is light a cigarette and hold it against them and watch them sizzle and squirm as they fall off. Too tired for anything but a shower. The day after, there we were with the honors of the Army report:

"In the course of a *ratissage* (mop-up operation), our forces have succeeded in discovering an enemy underground hideout. Several enemy agents were killed. An important amount of documentation was captured." Unquote. That's the end of that.

June 4. The bliss of a day's rest in Hanoi: clean bed sheets, a ceiling fan, a cold shower. Then a long swim at the "Cercle Sportif." Up in the deep-blue sky, twin-engined C-47's were flying formation in triangular groups of three and nine planes. Here and there, they would swoop low in formation, then gain altitude again and resume their lazy circles.

There was something strange about them, which I finally pinned down; they did not bear the tricolored bull's eye of the French Air Force but the blue lightning of the "Aigle-Azur" airline and the green-and-yellow dragons of "Air Viet-Nam," the two civilian airlines then operating in Indochina. But what were they doing flying formation over Hanoi?

"Oh, that's simple enough," said the lean paratroop lieutenant sunning himself next to me. "There's no doubt going to be a big push on within a few days and as usual we're short of both pilots and airplanes. So, the civilian planes and pilots are being requisitioned to fly the operation, and the civilian pilots are being trained to keep formation so that they won't strew us all over the countryside. Those civilian pilots are good, but to drop paratroopers in tight 'sticks' takes a special type of skill you don't pick up carrying honeymooners from Paris to the Baleares."

Yes, to fight a war does take special skills of all kinds. Up there, the civilian pilots were still flying their lazy circles.

5

Laos Outpost

"LIKE CHRIST off the Cross" was an expression which became current in Indochina to describe survivors from those harrowing retreats through the jungle. And usually that is exactly what they looked like: worn down to skeletons from hunger and dysentery, sunken eyes, the typical tropical pallor in contrast to the bronzed skins of the "white hunters" made popular by Hollywood, their emaciated faces curtained by shaggy beards, and their skins covered with festering sores, from heat rash to leech bites and jungle rot.

Sergeant René Novak was no exception as he and two Laotian soldiers staggered into Phong-Saly, the last French outpost in northern Laos, on May 22, 1953. He was only twenty-five years old, but he looked fifty; he kept on walking like an automaton to the center of the post before he was stopped by some of the men staring at him as at a ghost. In a way, Novak was a ghost, a *revenant,* as the French say, someone who had come back from the dead; he and the two Laotian soldiers were so far the only survivors of the garrison of Muong-Khoua.

They were followed two days later by one more survivor, Staff Sergeant Pierre Blondeau, a much-decorated combat veteran who had voluntarily stayed on in Indochina. Blondeau had spent 57 hours hidden in the bushes near Muong-Khoua before being able to slip through the Communist cordon; he had marched, alone, without food or compass for three days before he had the good luck of encountering a Kha-Kho mountaineer who had once known him and who furnished him some food and showed him the way to Phong-Saly. Never sleeping in a village, never resting on the path but tearing a hole into the thick underbrush with his bare hands and hiding himself in it, Blondeau reached a village a few miles from Phong-Saly, where an inhabitant lent him one of the small ponies which abound in northern Laos. Looking like a battered Don Quixote, Blondeau reached Phong-Saly on May 24.

The four men had performed a near miracle. They had crossed 80 kilometers of enemy-held territory after surviving a month long siege in a post whose name was to become a byword for heroism in Indochina: Muong-Khoua.

When the Viet-Minh invaded Laos early in 1953, the French High Command was faced with two choices: evacuate the whole country altogether until sufficient forces were available for its reconquest or try to hold on to a series of strongpoints throughout the country which would hold off the bulk of enemy forces until such time as the two capitals of the country, Luang-Prabang and Vientiane, were in shape for a prolonged defense. Since the King of Laos had refused to budge from his royal residence in Luang-Prabang, the political necessity for holding on to Laos prevailed over the military factors, which would have dictated total evacuation of at least the northern half of the country.

Dozens of outposts throughout northern Laos were given

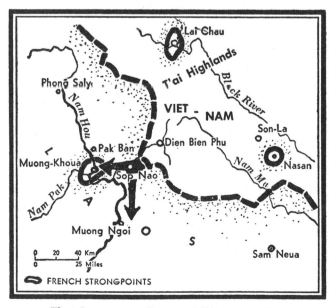

The Communist Spring Offensive, 1953.

the assignment to stay put and fight as long as they could in order to delay the advance of several Viet-Minh divisions now marching into the kingdom. Some of the posts had no choice; they were isolated in roadless territory and, in the middle of the rainy season, inaccessible to aircraft or trucks. Others were given specific missions to hold out for a minimum number of days in order to give the French Command in Laos time to construct a second line of defense. One of the key posts given such an assignment was Muong-Khoua.

Situated at the point of confluence of the Nam-Pak and Nam-Hou rivers, Muong-Khoua was an ideal site to delay the enemy advance for a short while. Together with its satellite outpost of Sop-Nao, defended by a reinforced platoon under Lieutenant Grézy, Muong-Khoua was given the task of holding out at all costs on April 3, 1953. On that day, the commander of Muong-Khoua, Captain Teullier, also assumed command over Sop-Nao. In the evening of the same day, a Viet-Minh battalion crossed the border near Dien Bien Phu and encircled Sop-Nao. For six days and nights, Grézy's men held out in the ruins of their post against the overwhelming might of their enemy. Finally, on April 9, Teullier authorized the survivors of Grézy's platoon to fight their way out and back into Muong-Khoua, 30 kilometers away across the jungle.

During the night from 9th to the 10th, Grézy and his men began their march out of the trap. As is usual in such cases, the Viet-Minh had prepared an ambush on the direct path from Sop-Nao to Muong-Khoua. However, Grézy was not new at the game; instead of taking the direct path, he and his men began to hack their own path through the jungle to the south of the post, thus shaking off for a time their Viet-Minh pursuers. But they were not to be shaken so easily. On the 11th in the morning, loyal Laotian tribesmen warned the worn-out Frenchmen and Laotian soldiers that two Viet-Minh companies had left Sop-Nao in pursuit and were in danger of overtaking them. In fact, they already had barred their most direct route towards Muong-Khoua.

Once more Grézy aroused his foot-sore men, who were still carrying with them all their equipment, armament, and radio sets, and decided to make a break to the north for Phong-Saly. Although farther away, Phong-Saly had the advantage of having an airfield. His first objective was the village of Pak Ban on the Nam-Hou river about 20 miles north of Muong-Khoua. This initiative had some extremely lucky consequences for the French, for at the same time a convoy of dugout canoes—one of the best means of transportation in Laos—loaded with equipment and ammunition destined to posts along the Nam-Hou came floating downriver from Phong-Saly, unaware of the Viet-Minh forces which had infiltrated the valley between Pak Ban and Muong-Khoua. After consultation with the convoy commander, the whole convoy, now burdened with Grézy and all his men, proceeded immediately to Muong-Khoua, which it reached the next day.

Teullier immediately realized that he had but little time left to clear out the noncombatants and surplus equipment from Muong-Khoua. Unmistakable signs of the imminent arrival of Viet-Minh troops had been in the air for several days; the village headmen around Muong-Khoua had become unfriendly when French patrols came through. In fact, they no longer talked to Frenchmen unless directly addressed, and in the village of Muong-Khoua, the population just simply disappeared. The market had been all but deserted for the past several days, with none of the Kha-Kho or Meo farmers coming down with their small gray pigs, fruits, or other produce. *"L'asphyxie par le vide . . . ,* the "choking-off by creating a void," had begun.

On April 12, 1953, Teullier assembled the dugout canoe convoy for a 40-mile dash down river to Muong-Ngoi, but once more the enemy had been quicker than the French. About 600 yards below Muong-Khoua, at a place where two sand bars narrow the navigable channel to a few yards, the whole convoy fell into a Viet-Minh ambush.

As usual, the Viet-Minh had been well prepared and perfectly informed. A small barrage of tree trunks had been floated across the navigable channel, and several machine guns and one mortar had been placed on the two sides of the river bed, thus insuring thorough coverage of the ambush area. Once more, however, luck had not been entirely against the French; by placing the ambush so close to Muong-Khoua, the Viet-Minh gave the French garrison an opportunity to intervene in the combat should the convoy survive the first salvo, which it did. As the first dugout was carried into the barrage by its own momentum, the sharp-eyed Laotians in the following dugouts immediately beached their craft against the sand banks and, using them for cover, went into action. In the ensuing fire fight, the Laotians coolly held their own but were soon in danger of running out of ammunition when four platoons of infantry from Muong-Khoua arrived and immediately counterattacked the Communists who soon abandoned the battlefield, leaving thirteen dead and four wounded. On the French side, two dugouts, which had been shot to pieces, had to be abandoned. There also were seven missing, one wounded, and one dead.

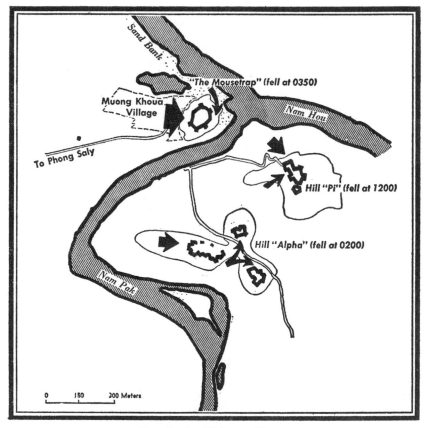

The End at Muong-Khoua.

It was very obvious that any further attempt at breaking through by the river had now become hopeless. The whole convoy returned to Muong-Khoua, to share its fate, and the defenders now grimly dug in for the siege and assault that was to come.

Muong-Khoua village was situated on a promontory formed by the junction of the Nam-Hou and the Nam Pak rivers. Covered on the Nam-Hou side by a fairly large sand bank, it was usually safe from floods. With its straight main street and its many clusters of green trees, it offered a fairly pleasant aspect. At the tip of the promontory, covered on one side by the sand banks and on the other by a steep embankment overlooking the Nam Pak, stands the fortified post of Muong-Khoua, dominating the river junction and the small city. It, in turn, is dominated by two hillocks on the right bank of the Nam Pak, forming with the post of Muong-Khoua an equilateral triangle whose sides measure 200 yards. Long before the attack on Muong-Khoua, Teullier had found it impossible to organize a defense of Muong-Khoua without also including in it the two hillocks on the other side of the Nam Pak. Naming the southern elevation Hill "Alpha" and the one to the east Hill "Pi," he had fortified them with trenches and earth bunkers and divided between them his meager resources and manpower.

In view of the fact that he now also possessed the equipment of the down-river dugout flotilla and the additional reinforcement of Grézy's garrison from Sop-Nao, he organized the whole position into a group of three independent but mutually supporting little forts. With a total garrison of one French captain, one French lieutenant and a handful of French noncommissioned officers supported by 300 *Chasseurs Laotiens* (Laotian light infantry) armed with a total of three 81mm mortars, two 60mm mortars and two machine guns. Teullier had little, if any, illusions as to his ability to hold out indefinitely against his much stronger enemy. Facing this little force was the whole 910th Battalion of the 148th Regional Regiment, reinforced by a heavy mortar company and other elements from the enemy's 316th Division.

April 13th was a calm day. A few old people and children had reappeared in the streets of Muong-Khoua and the garrison of the three-hill position felt in good spirits in view of the events of the day before. At 1100, Teullier received a coded radio message from Colonel Boucher de Crèvecoeur, the commanding officer of French and Laotian forces in Laos:

"You are to hold the position of Muong-Khoua for a minimum of 14 days with all means at your disposal. You will be re-supplied by airdrop and receive adequate air support . . ."

Muong-Khoua's fate was sealed. It was perhaps with a sort of prescient irony that the garrison of Muong-Khoua had named the main fort in Muong-Khoua village, "The Mousetrap."

The Viet-Minh command was eager to finish with Muong-Khoua, which would remain a thorn in the side of its communication lines, if the French were to hold it. At about 2300, April 13th, the first enemy mortar shells fell on the rolling, easily accessible slopes of hill "Alpha." The siege of Muong-Khoua had begun.

From that moment until the end, more than one month later, the defenders of Muong-Khoua were under fire every single night. On the first assault, the Viet-Minh had left 22 dead in the barbed wire of the French position. They now abstained from mass attacks and reverted to a strategy of gnawing away inch by inch at the entrenched positions—in tactics they were to develop to a fine art one year later at Dien Bien Phu. To be sure, during the day, French B-26's, fighter-bombers, and supply aircraft flew over Muong-Khoua, ferreting out Communist gun positions or parachuting in urgently needed supplies and surgical equipment; or at night, when Viet-Minh pressure would be too heavy on one of the outposts, a "Luciole" (firefly) reconnaissance aircraft would parachute light flares over the battlefield to help the defenders direct their fire.

But Muong-Khoua was low on the totem pole of French priorities in northern Indochina. Even within Laos itself, the Viet-Minh pressures on Luang-Prabang and Vientiane, though diminished in strength, had lost nothing of their menace and thus were more important than the small outposts far away in the north, fighting for their lives.

But, miraculously, the garrison survived. On April 27th, 14 days after the first major assault, the French High Commander in Hanoi parachuted to Teullier his own Legion of Honor and a number of *croix de guerre* for his men: They had kept their promise and held Muong-Khoua for 14 days.

Teullier himself waded through the Nam-Pak with an escort, scaled the steep slope of Hill "Pi" and the mortar-pitted ruins of what was left of Hill "Alpha," to decorate in person those men who had received their medals; returning late in the evening to the "Mousetrap." This was the last time that Teullier was to see his whole garrison. And on the Communist side, pressure increased to finish off the lonely outpost which effectively prevented the Communists from using the strategically important Nam-Hou river as a line of communications for their troops operating in central Laos.

As occurred much too often in the Indochina war, a post surviving desperately in a hopeless position had been elevated to a symbol, with newspapers all over the world broadcasting the name and fame of the defenders of Muong-Khoua. This publicity made its eventual fall, which in the eyes of the French High Command had been a foregone conclusion, a much more serious blow than it should have been.

All this was almost unknown to Teullier and his gallant 300 men. For them, the war had become a very personal matter of surviving through each night until the next morning, particularly through the dreadful hours of the monsoon period's *"crachin"* when a dense, milky-white fog laid itself down like a blanket on the countryside at around 2100, and usually not lifting before 0900 the next day.

But so far, Muong-Khoua had been in luck. The village itself had become a completely deserted no-man's land which French patrols would reconnoiter during the daytime, pushing at times as far out as the empty Laotian National Guard barracks, without ever making any contact with either the population or the enemy. Except for the hours of night combat, an eerie silence had settled down on the countryside—a silence which hid very well the hum of activity around the camouflaged Communist positions at the base of the two hillocks and around the "Mousetrap." Teullier had kept his men active with all-around patrols, even leaving them at night in ambush within the deserted village of Muong-Khoua, thus keeping them alert and giving himself the precious extra few minutes of warning in case of a general attack.

The days passed, and, against all expectations, the Communist forces in central Laos began to withdraw once more towards the Vietnamese border. Xieng-Khouang, the capital of a neighboring province to the south of Muong-Khoua, had been liberated from the Viet-Minh on May 13th; on May 17th, French forces were on the lower Nam-Hou, about 80 kilometers from Muong-Khoua. That evening, again one patrol had left the "Mousetrap" for its night round into the ghost town in darkness made even thicker by an extremely dense fog.

By 2200, it was impossible to see one's hand in front of one's eyes in Muong-Khoua. A few dogs, no doubt abandoned by their masters during the precipitous retreat into the surrounding hills, were howling in the darkness, their noise muffled by the settling fog. All of a sudden, there was the high-pitched yelp of unexpected hurt so well known to all dog owners; someone had stepped on a dog's tail accidentally or had kicked him! At about 2300, the French patrol saw dark shadows appear out of the fog along Muong-Khoua's main street: the enemy was here. In silence the patrol began to fall back to the "Mousetrap." Full alert was given to the garrison, and the two hill positions were notified by radio at midnight of the impending attack.

At 0030, May 18, 1953, the first mortar shell fell into the courtyard of the "Mousetrap," soon followed by a hail of other shells of various calibers, including those of a 57mm recoilless cannon and 120mm Soviet-made heavy mortars. Phosphorous shells, which had set afire some of the wooden bulwarks of the post, added their greenish light to the inferno. In the CP bunker, already filled with moaning wounded—there was no doctor in Muong-Khoua—Teullier yelled to Sergeant René Novak, the radio operator of Muong-Khoua:

"Get GATAC North*! Tell them to send a 'Luciole' and if possible some fighter-bombers. We need help bad."

To the south of Muong-Khoua, flashes of mortar fire could be seen around the easily accessible slopes of Hill "Alpha" where one reinforced Laotian platoon under a French senior NCO was likewise being torn to pieces by heavy Viet-Minh fire. Only Hill "Pi," under the command of Lieutenant Grézy, had succeeded

---

*GATAC: *Groupment Aèrien Tactique*, one of the five regional air commands in Indochina.

Viet-Minh Troops.

in shaking off the enemy. Its lone mortar was laying down pre-arranged supporting fires in front of the "Mousetrap" and on Hill "Alpha."

At 0110, the western corner bunker of the "Mousetrap" began to crumble under the impact of several direct hits and massive chunks of brick and concrete tumbled over the steep cliff into the Nam-Pak. The agony of Muong-Khoua had begun. At about 0130, Sergeant Novak had Hanoi's answer to the request for air support:

"Total QGO* over all delta airfields. Will send support as soon as feasible."

At 0230, a muffled yell was heard on the Viet-Minh side, becoming increasingly distinct as the first shadows of Viet-Minh shock troops began to appear over the parapets of the battered

*QGO: International Morse Code signal for lack of visibility.

French positions: *"Tiên-lên, Tiên-lên"!* (Forward, Forward!)
But Teullier's men were not giving in easily; twice, the assault
waves of the Viet-Minh were thrown back by the concentrated
automatic weapons fire of the defenders. Then, however, taking
advantage of the fog, one part of the enemy force by-passed the
"Mousetrap" to the north by following the sand bank along the
river under the cover of the fog, and now the fort was also attacked on its northern flank. Four more assaults were contained
but the assailants finally succeeded in gaining control of the fort's
platform. Hand-to-hand combat developed for each of the buildings and bunkers. Finally, at about 0350, the last defenders were
cornered against the wall of the fort overlooking the cliff of the
Nam-Pak river and the guns fell silent at Muong-Khoua. Hill
"Alpha" had met its fate about half an hour earlier when the last
bunker had been plowed to rubble by the enemy's heavy mortars.

This left Grézy and his two platoons up on hill "Pi." He and
his men had watched the end of the defenders in the "Mousetrap"
as if sitting in the front seat of a vast theater, watching the brief
bursts of the French machine guns trying to save ammunition and
the columns of flame as the superheavy 120mm mortar shells of
the enemy hit the bunkers of the "Mousetrap" with unerring accuracy. When the shooting died down at the two other posts, the
men of hill "Pi" knew that their turn had now come.

There was no panic, no outward sign of fear. Yet Grézy's troops,
like most of those in Muong-Khoua, were relatively recent Laotian
levies, run-of-the-mill troops of the Laotian army; not commandos
handpicked for a suicidal mission. But led by French Army
professionals, they performed as heroically as any carefully selected
crack outfit. When the first French reconnaissance plane arrived
over the area at about 0900 May 18th, it found the charred remains of what had been the French position in Muong-Khoua and
on Hill "Alpha." But around Hill "Pi," it found one vast cloud of
brownish dust, kicked up by the murderous concentration of enemy
heavy weapons on the little position. Here and there, a small cloud
of dust appeared on the side where the enemy must have been—
Grézy's lone mortar apparently was still in action. A little while
later, two lumbering C-47's appeared over Muong-Khoua with
their regular supply drop for the garrison. They circled the battle-

field and then returned whence they had come. At 1200 the red flag with the three white elephants of Laos and the French tricolor disappeared from atop the central bunker of hill "Pi."

Muong-Khoua's lightly armed garrison had held off a heavily armed force for *thirty-six days*. It had fulfilled its mission to the last cartridge and the last man.

Communiqué No. 14 of the French High Command in Indochina, for the period between May 10 and May 24, 1953:

> "During the night of May 17 to 18, the post of Muong-Khoua, which had victoriously resisted since the beginning of the Viet-Minh offensive, succumbed under the overwhelming mass of assailants."

Three lines out of two hundred—that was all that could be spared for gallant Teullier and his three hundred men.

Another chapter in Muong-Khoua's history was written six years later. In July, 1959, the tiny post of Sop-Nao was again held by a single platoon, this time of the Royal Laotian Army, for the last French combat troops had left independent Laos in 1955.* Evacuated by the Communist-led *Pathet-Lao* rebels since late 1957, Sop-Nao had been a quiet garrison, with little else to worry about than a few smugglers from North Viet-Nam, bringing in opium in exchange for some Western goods that could be found in Laos.

The commander of the little garrison was Lieutenant Déo Van Khoun, a scion of the famous Déo family of Black-T'ai chieftains, who until a few years ago were ruling the mountain provinces of northwest Indochina with an iron hand. There was old Déo Van Long who was the head of the T'ai Federation, whose capital had been Lai-Chau, now in Communist North Viet-Nam; there were Déo Van Cam and Déo Van Tri, provincial chieftains, and the many liege lords in Son-La and Phong-To. And there were the Déo of Dien Bien Phu, whose ancestor, by allying himself with the French consul Auguste Pavie, made possible the French penetration into northern Laos and the mountain areas of North Viet-

---

* The Western defeat in Laos in 1961-62 (see chapter 13) brought about the evacuation of all U.S. military personnel and the phasing out over five years of the French training mission. The last French air base in Laos, Séno, was transferred to the Lao neutralist regime in December 1962.

Nam. Déo Van Khoun, now a lieutenant in the Royal Laotian Army, was, therefore, "at home" in the area to which he had been assigned. His own people roamed the hills on both sides of the border and he had nothing to worry about.

In fact, he felt *so* confident that he would be warned of any untoward event that, instead of sleeping in the post with his men, he had taken up quarters in the village, where he lived with his wife in a Laotian house built on stilts, as most of them are. July 1959 had been a very warm month in northern Laos. The young rice was growing well in the narrow valleys and for weeks, Sop-Nao had been completely quiet. There had been very little patrolling going on since the rains had swelled the rivers. This, of course, does not make patrolling impossible; it merely makes it uncomfortable, but nothing in the present situation made long-range patrolling seem urgent.

But when the moon set over Sop-Nao in the night of July 29-30, 1959, dark shadows seemed to emerge from the whitish ground fog shrouding the hills. One or two dogs attempted to yelp, but were quickly disposed of by some well-directed stabs of long mountaineer daggers. Without hesitation, the bulk of the dark shadows went to the Lao post sitting above Sop-Nao on a bare hill—that is, it had been a bare hill when the French were there. Since then much of the low shrubbery had pushed up again with the fantastic rapidity of the tropics and provided again ample shelter for any assailant. The shadows encircled the small post in silence and then settled down to wait for their signal.

In the meantime, a smaller group of black-clad men had marched rapidly into Sop-Nao itself. Without hesitation, it went directly to Déo Van Khoun's house. A few men surrounded it while four men entered the six-foot high storage area under the house. So far, not a word had been spoken, not the slightest noise had been made by anyone in the two parties.

The deep silence was suddenly broken by the husky chatter of a sub-machinegun fired in a confined space, followed almost immediately by screams of pain; the four men under Déo Van Khoun's house had fired through the plank ceiling into the bodies of the lieutenant and his wife lying, Laotian fashion, on rice-straw mats on the floor. The very first burst hit Déo Van Khoun in the chest and groin, while his wife sustained a lighter wound in one of her thighs.

This was the signal the group encircling the hill post had been waiting for. They began spraying the post with sub-machine gun and BAR fire, jumping methodically from bush to bush. Within a few minutes, the struggle was over and the post in enemy hands. In fact, the very unpreparedness of the Laotians and the over-preparedness of the attackers finally saved the Laotians from annihilation. Had they resisted for several hours in the post—as the assailants had expected them to—daylight would have made any escape impossible. As it was, the confusion of attack allowed the bulk of the platoon to flee from the post, with the very bushes which prevented the sleepy sentry from noticing the attackers now preventing the latter from shooting at the fleeing soldiers. In Sop-Nao itself, the enemy commando had fallen back, as ordered, on the military post, abandoning Déo Van Khoun and his wife to their fate. This again was to the advantage of the Laotians, for Déo and his wife, with the help of the now-awake villagers and the fleeing soldiers, were able to head for the dugouts lying on the shore of the Nam-Houa, a small tributary of the Nam-Hou. Paddling frantically downstream towards Muong-Khoua, they escaped the attackers who were still in the captured post, sorting out the spoils— weapons, clothing, rations and an always precious field radio set.

Lieutenant Déo Van Khoun died during the boat trip to Muong-Khoua, which the exhausted survivors of Sop-Nao reached the following day. The garrison there was in battalion strength, reinforced by a half-dozen heavy mortars. Also, since the earlier defense of Muong-Khoua, an airstrip practicable for small planes had been hewn out of the brush. But within minutes after the arrival of the garrison from Sop-Nao, the news of the fort's capture had made the rounds of Muong-Khoua, and again minutes later, through the miraculous osmosis that is almost a sixth sense in Asia, the population also knew that the Laotian battalion would not fight for Muong-Khoua. It is, in fact, doubtful whether the process was one of the soldiers telling the population that they wouldn't fight, or one of the population—which had been occupied by the Communists from the time Teullier died in 1953 to the time the Royal Laotian Government signed an agreement with the *Pathet-*

Lao in November 1957—telling the soldiers that it was useless to resist such a Communist invasion. For there was no doubt in the population's mind that an invasion had taken place.

The number of assailants and their nationality had thus far not been made clear; it turned out later that there were about 80 and that they were Black T'ai from the North Vietnamese side of the border. But as far as the Lao commander in Muong-Khoua was concerned, they might as well have been the whole 316th Division, Viet-Nam People's Army. The same evening, the whole garrison of the fort of Muong-Khoua, American-equipped and French-trained, evacuated the post and withdrew into the surrounding mountains—*without having seen an enemy and without having fired a shot in anger.*

It was to stay up in the hills, watching its own deserted post, for several days until, in the obvious absence of an "enemy," it decided to reoccupy its quarters. The population of Muong-Khoua, which had stayed put to a large extent, received its "defenders" with barely a smile, but the effect of the episode on the unit's morale as well as upon the civilian population of the area had been devastating.

On August 2, 1959, a communiqué of the Laotian Army announced that "the post of Sop-Nao had been reoccupied after a struggle which lasted three hours," and a Laotian Government communiqué was to add on August 5, that, far from an "invasion," the attacks had been carried out by "small groups of partisans, benefiting from the effect of surprise to overrun small garrisons of the Lao National Army." And the report further added: "It seems that the number of reported assailants had been somewhat exaggerated in the first reports."

But the first reports were already going around the world, and people again began to talk of a "war in Laos." And it is perhaps a good thing that the newspapers' memories are so short as not to remember how the same little outpost had held off a Communist division for a month a few years before, for that would raise several uncomfortable questions—and the Indochina of today is not a place to ask uncomfortable questions.

6

Diary: The Women

T HIS WOULD have been a rather un-French war if women had not played an important rôle in it. First of all, there was the hard fact of a still-existing French civilian population—not only dependents of military or administrative personnel, but the wives and children of merchants and truckers, doctors and schoolteachers, about 80,000 in all. There were thousands of them to whom "home" was Saigon or Hanoi, Tourane or Vientiane—not the cold, misty climate of mainland France. Their children were a hardy, enterprising lot who had survived Jap concentration camps at the age of five or eight, lived through the Viet-Minh attacks of 1945 and 1946; were going to school in the knowledge that a hand grenade might maim them on the way back, but who still placed very well in the French competitive examinations and regularly won the French high school swimming championships every year. After all, you can swim all year round in Indochina, and many schools in France don't have winterized pools.

In a country where polygamy is legal (it was abolished, on paper, in 1958), the whole approach to womanhood and sex is different from that in a Western country. The existence of easy-to-get sex is treated matter-of-factly by everyone and thus, some believe, it presents far less of a problem than in most other countries. For example, the Ladies' Pagoda near the Great Lake of Hanoi, displayed the following poster inside the entrance, quite explicit in its pithiness:

"Il est formellement interdit aux amoureux d'amener leurs concubines dans ce temple pour y faire la noce. Ce temple est un endroit sacré."

("It is formally forbidden for all lovers to bring their girl friends into this temple to make whoopee on the premises. This is a holy place.")

131

This is a change from the warning posters which I saw inside Manila City Hall during an earlier trip, one of which read: "Please deposit your firearms with the guard at entrance," while the other read: "No agents, brokers, fixers, ten-percenters allowed within the premises of City Hall."

This approach is even reflected in the government information bulletin *Vietnam-Presse,* whose northern edition, at least, was not yet infected by the depredations of high-class morality which was to descend upon Saigon in later years. In any case, its copywriter had developed a classical style of his own, to report untoward events in the city's love life.

> Title: *"Chérie, do you prefer love or money?"*
> Story: "Mr. Cao Van Hop, 50, declared this morning to police that Miss Nguyên Thi Xuan, who had spent the night with him in a hotel, had taken advantage of his sleep to steal from him 5,000 piasters. The police is investigating."
>
> Title: *"Since he was not loved . . ."*
> Story: "Mr. Nguyên Thiên Thuat has beaten up in a beastly manner Miss Nguyên Thi Ninh, his girl friend, who had refused to make love to him."
>
> Title: *"4,300 piasters as a trade on wife."*
> Story: "This is the funny story which happened to the Chinese Soun Pieh Sang, 49, whose new wife left him for a brothel, where he found her. Mr. Sang filed a complaint with the police because the manager of the brothel now asks him for 4,300 piasters in exchange for his wife."

The French Army, like all other armies in the world, was to make its own contributions to the love life of the country, but perhaps in more variegated ways than any other army.

First of all, there was that hallowed institution of French colonial forces, the B.M.C. Originally, the three initials had stood for *Bataillon Médical de Campagne* (Medical Field Battalion), but, in the course of things, had become attached to another institution whose French name is *Bordel Mobile de Campagne,* or mobile field brothel. Over the years, the problem as to whether or not to abolish the institution has found partisans on both sides of the question. On the negative side, the argument is that which is used against any type of legalized prostitution—it is basically immoral and it does not cut down on venereal disease.

On the other side of the argument—and thus far, in the French Army at least, it has withstood all attacks—the B.M.C. has the advantages of providing the soldiers with a controlled sexual release, thus cutting down on desertions, on rapes of hapless girls of the surrounding civilian population, and also on venereal disease, since both the soldiers and the girls of the B.M.C.'s are checked regularly. As to the immorality issue, the girls themselves are volunteers, usually from the Oulad-Naïl tribe of Constantine, whose beautiful women have made it a century-old tradition of serving as prostitutes throughout North Africa, until they had assembled sufficient amounts of money for their dowry. Once they have their dowry, they return to their villages, settle down with the home-town boys and become devoted family mothers ever after.

I remember having served in a Moroccan Division which was provided with such institutions and thus made us the envy of our neighboring American outfits. In fact, it was said that the late General Patton, who always understood the needs of his troops, would have been quite willing to experiment with the idea but finally gave it up when he was made to realize that the ruckus kicked up by the outraged wives and mothers of America would probably result in a Congressional uproar that would slow down the war by several months.

In Indochina, the B.M.C.'s functioned admirably well, and it made for a pleasant change in the monotony of an army convoy all of a sudden to spot a 2½-ton truck loaded with the Oulad-Naïl in their gaily colored Algerian garb, shouting jokes at the soldiers. The B.M.C.'s would travel with units in the combat zones—for that matter, *all* of Indochina was combat zone—and some of the girls died heroically, serving as emergency nurses under fire. Of course, their presence was pure poison to the women army personnel—as some wags put it, because they constituted "unfair competition"—and in general, the French Army in Indochina kept them pretty much out of sight of American newsmen and officials.

"You can just imagine the howl if some blabbermouth comes out with a statement to the effect that American funds are used to maintain bordellos for the French Army," said one colonel. As it was, the girls didn't cost the Army one penny, anyway, since the men paid them (at standard tariff rates) for their "services."

There was one case, however, where two B.M.C. girls nearly ended up with the *croix de guerre* for services beyond the call of duty. This occurred in Lai-Chau, a French airhead 200 miles behind Communist lines, where two French battalions held out, encircled by the Viet-Minh, for more than a year. However, farther north, Lai-Chau had a tiny platoon-size outpost at Tsinh-Ho, which covered one of the approach routes to Lai-Chau itself.

When a B.M.C. was airlifted into Lai-Chau, Lieutenant Laurent, a tall, handsome mulatto from Martinique who combined the functions of artillery operations officer and "morale officer" for the airhead, felt that the men in Tsinh-Ho richly deserved their share of earthly joys, but the outpost could only be reached by following a treacherous 30-mile jungle path which, more often than not, was ambushed by the Viet-Minh. Laurent called the girls together, explained the situation to them—and asked for two volunteers to go on the trek, with an infantry commando escort. Without hesitation, several of the girls volunteered and two of them were picked. They left with the commando force, equipped in jungle boots and fatigues but with their flowing robes in their knapsacks, and covered the 30 miles in a harrowing 48-hour march.

They did indeed fall into an ambush on the return trip— perhaps the Viet-Minh wanted its share, too—but behaved as coolly under fire as the seasoned troopers they were and returned to Lai-Chau to the cheers of the garrison. Laurent wrote up two ringing citations for the girls and forwarded them to Northern headquarters in Hanoi. But Hanoi, mindful of the kind of flavor this episode would give to our "crusade," told Laurent in no uncertain terms that the awarding of the two medals would be "inopportune" at this time. We were all greatly disappointed, for we felt that the girls had richly earned them.

A B.M.C. was also present in the ill-fated fortress of Dien Bien Phu, and once more the girls performed heroically as auxiliary nurses, without, however, receiving the kind of publicity given the gallant French nurse, Geneviève de Gallard-Tarraubes. But many of the soldiers who were wounded in the battle will never forget the soft touch of a little brown hand or the guttural French of the little Oulad-Naïls, doing their rounds in the hell of the underground dressing stations.

It remains a matter of conjecture whether the element of "vice" which they added to the war was not outweighed by the element of femininity, even of humanity, which they added to it. Official histories do not like impure heroes and even less impure heroines, but I, for one, hope that on the day when the last war will have been fought and the histories of all wars will have been written, a small scholarly footnote will at least be reserved for the girls of the B.M.C.

At the other end of the scale were the 73 known French prostitutes residing in Indochina, mainly in Saigon, accessible only to rich businessmen, senior officers, airline pilots, and other persons with either means or connections (airline pilots, with their access to the dollars and gold of Hong Kong were considered particularly desirable). They had been a thorn in the French Army's side for many years but their connections made them fairly invulnerable to official harassment—at least until the arrival of Marshal de Lattre de Tassigny.

Endowed with both military and civilian powers, de Lattre decided to make a clean sweep of the French prostitutes. Within a short while he had signed orders of expulsion against all of them in spite of impassioned pleas by influential men throughout the community. De Lattre stood firm as a rock.

But one day, de Lattre's chief of intelligence, who had been out of Indochina on a trip, stormed in, obviously in great agitation: *"Mon Général,* you just can't do this to me!"

The icy stare of de Lattre would have frozen a braver man.

"And, pray tell, why not?"

"Because they're all on the intelligence payroll, as well!"

P.S. They were nevertheless expelled, but in a more gradual manner, so as to permit the distraught chief of intelligence to replace his charming operatives with "local talent."

A Communist propaganda leaflet in my possession accuses 60

---

*De Lattre was made a field marshal posthumously.

French soldiers of having raped 700 women in one afternoon. This works out to an average of eleven women per soldier. Such a compliment paid to French virility by the enemy!

Like all modern armies, the French Army has its women soldiers, called PFAT *(Personnel Féminin de l'Armée de Terre)*, with the standard problems and jokes this entails. By 1954, a total of more than 2,000 women served with the French ground forces in Indochina, with an additional 120 serving in the Air Force and 30 in the Navy. Another 470 women, wives of military or civilian personnel in Indochina, were recruited locally.

Assigned on an individual basis, or in very small units to various headquarters even in the combat zone, they performed their duties extremely well, in spite of the murderous climate, often doing jobs that were as dangerous as that of any man. Close to one hundred of them were killed in action.

Among the women as a group, one of the most respected was that of the ambulance drivers. Generally in their late twenties or early thirties, those girls would pick up their wounded in the worst of the fighting, in spite of the fact that the Viet-Minh would often make a special target of the vehicles marked with a red cross. Aline Lerouge was one of the best known, having in several cases raced her U.S.-made ambulance clear through friendly and enemy lines in order to pick up wounded left behind in an ambush.

Another woman who had left a deep impression was Captain Valérie André, M. D., command paratrooper and helicopter pilot. Piloting her own little Hiller 'copter, she had rescued 67 men from behind the Communist lines. Being not only a pilot but a full-fledged M.D., she was able to save the lives of dozens of men by giving them emergency aid before flying them out to a hospital.

Another girl of that elite group of the IPSA—I no longer recall the meaning of all the abbreviations of the French "alphabet soup" which is about as varied as its American variety, but IPSA had something to do with Flying Nurses Service—was Paule Dupont d'Isigny, a tall woman with immense dark eyes, wearing her hair in a tight bun and preferring the green combat fatigue uniform to the more conspicuous "suntans." She, like many others in her field, was a "graduate" of the French Resistance and of a

Nazi death camp; and, like Captain André, was a pilot and
paratrooper with 4,200 flying hours, thirty combat missions
and enough medals for bravery to last a regular army officer
from military academy to retirement as a general: Indochina
croix de guerre with two palms, the *croix de guerre* 1939-45 with
one palm, and the Legion of Honor for military valor.

There were other categories of girl soldiers whose jobs, though
less glamorous, were just as essential. This was the case of the
parachute riggers of the airborne units. There, in the hellish heat
of the parachute drying sheds, each crew of two girls would fold
one parachute every seven minutes. Most of the girls were paratroopers themselves—a sport which has attracted quite a few
women in France in recent years. (A French fashion model,
Colette Duval, has held the women's world record in free-fall
jumping for the past several years.)

The auxiliaries recruited in Indochina itself often were admirable types, women with families of their own, but serving in the
army as officers or enlisted women. There was one comical case
of one woman who enlisted in order to be near her husband in
North Viet-Nam. Through the usual vagaries of military red tape,
she found herself as a nurse in an encircled outpost behind Communist lines—while her beloved husband held down a safe desk
job in Hanoi.

But perhaps one of the most touching cases of devotion was
that of Madame S. White-haired and close to sixty years old,
she belonged to one of the *grand bourgeois* families of France.
When her son, a lieutenant in the infantry, was transferred to
Indochina, she enlisted in the PFAT to be near him and was assigned to Hanoi as director of the maternity hospital for army
girls who'd gotten "into trouble." There weren't too many of
them, but in any case, the French Army had taken the realistic
attitude that a girl, pregnant or not, still made a good radio
operator or secretary-typist. Thus, in case of pregnancy, the girls
were not discharged but merely sent on sick leave within the
theater itself, to return to active duty after confinement.

Petite and dignified in the immaculate white uniform of the
PFAT, Mme. S. would be seen zooming through the streets of
Hanoi on her white motor scooter, going briskly about her busi-

ness while awaiting the next leave period of her son. Her son, while no doubt touched by this extreme demonstration of maternal solicitude, felt that his mother was definitely cramping the style of his leave periods, and, in turn, sought any sort of assignment that would get him as far as possible from Hanoi, but to little avail. When last seen, Lieutenant S. was in Haiphong, hiding behind dark glasses and asking all his friends please not to tell *maman* that he was taking his vacation elsewhere.

Then there were women who were strictly one-of-a-kind, such as Brigitte Friang, one of the civilian reporters of the French Information Service. Brigitte, in her early thirties, had been through a lot. Having served in the French underground against the Nazis, a tattooed serial number on her forearm testified to her acquaintance with a concentration camp. In Indochina, her reporting of military operations equaled that of the best male reporters in matter-of-fact description of military situations without the gushiness and cuteness of her Anglo-Saxon sisters.

She never made the headlines of the world press with photographs of her face covered with road dust, but Brigitte had earned her paratroop wings in Indochina and had made several combat jumps with French paratroops, including the desperate jump of the 6th Colonial Paratroop Battalion at Tu-Lê. And she followed the 6th in its harrowing retreat on foot across the hills of the T'ai country, back to the French lines, carrying her own pack and steel helmet, back from a mission which, in the United States (or in Korea) would have earned her a Pulitzer Prize for sheer physical stamina alone. But in Indochina, this was taken as a matter of course, coming from little Brigitte.

Impeccably attired in black tulle evening gown, Brigitte Friang looked like any girl should look, except for her gray-blue eyes. No matter how gay the conversation, how relaxed the evening, Brigitte's eyes never seemed quite reconciled to smiling. Perhaps they were still seeing the gas chambers of Zwodau or the paratroopers impaled on the barbed wire of Tu-Lê.

No one who was in northern Indochina will ever forget Dung (pronounced "Zung"). She was a Vietnamese girl from Thanh-

Hoa, who had, contrary to the majority of her compatriots, an extremely shapely figure. Her career in North Viet-Nam closely paralleled that of a true courtesan of the Renaissance or of the old Chinese court.

After several affairs with increasingly senior officers, she had finally become the *maîtresse-en-titre* of one of the regional commanders, and soon her rising affluence began to show the extent of her equally rising influence. It was soon said that no one could be promoted without her say-so, or at least, that she could effectively block or delay the promotion of someone she disliked. Driving around in a Peugeot convertible, owning her own modern villa, Dung also had a "courtesy pass" at the customs station of the airport, which allowed her to participate in a brisk currency and gold trade with Hong Kong.

Every afternoon, she held court at the swimming pool in her emerald green one-piece bathing suit, showering her favors upon an athletically built paratroop noncom who acted as pool guard. When the general's tour of duty had come to an end, he begged her to return to France with him (the more so as she had borne him a small daughter) but Dung refused. In Indochina, she *was* somebody, in France she would merely be the mistress of a general without a command.

Dung stayed on in Indochina, carefully transferring to South Viet-Nam all her belongings as the situation worsened, and selecting her new protectors with equal care. Soon after the cease-fire she was seen with an American colonel from the United States Military Assistance Advisory Group (MAAG). Her villa in Saigon was even more lavish than the villa she had owned in Hanoi; and the French general died in Paris without having seen her again.

It was in 1957 in Saigon, in the famous "Arc-en-Ciel" (Rainbow) Chinese restaurant, that I met Dung once more. She was sitting in a stall in an iridescent green Vietnamese dress with a very high collar accentuating the graceful line of her neck. She was still beautiful, though perhaps not quite as fresh-looking as in the Hanoi days, and she smiled at her interlocutor, a swarthy looking heavy-set man.

"Well, she's changed protectors again," remarked my Vietnamese friend. "That fellow is a big cheese in one of the American engineering firms executing a multi-million dollar contract here. I wonder what she's getting for free now? That colonel she went with nearly went broke over her."

Her eyes crossed mine for a fleeting moment as I passed by. Obviously, she was trying hard to remember where she had seen me before. But Hanoi had been a long time and many men ago.

There were also those women whom Fate seemed to have singled out for tragedy. One of them was Marie-Rose M. She was a quiet, blonde woman in her early thirties and worked on the staff of the French Air Force Command, North Viet-Nam. Marie-Rose's first husband had been killed in May 1940, during the 90-day *Blitzkrieg* when Hitler's panzer divisions overran France. She remarried and her second husband was posted to Indochina. He was killed by the Japanese on March 9, 1945. Her third husband, Army doctor Didier Michel, died in an airplane crash near Gao, in French West Africa in 1948. Marie-Rose requested to be reassigned to Indochina again, and somewhat of a romance had blossomed out between her and Brig. Gen. Hartemann, the northern Air Force commander. But Marie-Rose was afraid, lest bad luck would again rob her of someone she loved. Hartemann, however, was hardly the type to be intimidated by fate.

On April 27, 1951, after lunch, when Marie-Rose was particularly despondent, Hartemann said: "Come on, Marie-Rose, there is no such thing as Fate! It's just bad luck, and your *série noire* has run its course." And, to change her mood, Hartemann took Marie-Rose for a brief ride in his American B-26 bomber converted into a command aircraft.

They were shot down by Viet-Minh antiaircraft artillery over Cao-Bang fifty minutes later and died on impact. I found the photograph of their destroyed plane eleven years later while going through the photographic files of the North Vietnamese Government, and told my escort officer the story of Marie-Rose.

"You know," said the Communist officer, "until now we had always wondered *why* General Hartemann had a female observer aboard on that mission."

Other problems which plagued the French Army in Indochina were the native common-law wives of the soldiers, and the wives of the local soldiers serving in French units. In the latter case, the state of generalized guerrilla warfare reigning throughout the country often exposed them to Communist reprisals, with the men's combat morale lowered because of fear that their families might be harmed in their absence. This problem was partly solved through the creation of the *camps des mariés,* settlements for local dependents either within or near a French Army base, where the families would live under the protection of nearby army units.

In other cases, the wives and children of the Frenchmen, North Africans or Senegalese would just travel with the unit, in the old tradition of the camp followers and share the fate of the unit, for better or for worse. Here again, this arrangement could work out well or prove disastrous. Some officers felt that a man who had his family near him in a fort could not afford to run away; hence, he would stand and fight, for the family's survival depended on him.

On the other hand, there were numerous cases on record where the *congaï*—the concubine, the common-law wife—had been "planted" in her rôle by the Viet-Minh to spy on French operations. In some cases, such women even committed sabotage or succeeded in opening a fort's gates. No less than one-third of all the posts which were successfully destroyed by the Viet-Minh, first fell victim to a successful act of treason or sabotage.

But against such isolated cases, there were the thousands of Vietnamese girls, or women from the mountain tribes, who remained faithful to their French husbands regardless of the consequences, which meant death in some cases and social ostracism by their countrymen in others. There was the story of Crey, the Bahnar wife of René Riessen, a commando leader on the southern mountain plateau, who threw herself in front of him to save him from a tommy gun burst; and there was the T'ai princess, the first wife of my friend L——, a French anthropologist, whom the Viet-Minh blew up with hand grenades because she refused to give away her husband's hideout after the Communists had invaded the tribe's territory.

I also remember a trip in a comfortable station wagon to Cape

Saint-Jacques, in South Vietnam, with Major T——, a comfortable looking, jovial southern Frenchman. It was a routine inspection trip along the newly rebuilt Saigon-Cape Saint-Jacques highway, now as peaceful as if war had never happened. As we passed through the village of Ben-Dinh, T—— slowed down at the tiny cemetery, where a few Christian crosses stood discreetly apart from the other grave mounds. He got out, and I could see him trying to find his way among the matted weeds of this cemetery which obviously had been left unattended for many years. Finally, T—— found what he was looking for; he bent down and, with careful gestures began to clear the weeds away from the cross, a simple wooden cross whose whitewash seemed to have suffered from the weather. It looked like the regular French G.I. issue to me, so that I thought that it might have been one of his men who had died here and whose tomb he had suddenly remembered.

But as I walked closer, I could read the inscription on the cross: "Christiane T——, *Morte pour la France*, February 13, 1948," and I could see the tears now streaming freely over the cheeks of Major T—— as I walked away.

T—— had been the commander of a convoy making its way from Saigon to Cape Saint-Jacques, and his wife, like many others who had been cooped up in Saigon for years and yearned again for the beaches and the sea breeze of the Cape, had begged him to take her along.

"After all, it was only a short trip," said T—— to me, "and nothing at all had happened on the previous trips, and I couldn't see why I shouldn't let her come along."

Indeed, the trip had remained uneventful until they were almost in sight of the Cape, near the fishing village of Ben-Dinh. It was there that the convoy was caught in a well-laid ambush. Christiane T—— was hit by the first machine gun burst and was dying by the time her husband got her out of the jeep and into the nearest ditch.

"And you know what she said? 'Don't worry about me, darling. I wasn't supposed to be with you anyway. Just do your job as if I weren't here.' Just like a woman who unexpectedly drops in on her husband in his office."

"And, of course, my men needed me. Well, we got out of the ambush thanks to an armored car platoon from Cape Saint-Jacques which had heard the ruckus and came to our rescue. But it was too late for Christiane; by the time I got back to her, she was dead. We decided to bury her here at Ben-Dinh, near the Cape Saint-Jacques which she wanted so much to see. She never really liked the atmosphere of Saigon."

We had started to roll again in our shiny station wagon. Ben-Dinh lay absolutely peaceful under the hot midday sun, looking as improbable a place to get ambushed in as a Long Island suburb.

"This is probably the last time I'm going to see Christiane," said the major. "After twenty years in Indochina, I'm shipping out next Monday, for good."

He lit a *Gauloise Bleue* cigarette, sucked in the acrid smoke and never once looked back.

7

"Street Without Joy"

FOR years, communications along the central Annam coast
had been plagued by Communist attacks against Road 1,
the main north-south artery along the coast. The principal
source of trouble was a string of heavily-fortified villages along
a line of sand dunes and salt marshes stretching from Hué to
Quang-Tri. By 1953, the French High Command had assembled
sufficient reserves in the area to attempt to clear up the threat
once and for all. In the meantime, losses had been heavy; one
French convoy after another passing on the road had been either
shelled or ambushed by the black-clad infantry of Viet-Minh
Regiment 95, a battle-hardened regular Communist unit infiltrated behind French lines. This inspired the French soldiers with
that kind of black humor proper to all soldiers, to christen that
stretch of Road 1 *"la rue sans joie"* or in English, "Street Without
Joy."

In July 1953 the French High Command decided to clean up
the "Street Without Joy." Called "Operation Camargue,"* the
action involved a simultaneous landing of troops along the sandy
coast of central Annam, coupled with two coordinated thrusts by
armored units, with airborne forces remaining in reserve to seal
off attempts at escape by the Communist forces in the trap. With
the elements of ten infantry regiments, two airborne battalions,
the bulk of three armored regiments, one squadron of armored
launches and one armored train, four artillery battalions, thirty-
four transport aircraft, six reconnaissance aircraft and twenty-
two fighter-bombers, and about twelve Navy ships, including
three LST's—this force was not very inferior in size to some of

*The Camargue is the name of the swampy coastal plain west of Marseilles.

those used in landing operations in World War II in the Pacific. Communist Regiment 95 and the few guerrilla forces around it, obviously, had very little chance of escaping the encirclement.

The attack was to be carried out by two amphibious forces, three land-borne groupments and one airborne force, under the overall command of General Leblanc, with each of the task forces under the command of a colonel.

Groupment "A" was to land on the coast on July 28 at dawn. Groupment "B" was to advance overland in the north about two hours later and veer south behind the line of advance of Groupment "A." Groupment "C" was to participate in the attack at about the same time as Groupment "B" at 0715, advance directly on the Van Trinh Canal and push all enemy elements west of the canal against the canal or across it. Groupment "C" was to pay particular attention to the coordination of its movements with Groupment "D" which was to land south of Groupment "A" on the northern peninsula of the lagoon.

Groupment "D" in turn was to land as early as possible, at 0300 for its amphibious elements and at 0500 for its infantry; and push northward across the peninsula in order to form a common front with Groupment "C" as soon as possible. The two airborne battalions were held in reserve at the disposal of the High Command and were to be committed only upon express permission of the latter. This was to have serious consequences when they were finally thrown into the battle.

At first view the forces assigned to this operation appeared impressive. Using a total of more than thirty battalions, including the equivalent of two armored regiments and two artillery regiments, the operation against the "Street Without Joy" was certainly one of the most formidable ever carried out in the Indochinese theater of operations. Yet the enemy, on the other side, amounted to a maximum of one weak infantry regiment. What made the operation so difficult for the French was, as usual in Indochina, the terrain.

From the coast, looking inland, the zone of operations divided itself into seven distinct natural strips of land. The first was the coastline itself, fairly straight, covered with hard sand and offering no particular difficulties. However, a bare 100 meters beyond began the dunes, varying in height from 15 to 60 feet, very hard to climb and ending on the land side in veritable ditches or precipices. A few fishing villages are precariously perched in the dune zone, which in certain places has a depth of more than two kilometers. Then comes a zone about 800 meters deep entirely covered with small pagodas or tombs and temples, which offer excellent protection to any defenders. This zone is followed by

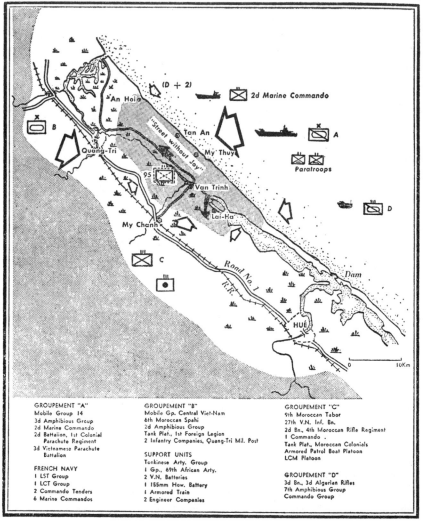

GROUPEMENT "A"
Mobile Group 14
3d Amphibious Group
2d Marine Commando
2d Battalion, 1st Colonial
   Parachute Regiment
3d Vietnamese Parachute
   Battalion

FRENCH NAVY
1 LST Group
1 LCT Group
2 Commando Tenders
6 Marine Commandos

GROUPEMENT "B"
Mobile Gp. Central Viet-Nam
6th Moroccan Spahi
2d Amphibious Group
Tank Plat., 1st Foreign Legion
2 Infantry Companies, Quang-Tri Mil. Post

SUPPORT UNITS
Tonkinese Arty. Group
1 Gp., 69th African Arty.
2 V.N. Batteries
1 155mm How. Battery
1 Armored Train
2 Engineer Companies

GROUPEMENT "C"
9th Moroccan Tabor
27th V.N. Inf. Bn.
2d Bn., 4th Moroccan Rifle Regiment
1 Commando .
Tank Plat., Moroccan Colonials
Armored Patrol Boat Platoon
LCM Platoon

GROUPEMENT "D"
3d Bn., 3d Algerian Rifles
7th Amphibious Group
Commando Group

"Street Without Joy."

the "Street Without Joy" itself, fringed by a rather curious system of interlocking small villages separated one from the other by often less than 200 to 300 yards. Each village forms a veritable little labyrinth that measures barely more than 200 feet by 300 feet and is surrounded by bushes, hedges, or bamboo trees, and small fences which made ground as well as aerial surveillance almost impossible. Regiment 95 had spent more than two years fortifying the villages with an interlocking system of trenches and tunnels, underground arms depots, and first-aid stations which no single brutal thrust by large mobile forces could uncover or destroy. Close to 20 miles long and more than 300 yards wide, this zone of villages constituted the heart of the Communist resistance zone along the central Annam coast.

On the land side, the "Street Without Joy" was preceded by another, less well-defined line of villages, the center of which was Van Trinh. This was protected in turn by a vast zone of swamps, sand holes, and quicksand bogs, extending all the way to Road 1. With an average width of about eight kilometers, it constituted an almost impassable barrier to tanks and other motorized vehicles of the French Army, except on the few roads crossing it, which were, of course, heavily mined and sabotaged. This, in short, was the fortress known as "Street Without Joy" which the French were now determined to crack in a combined air, sea, and land assault.

What further complicated the situation for the French was that the villages had retained their civilian population of small farmers and fishermen. Since this population was, theoretically at least, to be considered "friendly," the French High Command distributed directives to all its units on the day before the operation began that they had to show a "humane attitude" and treat civilians respectfully. Above all, they were not to bombard villages or set fire to them. It is certain that the limitations placed upon the employment of their weapons reduced the effectiveness of the French assault, particularly when it came into direct contact with major Viet-Minh resistance centers.

H-Hour was at dawn on July 28, 1953. The lumbering LST's had left their assembly areas the evening before and had steamed throughout the night toward their landing zone in the center of the coast facing the "Street Without Joy." Disembarkment of the amphibious landing craft began at 0400 in a clanking of metal and a howling of engines, as the Crabs and Alligators of the 3d Amphibious Group took to the water.

The Crabs and Alligators were French nicknames for two American-built amphibious vehicles. The Crab was an amphibious cargo carrier 29-C and the Alligator a LVT (landing vehicle, tracked) 4 or 4A. As their names indicated, the Crabs were never destined to become a combat vehicle, but the French in Indochina soon found that whole squadrons of Crabs could render immense service as carriers of amphibious task forces operating in the roadless swamps and rice paddies of Vietnamese lowlands and coastal areas.

At first these unarmored vehicles, lightly armed with a few machine guns and mortars, became the victims of enemy bazookas. This led to a change in tactics and by 1953, the Amphibious Group and Amphibious Subgroup had become regular units of the French Armored Forces in Indochina. It was regularly composed of two squadrons of 33 Crabs each, which were used as reconnaissance and pursuit elements; three squadrons of Alligators (LVT's) which formed the breakthrough force, since they were both armed and armored; and, finally, one platoon of six LVT's armed with howitzers providing the group with its own mobile artillery.

On the negative side, both types of vehicle were considered fragile and required a great deal of maintenance, which was often hard to come by in the swamps of Indochina. The Crab—initially built for carrying cargo in Alaska!—lacked floatability in water and towered too high on land, thus offering an easy target to enemy gunners who soon found out that it was not armored. On the other hand, it was small enough to be transported on an Army truck when not in use, or could be embarked in light landing craft or barges. The Alligator, much heavier and armored, took well to the water but was too heavy on land for its fragile tracks and its relatively weak engine. Also, it could not travel great distances on land but had to be transported on special tank carriers, since it was too big and too heavy to be transported on trucks.

Yet, it was an impressive sight as the 160 vehicles of the 3d Amphibious approached the central Annam coast, each leaving a wide wake in the leaden-colored water, with the bright recognition streamers of the various squadrons flapping in the morning breeze on the tips of the radio aerials. At 0600, the first landing wave of the Amphibious Group hit the beaches, immediately fanning out through the coastal villages and occupying the first hill crest line overlooking the coastal dunes. The French assault against the "Street Without Joy" had begun.

The regular infantry elements of the Tonkinese Mobile Group had a tougher time of it. Of the three battalions, only one—the 3d Battalion of the 13th Foreign Legion Half-Brigade—had had any experience in sea-borne operations; the two other battalions, the 1st Muong Mountaineer and the 26th Senegalese Rifle Battalion, had had no such experience. Unfamiliar with the landing ship's cargo nets, the rocking landing craft, and plagued with seasickness; it took them close to four hours to get ashore instead of the two hours assigned to that part of the operation. In the meantime, the men of the 3d Amphibious Group were struggling with their vehicles atop the dune line. Many of the heavily-loaded Alligators had bogged down in the sand as soon as they had left the coastal strip and had to be unloaded on the spot. In many other cases the lighter Crabs had pushed on atop the dunes only to find themselves face-to-face with a deep precipice. However, they finally found a break between the fishing villages of Tan An and My Thuy, and soon began pushing inland on their own. Communist resistance was almost non-existent. A few men were seen fleeing the first line of fishing villages near My Thuy and farther to the north two enemy platoons were seen pulling out.

In the meantime, Groupment "B" under the command of Colonel du Corail had not remained inactive. By 0630, two battalions of the Central Vietnamese Mobile Group reached and crossed the Van Trinh Canal and by 0745, the lead elements of Groupment "B" saw the squattish shapes of the 3d Amphibious Group's Crabs crawling over the hill line; the "Street Without Joy" was sealed off to the north.

To the right of the Central Vietnamese Mobile Group, the

6th Moroccan Spahis was not as lucky. It ran head-on into the bottomless swamps and sand holes east of Road No. 1 where most of its vehicles, with the exception of the M-24 light tanks, soon bogged down. It succeeded in reaching the canal—which was to be the line of departure for the mopping-up operation on the land side—at about 0830. In its sector also, there was no evidence of enemy opposition. In fact, the whole countryside seemed absolutely dead. No farmers were to be seen on the roads, and in the small villages the population stayed in their houses. Throughout the whole desolate landscape, the only moving objects were the French armored columns and truck-borne infantry, as they struggled through sand dunes and morasses to the Van Trinh Canal.

Only at the extreme right flank of Groupment "B" was there any shooting. There, an Algerian rifle company ran into unexpected fire from what appeared to be no more than 20 or 30 Viet-Minh. Private Mohammed Abd-el-Kader of 2d Company, fell forward as a BAR burst of fire caught him directly in the chest. Warily, his comrades fanned out in skirmish formation and shot back at the invisible enemy hidden behind clumps of bushes and in sand holes. Abd-el-Kader was the first French casualty in the assault.

To the right of Groupment "B," Groupment "C" under Lieutenant Colonel Gauthier had to execute the most complicated maneuver of the operation. The bulk of its troops crossed Road No. 1 in the direction of the canal to the north of My Chanh. A second column started along a path running parallel to Road No. 1, then veered sharply to the right to reach the canal between the village of Van Trinh and the lagoon. Lastly, the 9th Moroccan *Tabor* (Battalion), embarked on landing craft, went ashore at Lai-Ha at 0630, secured a beachhead, and then swung southeast along the inland coast of the lagoon in order to complete the sealing-off of the "Street Without Joy" on the land side. By 0830, it had reached Tay-Hoang and completed its part of the operation's first phase.

Groupment "D," under Lieutenant Colonel Le Hagre, was to seal off the long peninsula reaching down along the lagoon almost to the city of Hué. Composed of experienced troops, it encountered little of the difficulties which had faced Groupment "A." The landing began at 0430, with the 7th Amphibious Group in the lead, followed in rapid succession by Marine commandos and the 3d Battalion of the 3d Algerian Rifle Regiment. The commandos and the Amphibious Group hit the beach almost without stopping; the Amphibious Group immediately headed north in the direction of the head of the lagoon, while the commandos secured the little city of Thé Chi Dong and, cutting straight across the peninsula, reached the north side of the lagoon at 0530. For all practical purposes, Viet-Minh Regiment No. 95 was trapped.

Now began the hardest phase of the whole operation—the mopping-up. General Leblanc ordered the Navy ships standing off-shore to move four miles to the north to the villages of Ba-Lang and An-Hoi in order to seal off any attempt of the rebels to flee by sea. On the northern end of the "Street Without Joy," Groupment "B" began a methodical sweep of every village, a painstaking operation which had to be carried out with the greatest of care, regardless of results. Each village was first surrounded and sealed off by troops. Then heavily armed infantry moved in and searched the houses while mine detector and bloodhound teams probed* in bamboo bushes and palm-tree stands for hidden entrances to underground caches in the midst of the sullen and silent population. As a matter of routine most of the young men from the villages were arrested and detained pending a screening by intelligence officers, but even this had become a sort of rite in which everyone concerned participated without any great conviction.

By 1100 in the morning Groupment "B" had worked its way about 7 kilometers south through the labyrinth of tiny villages, without having encountered any resistance, when it reached the village of Dong-Qué, located almost in the center of the "Street Without Joy" at the intersection of several paths leading across the dunes toward the Van Trinh Canal. In the old days it had contained a customs post whose brick structure was still standing and this also gave it a certain importance.

---

*The French Army had "K-9" teams in every major unit. Their successes were extremely variable, considering the effectiveness of Viet-Minh concealment.

Dong-Qué lay in the hot midday sun, snugly nestled in its swaying bamboo hedge, the very image of rural peacefulness in the monsoon season, when there is little else left for the farmer to do but to pray for rain and watch the rice grow from a tender green to a rich brownish yellow. But now, Dong-Qué was the target of the M-24 light tanks of the 6th Moroccan Spahis. In fact, the whole northern thrust seemed to be a Moroccan show, what with the Spahis being screened by the 1st Battalion, Moroccan Rifles, and the whole force being covered by the howitzers of Colonel Piroth's 69th African Artillery Regiment which, in normal times, hailed from Fez, in northern Morocco. These were battle-hardened troops; they had fought Rommel in Tunisia, waded through the Rapido and clambered up the Petrella in Italy; knocked out the German 19th Army in the Black Forest and raced the Americans to Berchtesgaden. They were the elite of France's North African troops and more Moroccans had risen to senior ranks—even to general—in the French Army than any other nationality. Here again, they were doing a workmanlike job clearing their sector.

Keeping their intervals carefully, the M-24 tanks had worked their way towards Dong-Qué at a pace which permitted the infantry to keep up with them. With the innate sixth sense which the Moroccans seem to have for detecting mines and booby traps, they had come to within 1,500 yards of the village without losing a man or a tank, but that same sixth sense told them that something was wrong with Dong-Qué. In silence, the infantrymen began to peel off the dike on either side of the tanks.

Atop the vehicles, the tank commanders had so far remained sitting on their open hatches, as much to see more of the countryside around them as to catch a breath of the breeze. (At the 1st Foreign Legion Cavalry, one crew which must have contained an ex-Nazi electronics engineer, actually succeeded in mounting a regular air-conditioner into an armored car. The story came to light when the vehicle got caught in an ambush and its crew went to unusual lengths to defend it, and, when it was disabled, to retrieve it. The men were duly decorated for their bravery and then, in true Foreign Legion tradition, were sent to the stockade for "taking liberties with Government property.")

The French planners: Generals Cogny, de Castries, and Navarre.

" . . . All this was pure, orthodox, 18th-century siege technique . . . " (p. 324)
Communist commander-in-chief Vo Nguyên Giap at
a staff conference in his command post near Dien Bien Phu.

" . . . Within a few minutes the
          whole column had disappeared
in the elephant grass, swallowed up
          as in a green sea . . . " (p. 211)

" . . . the war of the vast empty spaces . . . " (p. 195)

" . . . he would be sent out
    again and again until his luck
ran out, his health broke or
    his mind cracked up. There
were no magical 'fifty missions'
    to look forward to, no end
to the ordeal . . . " (p. 271)

" . . . It is difficult to imagine
    life in such a commando
group . . . " (p. 272)

" . . . men who after 57 days of combat, had simply been marched to death . . . " (p. 300)

" . . . both garrisons were practically smothered by the sheer fury of the artillery fire and the masses of enemy infantry . . . " (p. 320)

Surviving PW's being loaded aboard French landing craft (p. 295)

" . . . After winding itself for weeks on end through empty villages, the under-strength "Condor" force had reached a point 40 miles from Dien Bien Phu when the fortress fell . . . " (p 325)

. . . The Viet-Minh artillery chose that moment to hack the ambulance plane to pieces . . . " (p. 323)

" . . . The T'ai women wear tightly draped skirts reaching down to the ankles, and blouses with silver clasps . . . " (p. 268)

Far right: Little girl from the Meo tribes.

The end at Dien Bien Phu: a Communist assault team hoists
the red flag above General de Castries' bunker.

The end of the road: French liaison officers escort the
first Communist troops entering the French lines in August 1954.

Major Derrieu, commander of the leading squadron, looked straight ahead into the small town; the road appeared clear of any obstacles or the suspicious mounds of hastily-dug mine emplacements. Nevertheless, the tank churned to a halt to let the mine-detector detail make one last sweep before rolling forward. Methodically, the tanned men with the long-handled frying pans and the earphones worked their way towards Dong-Qué, still quiescent under the tropical sun. Later, it was impossible to decide who had fired first—the Moroccan sergeant at the head of the demining detail who saw a rifle barrel flash in the sun, or a nervous Viet-Minh who felt that the Moroccans were getting too close for comfort. In any case, the fire fight developed with incredible violence at very short range. It was only due to the hair-trigger reactions of the Moroccans atop the road, who simply dropped to the ground and rolled off into the saving mud of the adjoining rice paddies, that none of them was seriously wounded.

The tanks were equally lucky that the Viets had probably tipped their hand ahead of time, for the two bazookas of the defenders opened fire only as the lead tanks already had left the dikes in a clatter of tracks and a howl of engines for the comparative safety of the deeper lying fields. Now "buttoned up" (i.e. with their hatches shut), the turrets swung out in direction of the suspected targets but still holding their fire. No point in wasting high-penetration shells against thatch huts when the machine guns could do a much more effective job. The infantrymen, in turn, had spread in an arc around Dong-Qué, but without moving closer. Behind one of the many grave mounds which always dot the Far Eastern countryside, the battalion commander had squatted down on his haunches in the mud, a map case on his knees and the combination earphone-microphone of his radio set in his hand. The set itself was affixed to the back of a Vietnamese "PIM"* who had also squatted down and who looked stolidly ahead under his battered hand-me-down campaign hat at the heat haze shimmering over the rice fields.

---

*PIM stood for *"Prisonnier-Interné-Militaire"* or "Prisoner or civilian internee arrested by the French Army," in contrast to detainees of the French or Vietnamese civilian police authorities. The PIM's often served as non-combatants in French units and became very devoted to their leaders. Others, of course, redeserted to the Viet-Minh.

The howitzers of the 69th got the range of their target within a few rounds, and minutes after the first radio call for support, Dong-Qué began literally to disintegrate under the impact of their high-angle fire. One by one the rice thatch of the roofs began to catch fire with a deep crackling sound that could occasionally be heard even above the din of the shells. Still, nobody ran; save for the agitation in the bamboo bushes around the village and the occasional flashes (hardly visible at high noon) of gunfire, the village might as well have been deserted. Then, all of a sudden, a tremendous explosion shook the village and a pillar of dense, black smoke rose in its center.

"The shells must've hit an underground depot," said Derrieu to his crew as he watched the shelling over the tank's scope. "Let's saddle up." With a howl, the idling tank engine shifted into high gear, and the lumbering vehicle, followed by the other tanks of the squadron, began to roll forward in direction of the inferno that had been Dong-Qué. "Follow in line," said Derrieu over the intercom, and, no doubt as an afterthought due to his farmer ancestry, "and watch where you're going. No sense in ruining their whole rice crop."

Now, small black figures began to appear seemingly out of nowhere; from the windows of the houses, the roof frames, and from dugouts on the side of the road, a veritable flood of human beings, completely blocking the advance of the tanks as they rolled into the village. This was phase 2 of the usual Viet-Minh defense pattern: once the position had become untenable or breached, use the civilians as a shield for the withdrawal of the combatants. But this time, the ruse failed. The tanks were not alone and the black-clad figures which now began to leave the village ran straight into the machine gun fire of the Moroccans. By 1300, it was all over for the 3d Company, Battalion 310 of the 95th Independent Regiment, "Viet-Nam People's Army," but its sacrifice had bought exactly what the commander of the regiment had needed—two hours of time to have the bulk of the unit withdraw towards the southern end of the pocket, where the Van Trinh Canal ended in a sort of marshy plant-covered delta which no one could effectively hope to seal off.

On the French side, General Leblanc also realized that the

enemy, far from fighting to the death, was trying desperately to buy time to last until the evening in order to withdraw into the nearby hills west of Road 1, and he ordered the dropping-in of the first of the two paratroop battalions still held in reserve. At 1045, the 2d Battalion, 1st Colonial Parachute Regiment, having flown in all the way from Hanoi, dropped into its assigned assembly area near the village of Dai-Loc, at the border of the dune zone close to Groupment "D" and immediately began its drive towards the mouth of the Van Trinh Canal. The race for the closing of the net around Regiment 95 had begun in earnest.

By mid-morning of D-Day, there were still wide gaps to the south of Van Trinh Canal near Phu-An and Lai-Ha as the 9th *Tabor* struggled through the sand pits and marshes to reach its line of departure. Apparently the Communists had correctly surmised that this was indeed the weakest point in the French perimeter and had reacted accordingly. At 0845, just as the Moroccans were about to enter Phu-An, heavy machine gun and small-arms fire began to smash into their ranks from the surrounding dikes. Silhouetted against the blue sky as they advanced over the dikes, and against the watery surface of the rice paddies as they plodded through them towards Phu-An, they offered perfect targets and immediately suffered heavy losses. Pinned down in the open, the 9th now began to call for help. It is here that its subordination to the faraway Groupment "C" rather than to the nearby amphibious Groupment "D" began to backfire; radio liaison to the Group's field CP at My-Chanh failed to function properly, and it was not until 0910 that Colonel Gauthier found out that things had gone sour on his extreme right wing.

But the Viet-Minh was not placing all its tactical eggs in a single basket. At 1100, smaller units of the Communist 227th Battalion also attacked the assault guns of the 1st Foreign Legion Cavalry with heavy mortar fire and followed up this attack with an equally heavy mortar shelling of the 2d Battalion, 4th Moroccan Infantry. By 0940, Gauthier decided to commit his last reserves, two companies formed from trainees of a nearby Vietnamese NCO school and three Vietnamese infantry companies hastily brought up from Hué. Finally two additional infantry companies were ordered into the Lai-Ha beachhead via LCM but landed only at 1500. They then floundered in the marshes for almost three hours until they finally reached the Moroccans. When they got their wind back, and had been beefed up by the reinforcements, the Moroccans counterattacked vigorously and finally occupied Phu-An at 1730.

In view of the difficulties encountered by Groupment "C," General Leblanc requested the dropping of the 3d Vietnamese Paratroop Battalion still held in reserve at Tourane. The order to use this second paratroop battalion was given at 1145, to be carried out at 1400. What then happened has remained somewhat unclear but according to the officers who participated in the operation, two separate errors had been made: one was in transmission of the order itself which delayed take-off time until about 1500; the second was in the weather forecast for the drop area. During the monsoon period, the winds which prevail on the Annam coast usually reach gale force late in the afternoon. This is a fact which is generally known along the coastal area, but which may, from time to time, escape the weather observers placed several hundred miles away from Annam in Saigon or Hanoi. The result was that when the C-47's of Air Transport Group "Franche-Comté" appeared over the drop zone at Lang-Bao, the wind was blowing gusts up to thirty miles an hour—twice the maximum usually permissible in the case of airborne drops. The French jump masters were looking down at the drop zone, with the trails of its smoke pots lying almost flat on the ground and shook their heads.

"Hell, you can't have these guys jump into this mess!" said one of them incredulously as he looked down. "They're going to be blown all over the place, light as they are."

In fact, their lightness had always been one of the problems and jokes among the Vietnamese paratroops. Jumping with American parachutes calculated to carry a 200-pound man with close to 85 to 100 pounds of equipment, the chute had proved much too vast for the small Vietnamese 100-pounders, who, even when loaded down with all their paraphernalia, still weighed only one-half of their American or European counterparts. Thus, a Vietnamese airborne unit generally floated longer in the air (offering a better target to ground fire) and also spread over a far wider area when landing. To load the Vietnamese down with more equipment was no solution either, because once on the ground they could not possibly carry it around. This lightness, coupled with the high wind speed, was to have disastrous consequences.

By now, the insertion of an additional battalion had become absolutely necessary on the peninsula in order to insure sealing off the Viet-Minh forces from the lagoon and the seashore. Thus, an additional battalion had to be dropped regardless of the consequences to the men themselves. At 1650, the first "stick" of Vietnamese paratroopers left the lead aircraft, followed within a few seconds by those of the other planes, and the hundreds of parachutes began to float down in the deep blue sky like a vast school of Portuguese men-of-war. Everything seemed to have gone all right. Only one parachute failed to open and the men of the ground party saw its human burden come down, feet first, held vertically by the drag of his unopened parachute, stirring up a small cloud of sand like an artillery shell as he smashed into the dune.

The strong wind caught the other paratroopers about 150 feet above ground. It was as if an invisible fist had been driven through them; some of them left the vertical position and began to fly off almost horizontally. Others, closer to the ground were slammed into it, dragged over the bushes, marshes and dikes at a speed of a racing horse. Two paratroopers were strangled to death by the shroud lines of their own parachutes as they desperately tried to liberate themselves before being dragged away. The equipment parachuted with the battalion suffered an even worse fate. Since most of the packages were somewhat lighter than the paratroopers, they floated even farther away, some of them falling into the sea and many of them drifting into Communist-held territory. When the battalion finally was assembled at about 1730 (some of the men had been dragged as far as two kilometers before they had been able to liberate themselves from their run-away parachutes) it was at best a weak rifle force. Close to ten percent of the men had suffered jump accidents, and most of the heavy equipment; mortars, machine guns, recoil-

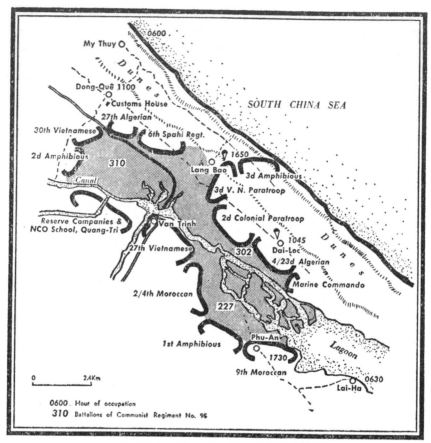

The Net Closes (D Day, Nightfall).

less rifles, and ammunition had been lost in the drop. But it was
in time to take up its position in the southern tip of the pincer
around Regiment 95, between the 3d Amphibian Group and the
2d Paratroop Battalion which had landed in the morning. By
nightfall, with Phu-An and Van Trinh occupied, the enemy had
now been constricted into a pocket about 14 kilometers long
and 4 kilometers wide. To all appearances, Operation "Camargue"
was a success.

However, this success was more one of appearance than of
reality. To be sure, one-half of the "Street Without Joy" already
had fallen into French hands—but without the expected booty of
enemy prisoners and equipment. This meant that the enemy forces

and equipment were still in the pocket. The latter, in order to be successful, had to become an airtight trap.

The trap, however, had *not* become airtight. Along the southern sector of Groupment "C," the last-ditch defense of Phu-An and the counterattacks of Battalion 227 had kept the French from reaching the natural boundary of the Van Trinh Canal. The result was that four French battalions had to guard a front close to 12 kilometers long in order to prevent the escape of about 2600 men. It was obvious that this pocket had several important gaps, particularly the whole network of tiny rivulets and canals cutting across the Van Trinh Canal towards Road 1.

To be sure, the amphibious Crabs and Alligators were stationed near, or even in, many of the canals; and hundreds of infantrymen spent an uncomfortable night standing in the knee-deep mud of the rice paddies watching the black expanse ahead of them, where the slightest noise could be that of a frog jumping, or of a Communist infiltrator stumbling over a branch. There is nothing that sounds more like a patrol seeking its way forward in the mud than a stray buffalo plodding to its stable.

The night of D-Day plus-one passed without major incident. Whatever shooting occurred was at fleeting shadows. Here and there, a French parachute flare lit up the pocket area in its ghostly greenish light before it fizzled into the wet underbrush, or the headlights of a French tank or amphibious vehicle probed the night to search out the sources of suspect noises. But nothing noteworthy was detected.

When dawn broke, the men resumed their march forward, this time on all fronts at once. The countryside appeared completely empty in the morning sun. The farmers again did not come out of the villages to till their fields, the little Vietnamese boys who are always riding the lumbering buffaloes out to pasture were nowhere to be seen with their charges. Again, the only things that seemed to be moving in the countryside were the French tanks, the amphibious vehicles with their long aerials dipping in the breeze, and long lines of grimy, weary, mud-caked infantrymen now plodding through the fields in an almost unbroken line from horizon to horizon.

By 1300, with the sun beating unmercifully on steel helmets

and berets or campaign hats, Groupments "A" and "D," along
with parts of Groupment "B," reached Van Trinh Canal throughout its whole length on the side opposite to Colonel Gauthier's
Groupment "C." The trap had been sprung on the "Street Without Joy." The steel jaws of a modern armed force, supported by
naval ships, amphibious tanks, and aircraft, had slammed shut
on a force of hurriedly trained farmers led by men, who, in only
a few cases, had received the training of corporals and sergeants.
A trap ten times the size of the force to be trapped, had shut—
and had caught nothing.

To be sure, "suspects" were found; that is, men of military age
who could not prove that they belonged to the village where they
were arrested and who could, therefore, be assumed to have
been members of Communist fighting units. A few weapons were
also found, and at the northern end of the pocket, where the
Viet-Minh had made its stand at Dong-Qué, some prisoners were
taken arms in hand. But on the whole, as of D-Day plus-36 hours,
Operation "Camargue" already was a failure. However, it was
not entirely over.

Some of the low-flying "Morane" observation planes had detected suspect movements in direction of An-Hoi—proof that some
elements of Regiment 95 had escaped towards the north. At 1300,
therefore, General Leblanc ordered a marine commando and some
infantry from Groupment "A" to carry out a seaborne raid on
An-Hoi. The raid was carried out swiftly enough; the troops
landed at 1500, mopped up rapidly whatever suspects could be
found and returned to their ships by 1800, their mission accomplished.

There remained one more task to be accomplished in the now
occupied villages, the methodical house-to-house search for hidden
entrances, camouflaged storage dumps and the one-in-a-thousand
chance of finding a really important Communist "cadre," one of
the unassuming black-clad *can-bô* who, often barely 20 years
old, really ran the war for the enemy. Hundreds of infantrymen
swarmed out with mine detectors or simply long metal rods,
thumping their rifle butts on the ground to detect suspicious
hollow areas; others would strip and, holding hands, form a chain
which would slowly walk through marshes and ponds in the hope

of finding weapons and equipment dumped into the water at the last moment—a sort of giant-size human rake slowly moving up and down the countryside.

Here and there, one of the members of the human rake would scream in pain and his friends would pull him up from the water, his foot pierced by a crude but effective caltrap—a small wooden plank studded with seven-inch long barbed steel arrowheads which would pierce a foot even through the thick soles of a jungle boot. What with the usual infection, the soldier would be disabled for three months or more. But the human chains and the mine detectors and bloodhound teams kept on with their monotonous and frustrating work, full of the knowledge of its futility.

Atop the sand dunes, the Crabs and Alligators of the 2d and 3d Amphibious Groups were still herding suspects towards the coastal village of Trung-An for combing out by Vietnamese and French intelligence and security teams. These were the *real* victims of the war, the hapless civilians caught in the bow wave of a French armored group plowing under in ten minutes a rice crop that had been the fruit of five months of back-breaking work; or caught in the ever-present clutches of a Viet-Minh "tax cadre" demanding his party's share of the crop's proceeds, after the farmer already had paid close to three-fourths of his crop to the landlord, the usurer, and the government tax collector. Too bad—there will be no shirt for little Hoang who was to go to the village school this year and there would be no pork to supplement the diet of rice and fish for the lunar New Year, the *Têt*—

By the end of D-Day plus-2, all organized resistance had ceased, and on the following day began the withdrawal of the first-line units, the paratroopers, amphibious groups, and marine commandos. Now came the real job of permanently controlling the newly-occupied area. Bridges that had been dynamited over the past years had to be rebuilt; roads cut into ribbons by Viet-Minh saboteurs had to be filled in, the whole artificial desert which the Communists had created around the "Street Without Joy" had to be eliminated. Vietnamese government administrators made their timid appearance in the face of a hostile or frightened population which, after a week's fighting and years of life in a state of siege, needed everything from rice to anti-malaria tablets.

"Funny," said Major Derrieu from the 6th Spahis, watching some of the new administrators in the village of Dong-Qué, "they just never seem to succeed in striking the right note with the population. Either they come in and try to apologize for the mess we've just made with our planes and tanks; or they swagger and threaten the farmers as if they were enemy nationals which—let's face it—they are in many cases."

"That may be so," said young Lieutenant Dujardin, standing on the shady side of his M-24, "but I wouldn't care to be in his shoes tonight, when we pull out. He's going to stay right here in the house which the Commie commander still occupied yesterday, all by himself with the other four guys of his administrative team, with the nearest post three hundred yards away. Hell, I'll bet he won't even sleep here but sleep in the post anyway."

"He probably will, and he'll immediately lose face with the population and become useless."

"And if he doesn't, he'll probably be dead by tomorrow, and just as useless. In any case, there goes the whole psychological effect of the operation and we can start the whole thing all over again three months from now. What a hopeless mess."

"Well, if the Vietnamese can't lick that, we certainly cannot. After all, it's *their* country. Let's saddle up." With a shrug, both men walked back to their tanks, climbing into the turrets with the litheness of long practice.

Below them, on the tiny square of ruined Dong-Qué, the young, earnest, Vietnamese administrator in his khaki shirt and slacks, was still talking to the villagers. They stood there, impassively, like so many wooden statues.

On August 4, 1953, the High Command called off Operation "Camargue." According to the newspapers, it had been a "total success, demonstrating once more the new aggressiveness and mobility" of the French and the value of great amounts of motorized equipment in swamp warfare. In their own reports, the French treated the operation with mixed feelings.

To be sure, Regiment 95 had, for the time being, disappeared as a constant menace along the central Annam coast. Two dozen villages or more had been placed under at least partial influence of the national authorities. But this had been no operation "on the cheap." Important numbers of troops and matériel had to be withdrawn from other vital sectors where they were sorely lacking and where their absence began to create emergencies of their own.

And the results in *actual loss of enemy combat potential* had been frustrating. For French losses of 17 dead and 100 wounded, the enemy had lost 182 dead and 387 prisoners, along with 51 rifles, eight sub-machine guns, two mortars, and five BAR's—and how many of the dead and prisoners were regulars of the 95th Regiment and not merely local farmers or members of the always-expendable *Du-Kich* (Communist village militia) remained open to question.

As regards swamp warfare tactics, "Camargue" had once more proved that it was impossible to seal off a pocket in an airtight fashion as long as a battalion had to hold more than 1,500 yards of ground—and most of the battalions along the southern flank of the pocket had held more than 3,000 yards. Thus, the fact that the bulk of the Communist forces could slip through the *"bouclage"*—the ring of French infantry and armor—was a foregone conclusion as soon as the slow progress of the infantry on the first day eliminated all hopes of constricting the pocket to manageable size by nightfall.

For the progress of the infantry had been slow. In fact, it had been a crawl of about 1,500 yards an hour, on the average. But here again the tactical commander was caught in a dilemma. The purpose of the operation was *not* the surface occupation of the villages but the *flushing-out* of the enemy from his well-camouflaged hiding places and underground installations; hence any speed-up of the advance would be at the expense of the thoroughness of the search for weapons, men, and secret administrative organizations. This dilemma was one that posed itself time and again in the course of mop-up operations and was never satisfactorily resolved.

But, basically, the major defect of Operation "Camargue" was one which was shared by practically all similar operations in the Indochina war: no sealing-off of an enemy force could be successful unless the proportion of attackers to defenders was 15 to 1 or even 20 to 1, for the enemy had in its favor an intimate knowledge of the terrain, the advantage of defensive organization, and the sympathy of the population.*

Another definite advantage of the enemy was its edge in combat intelligence. Very seldom did the French know exactly what they were looking for in the case of such a mop-up. On the other hand, the very size and mechanization of the units employed against the Viet-Minh sooner or later gave away French intentions and even their order of battle; for the positioning of large units required the prior arrival of reconnaissance detachments and liaison officers whose presence rarely remained undetected. Thus, tactical surprise was, with the exception of airborne raids, non-existent and the terrain itself precluded the use of high speed as a compensating factor.

Viet-Minh Regiment 95 lived to fight another day. In the spring of 1954, it again began to infiltrate back into its old hunting grounds, where it ambushed several convoys on Road 1, and even attacked a Vietnamese battalion stationed near Hué. Communist forces had to evacuate the area in July 1954, when the Geneva cease-fire split Viet-Nam in two at the 17th parallel which runs a bare ten miles to the north of Quang-Tri. Once more, the men of Regiment 95 emerged from their hide outs, picked up their weapons from the marshes and swamps, and now marched north in broad daylight along that Road 1 for which they had fought so bitterly. Here and there along the road were stationed some of the tanks of the 6th Spahis, guns elevated and turret hatches open.

---

*To quote one example of a successful anti-guerrilla operation behind the Russian front during World War II, the German LV Corps used the following units to wipe out a 3,000-man force north of Briansk (Operation "Freischütz"— May 21-30, 1943): 5th Armored Div. (less one infantry regiment), 6th Infantry Div., 707th Security Div., 747th Inf. Regt., and "Oststab" (Russians fighting for the German Army) Regt. 455.

In Malaya, a total of 250,000 British, Commonwealth and native troops and militia fought twelve years to defeat a maximum of 8,000 Communist guerrillas.

In 1964, Viet-Cong regulars inside South Viet-Nam were estimated at over 35,000 grouped in 45 standardized battalions and supported by over 90,000 part-time peasant guerrillas. Given the known 10:1 tie-down ratios, they could hold their own even against a one million-man force. Yet, the total South Vietnamese forces (regulars and paramilitary) number hardly 500,000.

Peace was going to be of short duration along Road 1. Early in 1962, several large-scale ambushes took place in the area which showed the sure hand of professionals and soon thereafter, the South Vietnamese Army announced that it had identified the enemy unit which operated in the area: Regiment 95 had returned to the "Street Without Joy."

8

Diary: Inspection Tour

WE took off in a roar of armored jeeps bristling with
machine guns, Willys station wagons for the press and
minor officials, and the Governor's Buick, at 0745, at
a clip of about 50 miles per hour over the worst roads I'd seen
in a long time, in the direction of the coastal areas north of
Haiphong. Governor Nguyên Huu Tri, a bigwig of the pro-fascist
Dai-Viet party and strong man of North Viet-Nam, had decided
to see for himself how the area, a bare non-Communist corridor
along the coast, was doing in the face of the renewed Viet-Minh
threat.

We crossed Doumer Bridge with its impassive Senegalese guards,
passed through dusty and drab Gia-Lam, and about two miles
beyond the airfield came to a French bunker with an adjoining
watchtower. There was also a road-block manned by Frenchmen
in white helmets with green bands—the men from the *regulatrice
routière,* the road traffic control. And next to the road, a big
wooden sign: "Isolated Vehicles, Stop Here! Form Convoys and
Proceed Only If Armed." Gay prospect, and we were heading
away from the front towards the rear area. But, of course, there
were no "rear areas" in this kind of war.

We were just waved on, but now the escorts in the armored
jeeps began their wary sweep of the countryside. To be sure, the
Governor's trip had been well prepared and a vast deployment of
troops had been placed on both sides of the road (deployment
that no doubt would be paid for by some successful Commie
ambushes in the areas where the troops had been pulled out).
But displays of force had never deterred the Viets from attacking
if they felt like it and were willing to pay the price. Right now,
we were driving through a quiet countryside lying placidly under

174

the hot sun, with here and there a farmer working out in the rice fields with his gray-black buffalo, the soldiers standing with their backs to the road at intervals of 50 to 100 yards, their rifles or tommy guns at the ready.

And there were now the French forts, some downright ridiculous in their exact imitation of the North African "Beau Geste" type (you would almost expect Gary Cooper and Marlene Dietrich to stand atop one of the crenelated towers in a tender embrace while soldiers with gold epaulets and caps with flowing neckguards would steadfastly look the other way), others of the squattish, ugly looking, deeply-dug-in modern bunker type. As I was to learn later, the fortifications in Indochina had had their "architectural periods" just like any other works of man, based upon the local terrain, the availability of building materials, the enemy's combat potential, and the state of the art of military engineering.

For example, in South Viet-Nam's dense marsh brush and jungle, high observation towers were at a premium, and the Viet-Minh's erstwhile lack of heavy weapons allowed the construction of high square belfry-type towers whose base was just slightly protected by tree trunks against direct bazooka hits. Even when the enemy acquired some recoilless SKZ's and other paraphernalia, the troops in South Viet-Nam did not depart from their beloved observation towers in one form or another. Some were now built directly into the concrete bunker (still reinforced with tree trunks), others were built atop it but in the form of a graceful derrick-type metal structure topped by an armored observation box. In fact, the forts not only became standardized, but they were actually assigned model numbers, just like automobiles, such as "FTSV-52" (Ground Forces, South Viet-Nam, 1952) so that the *afficionados* would immediately know what you were talking about.

In North Viet-Nam, where the Viets had received heavy weapons from the Chinese Reds as early as 1949, the high crenelated towers and "Beau Geste" forts soon went out of business as serious means of defense; wherever they remained, they were retained only as road checkpoints during the day or (in the case of the forts) as housing for garrisons. In their place appeared the reinforced-concrete bunkers with their tiny firing slits, first as elements in a fortified belt around a particular point, and as of 1951, as part of a gigantic attempt on the part of Marshal de Lattre de Tassigny to seal off the 7,500 square miles and eight million inhabitants of the Red River delta from the surrounding Communist areas. French combat engineers, Foreign Legionnaires and Vietnamese auxiliaries poured 51 *million* cubic yards of concrete into the 2,200 pillboxes of what was to become known as the "de Lattre Line," and all to no avail.

But even those standardized bunkers had their architecture and yearly style changes, as the enemy's attack patterns altered or his weaponry improved. There were the multi-chambered block which appeared in the spring of 1951, followed by the three-chambered block of the middle of 1951. Then came the round block of the end of 1951, containing a specially protected command chamber in the middle; and the easier-to-build hexagonal block of 1952. In 1953 came the hexagon with a small square attachment, and finally there was the small, squarish block of 1954, with a square attachment, capable of withstanding several direct hits by 105's and even an occasional 155mm shell, with its armor plate door and porthole covers; its central radio room, measuring 6 by 4 feet (aptly known as "the tomb"); the whole sometimes adorned on top by a tank turret with gun.

Sometime the bunkers were adjoined to other fortifications. Connected with other bunkers by barbed-wire entanglements and trenches and surrounded by walls, moats, and mine-fields, they then became forts with their own electric generators, fan-driven aeration systems, their own artillery, even their own tank platoon, and, in many cases, their own airstrip for light planes or helicopters. The sort of thing one could show off to the journalists, with regular Navy-type bunks where they could stay overnight, hear a machine gun clatter (sometimes the post commander would fire one for the journalists out of sheer courtesy) and feel that "they were right there, in the middle of things" without being actually too uncomfortable; just like being out in the rain with rubber boots, a waterproof coat, and an umbrella. And that sort of "rich fort" would even have its full name neatly laid out in white tiles or stones atop the bunkers' roofs, like Ké-Sat, for example, so that the airplanes could use them as giant-size road signs.

But on the other end of the social scale was the anonymous nine-men-and-a-sergeant bunker of the "de Lattre Line," with no name on its roof, with no identity whatever, in fact, except a whitewash scrawled "PK" followed by a number. "PK" stood for *poste kilomètrique,* kilometer post, followed by the number of kilometers that lay between the post and the point of origin of the road or some other point of reference. And if the post only possessed "a poor little gun without any pull or any relations higher-up at headquarters," as someone aptly put it* then it was perhaps only entitled to 30 shells a month, or less, and could not clamor for air support and artillery barrages. When the Viet-Minh came at night and blew up its barbed wire entanglements (strictly rationed, too; if you didn't have enough, use sharpened bamboo sticks) with bangalores and his "Death Volunteers" threw themselves with TNT satchel charges against the bunker's ports, the little bunker had to wait its turn for help if the Viets attacked at the same time one of the "luxury motels" in the area. And if it was too late, then, to help the little fellow, it still did not even rate a footnote in GHQ's morning report.

Perhaps the sector's operations officer would say, over the morning coffee, to one of his colleagues: "Did you hear about what happened to PK 141 (for even in death it did not become 'the little bunker at Tho Lam or Binh Dong, commanded by Sergeant Dupont')? Got clobbered last night. The Morane flew over it this morning and nothing stirred. Also looked a bit charred around the ports, the pilot said. Well, we'll send the tank platoon up to see what's what, clean up the mess and get the bodies back."

"Damn!—this is the third bunker this month. There goes another 57, two machine guns, the grenades and the radio set. Hanoi is going to bitch like hell."

And that was all the requiem PK 141 ever got.

Yet life in the 30 x 30 pillboxes was sheer hell even without combat; it meant sitting in a hot, airless, constantly dank cube of concrete embedded in the stench of its own human excrements

---

*J. P. Dannaud, *Guerre Morte*, Paris, 1954, p. 2.

added to those of the "night-soil" used by the farmers in the surrounding rice fields; it meant eating, day in, day out, monotonous
F.O.M. rations (the French equivalent of C-rations) hastily
cooked over a gasoline stove—that is, if anyone bothered to cook
them. It meant patrolling during the day, cutting the grass around
the fields of fire and barbed-wire entanglements, and staying awake
at night trying to listen to the suspicious clanking of the empty
ration cans hung on the barbed wire as warning bells. They
often rang under the push of a rat or of the night wind, but on
the hundredth or hundred and twentieth time, after months of
calm, they would ring for the Viet-Minh "Death Volunteer" pushing a TNT charge atop a long bamboo pole under the wire and
against the wall of the pillbox. If done well, the noise alone could
burst the ear drums of the men inside. Or the blast would dis-
able one of the heavy machine guns before the battle even began;
or a lucky bazooka round would enter one of the ports and the
bunker's crew would die instantly in the searing blast of its own
exploding ammunition boxes.

But sometimes, the bunker was lucky; it would hear the
enemy in time, would repel the first assault and would settle down
to the grim in-fighting, the deadly game of patience called "Defense of a Bunker." The game had its own precise rules, one of
the most important being its duration. It generally lasted seven
hours, depending on the moon or the season. Since the Viet-
Minh would attack the pillbox only during moonless nights or
after the moon had set, certain parts of the month, and the longer
winter nights in particular, would be particularly favorable for
the job.

On the other hand, the Viet-Minh knew that the French would
come to the help of their post shortly after daybreak; with infantry if the roads could be cleared, with fighter-bombers in any
case, when they were available. The post was covered by the
guns or mortars of the neighboring larger forts, or even by the
huge 155mm "Long Toms" of one of the artillery strongpoints
which covered most of the delta. And if everything went well,
the first friendly shells would begin falling around the bunker
within a few minutes after the beginning of the battle, directed by
the bunker's radio; adding their sharp "thump-thump" to the

staccato of the pillbox's own automatic weapons and to the blasts of the enemy's bazookas and SKZ's.

The bunker's crew would fight in absolute pitch-black darkness, since light inside the bunker would outline its portholes to the Viets or impair the men's night vision. Flare shells from the artillery or the flashes of their own weapons would provide for some visibility outside. After a few minutes' intensive fighting, the cordite smoke of the fort's own firing weapons would make the air inside the concrete cube almost unbreathable. Eyes would begin to smart, and throats, already constricted by exertion and fear, would choke from want of clean air. And so it would go on—for hours.

And then, all of a sudden, there would be silence and the gunners would distinguish a few shadows disappearing in the milky-gray dawn: the Viets were breaking off the fight. This had not yet been the final hour for PK 141, or 63, or another of the hundreds along the line. And later in the morning, combat engineers would arrive with an armored car or two, inspect the damage, noting how the box had stood up—perhaps next year's pillbox model would have an improved aeration system or narrower firing slits—and the trucks would replenish the ammunition and take with them Sergeant Dupont's report for the sector commandant. If there had been casualties, an ambulance would have come along as well. And the post would patch up the wire and look for indications as to the enemy's identity. A well-made helmet with a camouflage net would indicate that the enemies had been Viet regulars; a piece of brown or black *cu-nao* cloth could show that, on the contrary, the attack had been mounted by regional troops. Local Communist militias seldom had the armament or the training for the attack of a pillbox. And if Sergeant Dupont himself was not too exhausted, he and a few men would push a recon. into the nearest village, a bare two miles away, a quiet village.

None of the farmers spoke a word of French—well, at least not since the past four weeks, anyway. And the local administrator had left two or three days before the attack to go and see his very sick grandfather in Hung-Yên; and the local little lady merchant who would sell the soldiers some "B.G.I. beer fresh from Hanoi" or some pretty moldy "Mélia Jaune" or "Lucky Strike" cigarettes and would take their wash in (the story had it that she was at times taking in more than the soldiers' wash, but that was just "men's talk"), said to the sergeant in frightened tones: "No, no, today I have no cigarettes, no *bière,* and no time for washing." And the sergeant nodded silently. He had understood. The post had "lost contact." No longer would the small *nhô,* the Vietnamese small fry, come and hang around the pillbox in their charming nudity, joking with the soldiers in pidgin French. And the little merchant would never again have time for washing, nor for visiting with the tousle-haired Corsican corporal.

The post had lost its usefulness as a link in the chain of forts of the "de Lattre Line"; as an obstacle to Communist operations in the area and, most importantly, as a symbol of French authority. In a very real sense, it had become "non-existent"; an "un-person," to use George Orwell's phrase. It was there, on the map, not yet a prisoner but no longer integrated into the defensive fabric—a sort of cattle-on-the-hoof for the enemy, from which the latter could obtain some precious weapons and an even more precious radio set whenever he really felt like paying the price for it. Remaining where it was, it could do the Viet-Minh no harm but deprived the French of men and weapons who could have been profitably used elsewhere, and who, in turn, immobilized a certain amount of artillery and mobile reserve potential for their constant protection.

As the war wore on and Communist infiltration became more general, the French, in North Viet-Nam alone, had locked up more than 80,000 troops in more than 900 forts (many of which had several pillboxes), using an armament of close to 10,000 automatic weapons, 1,200 mortars and 500 artillery pieces. At the same time, the whole Viet-Minh forces *inside* the Red River delta—for the "de Lattre Line" had never had more retaining power than a sieve—amounted to three regular regiments, 14 regional semi-regular battalions and about 140 *dai-doi Du-Kich,* the local peasant militia companies; a total of perhaps 30,000 combatants.

For one last time, the "Maginot Line" spirit had prevailed

and it led straight to the biggest pillbox of them all: the fortified camp of Dien Bien Phu.

Back to the road to Haiphong. Halfway between Hanoi and the seaport of Haiphong was the city of Haiduong, a dusty, sprawling place that was important because it was the junction of our rail and road lifeline with the canal network leading to the southern part of the delta. The administration had completely passed into Vietnamese hands, with one Frenchman, Monsieur de Saint-Hilaire, remaining as an adviser. He and his young wife lived in a vast house at the outskirts of town, overlooking the water-covered rice paddies.

"Actually, we live here on the outpost line," said de Saint-Hilaire, pointing to a skimpy string of barbed wire crossing the rice field opposite the house, "but the view is so magnificent and the place so comfortable that we couldn't decide to give it up."

"We did have two attacks," said Mme. de Saint-Hilaire, "but we beat them off handsomely."

"She's a very good shot," said de Saint-Hilaire.

The table was beautifully laid, and the sandbag breastworks on the veranda barely spoiled the view.

As we passed through Kien-An, the Vietnamese flag over the watchtower was flying at half-staff. Since I shared my vehicle with the "Pacification Commissioner" (the anti-guerrilla warfare chief) for North Viet-Nam, a Vietnamese named Thuan, we stopped in the district chief's house to see the reason for the ceremonial, only to find that his house was filled with wailing women in white, the color of sorrow. A rapid fire conversation in Vietnamese ensued between Thuan and a Vietnamese noncom; both disappeared in an adjoining room, and Thuan returned a few minutes later, his jaw set. The deputy chief of Kien-An Province had been killed during an anti-guerrilla patrol—shot in the back by his own adoptive son who had been converted to Communism. The fellow had escaped, of course.

Kien-An is another example of a swell boondoggle. Somebody decided that we needed a large bomber base in North Viet-Nam and Kien-An was chosen for it. Millions were spent in carting stones from far away mountains to the site of the runways because the water-logged soil of the Red River delta doesn't lend itself to the building of long concrete runways. For nearly two years thousands of coolies worked feverishly at the project. Then the first heavy plane landed and the runway promptly buckled under its weight. Result: Scratch one airbase and 20 million dollars.

Past the port of Haiphong begins Viet-Nam's coal country, its main hope for future industrialization, with broad coal seams close to the surface permitting open-pit mining and direct trans-shipment to high-seas ships of first rate anthracite. In the bare hills beyond the Quang-Yen coal fields, in part with the intention of protecting them, the French had installed another factory—a factory to turn out the fifty-two *Tieu-Doan Kinh-Quan* (TDKQ), the new commando battalions of the young Vietnamese National Army. Trained for combat in the rice fields and marshes of their native land, they were to become the units destined to seek out the enemy on his own terrain, out-foxing him at his own game. They were to be the hunting pack which was to corner the quarry against the guns of the hunter—in other words, who were to flush out the Viet-Minh from its hide-outs into the open where the heavy firepower of the artillery and tanks could get at them.

Here at Quang-Yen, they just looked great and morale seemed high. Governor Nguyên Huu Tri was received with all the honors due his rank and he addressed the five battalions—the first units off the "assembly line"—on the barracks square. Unfortunately, something had gone awry and the Governor had begun his speech before the troops could be ordered to "parade rest." They remained there, stiffly in the position of "present arms" (possibly one of the most uncomfortable of the whole manual of arms) for a full forty minutes while he addressed them.

"That alone would inspire me to hate the guy for the rest of his life," said one of the French training officers next to me. "I don't think the kids'll get anything out of his speech except sore wrists."

When the speech finally ended, the shout of relief of the sorely-tried soldiers sounded like a genuine ovation and made everybody feel even better. Food at the mess was excellent. Major Collinet, the French training commander, had instituted a schedule which provided for French-type meals three days a week and for Vietnamese food on alternating days, with Sundays rotating between the nationalities, with the happy result that all Frenchmen present could eat with chopsticks and learned to appreciate a diet on which they might well have to depend for survival; while Vietnamese officers would learn how to handle a Western meal, which would stand them in good stead should they be assigned abroad to an advanced school, or as military attachés.

Soon the idea of the TDKQ's caught on throughout Viet-Nam; another training center sprang up in South Viet-Nam, and the French legislators at home already began to have visions of vast hordes of Vietnamese commandos overrunning demoralized Viet-Minh guerrillas hiding out in the jungle.

Then Psychological Warfare and the Army's Public Information Office got hold of the concept; from the light infantry battalions which they were—they had neither the technical skill nor the tactical training of commando forces—the TDKQ's were promoted to become the "secret weapon" to win the Indochina war before they had ever been tried in combat. A rather unfortunate motto also began to dog their steps as they emerged in their brand-new battle dress from the training camps: in order to emphasize their psychological role of wooing the population as much as their role to combat the enemy, someone had thought up the formula "With a guitar in the left hand and a tommy gun in the right," which may have sounded fine in the air-conditioned offices of GHQ in Saigon, but made the hapless types the butt of poor jokes throughout the command even before they appeared on the battlefield.

In the eyes of the enemy, the problem had become obvious. The TDKQ's had to be smashed right at the outset, their reputation ruined in the eyes of both the civilian population and their own comrades-in-arms. The Vietnamese National Government unwittingly lent itself to the maneuver. The first new commando battalions were assigned to the Bui-Chu sector in the southern corner of the Red River Delta, where strong elements of two regular Viet-Minh regiments had established themselves over several months. Those were not armed peasants, but regulars of the enemy's core force—and they were now faced with a couple of

under-strength battalions which, already handicapped by the very
lightness of their armament in the face of well-armed regulars,
were almost completely made up of raw troops. The result was
what might have been expected; the Viet-Minh made mincemeat
out of them and the reputation of the TDKQ's was shattered
forever. The idea of the TDKQ's, good as it may have been in
theory, was quietly dropped after the cease-fire by the Vietnamese
National Army and its American instructors.

The last stop on the way back to Hanoi was the *Bao Chinh Doan*
(National Guard) anti-guerrilla training school, located on an
island in the middle of the Red River, west of Haiphong. A handsome Vietnamese major and two dignified civilians were the school
leaders. The school taught sabotage and anti-sabotage measures,
the detection of booby traps and ambushes and other arts essential
to survival here.

"And *they* know their stuff," said Thuan. "After all, they were
part of a Communist sabotage group before they came over to
our side."

Our convoy reached Hanoi just in time for the "closing of the
road," with the trucks picking up the outguards along the highway,
the bunkers closing the gaps in their barbed-wire entanglements,
and with two armored cars and two half-tracks taking up position
near the traffic control check point near Gia-Lam, ready to come
to the rescue of any hapless vehicle which may have missed the
final closing, or to support the nearest posts around the defense
perimeter of the city itself.

Night began to fall over the four thousand villages of the Red
River delta, and the night belonged to the Viet-Minh.

9

End of a Task Force

EVEN prior to the fall of Dien Bien Phu on May 7, 1954, the Viet-Minh counter-offensive had gained momentum in other sectors, particularly on the southern *Plateaux Montagnards* (Mountain Plateau) which includes Indochina's shortest north-south route, and one that was largely invulnerable to French aerial observation and bombing.

Consolidation of the Communist strangle hold on the plateau would have rendered impossible a prolonged defense of southern Laos, opened hitherto quiet Cambodia to full-scale invasion, and directly menaced the small but important French toeholds of Hué, Tourane and Nha-Trang along the Annam coast.

To feed the battle of Dien Bien Phu and the full-scale onslaught on the vital Red River delta position which was bound to follow, the French High Command had to strip the plateau area of the bulk of its mobile forces, leaving its defense in the hands of the static 4th Vietnamese Mountain Division and of small deep-penetration commando units (see chapter 10). One Vietnamese Mobile Group, No. 11, was entrenched at Ankhé but had limited offensive value. Thus, the burden of the whole defensive system was placed upon one single highly mobile regimental task force, the *Groupement Mobile* (G.M.) No. 100.

Groupement Mobile 100 was one of the best and heaviest units of its type. The hard core of its troops were the veterans of the French battalion from the U.N. Forces in Korea, battle-hardened elite troops, many of whose officers and men had taken a down-grading of two or more ranks in order to be able to serve with the United Nations forces. In Korea, the French battalion had fought in the ranks of the 2d U.S. Infantry Division and had covered itself with glory at Chipyong-ni, Wonju and Arrowhead Ridge. Transferred to Indochina after the conclusion of the Korean cease-fire in July 1953, the *Bataillon de Corée*, reinforced by its own reserves and the incorporation of two Vietnamese companies and the famous Commando Bergerol,* had formed the "Korea Regiment." Joined in turn by the 2d Group of the 10th Colonial Artillery Regiment, and the *Bataillon de Marche* ** (B.M.) of the 43d Colonial Infantry, a composite unit made up of tough and jungle-wise French and Cambodian troops, it was activated as Groupement Mobile 100 on November 15, 1953.

More than usual care was given to both the training and equipment of this elite force. Under the orders of its new CO, Colonel Barrou, and his chief of staff, Lieutenant Colonel Lajouanie, the G.M. installed itself in comfortable quarters at Gia-Dinh, not far from Saigon. Until November 29, the G.M. was thoroughly retrained, carried out firing exercises in combination with its own artillery (a rarity in Indochina, where it was often thought that "the best training is to send 'em out to face the Viets. . ."), and during the 29th and 30th of November, went on night bivouac. Soon reinforced by the 3d Squadron of the 5th ("Royal Poland") Armored Cavalry, the G.M. now counted, including its own headquarters company, a total of 3,498 men. Well-equipped and in splendid physical condition after several months of peace and refitting in Korea, the bulk of the G.M. was more than ready to face the enemy. That day was not long in coming.

On December 4, the whole G.M. carried out a mopping-up operation in the *rachs* (arroyos) of the Saigon river delta, and within a few minutes after the beginning of the operation, it had its first dead: Lieutenant Masagosa, of the Artillery Group, stepped on a mine as he was seeking an emplacement for his battery. It also had its first taste of Viet-Minh tactics. After a whole day of painful progression along irrigation ditches and dikes that were

---

*In the French Army, a small shock troop unit (commando) often carries the name of its creator or commanding officer; hence Commando Bergerol, Vitasse, Vandenberghe, etc.

**There is no regular American equivalent to the so-called "march units" of the French Army. While at times assembled for a specific purpose only, like an American task force, they often tend to become permanent composite units. In Tonkin, there were two *divisions de marche* and the Foreign Legion has a famous *régiment de marche*.

thoroughly mined and booby trapped (and in the course of which it lost another four men to mines) the whole group had found exactly one hand grenade, a few documents and 400 kilos of rice. The operation, dubbed "Canter I," was carried into the following day, in the searing heat and stench of the *rachs*. One soldier collapsed from heat and at 1115, three more men were blown up by

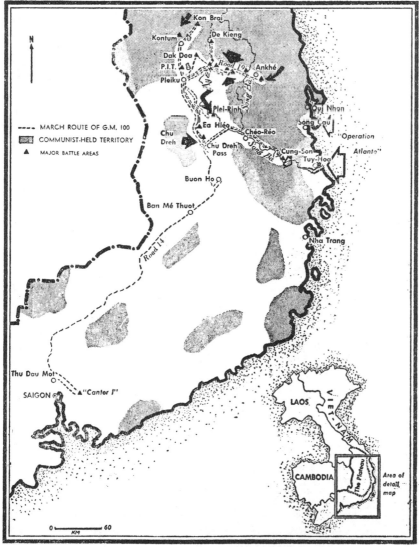

The Campaigns of Mobile Group 100.

mines. At 1600, out of a bush thicket, the 2d Korea Battalion was hit by accurate and heavy grenade-launcher fire, suffering 15 wounded within a few minutes. On December 6, the operation was called off. The losses: 26 wounded and 3 dead for the G.M.; 3 grenades and 3 prisoners for the Viet-Minh.

On December 10, the G.M. began its movement towards the southern part of the Mountain Plateau in order to assume its rôle as the mobile "backbone" for the defense of the whole plateau region. By December 17, the movement was completed and the whole unit again assembled at Buon-Ho, a tea plantation hacked out of the dense woods 40 kilometers to the northeast of Ban Mé Thuot. The men set up their tents in silence and prepared their bivouac for all-around defense. The nearest friendly unit was about 20 miles away with nothing but dense forest in between—no lines of trenches, no barbed wire, no minefields, no tanks and no corps artillery.

This was not like Korea.

In the meantime, the Viet-Minh had not remained inactive. After a brief but successful stab against the line of French garrisons in southern Laos, the enemy had melted away into the jungle of the plateau, leaving two local regiments, the 108th and the 803d, for further operations. In rapid succession, the 108th attacked and destroyed a whole string of posts to the north of Kontum, the French northern anchor on the plateau, while the 803d, in a sweeping movement to the south, menaced Chéo Réo and the string of posts along the Song (River) Ba.

The G.M., which had passed an uneventful Christmas at Buon-Ho, suddenly received orders to interrupt its training schedule to reinforce Chéo Réo as soon as possible. The distance between Buon-Ho and Chéo Réo is less than 30 air miles, but close to 60 land miles over a miserable secondary road. Having left at dawn on New Year's Day, four rifle companies on trucks and the armored squadron reached the ferry northeast of Chéo Réo late at night and immediately began ferrying across. Night ferry operations are hazardous at best. When the operation has to be carried out with one flimsy boat across an uncharted river, the perils increase accordingly. By 2300, the ferry was stuck on a sandbank in the middle of the river and the advance element, now split in two, went into bivouac on the spot. On the following day, the remainder of the G.M. arrived at the ferry, which was unstuck from its sand bank only at noon. The ferrying operations continued with desperate slowness until on the following day, the combat engineers were able to rig up a floating platform propelled by outboard motors. On January 4, finally, the whole Mobile Group was once more assembled at Chéo Réo.

Without respite, the G.M. was now thrown into the difficult operation of reopening Road 7, and keeping it open over a distance of more than 70 miles in the direction of the South Annam coast, where a naval landing operation was to inaugurate Operation "Atlante" on January 20. In the stifling heat, the men of G.M. 100 worked slowly and methodically, de-mining an always empty road and reconstructing bridges blown up by an invisible enemy. Another enemy regiment, the 84th, was briefly identified, but broke contact. Combat patrols found only empty camps in the nearby jungle. A commando composed of mountain tribesmen and commanded by Captain Vitasse now joined the G.M. to become its screening and reconnaissance unit, and by January 28, the G.M. was almost in view of the coastline near Tuy Hoa and made its link-up with the landing forces.

But on the very same day, the 1st Korea Battalion received orders to reinforce Pleiku, the central anchor of the plateau (the southern anchor being Ban Mé Thuot), now also menaced by the 108th Viet-Minh Regiment, while two rifle companies and one battery of the 2d Korea Battalion were ordered to continue directly towards Kontum—treks of 160 and 220 kilometers, respectively. Men and vehicles of G.M. 100 had now been on the march for 30 days and began to show the effects of their ordeal.

Looking back upon the problems of his Group during the shake-down just past, Colonel Barrou wrote in his war diary:

> The most delicate problem remains that of the protection of the artillery and of the means of command and communications, since the largest possible number of infantrymen must be left free to search out the enemy and fight him.
>
> The very means of support and coordination which make the strength of the G.M. also create some enormous obligations in a mountainous area where roads are rare and of poor quality.

Considering the later fate of the G.M., those words were prophetic.

By February 1, the menace upon the whole northern part of the plateau had become precise enough for the entire G. M. to move to Kontum, where a state of near panic existed among the civilian population. To the north and northeast of the town, the mountain tribesmen partisans had either withdrawn into the jungle or, undermined by Communist propaganda, had murdered their French NCO's—and this time, the enemy did not avoid contact. A strong patrol from the 2d Korea to Kon Brai, led by Lieutenant de Bellefont, fell into a well-laid ambush, in which the whole platoon was nearly wiped out, leaving seven dead (including the lieutenant) and thirteen wounded, while the Viet-Minh lost five dead.

At 1300, on February 2, all the posts to the northwest of Kontum, including the important post of Dak-To, were simply submerged by enemy troops in battalion strength attacking in several waves. Air support, called in from the fighter-bomber fields in Nha-Trang and Séno, continued strafing missions around Dak-To until nightfall, but only a handful of survivors succeeded in reaching the outposts of Kontum. The 2d Korea continued its patrol activities in the direction of Kon Brai and suffered casualties from mines and booby traps.

Slowly, the 803d Viet-Minh Regiment continued to narrow its strangle hold around the G.M. In a wide sweep beyond the city it attacked the post of Dak Doa, 28 kilometers to the southeast of Kontum, which suffered 16 casualties but continued to hold. On February 5, the enemy blew up several bridges to the north of Kontum, thus prohibiting any jeepborne patrolling north on highway 14. It was only a matter of hours before the G.M. would be totally encircled in Kontum, but the High Command decided not to defend Kontum; the evacuation of the town by all troops, European civilians and Vietnamese civil servants was completed without major incident by February 7, and the G.M. now grimly dug in around Pleiku for a last-ditch defense of the central region of the Southern Mountain Plateau.

Colonel Barrou decided to hold Pleiku offensively in order

to avoid the progressive crowding of his troops into an area too small to allow for maneuver. The command post of the Group was established to the north of Pleiku, at La PIT* while the composite battalion of the 43d Colonial, reinforced by a battery of the 10th Colonial Artillery, was posted midway between Dak Doa and Pleiku, posting in turn two platoons at Dak Doa itself. One battery of 105's from the 10th was sent 75 kilometers east of Pleiku to reinforce the garrison at the Mang-Yang Pass.

The Viet-Minh had not remained inactive in the meantime. Two companies of the ubiquitous 803d Viet-Minh Regiment ambushed a patrol of the 2d Korea, killing Lieutenant Miolletti and two of his men, wounding ten others. Once more, the dreaded pattern of the *grignotage,* the slow gnawing away man by man, platoon by platoon, was setting in, regardless of the G.M.'s attempts not to be sucked into a static defense position. The ambush of the 2d Korea's patrol was immediately followed by a counter-offensive stab into the Dang Roia mountain massif north of Pleiku, from where the attackers had presumably come. No trace of them was found, of course.

On February 11 at midnight, Dak Doa was attacked once more by Viet-Minh elements which had infiltrated as far as the barbed wire entanglements. The G.M.'s artillery, aided by a "luciole" ("Firefly"—a light plane equipped with flares) and a flight of Grumman "Goose" planes equipped for strafing, succeeded once more in holding off the assailants, but the strength of the defenders of Dak Doa, almost continuously under fire for seven days and nights, was spent. The following day, two reinforced platoons of the 1st Korea relieved the garrison, while the rest of the battalion replaced the 43d on the road to Dak Doa.

But there was to be no respite for Dak Doa. Its barbed wire entanglements, blown to bits by bangalore torpedoes and mortar shells, offered little, if any, hindrance. Its earth-covered bunkers offered protection of a sort, but not against direct hits. By February 17, the road leading from Pleiku to Dak Doa was under almost constant harassment; one last convoy brought in supplies that afternoon, along with Lieutenant Boissinot from the 2d

---

*La PIT is the abbrevation for "Plantation Indochinoise de Thé," one of the many tea plantations of the plateau area.

Korea who was to become the commander of the outpost after the relief of the 1st Korea and who made the trip to familiarize himself with the terrain. He decided to spend the night at Dak Doa and to return to Pleiku with the next convoy.

The attack which followed during the night of February 17 to 18 was a model in careful execution and brutality. As of 2300, one battalion of the 803d Viet-Minh Regiment began its by now habitual harassment of Dak Doa with 81mm mortar shells and machine-gun bursts designed to keep the defenders under cover. In fact, Lieutenant Garnier, the artillery forward observer (FO) at Dak Doa, had radioed his battery over at the bivouac of the 1st Korea that "things seem to be going quietly tonight," amending his view at about 2200 to ask for a prearranged fire on a presumed Communist assembly area.

At 0250, scattered mortar fire against the CP of the Group at La PIT pinned down reserves there, while enemy patrols began to engage the bivouac of the 1st Korea. Within less than an hour, the whole Group was engaged in a fire fight of moderate intensity and preoccupied with the immediate security of its own position and equipment.

This was the moment the Viet-Minh chose for its final attack on Dak Doa. At 0335, the enemy fire on Dak Doa increased to an unheard-of intensity and deadly accuracy. The first mortar salvo landed directly on the electric generator of the post, setting afire the jerrycans of gasoline standing nearby and knocking out at the same time the post's electrical system, including the vital searchlights used to illuminate the fields of fire around the post. The second salvo fell on the sleeping quarters of the guerrilla tribesmen housed in the post, which collapsed on top of them. The third salvo knocked out the post's main radio set, but the post maintained radio contact with the FO's set. The young second lieutenant who commanded the post, Tougeron, was severely wounded at 0345. It was probable that the visitor from the 2d Korea, Lieutenant Boissinot, assumed command at that moment.

In this pandemonium, lit up by the flaming gasoline which had set afire the CP bunker, rose the dreaded, high-pitched, *"Tiên-lên! Tiên-lên!"* of the Communist infantry streaming over the barbed wire entanglements. At the request of the FO, the battery of the 1st Korea was now sending a steady stream of shells directly into the forward works. But the Viet-Minh, in battalion strength, already had reached the connecting trenches of the forward bunkers, mowing down the defenders.

At 0350, Lieutenant Garnier, the FO, sent his last message: "They've got one-half of the post. Keep up the fire."

At the CP of the 1st Korea, the local attacks had been identified as what they had been intended to be—diversions from the main thrust at Dak Doa—but nothing could be done for Dak Doa until daybreak for it was axiomatic that an ambush would be awaiting the 1st Korea along the road precisely in the hope that the plight of their friends would lead the battalion to throw all caution to the winds. As it happened, it would have been too late anyway. At Dak Doa, the set of the FO continued to function, and at 0410, an unknown voice said in excellent French: "Cease fire; the post is taken." Artillery fire, however, was maintained, since it was possible that the set had fallen into Communist hands while the post was still fighting.

Fifteen minutes later, however, there could be little doubt as to the fate of the post: "This is Sérignac," said the voice. "Please cease the artillery fire." Sérignac was one of the French sergeants at Dak Doa, and a moment later, a very weak voice, perhaps Lieutenant Tougeron's, confirmed the request. At 0425, Boissinot transmitted the last direct message from Dak Doa, confirming that the post had fallen and that he was in Communist hands.

Then silence fell on Dak Doa, but 4th Company of the 1st Korea picked up, on its "walkie-talkie" net, a last message. Somewhere out there in the dark, in the jungle, among the smoking ruins of what had been the post of Dak Doa, someone was whistling the *Marseillaise*, the French national anthem. A Viet-Minh bit of psychological warfare? A French prisoner in the FO bunker who saw that the set was still tuned in and who wanted to show that he was still alive? It will never be known.

The 1st Korea was in a cold rage. In silence, the men loaded their spare ammo clips. At daybreak, the battalion was ready for the push on Dak Doa, if need be, by fighting its way over the 20 kilometers of road. But as the first company left the bivouac, a message came in from the Group's CP: "Break camp, fall back to Pleiku. No attempt will be made at this time to re-occupy Dak Doa. The Dak Doa affair is closed."

A wave of incredulousness swept the battalion, from Major de Turbet to the last man, "You mean, we're just going to let 'em lie there for the buzzards? Maybe we could find some of the wounded alive. Up here, the Viets generally leave them on the spot," said Lieutenant Antonetti. But Group Headquarters refused to be budged; in fact, it had only transmitted an order received from the CG of the Plateau Zone, which held the Group respon-sible for the defense of Pleiku, "disregarding all other matters." A request by the 1st Korea to send five unarmed ambulances to Dak Doa—at times, the 803d was amenable to chivalry—was turned down at 1130, also upon direct order of "Grand Pasha," code name for the CG, General de Beaufort. Camp was broken slowly, as if in hope that orders would be changed at the last moment.

At 1440 of February 18, Private Mohammed Ballas, a wounded survivor from Dak Doa, staggered into camp. He had played possum after the Viets had captured the post and stripped it of its equipment—they would never stay in a post any longer than necessary for fear of artillery or aerial bombardment—and then had just walked away. Ballas confirmed that there were many wounded in the post. This further angered the men of the 1st Korea, but Hq. remained inflexible. Finally, on February 21, at 0730, Private Marcel Millet, a wounded prisoner from Dak Doa, arrived at Pleiku with a message from the CO of the Com-munist 803d Regiment: four gravely wounded Frenchmen would be left on the road from Pleiku to Dak Doa and could be picked up by an unarmed ambulance. This time, Zone relented and an ambulance was sent out and brought the men back at 1100.

Dak Doa had cost Mobile Group 100 a total of more than 80 Frenchmen, including three officers, and about 30 native partisans. And this was only the beginning. Any movement out of the fortified camp of Pleiku now became a military operation of its own. On February 23, the bulk of the G.M. attempted a reconnaissance in direction of Dak Doa, but found nothing. Upon

returning to camp, however, the rear-guard platoon was ambushed by a reinforced company of the 108th Viet-Minh Regiment
and nearly hacked to pieces. It was saved in the nick of time by
tanks from the 5th Armored and providential strafing by a flight
of fighter-bombers returning to Nha-Trang. The 1st Korea again
lost 19 men, including 12 missing, but at least had the consolation
of being able to count 55 Communist dead on the ground. In a
message to his men, Colonel Barrou commended them "for this
war action, in which, in spite of 56 days of continuous operations,
all the elements of the G.M. have shown resolute spirit and aggressiveness, thus avenging the Rebel success at Dak Doa." But in his
unit's war diary, there was this telling line, "The morale of the
men remains good, but they are tired."

The month of March became a nightmare of its own, but for
an entirely different reason. This time, the enemy, far from pursuing his apparent advantage around Pleiku, again melted away
into the jungle. Footsore and weary, plagued by mosquitoes and
leeches, pushing and dragging its artillery, tanks and vehicles, the
G.M. advanced east along Road 19 in the direction of Plei Bon
in support of Airborne Group No. 3*, dropped in on March 1
to attempt to seal off the elusive 803d or 108th Viet-Minh regiments—whichever would stand battle. After several days of rain,
the unimproved road to Plei Bon had turned into ankle-deep mud
which the vehicles of the Group promptly churned into a bottomless quagmire.

In the searing damp heat, the men kept pushing forward with
the strength of despair—the enemy *had* to be somewhere! But the
war diary of the 1st Korea stated tersely, on March 13, "The impression of emptiness continues." This was what the French General Staff Manual for Indochina calls *la guerre des grands vides*—
the war of the vast empty spaces—entirely unlike that fought in
the plains and rice paddies crawling with people living in thousands of villages. Here, an entire day could pass without coming
in sight of a human being; to be sure, a few huts would be found
here and there, but empty of any inhabitants. Whatever tribesmen

---

*A French Airborne Group (G.A.P.) was composed of three paratroop bat-
talions and attached airborne artillery and service units.

had remained loyal to the French were now in the posts and camps, and the remainder had retreated with the Viets into the inaccessible hills a few miles off the paths and roads.

A last stab by the Airborne Group to the north of Dé Kyeng, supported by an artillery battery of the G.M., brought no results, save a few camp sites already three to five days old—and to the north of Dé Kyeng begins the zone marked on the maps in the yellow color of "relief and alignment uncertain or unknown." On March 14, the operation was called off, as the paratroops were withdrawn to be dropped into Dien Bien Phu and the G.M. was assigned the task of protecting the monthly convoy making its way along Road 19 to the fortified camp of Ankhé, 100 kilometers to the east of Pleiku. Once more the enemy had escaped, and once more, the dead-tired G.M. had to cover 130 kilometers in two days to face a new thrust of its old enemy, the 803d, now reported near Do Dak Bot, at the cross-roads of highways 7 and 14.

By now, the two Viet-Minh regiments in the central plateau area had worked out their tactics in fine detail: unhampered by heavy equipment, unburdened by such matters as keeping open several hundred kilometers of roads, they were always able to move faster than any motorized force opposing them which, by necessity, had to operate from the peripheral roads. With the adroitness of seasoned team players, the 108th had drawn the G.M. far into the road-less north; while the bulk of the 803d, the 39th and 59th battalions, rapidly moved south along the Dak Ya-Ayun, reaching the cross-roads about two days before the Mobile Group began its movement. By the time the Group set up shop around Plei Rinh, the Viet-Minh had once more set its trap. It was sprung on March 22, at 0245.

The bivouac of the G.M. at Plei Rinh was centered around the small army post located there, a thatch hut and barbed wire affair more designed to provide shelter against the tropical rains for the platoon of local levies than as a military installation. In wagon-train fashion, the G.M. had drawn a semicircle anchored on the Dak Ya-Ayun. Its CP, artillery and tanks were in the center and the three infantry battalions on the edges. The fairly flat valley offered favorable fields of fire broken at places by clumps of bushes. The outposts ahead of the Group's MLR reported nothing suspicious until about 0245, when in the sector of the 2d Korea some movements were reported in the vicinity of the Dak Ya-Ayun.

At 0254, the whole area of the G.M. was hit by extremely violent mortar fire, accompanied almost immediately by accurate and concentrated fire of rifles and several heavy and light machine guns. The CP of the 2d Korea was almost immediately hit by several mortar shells, and at about 0330, the dreaded screams of *"Tiên-lên!"* were heard again in the 2d Korea sector as black clad Viet infantrymen broke into the position of the 2d Korea's 5th Company, wounding and capturing Captain Charpentier.

At the same time, the diversionary attack against the post of Plei Rinh was making progress. The post, attacked by Communist SKZ's recoilless cannon), soon burst into flames, lighting up the battlefield, and joined a few minutes later by two trucks of the 2d Korea, hit by mortar shells. The flames proved advantageous to the defenders, for they facilitated the intervention of the 5th Armored's tanks, which now began to rumble into the 2d Korea's sector, saving 5th Company from annihilation; the survivors of the company counter-attacked and were able to liberate Captain Charpentier.

A few determined Viet-Minh got as far as the Group CP, but were shot down at the last minute by the men of the Hq. Company. By 0430, the 803d had enough. As rapidly as they had appeared, the Viets dissolved into the nearby jungle. Fighter-bombers and reconnaissance planes called in at daybreak found, of course, nothing. A later ground reconnaissance by the 1st Korea found the empty CP and camp of the 803d. A large amount of bloody dressings indicated that the fight must have been costly to the Viets as well. Thirty-nine dead were found on the battlefield and two wounded were taken prisoner.

But on the French side the losses had been heavy—36 dead, including one captain; 177 wounded, including Major Kleinmann, CO of the 2d Korea, and 13 other officers; and 8 missing. In addition, the G.M. had used up most of its ammunition and all of its medical supplies. It was still capable of fighting but it had been severely mauled.

In an order of the day, Colonel Barrou congratulated his troops for their courage and for having inflicted upon "the invincible and ever-elusive 803d the shame of having to abandon part of its dead and wounded on the battlefield."

"Let me express to you," he continued, "my pride, my affectionate confidence and my faith in the future and in our victory."

But the past days had been hard on Mobile Group 100. The 1st Korea had shrunk from 834 in December to 532. The losses of the 2d Korea and of the *Bataillon de marche* of the 43d Colonial were hardly less severe—and the worst was yet to come.

With its wounded barely evacuated and ammunition and fuel barely replaced, another emergency around Ankhé forced the G.M. again to take to the road. Until now, Ankhé had been considered a relatively quiet sector, infiltrated to be sure, but not in immediate danger of being overrun. Thus, its defense had been in the hands of Mobile Group No. 11, entirely recruited from among South Vietnamese lowlanders who were more at a loss in the jungle inhabited by "savages"—the Vietnamese name for the highland tribesmen, *Moi*, meant exactly that—than were the European French. The Viet-Minh command was not one to let this opportunity go unexploited .

On March 30, two independent battalions from the neighboring "Inter-Zone V" fell upon the unsuspecting Vietnamese garrison at Déo Mang pass, controlling the eastern approaches to Ankhé. When dawn came, the post had been annihilated and the equipment of a whole infantry battalion as well as four 105mm howitzers had fallen into Communist hands. At the same time, intelligence reported the reappearance of the 39th and the heavy weapons battalion of the 803d Viet-Minh regiment a few kilometers south of Road 19, in a move apparently designed to cut off Ankhé from the west.

On April 1, the whole G.M.—trucks, tanks and artillery—had to cover once more the 140 kilometers to Road 19 to assume a semi-static defense mission for the whole central plateau area, with Colonel Barrou taking over command of the zone of Ankhé and of the Bahnar tribal area, relieving the badly demoralized G.M. 11. Once more, the trek began from Plei Rinh to Pleiku with its Far West atmosphere, where the few remaining French tea planters congregated every evening at the "Embuscade Bar" with Colt .45's on their hips and their jeeps chained to a hitching post in front of

the bar lest they be stolen by a passing unit. Without even stopping, the convoy wound its way past the old bivouac of the 1st
Korea and the crossroads where the men of Dak Doa had fought
their last battle. It crossed once more the Dak Ya-Ayun river,
where it had, one month ago, vainly pursued the 108th Regiment
into the unknown vastness north of Plei Bon, and now it pushed
on along Road 19, towards Mang Yang Pass and the heavily
fortified post beyond it, PK 22, exactly 22 kilometers from Ankhé.

Road 19 was unsafe for anything but convoy travel, and Colonel
Barrou's trip to Ankhé was a military operation in itself with the
1st and 4th companies of the 1st Korea and two companies of the
43d Colonial opening the road as far east as PK 11 while G.M.
11 sent out three companies from Ankhé west to PK 11 to escort
the colonel and the gasoline supplies into the fortified camp. The
whole operation seemed to have gone off without incident and at
1445, Colonel Barrou, the command vehicles and the now empty
gasoline trucks returned through the safety corridor beyond PK 11
into the zone held by the forward troops of the 43d Colonial and
the 1st Korea.

Now began the "telescoping" process of the withdrawing units,
a delicate operation in which the units leapfrog each other, with
the leapfrogged unit remaining in firing position until the withdrawing unit had, in turn, established itself in a defensive position
—a dreary process which the 1st Korea had worked out to the
precision of a ballet.

At 1520, the message had come in from the CP at PK 22:
"Convoy safely arrived. Fall back." And the ballet had begun; the
two companies of the 43d began their westward movement, on
foot since they had been closest to the CP, with the 1st company
trailing.

"Looks like we've made it once more," said Lieutenant Muller
to the company CO, Captain Léouzon, as the column began its
march amid the usual clatter of equipment and weapons with
which an infantry unit travels when it is tired and feels safe. A
rifle squad under Sergeant Li-Som, a Cambodian—the bulk of the
43d was recruited in Cambodia—was in the lead. The time was
1530, with the sun still high in the tropical sky, and the Colonials
were now about 2 kilometers west of PK 15.

All of a sudden, Sergeant Li-Som stopped dead in his tracks. "What's the matter, Li-Som," said Léouzon. "See something?" As the men of the G.M. well knew by now, some of the worst ambushes had happened at the end of an uneventful patrol.

"No, Sir," said Li-Som, his face wrinkled with concentration, "machinegun fire. They've caught the 1st Korea again."

Now everybody in 1st Company could hear it: rapid machine gun bursts and the heavier thumping of the SKZ's. This was it, a big ambush, and the prize was worth it—two companies, ten trucks and a platoon of armor. Léouzon's company needed no further orders. At about 1530 they began dogtrotting back to PK 15, overtaken five minutes later by the 4th Platoon of the 5th Armored, barreling by under the personal command of the squadron commander, Captain Doucet.

All hell had indeed broken loose at PK 15. The 4th Company of the 1st Korea had just telescoped through the 1st Company and was about to take up position farther up the road when, without a sound of prior warning, all trucks of the company were taken under a stream of machine-gun and rifle fire from the southern edge of the road. Before the men had even time to stop the vehicles, the lead truck exploded in a sheet of flame, blocking the road, with the second truck piling into the first. A few instants later, again the shrill cry of "*Tiên-lên!*" and Viet-Minh regulars (Battalion 19 of the 108th and Independent Battalion No. 30 from the nearby Inter-Zone V) began pouring from the thickets.

The 4th Company was composed of seasoned troops; whoever was left in fighting shape struggled off the trucks and headed toward the higher northern edge of the road. By 1525, exactly at the moment when Sergeant Li-Som had first heard the firing, the survivors of the 4th, now commanded by corporals (for all senior noncoms and all officers already were casualties), had dug in for a last stand. In fact, they had rallied enough to launch two ineffective counterattacks against the enemy in the hope of saving some of the wounded from frying in the burning vehicles or from being used as shields by the Viet-Minh advancing across the road. Moreover, a radio message had got through to the CP, and every available unit of the Group was en route to PK 15. The 1st Company of the 43d Colonial never received the message, but already had begun its return march on its own initiative.

The first to arrive on the spot was the rear guard company, with its two light tanks and the lead half-track running hell-for-leather into the center of the ambush, hoping that the appearance of armor would at least startle the Viets and give the 4th Co. a chance to regroup. But the Viets were also seasoned troops. Half-track

At PK 15.

"Dingo"* was stopped dead with an SKZ shell in its front axle; while the ensuing raking of the open vehicle with machine-gun fire wounded Sergeant Lem, the vehicle commander, and its gunner, Corporal Tran Van Srey. Extremely dense and accurate fire on the slits of the following tanks also wounded some of their crews, and Viet infantry began to climb onto the vehicles.

What saved the whole unit from annihilation was the providential arrival at that moment of the 4th Tank Platoon under Captain Doucet. Driving his tanks with all guns firing into the stalled column, he cleared the road sufficiently for the armored vehicles to form a square into which now poured the survivors of the infantry companies. This slowed down the Viet-Minh only for

---

*All French armored vehicles have names, with all the vehicles of the same squadron having names beginning with the same letter.

the moment. From 1600 to 1700, they launched four assaults against the tanks, apparently with total disregard for their own losses. Twice they climbed on top of tank "Diable" and the disabled "Dingo," only to be thrown back in hand-to-hand fighting, and for a moment it seemed that the end had come for the tanks, also running low on ammunition after nearly 90 minutes of intensive combat.

Strangely enough, the artillery of the Group had remained silent. "Where in hell is the artillery?" Doucet radioed to Group CP. "Can't intervene yet," was the answer, "there is one of our *mouchards* above you." In the din of the battle, the *mouchard*—French slang for "snooper" or "stoolie"—a small, dainty-looking observation plane, had been totally overlooked, but now his noise could be heard clearly. And behind the puttering of his engine, there was the throatier sound of heavier planes—the B-26's from Nha-Trang, diving in steeply, their high tailfins shining in the setting sun. The Viet-Minh had heard them, too, and they promptly broke contact to withdraw into the deep woods, but not fast enough for the B-26's. In a wild carrousel, the still smoking vehicles of the 4th Company serving as marker, they came down at tree top level, jettisoning their black, cigar-shaped canisters. A swoosh, a moment of silence, and then a sheet of flame immediately topped by an enormous black billow—napalm, jellied gasoline which sticks to skin and clothes.

The arrival of the 3d Co. of the 1st Korea, along with a truck of ammunition for the tanks, now gave the hedgehog the strength for one supreme effort. With the Viets held down by the B-26's, the French counterattacked for the last time at 1715. Supported by tank "D'Arc II" and the self-propelled howitzer "Duroc," Lieutenant de La Brosse's 3d Co. and some elements of 1st Co. worked their way through the column, pushing damaged vehicles off the road and starting up the others, while still under enemy fire. By 1900, all the wounded and dead of the three companies and of the shot-up tanks were loaded on the trucks. The battered task force began its retreat to PK 22 when once more the rear guard, this time de La Brosse's company and armor, were attacked.

Jungle fighting is unpleasant at best. In the dark of the tropical night, it is hellish. About 15 Viets swarmed over "Duroc" whose driver had seen them at the last moment and had accelerated, crushing three of them to a pulp under the howitzer's tracks. But the Viets were not to be shaken; Sergeant Piccardat, the tank commander, was shot in the face, while the driver, Corporal Bonnat, received a mortal wound in the chest. The driverless vehicle smashed into the ditch, with the Communists still clinging to it. Piccardat was dragged out and the second driver, Danh Kuong, was tied up and about to be dragged away when Sergeant de Temmermann's "D'Arc II" appeared around the bend, headlights blazing and machine guns firing.

Coolly, as if on an exercise, young de Temmermann climbed out of his tank with two of his men, climbed into "Duroc" and removed its radio set, the gun's breech block and the vehicle's documents, then gave first aid to Piccardat and the dying Bonnat, and placed them with the other two crew members on the rear deck of his tank.

But this was not the last fight of the day. Captain Doucet's own armor escorting the bulk of the infantry back to the camp at PK 22, ran into yet another ambush at 2000. The pattern was exactly the same: direct assault against the tanks. Another of the lightly armored self-propelled howitzers, aptly named "Don Quixote," was hit and two of its crew members wounded. Within a few minutes, Viets had swarmed over the tanks, with each tank lighting up the preceding vehicle and "cleansing" it by spraying it with machine gun fire. The surrounding infantrymen could not intervene effectively for fear of hitting the tank crews or of being hit themselves. Like huge elephants attacked by tigers, the tanks finally shook off their assailants. At 2300, the last armored platoon rumbled into the defensive perimeter, dragging behind it like wounded animals two of the half-tracks shot up during the fighting of the afternoon. The crews had spent nine to twelve hours in steel hulls with an interior temperature of 110 degrees Fahrenheit.

A strong reconnaissance the following morning by the 2d Korea and a company of the 43d Colonial at the spot of the ambush yielded another seven bodies of Frenchmen apparently missed the evening before, as well as 23 Communist bodies—and again a gesture of chivalry on the part of the enemy; one wounded Frenchman lying in the middle of the road, bandaged and fed.

Once more, the score had been murderous; the G.M. had 90 casualties, including one lieutenant killed, against 81 known enemy dead. From 175 men each, the 1st Co. of the 1st Korea had melted to 67, the 2d Co. to 83, the 4th Co. to 94. Mobile Group 100 had had a dress rehearsal of its own end ten weeks before it was to occur, and a bare mile from the spot where it would happen. The stage was set on both sides for the last chapter.

The severe battering which the G.M. had received did not change its mission. It was to relieve G.M. 11 at Ankhé, considered too demoralized for an all-out defense, and it was to hold Ankhé with a smaller number of troops against a larger number of enemy forces than ever before had been assembled in the area. In the meantime, Headquarters for the Mountain Zone professed to be optimistic. In fact, G.M. 100 was the object of a special order of the day on April 9, 1954, retracing the whole history of the Group's desperate battle on the plat au:

> . . . By a rapid descent along the Song Ba, you attack the western flank of the enemy and take Cung Son. And, in one single leap you turn to Kontum and beat the enemy to an area which he sought to reach . . .
>
> . . . You fought this enemy to a stop during the admirable defense of Dak Doa (and) a few days later, you surprise him at La PIT and— in the furious rush of armor and the hand-to-hand struggle of the rifleman, supported by the fires of the artillery—you inflict upon him a bloody defeat . . .
>
> . . . You leave no respite to this fanatical adversary. A race now begins between him and you between Road 19 and the valley of Plei Bon. You are faster than he (and) the speed of your reaction and the fierceness of your resistance carry the day against the violence of the enemy attack . . .
>
> . . . You have again beaten the enemy in his race to Ankhé. His forces had the mission of destroying you. It was his forces which were mauled in the course of the fierce battle fought on the evening of April 4, 14 kilometers west of Ankhé . . .
>
> . . . What is the result of all this? The abandonment by the enemy of all hopes of capturing Ankhé and of destroying our reinforcements . . .

The proclamation, read at morning report to the various units of the Group was received with barely a smile. "Oh, well, they *had* to say something," said one lieutenant, and Lieutenant Colonel Lajouanie, the CO of the Korea Regiment, added: "True enough, but Headquarters could have dreamed up something which was closer to realities than that. And what we need now is not citations, but reinforcements."

But reinforcements were nowhere to be had. Dien Bien Phu was eating into the entrails of the French Army in Indochina like a cancer, and Tonking had an additional priority. Then followed Laos and South Viet-Nam (for political reasons, since the country's capital was there) and, lastly, the plateau area and quiescent Cambodia.

Since December, the Group had fallen to 25 percent below its full strength, and the recent events had drained it of its most important combat specialists. Even before the ambush of April 4, the Group had been short of twelve rifle platoon leaders, five heavy weapons platoon leaders, twelve medical corpsmen, and about twenty signal personnel. "*Débrouillez-vous* (muddle through)," was the invariable reply from Headquarters, along with reassurances that replacements were going to come "soon." But in the face of the determined attack by three reinforced regiments, "soon" was not going to be early enough.

Now began a brief period of respite for the Mobile Group. Having relieved the 11th Mobile Group at Ankhé it settled down to a routine of building field fortifications around the camp, improving its airfield so that it could take C-47's (for by now, Ankhé was completely surrounded and received all its supplies and reinforcements by an improvised airlift), and preparing for the final showdown battle—its "own personal Dien Bien Phu," as some of the men grimly joked.

As in all encircled fortresses which are not under immediate attack, morale, good until then, began to sink off. Fourth Company of the 1st Korea reported desertions as well as self-inflicted wounds: on April 15, Private Hiem Rum deserted with his weapon at 0310; on the following day, Private Pham Van Muoi wounded himself in the foot with a sub-machinegun bullet, and two days later, another Vietnamese soldier of 4th Co., Private Tran Van Loi, also shot himself in the leg.

On the day of Dien Bien Phu's fall, May 8, 1954, the beleaguered men in Ankhé could hear the mocking voice of a Communist loudspeaker echoing eerily across the plain: "Soldiers of Mobile Group 100! Your friends in Dien Bien Phu have not been able to resist the victorious onslaught of the Viet-Nam People's Army. You are so much weaker than Dien Bien Phu! You will die, Frenchmen, and so will your Vietnamese running-dogs!" Brutal, but effective, at least on the Vietnamese, and this was to become a key problem.

The G.M. had inherited, for the defense of Ankhé, a Vietnamese unit, the 520th *Tieu-Doan Kinh-Quan* (TDKQ or Commando Battalion), one of the series of newly-raised units designed to seek out and destroy the Viet-Minh by using its own methods. But, as the wags soon began to say, the TDKQ's "were neither commando nor battalions." Created in 1953, the TDKQ's had become, by and large, totally unreliable as an autonomous combat force by spring 1954. This was to have tragic consequences for the ultimate fate of G.M. 100.

The month of May 1954 was kind to Ankhé. Facing difficulties of its own along the South Annam coast, where Operation "Atlante," after months of bogging down, finally got off to a slow start, the Viet-Minh forces on the Mountain Plateau deferred their direct attack upon Pleiku and Ankhé.

But by the third week of June, the Communists were ready for the final push deep into the plateau area in the knowledge that no French reserves were available. The French High Command had realized the Communists' intentions, and orders were now given to G.M. 100 to evacuate Ankhé and to fall back to Pleiku, across 80 kilometers of enemy-held road. A steady airlift of C-47's and lumbering "Bristols"—British-made two-engine planes with frontal clam-shell doors—carried out of Ankhé the most precious equipment and eleven hundred civilians. All the equipment and ammunition which could not be taken along on the trek was stocked near the airfield to be destroyed by French bombers after the withdrawal of the last troops. On the 23d of June, however, intelligence reports began to come in that a large Viet-Minh force, probably the whole 803d Regiment, was on its way to Road 19 in the hopes of intercepting the evacuation force. The departure schedule was set one day ahead to June 24 at dawn and Colonel Barrou decided to cover the distance from Ankhé to PK 22 in one day instead of regrouping the convoy around PK 11.

This entailed faster traveling, less roadside security and greater convoy discipline, but, under the circumstances, Barrou felt that the game was worth the gamble, the more so as Mobile Group No. 42, recruited mostly from local mountaineers, had reached Mang Yang Pass and was soon to be reinforced there by Airborne Group No. 1.

The evacuation began at 0300 on June 24, 1954, with the various elements of the G.M. pulling back from the outposts to Road 19 west of Ankhé. The battle-tested Cambodians and Frenchmen of the 43d Colonial again led the way, followed by the 2d Korea, with the 1st Korea closing the column. All three battalions had dismounted and were forming a screen around the vehicles of the Group, with the 43d also screening the 520th TDKQ, which was not included in the infantry screen. Each of the battalions also received an artillery battery. Headquarters Co. and the Group's rolling command post were placed in the convoy behind the rear elements of the 520th, and the march began in the early dawn. By the time the column reached the open road, the first French B-26's arrived over the now deserted post of Ankhé and began bombing the ammunition dumps which had been left behind. Black billows of smoke rose over the mountains, but barely anyone in the column bothered to look back, save perhaps the last remaining civilians—300 perhaps—who followed the military column at a brief distance. They had not found space on the last departing airplanes when the decision was made to evacuate Ankhé prematurely, and now they had decided to stay with the column in spite of strict orders by Zone Headquarters not to allow civilians to follow the troops. Too many movements had been betrayed by "refugees" and other camp followers.

In the case of G.M. 100, however, there was no question of maintaining secrecy. The Viet-Minh had seen the stream of aircraft, had been informed of the evacuation of all heavy equipment and of the civilians, and had drawn its own conclusion. The operation simply became a footrace between the 803d and the

Group as to which would be able to hold Road 19 in required strength at the right moment. The French still had one ace up their sleeve—the jungle-trained tough Bahnar tribesmen of Captain Vitasse and his commando still held out in the brush to the north of Road 19. Any Communist unit which would try to cut across Road 19 from the north would have to cross their path sooner or later and give the French a small measure of advance warning. As it turned out, Vitasse and his men did their job admirably.

At first, as long as the column moved in the open plain around Ankhé, progress was not too difficult and spirits began to rise accordingly. At about 0900, the rear guard of the column had reached Kilometer 6 when it received fire from several automatic weapons. Second and Third companies of the rear guard 1st Korea fanned out in the now routine ballet of leapfrogging each other while fighting back. Several men screamed in pain as enemy bullets found their marks. The medical corpsmen began crawling forward. At 0930, as suddenly as it had begun, the enemy's fire ceased. Both companies fell in again and the march continued.

The rear guard reached Kilometer 8, near the Dak Jappau river and plantation, at about 1100, when Private Fauret screamed and doubled over in pain. Not a shot had been heard. For one second, the men stood about in bewilderment; then Sergeant Lefranc, in one smooth, long-practiced movement, hit the dirt, brought up a hand grenade from his belt and threw it while yelling at the top of his lungs: "Get down . . .! *Flêchettes!*" The men of the 1st Korea had just made their acquaintance with another nicety of the Indochina war of which nobody in Korea had ever dreamed—poisoned darts fired from blow-tubes, an unerring killer in the hands of an experienced Bahnar or Hré tribesman. The men of 3d Co. were now crying with frustration, firing wildly or grenading the nearest clumps of bushes. But once more the enemy broke off contact in silence and disappeared as suddenly as it had come.

At about the same time, the bulk of the convoy had reached PK 11, the initial target of the first day's march but now only a rest stop. From there on, the road again entered the thick highland jungle, with trees fringing the road on both sides and with rock cliffs and overhangs providing ideal sites for an ambush. Both

Colonel Barrou, as the Group's commander, and Lieutenant Colonel Lajouanie, as CO of the Korea Regiment, decided to split up the convoy into four elements, each a self-contained unit with its own infantry and artillery, in order to forestall the simultaneous falling of the whole convoy into one single trap.

The new convoy arrangement was formed rapidly enough, and after a brief rest, the first element left PK 11 at 1250, followed by the second element at 1300, the third at 1330, and the fourth, delayed by 2d and 3d companies of the 1st Korea carrying their wounded since 0930, at 1400. Contact between the various elements was maintained via radio and constantly one of the faithful *"mouchards"*—the small reconnaissance planes—hovered within hearing distance of the convoy. Fighter-bombers were stationed on call at Nha-Trang and but eleven kilometers were left to cover between PK 11 and the safety of Mang Yang Pass.

"I guess the luck of G.M. 100 is going to hold out once more," Lajouanie was heard to say as he rolled off in the second convoy element. In fact, luck was for once with the Mobile Group; a few minutes after starting out, the radio truck picked up an urgent message from Captain Vitasse and his junge commando: "Important Viet-Minh elements 3 kilometers north of Road 19." At almost the same moment, one of the reconnaissance planes had spotted another Viet column at Kon-Barr, about 8 kilometers north of PK 11. Group Headquarters acknowledged both messages at 1330, and a few minutes later, the 105's of 4th Battery, still at PK 11, began to slam at the enemy concentration near Kon-Barr, soon followed by the B-26's of the French Air Force. Coordination was good; for once, the Group was forewarned, and air cover was available. Very little could go wrong now.

But something *did* go wrong—the tiny human error which, even in the Atomic Age, still can shape human destiny. The information that the Viet-Minh were 3 kilometers north of the road had been received by the Headquarters radio truck on the road and been duly relayed to the other units along the road: the 520th Vietnamese Commando Battalion, the 2d Korea, the 1st Korea, the 10th Colonial Artillery . . . *to all units except the lead battalion,* the *Bataillon de Marche* of the 43d Colonial Infantry. How this omission occurred will never be known, for the radio personnel and its documentation perished in its truck a few minutes later; but perhaps one explanation can be found in Colonel Barrou's complaint to GHQ in late March that he was short twenty radio operators, including five radio crew chiefs. Unwarned, the first convoy element marched on, toward Kilometer 15, scene of the great ambush of April 4. At 1400, air reconnaissance warned Colonel Barrou that rocks had been placed across the road at Kilometer 15, but that the area seemed clear, otherwise.

As the battalion of the Group with the greatest amount of jungle experience, the 43d did things right by instinct. Just as it had come to the rescue of the 1st Korea on April 4 before it had been ordered to, it now again saved itself from total annihilation by obeying one of the iron laws of jungle warfare—reconnoiter always as much as you can.

Near Kilometer 15, Road 19 emerges onto a small plain covered with dense, six-feet high elephant grass, in which the road winds toward the west in a wide arc. A slight wind stirred the otherwise unruffled surface of the yellow-greenish mass. Not a soul was in sight. Neither were there any birds.

Captain Léouzon, CO of the 1st Co. of the 43d, stopped in his tracks on the left side of the road and looked out over the plain. The whole thing looked calm. Much *too* calm, in fact. He walked over to Major Muller, the battalion commander.

"Look, this whole thing looks fishy to me. If the Viets are going to pull something over us, this looks like the ideal place. Open fields of fire for them, with easy paths of retreat into the high jungle, and as little air observation as possible. I want to send out a screen and see whether we can stir up something."

"Frankly, Léouzon," said Muller, "I feel the same way about it, but sending out a screen in depth will just make us lose time, and if you get involved in a battle way off the road, I'd have to pull off 2d and 3d Co. and that would leave the whole convoy wide open."

"Well, then let's cut the problem halfways," said Léouzon. "I'll leave the road with my company and just cut across the arc of the road through the high grass. If there is nothing that close to the road, it'll give us an additional screen, and if I get caught, it'll give you an early warning and permit you to support me without having to weaken the convoy."

Muller approved and Léouzon's 1st Company left the road embankment to begin its march in the high grass in a rustle of knife-sharp grass blades and the stifling heat of the midday sun. Within a few minutes the whole column had disappeared in the elephant grass, swallowed up as in a green sea, and was about to climb a small hillock which, though also grass-covered, would afford a better view over the whole area. Then, Sergeant Li-Som stopped and motioned his squad to be silent.

"Quiet!—I want absolute quiet!"

Within a few moments, the whole column fell completely silent. Nothing could be heard now save the slight rustling of the wind in the top of the grass blades—and a slight knacking: knack—knack—kna-a-ack. This was what Li-Som had been listening for—the slight knacking sound which high jungle grass makes a few minutes after the passage of a large body through it, as the long, resilient strands return to their normal position; the knacking continues even a few minutes after the strands have returned to their normal position, making the ear (as often in the jungle) a more precious auxiliary than the eye. To Li-Som, the message was clear. The Viets were here. The big, the final ambush to engulf all of Mobile Group 100, was ready to be sprung. Viet-Nam People's Army Regiment 803 had kept its promise. The Communist troops spotted earlier north of Road 19 by Vitasse and the Air Force had either been decoys or merely reinforcements. The main Communist striking force was already in place, its weapons poised, while the French were strung out along a road where their heavier firepower could hardly come into play.

Two Communist machine guns opened up at a range of about 30 yards, catching Léouzon's Cambodians broadside. But Li-Som had not stopped; as soon as he had realized what was happening, he had stormed forward—as much as one can "storm" in tall grass which has the consistency and stopping power of as many feet of water.

"Second platoon with me!" he had shouted as he ran towards the hillock, throwing a hand grenade as he ran. Death came kindly to Li-Som, the Cambodian sergeant of the French *Infanterie*

Coloniale; he caught a burst from the second machine gun in the chest just as his grenade silenced the other gun in a billow of exploding ammunition and seared human flesh.

"Get Li-Som!" shouted the men from 1st Company. Li-Som had been a sort of good omen, a reassuring presence, always doing the right thing at the right moment. His own platoon, caught on the slope of the hillock, resumed the climb under the murderous fire of the remaining machine gun, now joined by rifles and tommy guns. Two more men were hit, but the platoon brought Li-Som back to the company, which now had fanned out into a narrow perimeter. But the small-boned Cambodian with the short, greying hair already was dead, his chest one wide-open bloody cavity. Somebody quickly threw a poncho over him, for there was more urgent business at hand.

It was exactly 1420 on Léouzon's watch, and he and his men knew that they were going to die right there, in the high grass in the narrow highland valley around Kilometer 15. And they also knew that the end had finally come for battered, mauled, harassed Mobile Group No. 100.

"We knew we were cooked," said Léouzon later, "so we tried to do everything by the numbers, just as it said in the book. Time no longer mattered."

As in a fog, the men of 1st Company went into action, no fear or panic showing on their faces, doing what they had to do quickly and with an unearthly calm, as if the whole thing were but a command performance for a visiting general, even muttering apologies if they jostled each other.

"I hope you won't mind, *mon Capitaine*," said the gunner of the 57mm rifle as he slumped down into position next to Léouzon, "but I'll have to kick up quite a bit of dust."

A few meters from there, Corporal Beausset, whose dream it was to become a driver of one of the big tank trucks which transport wine in southern France, struggled with the SCR 300 radio set, trying to raise battalion CP, only to give up in disgust when he found that a .50 caliber slug had smashed into it.

"It's really impossible to do my work properly under such conditions," said he, carefully smashing the remaining tubes of the set with his carbine butt, so as to leave nothing usable for the Viets.

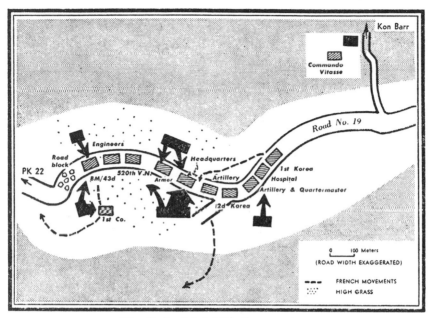

The End of Mobile Group 100.

A slight pall of smoke, acrid with cordite, began to rise over the grass and from the edge of the jungle, where the Communist gunners were working feverishly at their heavy mortars, recoilless cannon and bazookas.

For the men of the 803d, this was the pay-off for six months of painful marches on roadless jungles, dragging thousands of pounds of food and equipment on their bleeding backs; of eating cold, clammy rice day in, day out, with barely a little rotten fish and a few drops of *nuoc-mam* sauce to add taste and provide for a few vitamins; of suffering from endemic malaria and dysentery without proper rest or drugs; of leaving their wounded behind at the mercy of cannibalistic savages, or to die unattended on the path unless they were eaten first by huge armies of black ants; of cowering in helpless terror and hatred as the French B-26's and Bearcats roared overhead with their deadly load of bullets, rockets and napalm.

This was the moment they had been waiting for, the battle which was going to repay them for hundreds of their own dead,

and which was going to give them control of the plateau area before the armistice negotiations were terminated in Geneva; the
battle, finally, which would wipe off the face of the earth the
hated Korea Regiment which still wore on its sleeve the white star
and Indian head of the 2d U.S. Infantry Division. But 1st Company's private agony was soon overshadowed by the same fate
befalling the other elements of the convoy as the ambush unfolded in all its hugeness.

In the Headquarters convoy the ambush looked quite different
from what was happening to Léouzon and the now fully-deployed
Bataillon de Marche of the 43d Colonial.* The armored platoon
—three half-tracks and two M-8 armored cars—traveled directly
ahead of the headquarters elements, with the exception of one
M-8 which went with the 2d Korea. The commanding officer,
Colonel Barrou, traveled in an open jeep, carbine within reach,
at the head of his convoy element, directly behind the armor. He
was in direct communication with his own radio truck. Thus, he
was informed by it that the tiny Morane *mouchard* circling overhead had reported at 1405 a light stone barricade at PK 15 which
apparently was not defended. The headquarters truck had acknowledged the message with a laconic *"compris"* [understood].

At 1415, Barrou all of a sudden noticed that the lead element
had picked up speed and that the armored platoon, following it,
had increased the distance between itself and the Headquarters
convoy it was supposed to protect. Barrou left his jeep, returned
to his radio truck, and personally ordered the armor to slow down.
The message was immediately acknowledged by the platoon commander and Colonel Barrou left the radio truck. At that precise
moment, a machine-gun burst was heard far ahead, followed by
the dull "thump" of a hand grenade. It was 1420.

As if swallowed up by an earthquake, the whole headquarters
convoy now disappeared in clouds of dust and shattered metal as
salvo upon salvo of well-aimed artillery and mortar fire slammed
into it. The armored platoon was simply knocked out of the fight
before it could even search out the guns which were destroying
it. Within four minutes, the three half-tracks and one M-8

---

* The material on the fate of the Headquarters element and Colonel Barrou
is the result of new research in Paris and Indochina.

were afire and exploding. The last M-8, though also immobilized, registered on a machine-gun nest which, from a nearby hilltop, was raking the stopped vehicles with its fire, and covered it with canister shells. At 1425, the Group's radio truck collapsed in flames, thus depriving the doomed task force of central control and its best communications with the outside world.

Barrou himself reacted immediately. Grabbing his carbine, he joined Captain Fiévet of Headquarters Company who had gathered together a few of his men for a counterattack against the hill crest to the north of the convoy, from which murderous machine gun fire still kept pouring into the massed vehicles. At 1435, the colonel was hit in the thigh by a BAR bullet. Captain Fiévet, like Sergeant Li-Som a few minutes earlier, was dying next to Barrou, his chest torn open by a machine-gun burst. The colonel, using his emergency prerogatives, conferred upon the dying young officer the Officer's Cross of the Legion of Honor *in articulo mortis*. But Fiévet, in all likelihood, did not live long enough to hear him.

Lieutenant Colonel Lajouanie, the commanding officer of the Korea Regiment, also had attempted a counterattack against the murderous hill crest. The canister shells of the last M-8 were beginning to have their effect, and for one fleeting moment it seemed as if the remnants of Headquarters Company would be able to reach the crest and outflank the ambush. At that moment, however, the armored car's cannon fell silent, its gunner killed; and at 1445, Lieutenant Colonel Lajouanie fell mortally wounded near where Colonel Barrou lay. Barrou conferred upon him also the Officer's Cross of the Legion of Honor. A few moments later, whatever was left of Headquarters Company was wiped out as a fighting force.

Letting himself roll down the slope, Barrou reached the disabled armored car and painfully dragged himself into the turret in the hope of being able to bring its gun again to bear on the ill-fated hill. But his metal rank insignia had caught the eye of an enemy soldier. A tommy gun bullet hit him in the other leg and he fell backwards into the dust. Dazedly, Barrou rolled into the road ditch; he knew that his capture was likely and he methodically tore up all his identification and other papers and removed his rank insignia in the hope of being able to slip away later. A medical corpsman sped by and stopped for an instant, not recognizing his colonel lying blood-spattered in the ditch.

"There isn't a damn' thing I can do for you, buddy," he said, "we've got no stretchers left and everybody at the aid station is pinned down. But I'll put a couple of dressings on you." In a few expert movements, he bandaged the colonel's wounds and raced onward to the 43d, which was suffering heavy casualties. Major Hipolite, the Korea Regiment's chief of staff, fell a few minutes later; and Viet-Minh infantrymen, well briefed as to where the key targets of the convoy lay, overran the Headquarters convoy. Ten minutes after the fight had begun, Mobile Group 100 not only was without central communications, but was leaderless as well.

In the spreading chaos, the least experienced troops cracked first. The truck drivers of the engineering troops of Ankhé abandoned their vehicles in the middle of the road at the head of the convoy; while in the second element—where the Group CP had been—the whole 520th Vietnamese Commando Battalion simply evaporated, leaving the survivors of Headquarters Company and of the 10th Artillery's Headquarters Battery to fend for themselves. At 1500, a mighty roar, reverberating from the surrounding mountains, shook the whole column while huge flames shot skyward and pieces of equipment and fragments of men began to rain down on the battlefield: the engineers' ammunition trucks had begun to explode under the impact of Viet-Minh shells.

This was the moment when the last two elements of the convoy, the 2d and 1st Korea and their artillery, arrived at Kilometer 15, saving the remnants of the Headquarters units from total annihilation. Like the men of the 43d Colonial at the head of the convoy, they knew that they were done for but they, too, were doing things by the book, to the end. Without stopping, the two lead companies of the 2d Korea opened themselves a path through the mass of wrecked vehicles and linked up with the bulk of the 43d which had regrouped at a distance from the still burning and exploding vehicles (they were to continue to explode until 1730) and attempted to clear the road for the following convoy elements. Under a withering fire which caused heavy losses, the Colonials got a few of the trucks started, but renewed Viet-Minh attacks again closed the gap after some of the vehicles broke through the ring under the benefit of the initial surprise. These were the only vehicles to break out of the trap and reach PK 22.

In the center of the pocket, in the meantime, the 1st Korea and the remnants of the other remaining units had regrouped and dug in around the convoy. Major Kleinmann, CO of the 2d Korea and now senior officer alive in the trap, had assumed command and at 1530, a welcome sound had added itself to the battle on the French side: in spite of serious losses and the constant shelling by enemy mortars, 4th Battery had again unlimbered its howitzers to fire at point-blank range, with fuzes at minimum setting, against on-rushing waves of Viet-Minh infantry. By 1620, both Kleinmann and Major Guinard, the CO of the 1st Korea—Muller, of the 43d, being out of reach—had decided that what remained of the Group was strong enough to hold a defensive perimeter and to prepare a drop zone for supplies, as ammunition began to run short.

The arrival of the Air Force's B-26's also helped to consolidate the situation, although not in the way it was expected. By the time they intervened, combat had reached the hand-to-hand stage in many places; the intervening aerial strafing froze everyone flat on the ground, enemy and friend intermingled and often only feet apart. As the silvery birds swooped down in a deafening roar of engines, the bursts of their nose guns raking the high grass like strong gusts of wind, men from both camps looked up at the sky in fear and hatred of blind fate which dealt death in almost impartial fashion. One of the radios of Headquarters Co. was heard to say, as if to settle a long-standing argument:

"This goes to show you again—this whole aerial warfare business isn't quite perfected . . . *ce n'est pas encore au point.*"

But as dusk began to fall, it was obvious that the position would become untenable. While the Viet-Minh's infantry pressure had lessened, its mortar fire was still heavy and accurate. On the French side, the guns of the 4th Battery had again fallen silent, their crews dead, most of the ammunition spent. More than a hundred wounded were moaning at the eastern end of the convoy, where Major Varme-Janville, M.D., was caring for them in a small square formed by overturned trucks and an ambulance; the medics, as usual, had done a magnificent job during the battle, against hopeless odds, becoming casualties themselves as they sought to help others, with the wounded themselves being wounded again as they lay helpless in the improvised dressing station. Finally, the stretcher cases were pushed under the trucks for greater safety, but there were too many of them, and often they were only within twenty yards of the actual firing line. It was obvious that none of the severely wounded would survive the next day unless they were soon removed from the battle area.

At 1715, Kleinmann received orders from Zone Headquarters to abandon the vehicles and equipment and to break through to PK 22 with his infantrymen and whatever wounded he could carry. Kleinmann acknowledged the order and again conferred with Guinard. The 43d, in the meantime, acting again with the independent horse sense which seemed to be the trade-mark of the outfit, had broken through the fire ring at the western end of the trap and had, on its own, begun the trek out of the pocket. For the two battalion commanders of the 1st and 2d Korea, the big problem was that of the wounded. They could not be simply abandoned and it was pure madness to try to carry them; in the thick jungle, each stretcher would need eight carriers and two armed escorts—if the paths were known. Here, where the paths were not only unknown, but mostly nonexistent, the wounded would soon find themselves abandoned piecemeal.

Both men made the decision that the wounded would be left on the road, provided with all necessary drugs and food and with the wounded medical corpsmen and volunteer medical personnel who were willing to share their fate. The 803d had been kind to the wounded before.

Major Varme-Janville was called forward. The little doctor from northern France looked at both officers. Bloodstained from head to toe, dead-tired, he knew the score better than anyone else.

"Janville, we've just received our orders. We're pulling off the road at 1900."

"And the wounded?"

"Janville—the wounded are staying here. You know there's nothing we can do for them once we're off the road."

"But perhaps we could ask for a truce to get the wounded out of the way? The Viets have been nice to them before in this area."

"We have neither orders nor the right to ask for a truce. The men in Dien Bien Phu didn't ask for a truce, either."

Varme-Janville blinked, and looked once more out on the road littered with gutted trucks, artillery and armored cars, at the men who had now been fighting without water, in the searing sun, for six hours, and who were here, in the middle of the road surrounded by mountains, sitting ducks for the enemy's guns. He knew that salvation lay only in a rapid withdrawal into the cover of the jungle, and that a request for a truce would give away the plans of the survivors. His wounded would have to fight one more battle—their last.

There was nothing left to do but go back to them.

"Gentlemen, I don't think I can be of much further help in this. They've got good doctors up in Pleiku but my men need me here. I'll stay with them."

This was no time for sentimentalities. A quick handshake, and Major Varme-Janville, M.D., returned to his wounded lying under gutted trucks, behind shot-up ambulances; a small, scholarly figure, but a man and a soldier.

Varme-Janville's sacrifice had been in vain. To be sure, the 803d did not kill the wounded on the spot; in fact, it used many of the trucks still in running condition to return the wounded to the empty hospital in Ankhé. Varme-Janville begged the Communists to let him operate on his wounded, offering that he would operate and care for the Viet-Minh wounded as well.

But at Ankhé he no longer dealt with the frontline Viet-Minh but with the Communist commissars. The answer was simple:

"You are no longer a doctor, but simply a dirty imperialist officer. Our wounded have no doctor. Your wounded have no doctor."

Within three days, the last of the twenty-odd severely wounded died for lack of the most elementary care in the midst of an equipped hospital—for the G.M.'s entire field surgical unit had been deliberately left intact. Almost all the other wounded died in the course of the murderous trek through hundreds of miles of jungle to the enemy's PW camps. Varme-Janville himself survived the march and was released at the end of hostilities, broken in health and spirit.

At 1900, the remnants of Mobile Group No. 100 gathered for the final battle as an organized unit: the breakout from Kilometer 15, from the steel trap which had been chewing them to pieces for the past six hours after gnawing at them for the past six months. In the dark night—night falls early in the tropics, even in June —there was a new series of blinding flashes as the men were stuffing incendiary grenades into the tubes of the artillery pieces, dousing equipment with gasoline and lighting it, and firing madly the last rounds from recoilless cannon and heavy machine guns before destroying them.

It fell upon the 1st Korea to lead the way, followed by the 2d Korea and the artillerymen, with the pitiful remnants of the 520th TDKQ closing the march. For once, the night played in favor of the French. In spite of heavy fire, the Viets did not succeed in stopping the breakthrough, the more so as it was not directed against the western flank of the trap (the logical escape route towards PK 22) but due south into the deep jungle. As the last survivors of G.M. 100 left the clearing, they could still see, on the road, some of the leg-wounded but otherwise battle-worthy remnants of the column fighting a last-ditch battle in the light of the burning trucks.

But soon, even those last resistance nests of disabled soldiers fell silent as the Viet-Minh began to strip the convoy of all its precious booty. They knew that they had to work fast, as the French Air Force could be counted upon to bomb and strafe the ambush area as soon as it could assume that the prisoners in the hands of the Viet-Minh were safely out of the way. By dawn, nothing remained after the previous day's carnage but the stripped vehicles and the silent mounds of French dead beginning to rot in the sun.

A few wounded, forgotten by the Viet-Minh, also remained on the site. Colonel Barrou was among them. For two days, he remained hidden in bushes near where he had been wounded, dragging himself painfully to a shot-up Dodge ambulance where two dying Cambodian soldiers were moaning softly, to drink some water from the vehicle's jerrycan. On June 26, a group of French soldiers suddenly appeared, but they turned out to be survivors of the convoy rather than a patrol of the paratroops at Mang-Yang. They built a stretcher for Barrou and slowly began the 50-mile trek to Pleiku. Three hours later, they ran straight into a hail of bullets—a Viet-Minh reconnaissance element watching Road 19 had intercepted them. Soon, Colonel Barrou and his companions followed their other comrades on the long trek to the prison camps.

In the meantime, the column which had broken out of the trap at PK 15 had soon hit upon deep jungle, which made simultaneous progress of a large body of troops impossible. Within minutes, the Viets would begin to race the column to PK 22 and surely destroy it. At 1930, therefore, the battalion commanders decided to break up the column into platoon-size groups under the command of an officer or a senior NCO.

For most units, including the spearheading 43d, it became a nightmare-like experience as individual groups and single men tried to hack their way through dense brush with their bayonets or bush knives, or would even tear at the bushes with their bare hands, with thorns tearing their clothes to shreds. Here and there, a man would collapse in silence, later to be killed just as silently by marauding mountaineers. In fact, progress became more difficult as they approached PK 22, for the Viet-Minh knew that they would eventually have to return to the road and had, during the night, sent elements ahead to intercept them.

Hundreds of men were again lost during the night of June 24, 1954, but when the morning dawned, the 1st Korea was still in the lead and was still more or less a fighting unit. With 3d Company acting as rear guard, it beat off three Viet-Minh attacks between 0630 and 0830 on June 25, within five kilometers of PK 22; and at 0800, 4th Company, at the head of the column, found itself face to face with a Viet-Minh ambush, charged it with the strength of despair, and killed twelve Viets.

By 1130, blue sky began to shine through the thick canopy of trees, and a slight breeze could be felt.

"Qui va là?" (Who's there?)

"Ne tirez pas . . . Français!" (Don't shoot . . . French!)

From a clump of trees ahead of 4th Company, three soldiers in mottled-green battle-dress emerged with their tommy guns at the ready—the paratroopers from the 1st Airborne Group at PK 22.

The men of the 1st Korea jumped forward, embraced the paratroopers as Frenchmen do the world over, and cried, from exhaustion, from repressed fear, from gratitude of having survived. They had survived as individuals, but Mobile Group No. 100 had ceased to exist at Kilometer 15, the day before.

PK 22 was itself untenable and the paratroops had held it only to serve as a collecting point for the survivors of G.M. 100. As they straggled in (the last elements were only to arrive at 1900, having marched and fought a total of 40 hours with almost no rest and little food), they were sent back to Mang Yang pass, where Colonel Sockel's G.M. 42 sorted them out and shipped the wounded by truck to Pleiku. Here miraculously, Captain Léouzon reappeared with the remnants of 1st Company of the Colonials, in shirt and combat boots, his trousers having been torn off by the thorns of the jungle.

On the enemy side, the Viet-Minh also had caught its breath, stripped the convoy of G.M. 100 of all its salvageable equipment, sent back its wounded to Ankhé, and received a fourth full battalion of reinforcements. It was now ready for the second part of the attack, the destruction of the Airborne Group and of G.M. 42, both slow-moving in view of their lack of transport and now burdened down by the exhausted remnants of G.M. 100.

Once more the trek began and this time it was a full retreat to the fortified camp of Pleiku, which the G.M. had left barely two months earlier as a confident combat unit. Now, however, the bloody lesson had been learned, and the column of mountaineers, paratroopers and units from G.M. 100, reinforced again by some of the tanks of the 5th Armored ("Royal Poland") Cavalry, moved slowly, with the infantry constantly deployed on both sides

of the road. On the evening of June 26, G.M. 42 had secured Phu-
Yên, 10 kilometers west of Mang Yang, and the remaining units
began to funnel through to the new position.

Target for the following evening was the bridge across the Dak
Ya-Ayun, 12 km farther west; here again it was the 1st Korea, now
leading, which had to bear the brunt of a well-laid ambush east
of the bridge. Once more, and with the help of the tanks, the
column broke through and wearily established its camp around
the bridge that same evening.

On June 28, the column could feel that it had almost reached
home base. Road 19 ran now through an increasingly wider plain;
some villagers were seen along the road and here and there tilled
fields began to appear. Pleiku itself was a bare 30 km away. By
1100 of the 28th, the leading elements—two companies of the
Bataillon de Marche, the remnants of the 1st Korea Battalion, the
4th Vietnamese Artillery Group and one platoon of the 5th Armored's 3d Squadron—had reached a point merely 3 km from the
junction of Roads 19 and 19-b, when again the ominous signs of

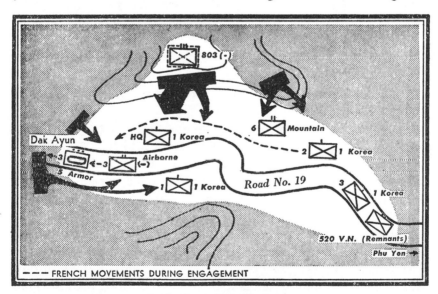

Ambush at Dak Ya-Ayun.

an ambush reappeared: the total silence, the absence of any birds,
and boulders strewn seemingly helter-skelter across the road.

This time, it was the 803d's sister unit, the Communist 108th Regiment, reinforced by the elite 30th Independent Battalion, which had prepared the ambush, and the prize was almost as high as on June 24. With the destruction of Mobile Group 42, much of the Plateau area would become totally indefensible. But the survivors of Kilometer 15 had learned their lesson. As the first shots rang out, the men of the 43d Colonial and of the 1st Korea went into an all-around defensive perimeter on both sides of Road 19, with the tanks of the 5th Armored covering the road, while the cannoneers of the 4th Vietnamese Artillery Group took up position in the center of the perimeter. Colonel Sockel's own CP was inside the pocket and directed the battle.

The trucks of G.M. 42's supply train were caught outside the perimeter by deadly volleys of Communist mortar and bazooka fire, and with a deafening roar, several vehicles loaded with ammunition began to explode. But here also, the bloody lesson had been learned: the native drivers did not abandon the vehicles, thus blocking the road for the troops coming behind them; on the contrary they kept on driving, pushing into the ditch the burning vehicles ahead of them, racing over the maimed bodies of their own comrades. Leaving ten burning trucks and dozens of dead and wounded behind, the convoy entered the perimeter at 1208. At 1215, the Communist infantry rose out of the grass and charged —and once more, the dead-tired survivors of the 1st Korea had to bear the brunt.

A whole fresh Communist battalion threw itself against the northwestern sector of the perimeter, thinly held by 1st Company. With no heavy machine guns left since the ambush of June 24 and with barely enough ammunition for its hand weapons, having lost twenty men the day before at the bloody ambush near the Dak Ya-Ayun, 1st Company nevertheless did its duty, at sixty men against five hundred. But it could merely delay, not stop, the human waves of the enemy. At 1235, 1st Company of the 1st Korea ceased to exist as a unit and enemy infantry surged through the gap towards the Vietnamese artillery position, whose guns, pointing almost in all directions at once, gave support at minimum distances.

With the Communists almost on top of the guns, Sockel gave

*The end of G.M. 100.
HQ convoy at right
bottom. Note two 105's
on the road. Photo by
French Air Force. (p. 216)*

*The massacred surgical
convoy. Photo by
French Air Force. (p. 219)*

Landing at "Street Without Joy." Photo by French Navy. (p. 145)

A Communist pack train, escorted
    by Viet-Minh infantry and Meo tribesmen,
on its way to the front.

Left: Viet-Minh infantry.
        Note Russian automatic rifles.

Viet-Minh female militia, in black peasant garb, tough and well-trained.

Mme Nhu's South Vietnamese "Gun Girls" (dissolved in November 1963) wore fancier uniforms and headgear unsuitable to ambush fighting.

Right: American-built Vietnamese fighter-bombers on patrol over Central Viet-Nam.
Photo by Sgt. Al Chang, "Pacific Stars and Stripes."

Sometimes the war laps across the border: Cambodian troops wounded in an encounter with "unknown Vietnamese elements."

A Communist weapons workshop operating somewhere in South Viet-Nam.

The Second Indochina War: U.S. Marine helicopters and South Vietnamese troops (p. 360)

The new armored personnel carriers add mobility to friendly forces, but they, too, bog down in Viet-Nam's irrigation canals. Photo by François Sully.

Bamboo fences do not always stop Communist forces from penetrating a just built "New Life Hamlet." Photo by Sgt. Al Chang, "Pacific Stars and Stripes." (p. 348)

The payoff: South Vietnamese troops survey battlefield covered with enemy dead; the booty includes British Lee-Enfields, a Bren gun, and French carbines.

The American stake: an American adviser, wearing Vietnamese rank insignia, brings in Communist prisoners. Photo by François Sully. (p. 346)

three platoons of the 1st Korea's 2d Company the authorization to counterattack. At 1300, the yell "*Corée!*" (Korea) was heard along the French line as 2d Company rose out of the grass, crossed Road 19 under fire and slammed into the flank of the Viet-Minh thrust. This no longer was the butchery of Kilometer 15: there was space to maneuver in, there were tanks, there were no cumbersome engineering troops and raw commando recruits, and the Vietnamese artillerymen stuck to their pieces and sent round after round at point-blank range into the enemy.

The faithful B-26's, barreling in from Nha-Trang, found (for once) the Viets in open terrain, too far from the protective canopy of the forest to do them any good. The bombers' machine guns and napalm canisters found easy targets and within a short time, it was the Viet-Minh who broke off combat and retreated into the forest, leaving behind scores of charred bodies where the napalm had found its mark.

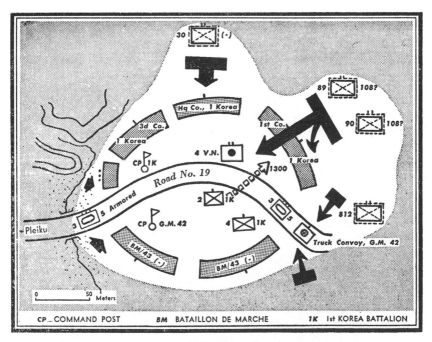

Ambush at Kilometer 3.

"It would even smell like fried pork," said one of the stunned survivors of 1st Company. "But it's that awful gasoline stench which spoils everything."

The men of the task force regrouped slowly along Road 19, as if surprised that they were still alive. The 1st Korea had again bled profusely; forty-two of its men—mostly from the sacrificed 1st Company—had died in slightly more than sixty minutes. And the ambush at Dak Ya-Ayun the day before had cost the lives of fifty-nine men. Five days of fighting on Road 19 had cost the 1st Korea more casualties than two years of fighting in Korea.

But this was almost the end of Calvary for the survivors of G.M. 100. After an uneventful bivouac at the road fork of Dak Doa, they reached Pleiku on June 29, where they found their new CO, Colonel Masse, and the nucleus of a new Group staff. For the first time in a week—in fact for the first time since December 1953—the men of G.M. 100 had time to take stock of themselves. They presented a frightful picture: unshaven, clad in rags, undermined by months of dysentery, covered with sores, they looked more like fugitives from a concentration camp than a regular fighting unit. And as a unit, their losses had been equally frightful: of the 222 men of Headquarters Company, 84 were left; the 1st Korea, the 2d Korea and the *Bataillon de Marche* of the 43d, which counted 834 men each at the outset, now mustered 452, 497 and 345 respectively; and the 2d Group of the 10th Colonial Artillery had shrunk from 474 men to 215. The latter, after having lost their guns, had fought as infantry on June 27 and 28. Major Arvieux, the artillery commander, had died beside his guns at Kilometer 15.

The losses in equipment had been equally heavy: 85 percent of all the vehicles, including the entire armored car platoon; 100 percent of the artillery; 68 percent of all the signal equipment and one-half of the machine guns and automatic weapons. On the other hand, nearly every man who got out alive from the battle, came out with his rifle or tommy gun—indication of the fact that these were troops seasoned enough to know that a man without his piece is a dead man in the jungle. Some of the men had even carried a second weapon with them, for the walking wounded who could still use them if the worst came to the worst, as it often did.

The G.M. had now become useless as a mobile force, both from the physical fact that it was understrength and without vehicles and weapons, and from that of combat morale. As long as they had been in mortal danger, the men—Frenchmen as well as Vietnamese—had fought well, but now the reaction set in. Yet such was the overall situation that the remnants of G.M. 100, on July 2, had to assume responsibility for the defense of the Pleiku sector, after the latter had been further weakened by the airlift of the First Airborne Group to North Viet-Nam and of the 4th Mountaineer Battalion to the South Annam coast.

In the meantime, Zone Headquarters began to scrape together equipment for the Group—three jeeps here, six trucks there, and three 105's for the 10th Colonial Artillery. A small detachment of reinforcements for the Korea Regiment also arrived finally; the men of the G.M. rested, ate and did their chores like automatons, but as far as they were concerned, the war was over. And, indeed, it was almost over. In far-away Geneva, the statesmen were hammering out the last details of the cease-fire. In France, Premier Pierre Mendès-France had promised on June 20 a cease-fire in a month or the resignation of his government and this was July 12. But Zone Headquarters was still dead set on a last offensive, properly dubbed "Operation Forget-Me-Not" (Myosotis).

"Forget-Me-Not" was intended to mop up the mass of Viet-Minh regulars which had infiltrated from the south and which now almost interdicted Road 14 between Pleiku and Ban Mé Thuot. Nestled in a range of low jungle-covered hills, the Chu-Dreh, almost exactly halfway between those two cities, their strength had grown, through the indoctrination of the surrounding Rhadé mountaineers of the Darlac Plateau. Now every supply convoy from Ban Mé Thuot to the positions in the north had become a major breakthrough operation requiring artillery, tanks and aircraft.

A mop-up operation such as "Forget-Me-Not" was, therefore, due sooner or later, but whether the operation had to be carried out at this particular moment, with troops which had just escaped from the jaws of death, was questionable. Lieutenant-Colonel Sockel, the CO of the 42d (Mountaineer) Mobile Group, who was to be the commander of the whole operation, argued against it with Zone Headquarters at Nha-Trang until the day before the operation was to be launched, but Zone remained adamant. The remnants of the *Bataillon de Marche* of the 43d having joined up with its mother regiment for refitting and the 2d Korea being committed to the defense of Pleiku, it fell once more upon the valiant 1st Korea to join in the fray. The 1st Korea had the real strength of about two-and-a-half infantry companies. Its men were exhausted from seven months of continuous fighting without rest in a debilitating climate; two of the companies were commanded by young lieutenants, and most platoons by sergeants. The news that the battalion was to go once more into operation was received with incredulity.

"My God, they want to kill us to the last man," said Corporal Cadiergue, who had earned himself two citations in Korea the year before. "Haven't we done enough?"

On Bastille Day, July 14, the task force, composed of the three mountaineer infantry battalions of G.M. 42, the 4th Vietnamese Artillery Group, the 1st Korea, and a reinforced armored platoon of the faithful 3d Squadron of the 5th ("Royal Poland") Armored Cavalry, took to the road again. This time the direction was due south on Road 14; the first objective was the post of Ea Hléo, 85 km south of Pleiku, lightly held by one company of mountaineer regulars supplemented by thirty local guerrillas. From there, the task force would push into the Chu Dreh massif, isolate the enemy and destroy him with the help of the local garrisons and of the French Air Force. At dusk of July 16, the various units had reached Ea Hléo. A-Day was at dawn of the 17th of July 1954.

At 0430, the 1st Mountaineer Bn. of the 42d G.M. pushed off, followed at 0500 by the 1st Korea. Both the 42d and the 1st Korea were veterans of the battles of Road 19, and all possible precautions were taken to avoid a surprise attack. The whole force advanced by short leaps, with the howitzers of the 4th Artillery Group covering the advance until the troops had reached a new defensive position. Then the artillery would limber up battery by battery and advance under the cover of the tanks. Using this method, the convoy had reached Ban Ea Ten, a tiny village about

2 km north of Chu-Dreh pass, at 0800. So far, there had not been the slightest evidence of the enemy's presence.

The order of march was now reversed and the 1st Korea became the rear guard, staying at Ban Ea Ten with the 4th Artillery, while the mountaineer battalions took over the screening of the task force over the next stretch of road which involved the extremely delicate passage of Chu-Dreh pass. While at nearly all other places the road was fairly open on both sides, at Chu-Dreh pass the mountains tower directly over the road, blocking all vision. Furthermore, the whole western side of the road is lined with thick brush. In short, if there were to be an ambush anywhere between Pleiku and Ban Mé Thuot, this would be the spot for it.

Carefully fanning out on both sides of the road, the 1st, 5th and 8th B.M.'s (Mountaineer Battalions) approached the pass with arms at the ready, looking for the small sign, the faulty camouflage, that would reveal the enemy's presence—but nothing stirred. The tanks and half-tracks of the cavalry platoon shuttled back and forth like so many worried sheep dogs, and by 1015, the lead elements of the infantry battalions emerged on the southern end of the pass, unscathed. At 1030, the Headquarters column of the 42d G.M. left Ea Ten and began its crossing of the pass, and at 1115 the rear guard 1st Korea and the artillery received their orders to begin the crossing.

The order was countermanded five minutes later, and the artillery, on the contrary, received urgent orders to execute a fire mission. The ever-faithful *mouchard* plane had discovered something suspicious to the south and west of the pass. The fire mission was stopped at 1145 and the Artillery Group received the order to limber up for the crossing. At 1200, the armored platoon met the units in a cloud of stirred-up dust midway between Ea Ten and the pass, followed in turn by the men of the 1st Korea, with 4th Company in the lead, Headquarters Co. in the middle and 1st Co. trailing.

Then it happened. At 1215, as the bulk of the convoy had emerged from the pass, well-hidden 81mm mortars, 60mm's, and the feared Viet-Minh SKZ recoilless cannon opened up at minimum range upon the "soft" vehicles—trucks and jeeps—of the convoy.

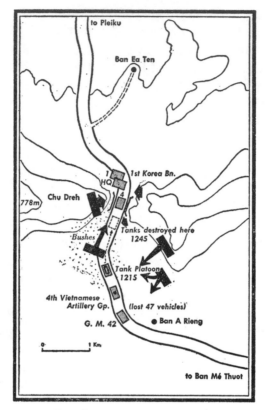

Slaughter at Chu-Dreh Pass.

Within a few moments a dozen or so were blazing fiercely, joined
soon by the ear-piercing crashes of exploding gasoline tanks and
ammunition crates. Fourth Company of the 1st Korea never had
a chance; it was caught in the middle of the pass, where there
were no road ditches, by Viet-Minh automatic weapons firing down
the center of the road as if on a target range. The complete butchery of 4th Co. gave Headquarters Co. and 1st Co. a fighting
chance. Digging in on the west bank of the road, they sought to
fight their way back to Ban Ea Ten, dragging their wounded with
them, including Major Guinard, the Battalion CO, and the lieutenant who commanded 4th Company.

This was the end of the line for the 1st Korea Battalion. The
troops who had defeated the Reds in Korea at Wonju and at the

Arrowhead, who had survived Ankhé and the hell of Kilometer 15, were going to die now, three days before the cease-fire that was going to end this eight-year old war. But still they kept on doing things "by the numbers." Headquarters Company dug in its automatic weapons and let itself be leapfrogged by 1st Co. dragging the wounded, and then repeated the process, leaving several men dying or dead every time the demoralizing process was repeated.

At the other side of the pass, G.M. 42 had held, despite the fact that forty-seven vehicles were now destroyed. Once more the B-26's had responded on call, but the very success of their intervention kept the men of the task force from hearing the agony of the 1st Korea. That battalion not only was dying, but it was dying completely alone—every one of its remaining radio sets failed either to function or to be heard, masked as they were behind the pass and the jungle. It was only at 1235 that the armored platoon, another faithful retainer of G.M. 100, realized that the Korea Battalion had failed to follow the artillery out of the pass. Without hesitation, the tanks and lightly armored half-tracks of the gallant "Royal Poland" raced back into the pass, unaccompanied by infantry.

The Viets did not even bother to blow them up with their bazookas; they preferred to storm them with infantry in the hope of capturing their guns and even more precious radio sets. Within seconds, black-clad Viets were crawling like so many ants over the armored vehicles, with wild hand-to-hand battles developing in the open half-tracks. Here again, the crews fought to the end, with the remaining vehicles trying to push their disabled comrades out of the pass. The diversion had been costly, but it did save the remnants of the 1st Korea from annihilation. At 1400, as suddenly as it had come, the Viet Minh attack ceased, the small, black-clad men disappearing again in the dark green hills of the Chu-Dreh.

The 1st Korea Battalion, flagbearer of France's contribution to the U.N. effort in Korea and the fighting backbone of Mobile Group No. 100, had ceased to exist. When the last stragglers had come in—and it took some of them, such as Sergeant Luttringer and Corporals Cadiergue and Levet, until July 25—there were exactly

107 men left. And of these, 53 were in the military hospital at Ban Mé Thuot. The 1st Korea had done its duty to the last.

Strangely enough, the enemy once more showed a short moment of mercy to the 1st Korea. On July 19 at 0800, the commander of Viet-Nam People's Forces in the Chu-Dreh area sent a messenger to Ea Hléo, informing the French that 37 wounded from the ambush of July 17 would be left on the road 10 km south of Ea Hléo and that they could be picked up by unarmed ambulances. The ambulances, in charge of Lieutenant Patrouilleau, M.D., and of Father Currien, a priest who could speak the mountaineer language, left Pleiku a few hours later, passed through Ea Hléo and disappeared south of the outpost for four days. A band of ambulatory wounded, seventeen in all, already had rejoined Pleiku on foot on July 22, and had reported that the ambulances had been held up by the enemy until their passage had been authorized by higher authorities.

In the meantime, the little outpost of Ea Hléo, which had harbored the remnants of the 1st Korea, was faced in turn with the advance from the south of the victorious Communist forces. During the night from July 19 to 20, twenty mountaineer partisans deserted with their weapons, leaving in the post seven Frenchmen —as in many of the hill posts, gendarmes rather than soldiers— another twenty mountaineers of doubtful loyalty and a handful of almost shell-shocked survivors from the 1st Korea. The post commander did the logical thing: on the evening of July 20—the day the armistice was signed at Geneva—he and his men took to the hills, and, instead of trying the obvious retreat to Pleiku, struck out across the deep jungle to the north of Ban Mé Thuot, thus avoiding the traps which the Viet-Minh had placed along Road 14. They reached Ban Don, north of Ban Mé Thuot, on July 24, exhausted but unharmed.

The declaration of the armistice made life on the Southern Mountain Plateau even more frustrating: under the pretext that communications between the various Viet-Minh units and their regional command were very poor (which, in part, was true), combat operations in the Plateau area continued for yet another month. Knowing full well that peace had been declared, the battle-weary men of the mobile groups on the Plateau had to continue to fight for their lives. In fact, the positions of G.M. 100 at Pleiku were attacked on July 27, and an outpost on Road 19 even had the disagreeable experience of being bombarded with 105mm shells fired from the howitzers captured by the enemy on June 24.

The armistice finally became effective on August 1, 1954, and on August 13, the remnants of G.M. 100—the 2d Korea, the survivors of the 1st Korea, the one remaining battery of the 2d Group of the 10th Colonial Artillery, and the 100th Headquarters Company—began their last march to Saigon and the Cape Saint-Jacques.

On September 1, 1954, the French High Command in Indochina dissolved Mobile Group No. 100. It was up to Colonel Masse, its last commander, to write the epitaph of the unit in his last order of the day:

> G.M. 100, thrown into battle right after it had been created, forged together by hard tests, ceases to exist as of September 1.
>
> Kontum, Dak-Doa, La PIT, Plei Rinh, Ankhé, Road 19, Road 14 and the Chu-Dreh—are many fierce battles which mark its brief but glorious history.
>
> This history, it is you who wrote it together; you, the men of the Korea Regiment, of the *Bataillon de Marche* of the 43d Colonial Infantry; of the 2d Group, 10th Colonial Artillery; of the 100th Headquarters Company. Beyond the diversity of your origins, nationalities and unit traditions to which you remained deeply attached, you have succeeded in acquiring a collective soul which has given its unity to G.M. 100 . . .
>
> I was proud to have had the honor of commanding such a Mobile Group. It is with profound regret that I see it disappear and I salute reverently the memory of our dead and bow with respect before your flags, standards and guidons. I wish you all a future which I hope to be worthy of the collective past of our Mobile Group No. 100.

Thus ended what at the outset was perhaps one of the best fighting units in Indochina, a unit one-third of whose men had survived two years of combat in Korea without noticeable slackening-off in spirit since they were all hand-picked volunteers and most of them professional soldiers. It is certain that the addition of the experienced composite battalion of the 43d Colonial did not harm unit morale—quite the contrary.

On the other hand, the addition of Cochin-Chinese (South Vietnamese) infantry when the Korea Battalion was almost doubled in size, caused at first some misgivings, which proved largely unfounded until the last weeks of the war, when the progressive physical destruction of the whole unit began to destroy its moral cohesion. Also, the mountain plateau constituted for the South Vietnamese a completely alien and hostile environment, and the six-months long separation from their families—while exposed to the threats and reprisals of Communist rebels—also affected their morale. Desertions, however, began to occur only after the armistice, when homesickness became unbearable and any further exposure to danger appeared senseless.

One psychological factor, however, cannot be overlooked: by and large, the troops from Korea had become used to standards of combat logistics which, to the French in Indochina, represented unreasonable luxury. For example, it became a standard joke throughout the theater that one of the Korea battalions, faced with 20 casualties, had requested helicopters for their evacuation and that the Zone commander had personally gone to the radio shack to roar back:

"Dammit, this isn't Korea. You carry your own wounded like everybody else!" There had never been more than ten operational helicopters in Indochina until April 1954.

The same went for artillery and air support, almost always in plentiful supply in Korea and rarely plentiful and almost never on time in Indochina. Also, the war in Korea, with the brief exception of the Inchon-Yalu campaign, was essentially a war of the most classical kind, with the front solidly anchored on two seas and most of the time organized in depth. Furthermore, the whole Korean front was about 180 miles long, with each front-line unit assigned its proper sector; while G.M. 100 would often cover 20 to 30 kilometers a day if conditions permitted it. During the six-months period of its active existence, G.M. 100 had covered close to *two thousand* miles, and all of it in areas of intensive combat.

Lastly, the very motorized equipment which gave it mobility, also bound it to the existing road system, with minimum cross-country capability, thus giving the enemy the immense advantage of the inner line. The incident where Communist Regiment 803 attacked the Group on March 14 on Road 19 and was ready to attack it again at Plei Rinh, six days later, is illustrative of the problem involved. The Communists had covered about 80 km through the jungle while it took the road-bound G.M. exactly seven days to cover the 150 km to arrive at the same place over the poor roads available in the area.

In the monsoon jungles of Southeast Asia, there is no cheap substitute for the most expensive commodity of them all—the well-trained combat infantryman; not the mass-produced item of the "divisional training camps" so dear to the Korean war, but the patiently trained jungle fighter who will stay *in* the jungle—not on the edges of it—and who will out-stay the enemy, if need be. The French had finally recognized this and their commando groups, once developed, showed surprising staying and hitting ability. But when the showdown came, there were too few of them —and they were too late.

*

G.M. 100 is dead, but its spirit did not die. The 1st Korea Battalion, like the proverbial phoenix reborn from its ashes, was reconstituted after the dissolution of the Group, lost its Vietnamese components, and became again a French infantry battalion of the "heavy" type, comparable in armament and effectives to those of the Foreign Legion. Its status in the French Army as the "bearer of the traditions" of the French forces assigned to the U.N. in Korea was made permanent. It left Indochina for good on July 17, 1955, the anniversary of the ambush of the Chu Dreh, for Algeria. A rebellion had broken out there, in November 1954, which was to last until May 1962.

A modest marker bearing in Vietnamese and French the inscription: "Here Soldiers of France and Viet-Nam Died For Their Countries" indicates the spot where Mobile Group 100 met its fate*. And by May 1955, its tough but gallant enemies, the 108th and 803d People's Army regiments, had disappeared silently north of the 17th parallel.

---

*I wish to thank here 1st Lt. Charles W. Raymond, 3d, for providing me in April, 1964, with a photograph of the still-existing marker.

But not for long. In November 1961, after a series of sharp attacks on Kon-Brai and Dak-To in which unsuspecting South Vietnamese garrisons were hacked to pieces, columnist Joseph Alsop reported from Kontum that American intelligence officers had clearly identified the re-infiltrated 803d as the author of the attacks. With its sister mountaineer regiments, the 120th and the 126th, it is again spreading havoc in the northern mountain plateau area, in spite of the many helicopter-borne units which now have replaced the roadbound G.M. 100 in the pursuit of the elusive enemy. And in April, 1964, the dreaded 108th Regiment also appeared again in Quang-Ngai, thus completing the build-up of regular Communist regiments who had operated there during the First Indochina War.

"This is a dirty, a disgusting way to fight a war. If we could corner them in open terrain, we'd clobber all the Communists operating in the Plateau in 25 minutes. That way, it takes weeks to find even fifty."

Those words were not spoken by Colonels Barrou or Lajouanie in 1954, but by a colonel from the U.S. Special Forces late in 1961, after a fruitless twelve-day pursuit of the 803d.*

In the unfolding tragedy of the Second Indochina War now fought by South Vietnamese and American forces, few have the time to remember the agony of the French Mobile Group—but the Jarai and Bahnar tribesmen among whom they fought still remember them, and so no doubt do the veterans of the 803d People's Army Regiment. And that is perhaps the way G.M. 100 should be remembered.

* * *

The attack on Plei-Rinh as seen by the enemy**

. . . The Party Committee finally decided to annihilate the post of Plei-Rinh in order to stab deeply into the enemy's calm southern rear areas. A month ago, the garrison of the post amounted to a platoon of Bao-Dai's

---

*Newsweek, January 1, 1962.

**The author, Hoang Duy, was an enlisted man in the coding section of the Hq. Company of the 803d Infantry Regiment, Viet-Nam People's Army. He spent the whole Indochina war in the Fifth Inter-Zone (Southern Central Viet-Nam) and is the author of several short stories published in the VPA's weekly news-

[Vietnamese Nationalist] army. But as soon as the enemy detected our presence, he reinforced the post by two companies of Europeans and Africans to take care of any eventuality. If we wanted to liquidate at the same time the new positions held by the reinforcements around the strong point, we had to force back the enemy into the central post or encircle him solidly. Our regiment already had become inured to that sort of operation since the fighting around Déo-Mang pass in 1953. So, no one was too worried about that part of it.

What bothered us [was] that we no longer were a regiment but in name. Our best battalion had left us to take part in the operations in the plain against [the French landing at] Tuy-Hoa. After the departure of one company for Road 14, we had, in fact, only five infantry and two heavy weapons companies left. And calling them "companies" was saying a great deal! We had had a great number of wounded and sick who had not been replaced. One evening, as the operation was explained on the [sandbox] model, a platoon commander complained about the lack of men.

"How many have you got left?" asked the regimental CO.

"I've got only 28 left."

Everybody began to laugh and the CO said:

"You're a rich farmer! You administer your effectives pretty well; all the others are nothing but poor peasants or landless farm workers in comparison to you." And renewed laughter was heard.

Nevertheless we decided to wipe out the two-and-a-half white companies and the Bao-Dai soldiers who were awaiting us in Plei-Rinh.

We were on the 16th day of the second lunar month (March 21); we'd have the full moon. At 5 p.m., my unit left the sparse forest and began the march forward. From the moment we left the bivouac until we reached Plei-Rinh, all we encountered were forests of dead trees* without a single leaf, and bare hills without a single spot favorable to camouflage. According to the plan, the operation was to be terminated at 3 a.m. to give us time to cross the [Ya] Ayun River and to march another fifteen kilometers until we came to an area offering cover.

Our march was extremely tiring. At 10:30 p.m., we reached our assembly area. Fifteen minutes later we were in position and attacked.

The [Viet-Minh] CP was installed in the bed of a dry rivulet. The sky was clear and the moon shone so brilliantly that one could read without a

---

paper. This story was published in the French-language book *Les premiers jours de notre combat*, published in Hanoi, Communist North Viet-Nam, in 1958.

The story is noteworthy for its insight into Viet-Minh command procedures. As will be seen, the Communists had an accurate knowledge of the number of French vehicles and units involved; French losses were, however, exaggerated. Words in [ ] are explanations added to the original text for further clarity.

*The unit was crossing a *ray*, a large expanse of forest burned by the aborigines to clear the land for their crops. After two or three crops, the whole tribe moves on to another stand of forest. The standing dead trees are often more of a hindrance to operations than the live forest.

light. Within myself, I meditated somewhat bitterly about my fate which
had made me a sort of "chairborne" soldier: I went close up to the front
without being allowed to hold a rifle to fire at the enemy!

Twelve-thirty a.m. The regimental commander yelled into the telephone:
"Open fire!"

The mortars, bazookas, the bangalore torpedoes and machine guns began
to spit flame in a deafening roar. I woke up completely and with a few
twinges of my stomach began to open my papers, ready to work.

The hand generator which fed the radio set began to crank with the
noise of a rattle; [that is why] as a matter of principle, we were authorized to operate our radio only once after the first shooting had begun. Two
minutes later, the messenger handed me a telegram from Zone Headquarters.

"Up there, they're never satisfied! I'll bet that we've forgot to send them
a report about some stuff and *now* is the moment they've chosen to ask
about it!" I remember having said this to myself, but as the [decoded]
words of the message began to make sense to me, I asked myself whether
I had been dreaming. I at first believed that I had made a mistake in de-
coding and verified the message immediately. But there was no error;
the text was correct. I leaped up and ran over to the CO.

"Urgent message from Staff."

He put down the telephone receiver, took the small piece of paper and
held it up to read in the moonlight. With my heart beating, I looked at
him, watching for the moment when his facial traits were going to change.
Without being a great strategist, I realized the importance of the message.
Our heavy weapons were still firing; under my feet the ground was trembling
in a tempest of fire.

The CO gave me a quizzical look and spoke with a slightly hoarse voice.
I was used to his look, but it appeared to me sterner than ever.

"Comrade, are you sure that you have decoded this right?"

I lost all confidence in myself. Had I committed some error after all? The
CO had called me "Comrade." He only did this on especially solemn occasions. Nevertheless, I regained confidence and answered without hesitation:

"Comrade, I guarantee that all this is perfectly correct."

"Good."

He talked the matter over rapidly with the Political Commissar*. There
were only two members of the [Army] command and the [Communist]
Party here, since the Deputy Commissar and the deputy of the CO had gone
to the [Tuy-Hoa] plain with the detached battalion.

The telephones transmitted the fire orders: "Curved-trajectory fire—mortars and machine guns, prolong fire mission by another five minutes—spend
all your ammo."

---

*Each Viet-Minh unit was directed by a "Command Committee" in which
the Political Commissar had the preponderant voice even in tactical matters.

What was happening?

All this occurred so long ago that I no longer recall the exact tenor of the message from [Zone] Staff, but the essential parts read as follows:

> We have learned from reliable sources that tonight enemy has brought to Plei-Rinh G.M. 100, the 4th Battalion of the 2d Foreign Legion Regiment and one armored unit*. His intentions are to begin a large-scale mop-up operation in the [Do] Dak Bot area to annihilate us. Air support [expected] from Tourane and Nha-Trang. For your information.

This meant that we were attacking a force eight times the size of ours, formed by European elite units with all their motorized equipment and artillery. One can well imagine the worries of my CO and the weight of the responsibility he felt on his shoulders at the thought of the fate of his unit. Our scouts had looked over the situation too summarily [the open terrain did not permit their coming close during daytime].

They had been unable to notice all the changes that had occurred during the last few hours. We now had to inflict a defeat upon the enemy during this very night, or he would be able to counterattack tomorrow morning. In this flat terrain favorable to the artillery and the air force, with effectives larger than our own, he could make things enormously difficult for us. We were decided to make up for the numerical inferiority of our troops by their revolutionary heroism, and to use to the utmost the factor of [tactical] surprise to win the battle.

Volley upon volley, the 81 and 60mm mortars, the bazookas and the machine guns tore the atmosphere in response to the given order. I was as happy as if I had personally pulled the trigger. G.M. 100 was an old acquaintance of ours. It was the third time that we faced this unit which had borne the insignia of the United Nations in Korea. The first engagement had been on the Kontum—Kon-Brai road, where the G.M. 100 had lost a platoon. The second had been the capture of Dak-Doa where it had lost a company. This now was the third time!

I distinctly heard the bugle calling for the charge. Red and green signal flares rose in the sky. . . .

. . . Then, above us, began the unrelenting whistling of the [French] shells like an immense flock of birds passing at high speed. Ah! I had deciphered my message well! Only the G.M. 100 could have such fire power! Little by little, the resistance becomes stronger, the enemy's fire becomes denser. The shells continued to pass over our heads and fall behind us in a noise like an earthquake.

But now I did not know whether I was to rejoice or whether I was to

---

*The enemy's intelligence was essentially correct. It probably mistook the 2d Korea Bn. for a Foreign Legion unit because of its size and overwhelmingly European ethnic composition. The armor was, of course, the 3d Squadron of the 5th Armored Cavalry.

worry. Rejoice at the fact that I had correctly and rapidly decoded the message and to see how my regiment had been able to surprise the enemy. Or to worry about the weakness of our effectives, as it was impossible for us to destroy 4,000 men and to establish a springboard to penetrate further into the south. . . .

Then the CO gave the order to fall back.

"The CP falls back upon yesterday's position. The [committed] units continue to keep up the pressure while establishing a plan for the evacuation of the dead, the prisoners and the booty before beginning the withdrawal."

The word "withdrawal" hurt my ears. For the second time during the spring and summer campaign [of 1954], my regiment had to break off combat without being able to follow it through to the end. My bag on the shoulder, my trench tool on my hip, I looked at my watch: 3:30 a.m. I jumped over the river embankment along with the CP cadres and began to cross the zone beaten by the artillery. It was a veritable race; we had to cover 15 kilometers before daybreak.

But there wasn't time enough. In the sky which became lighter little by little, the sun rose brilliantly. Tough luck! Three planes in dark-grey coming in from the north [i.e., Tourane] dived right down on us like crazy pirates. They flew into the cloud of smoke above Plei-Rinh and launched sticks of bombs into that sparse forest of leafless mulberry trees.

We carried a camouflage of dry grass on our heads and backs. We alternately ran and flattened ourselves on the ground and, after a long run, arrived at 9 a.m. at our withdrawal area.

It was only the evening thereafter that the CO himself arrived, dead tired, his eyes shining deeply in their sockets. Having read the mail and messages, he remained taciturn. Crouching next to him, I awaited his orders while chipping away at a piece of dead wood. He turned towards me and asked in a low voice:

"We must have killed at least a company, don't you think so, older brother?"

It was the first time that he had called me "older brother"* and it was also the first time that he had asked my opinion on a matter outside my functions. I answered not without some temerity:

"Oh, there must've been more than that! The riflemen say that the enemy had many dead, all white men."

"The comrades have a habit of exaggerating. If we killed a company's worth, that already would not be bad. If we killed more than that, it would be a wonderful stroke of luck." He remained absorbed in his thoughts. "Did you already send a report to Zone Staff on our own losses?"

"Yes, I sent in a preliminary report which evaluates them at about a platoon."

*"Older brother" (anh) is a Vietnamese expression of endearment.

"Well, that's about it. I don't think we lost much more, in spite of the fact that not everybody has yet returned."

In the middle of the night, the messenger shook me vigorously and handed me five sheets of coded messages. "Urgent!" Always "Urgent!" They must make a terrific consumption of "Urgents" at Headquarters, I said to myself while beginning to decipher the first line. We had marched like mad for the past two days to get to a more sheltered area and the nights without sleep were burning my eyes. Almost dead from fatigue, I only wanted to sleep. But the lines I decoded filled me with enthusiasm:

> According to reliable sources, the G.M. 100, the 4/2d Foreign Legion, one artillery group and an armored unit attacked at Plei-Rinh have suffered heavy losses.
>
> According to first news, casualties (dead and wounded) amount to more than 900; 20 vehicles destroyed, 200 vehicles, tanks and artillery pieces damaged. The heaviest losses had been suffered by the G.M.'s CP. During the whole day today, helicopters shuttled forth and back in order to evacuate the dead officers and the wounded.
>
> G.M.'s 4, 2, 7, and 21 have sent their condolences to G.M. 100, and flags will be flown at half mast for three days on the Plateau . . .

We had done our job well, after all! Those among you who have worked in a regimental CP will remember how often the staff cadres complained about the "Three manys" and the "Three fews" (much work, much responsibility, much bawling-out; and little authority, few material advantages, and few citations and promotions*) which plague them.

A few days later, I was present during a conversation between a battalion commander and the CO.

"Our curved-trajectory fire fell right into their bivouac," said the CO. "And our machine guns just raked them over at a distance of one hundred meters. They had arrived the same evening and believed that they were safe; they had contented themselves to put up their tents and to sleep on the ground half naked. How could they expect an attack? When we began the assault, some of them had not even been able to get out of the tents and the intensity of our fire did not leave them the time to get organized. If we only had had more ammunition, it would have been terrible . . ."

I now was happy with my job. Without staff work, without men who were doing boring work like mine, such battles would be impossible. . . .

Postscript

On July 2, 1964, an ammunition convoy of the Vietnamese Army, shepherded by a U.S. Army helicopter, proceeded on Road

---

*The use of such numerical jingles for propaganda slogans is widespread in Asian Communist countries. Here, apparently, the Viet-Minh staffers seem to have the same complaint as soldiers in the same category the world over.

19 from the coastal town of Quang-Ngai to Pleiku.

It had passed Ankhé without incident and at 1115 had entered the small valley which precedes the entrance to Mang-Yang Pass, when its lead trucks blew up on the well-concealed land mines which barred the road. Within a few minutes the Viet-Cong ambush unfolded fully and the stunned Vietnamese fought for their lives around the remaining trucks while the helicopter, though unarmed, flew low runs over the battlefield in order to confuse the assailants. Armed helicopters which arrived later saved the surviving soldiers from being overrun but could not prevent the partial stripping of the convoy of its cargo and weapons. The Communists broke off their attack at 1600.

The ambush had taken place at the foot of the monument commemorating the end of G.M.100—ten years, eight days and three hours earlier.

10

Diary: The Men

A NY war—and particularly a jungle war—is fought by men, regardless of the amount of equipment which may be at their disposal. In Indochina, where there never was such a thing as a "front," every unit commander, from the lowly sergeant holding a bunker on the de Lattre Line to the major general commanding North Viet-Nam or Cambodia, had to rely upon himself. In a continuous front, two solid neighboring units can be counted upon to "carry along" a weak one; or a weak commander could, if necessary, be propped up by more energetic colleagues or prodded into activity by an always present higher commander. In Indochina, where division headquarters merely served administrative purposes and the actual fighting was, of necessity, in the hands of the colonels commanding the Mobile Groups; where it was not unknown to shift paratroop battalions or artillery batteries for one single operation over distances equivalent to those between Seoul and Tokyo, enormous responsibilities rested upon single individuals.

The Leaders

Rare was the commander who lived long enough to make the same error twice, and even rarer was the second-rate unit which could remain intact by simply "muddling through" or "minding its business." In one area in North Viet-Nam, a clash of personalities had developed between a Vietnamese unit commander and his compatriot who was the chief of the province, over a matter of protocol the importance of which probably would have seemed minor to the average Westerner. Both men instructed their own subordinates to do only what was strictly necessary to "co-exist" with the representatives of the other. Commanders of military posts would help an attacked police post only if the latter was about to be destroyed, and the village mayors and policemen would never

251

report the infiltration of suspects unless the Vietnamese Army unit on the spot would directly ask them to do so. The Communists knew about this situation and within a short time that province was the most heavily-infiltrated area inside the Red River delta.

In such a war without fronts, no one was safe and no one was spared. Lieutenants died by the hundreds, and it was calculated that to maintain major communication lines throughout North Viet-Nam cost on the average three to four men *per day* for every hundred kilometers of road. Senior officers died also. General Chanson was assassinated by a terrorist in South Viet-Nam; Air Force General Hartmann was shot down over Langson; Colonels Blankaert, Edon and Erulin were killed by mines while they were leading their mobile groups through the swamps and rice paddies. And the war did not spare the sons of the generals, either. Lieutenant Bernard de Lattre de Tassigny was killed in the defense of the rock spit which was the key to the fort of Ninh-Binh. He was Marshal de Lattre's only child and his death broke the man's heart. Lieutenant Leclerc, son of Marshal Leclerc, died in a Communist PW camp; and Lieutenant Gambiez, son of the chief of staff of General Navarre, was killed at Dien Bien Phu.

These men, and thousands of others, from Martinique to Tahiti and from Dunkirk to the Congo, from all parts of the Indochinese peninsula, and Foreign Legionnaires from Kiev in the Ukraine to Rochester, N.Y., made up the *Forces de l'Union Française*— no doubt France's last, and largest, army ever to fight in Asia.

The "Hotel Métropole " in Hanoi, opposite the residence of the Governor and next to the massive Bank of Indochina building, was "*le dernier salon où l'on cause*," the last really fashionable place left in Hanoi. Louis Blouet, its manager, had succeeded in exacting high standards of performance from his staff which was as well-styled as that of his brother's "Hotel George V" in Paris and whose tipping scale was considerably lower than that of the Paris establishment. The headwaiter—a former colonel in the Chinese Nationalist forces—was as suave as his Paris counterpart and the barman could produce a reasonable facsimile of almost any civilized drink except water.

It was at the "Métropole" that one could find the wealthier of the French merchants, those among the journalists who had got tired of the professional inbreeding resulting from an overlong stay at the Press Club, and the senior officers of the northern command who were on leave from their posts in the "paddy" (i. e., in the rice fields) and who needed a psychological shot-in-the-arm of French civilization and manners before returning to the bunkers, leeches and stench of Hung-Yen or Nam-Dinh. Here and there, one of us younger men would sneak in and see how the other side lived.

The commanders of the Mobile Groups, by virtue of their particular assignment, were an element quite apart from the rest. Their problems were different from those senior officers whose troops were pinned down *"dans le béton"*—"in the concrete" of the bunkers of the de Lattre Line. Constantly on the go save for short rest periods, their life resembled more that of ships' commanders in a period of cruiser warfare and one could almost speak of a G.M. "putting into port" when it was stationed around Hanoi or Haiphong, Hué or Bien-Hoa for refitting, and each commander after a while had become identified with his G.M. much the same as a captain is with his ship or a feudal lord with his fief. There was Col. Némo, with a dark-eyed, narrow face, and the dying butt of a *Gauloise Troupe*—the harsh black-tobaccoed French G.I. cigarette—always in one corner of his mouth; Dodelier who camouflaged a keen mind in the unprepossessing exterior of a "tough kid" from the Paris streets; or the aristocrats (by virtue of title or exterior aspect) such as Blanckaert with his always-impeccable shirts and his eyeglass; or the intellectuals, men of true erudition and broad views who were able to look at themselves and at the whole Indochina war from a distance, "in profile," as they said. They felt that, bearing the brunt of the war, they were entitled to express their opinions about it. No matter what can be said about the French officers corps, the stigma of being unblinking "yes-men" or Prussian automatons is not one which can be fairly applied to it.

Perhaps one of the most interesting men in that category was Colonel Wainwright.* Wainwright ("My grandfather was an

---

*We also had a Lieutenant Colonel MacCarthy in Indochina, commanding the 10th Moroccan *Tabor*, I believe. As one can well imagine, the man was the butt of quite a few puns during 1952-54. The French armed forces contain a

English officer captured by Napoleon who never got over his taste for French women and stayed after the whole thing was over") was one of the senior armor officers in North Viet-Nam. His armored group would relentlessly plow through the rice paddies of the Tonkinese delta, spend hours in the broiling sun of the dikes until any unprotected contact with the steel hulls would produce serious burns and, having shaken off human wave attacks and bazooka salvos at a range of 10 yards, would return only to its base long enough to fuel up, unload the dead and wounded, patch up the vehicles and roll off again. The *Groupement Blindé* (Armoured Group, or G.B.) was truly one of the fire brigades of the northern command, thrown in at the behest of the theater commander wherever danger threatened, often covering more combat mileage in a week than a similar unit would cover in Korea in six months. Small-boned and wiry, soft-spoken with his gray eyes looking directly at his interlocutor, Wainwright was almost instantly liked by everyone. Rarely seen in anything else but his British army shorts and a plain suntan shirt with the black-and-silver rank stripes of the Armoured Corps, he looked anything but the tough combat leader he was.

It was Wainwright who always had a vast store of authentic Kipling-ish tales about what people were likely to do under stress. Speaking of one of his young squadron leaders, he said: "The man is *so* polite that it sometimes drives me crazy! Mind you, he is not obsequious—he's just naturally polite. He doesn't lose his good manners even in combat; the other day I talked to him over the tank intercom when his vehicle had to use its piece and S—— said:'Excuse me, Sir, but I MUST fire. . .' and then calmly resumed the conversation after the fire mission was completed."

"Or on his very polite days," said Wainwright, "he would add 'Could you please wait a minute? I have some business to attend to here.' "

It was also Wainwright who told the story how a stock clerk in Korea nearly fouled up an operation in Indochina. By a freak accident of cloud ionization, the G.B.'s radio traffic one day was

---

fairly large number of officers with Irish and Scottish names, descendants of men who had fled to France after having been the losers in one of their countries' recurrent rebellions against Britain.

almost drowned out by a twangy American voice in a supply depot in Korea reciting a long list of equipment items. It came through loud and clear over a distance of 4,000 miles and proved impervious to all pleas (in French, of course) to shut up for a while. Fortunately, Colonel Harris, an American MAAG observer with the French, happened to be near-by and in a tone whose American origin (and authority) was unmistakably clear to the supply sergeant in Korea, he roared: "Get the hell off this radio channel! There's a war going on here!" Compliance was immediate.

In another instance, the ever-so-polite S——was caught in a rather unforeseen dilemma. In Indochina, where both men and women peasants wear almost identical clothes and hats and where the women are almost as flat-chested as the men, Communist guerrillas very often tended to pass themselves off as women if they were cornered. Final indentification, was therefore, possible only through physical search. Once faced with such a task, S——, who at that time had freshly come in from France where this particular situation had not been taught at Armored School, radioed for instructions to his higher commander and promptly received the clear-cut reply: "Shove your hand up their arse, Captain!"

That particular message had been, however, intercepted by the monitoring command net in Hanoi, whose job it was to listen in on radio traffic to see that proper security and other regulations were obeyed by the unit radio operators. The command net was operated by French Army WAC's and the contents of that particular message nearly shocked the earphones off the girl operator, who immediately reported this highly improper message through the usual channels.

The Armored Group duly acknowledged that the message had been sent, but in turn, asked whether the WAC personnel would be more satisfied if the message had read: "Please insert your hand into the vagina—if any—of the suspected rebels." There was no further reply from the WAC detachment.

By early 1953, with the war in Korea obviously drawing to its inconclusive end, most of the French commanders shed any illusions about the possibility of any successful conclusion to the Indochina war. The signature of the cease-fire in Korea in July

1953, brought a wave of exasperation and hopelessness to the senior commanders that—though hidden to outsiders—was nevertheless obvious.

It was one of the Mobile Group commanders who, during a lunch at his CP, came out with a clear definition as to how things were going.

"This is not a military war in the old sense. It is not even a political war. What we're facing here is a *social* war, a class war. As long as we don't destroy the mandarin class, abolish excessive tenancy rates and do fail to give every farmer his own plot of land, this country'll go Communist as soon as we turn our backs."

"As long as we don't give the Vietnamese the only program they could really be expected to fight for, we're doomed to fight this war without any hopes for success and die here like mercenaries. I'm getting close to a thousand dollars a month in pay and allowances for fighting in the rice paddies, and my sector killed one thousand Commies last month; that makes it one dollar per Commie on my pay."

"And what about the junior officers?" said someone around the table. "What can they be expected to believe in? After all, they're paying *les pots cassés* (the smashed porcelain), they're laying their lives down for it at the rate of one a day?"

"Oh well," said the colonel, puffing at his *Gauloise,* "they believe they're doing the right thing and that's the way it's got to be. If they knew they were dying uselessly here, it would be like shooting them in the belly and kicking them in the behind at the same time. And when my aide eventually fries in his tank, I want him to believe that he's frying for the good of the Country. That's the least thing I can do for him."

Wainwright sat there, nodding. This view of the war seemed to be pretty much a consensus. "The Americans," he said, "have been paying an increasing share of the war costs since 1952, with us expending the francs here and their dollars going into our Treasury at home. At least we have the consolation of paying for the prosperity of the Frenchmen at home, even though they don't know it. We're getting to the point of Rumania under Bismarck, when Bismarck said: 'To be Rumanian is not a nationality. It is a profession'."

News Items:

• A legislator recently asked the French Government what it intended to do about hospital trains with wounded from the Indochina war being stoned by French Communists as they stopped in the stations to unload men in their home towns.

• We were so short on helicopters that several French cities, notably Bordeaux, collected money in the streets to buy the French Army in Indochina a few whirlybirds to transport our wounded. Even at the end of the war, we never had more than about three dozen for a territory *four* times the size of Korea, the bulk of which arrived in Indochina a few weeks before the end of the war.

• According to a French parliamentary inquiry, about *forty* percent of the equipment delivered to Indochina arrives with evidence of sabotage: sugar in gasoline tanks, emery oil in transmission gears, torn or broken electrical wiring. Even equipment delivered directly from the United States to Indochina is often sabotaged.

• On the gayer side, we just received a shipment of tanks from the United States, each of which bore on its sides in large chalk letters the word STEVENSON—courtesy, no doubt, of the longshoremen of the port of New York. That must have been as far as American political advertising ever traveled.

• American efficiency is admirable. While in Lai-Chau, the airhead behind Communist lines, a mailbag was parachuted in to us, since the airfield was flooded. It contained a letter for me which had followed me, through all my changes of address, from Syracuse, N.Y., to France, Hanoi, and the postal unit of our Airborne Resupply Group. It was a court summons issued for a parking violation committed while a graduate student in Syracuse. [P.S. I went back to pay it one year later, but the judge dropped the matter when he heard under what circumstances the summons had been delivered.]

The other day, Wainwright came back again after having spent a week in the rice paddies with his tanks. He looked like a ghost of his former self and had a noticeable limp; yet he managed to come down for dinner since the chief of staff of the northern theater commander had come over to the mess. Wainwright, usually a good conversationalist, was almost silent. It was obvious that he was in pain. The way he told it, he had been sitting on the edge of his tank turret when part of a dike gave way under the weight of the vehicle and he had lost his balance and fallen into the tank. He had scraped both his legs against the raw edges of the armor and also bruised his shoulder against the gunbreech.

As always happens in the tropics, the leg wounds left unattended, had become infected and now, both legs were blue and swollen. By 10 p.m., Wainwright could stand the pain no longer; he excused himself and went to bed. With the fool's privilege of the outsider, I suggested to the chief of staff that the garrison doctor should see Wainwright immediately since, when asked to see the doctor on his own accord, Wainwright had refused to do so. The chief agreed, and we both went to get the doctor at Headquarters.

He didn't look very happy—he told us later that, plagued with insomnia and the heat for several nights in a row he had taken a sedative that evening to get a good night's sleep—but he snapped to when he recognized the colonel and was ready in a few minutes. Wainwright was still awake—he had taken aspirin which, of course, had no effect on the acute pain he suffered—and, after a few weak protests, submitted to the examination while we waited outside in the corridor.

A few minutes later the doctor came out, looking glum.

"The leg scratches are all right; a few shots of penicillin will take care of them. But it's the guy's general state of health I'm worried about. Forty-eight years old, two years in the rice paddies —it's a miracle he's even alive and on duty at all. He told me that he had lost sixteen pounds during the past ten days. I suggest you relieve him immediately from further combat operations."

There was a moment of shocked silence. Wainwright, with his keen sense of humor and good spirits—could he be so near the end? The chief was an old friend of his and what the doctor had said must have upset him.

"Hell, the guy's finished right now. You're using too many old men in that cr—," the doctor went on, obviously warming up to a subject he must have given a great deal of thought. "You ought to know that it means a death warrant for a man of his constitution to stay under that kind of pressure. You're exploiting the man's dedication to duty to keep him going. He'd rather die than complain."

"Look, Captain," said the chief, and he was now addressing the doctor by his lowly rank, as if to remind him of the military proprieties, "I want you to keep all this under your hat. You will make a full examination of Colonel Wainwright tomorrow and report to me directly. In any case, he *must* hold out another month. Dope him, feed him vitamins, do anything, but keep him going another thirty days. We're short on senior armor officers and it'll take me that long to scrounge for a replacement in France. Is that clear?"

It must have been to the doctor, for he made a smart military salute and strode back to his jeep.

And I guess that his cure worked, for a few days later, Wainwright, more gaunt than ever and with one bandaged shoulder— he had suffered a splintered bone in that fall in the tank—and two lanced and bandaged legs, propped himself into the turret of his M-24 named "Saumur"*. He then took part in a three-hour parade under the broiling tropical sun in honor of some visiting fireman, before returning once more to the stench, the swamps and the Viet-Minh bazookas of the delta.

"There is a difference between us French and Don Quixote. Don Quixote rode against windmills believing they were giants, but we ride against windmills *knowing* that they are windmills but doing it all the same because we think that there *ought* to be someone in this materialistic world who rides against windmills," Wainwright once said.

On the way back from seeing Wainwright being put under the doctor's care, I met Art Deschamps from the local U.S. Information Service (USIS) post. Gave me the latest lowdown on what was wrong with France, her army, her government and her people.

---

*French town where the Cavalry School is located.

"The whole damn' country is degenerate, admit it. And man for man, the French are scared of the Germans, and the whole damn' French Army is here in Indochina just to make money and they have no fight left in them, anyway."

I was too tired for an argument.

While at the hospital for treatment of my own jungle rot, saw a Vietnamese soldier who had been hit by an incendiary shell, and nearly retched then and there. His legs were completely roasted, with his thigh muscles just plain burned off. Two surgeons were working on him; the way I understood it they were pulling down part of his buttock muscles to give him something to pull his thighs with so that he could later on be put on crutches once his legs were amputated. Same job on his hands (he had been crouching behind a machine gun and got hit sideways, with the blast missing his body but hitting his limbs), where the surgeons were transplanting whole skin to cover them.

Air War in the Jungle

The French pilots in Indochina called their aircraft *"les pièges"* —"the traps." And traps they were indeed, for to be shot down in the jungle even without a serious injury was in most cases equivalent to a death sentence, even with survival kits and survival training. Thus, for an air force which, until the last months prior to the fall of Dien Bien Phu, never fielded more than 275 aircraft, the losses suffered were very high.

FRENCH PILOT LOSSES IN INDOCHINA

	Killed in action	Missing in action	Totals
Officers	61	85	146
NCO's	160	243	403
Other ranks	49	52	101
	270	380	650*

*About 70 civilian crew members were also lost on combat missions.

If much of the Indochina war was fought on a thin shoestring, the air war was fought on one that was also badly frayed and had to be held together by knots at several places. In 1946, the French

Expeditionary Corps fielded a total of sixty British "Spitfires" whose wood and canvas components literally rotted off the aircraft in midflight, since the "Spits" were not designed for tropical combat. Until 1950 the backbone of the transport and bomber force was made up of German Junkers-52 tri-motor planes assembled from booty stocks found in Germany. In many cases the same planes fulfilled transport and bombing missions, with the "bombardiers" simply lobbing bombs and napalm canisters out of the plane's side doors.

By late 1951 enough American aircraft became available through the Military Assistance Program to re-equip the French Far Eastern Air Force to a point where it could fulfill its transport and ground support missions. It never received any aircraft for the purpose of strategic bombardment, with the exception of eight French Navy "Privateers." Thus it was impossible to interdict Viet-Minh roads (and road convoys) close to the Red Chinese border; a fact which was to have disastrous results at Dien Bien Phu. Not that it could have been hoped to save Dien Bien Phu through air superiority alone: but by compelling the enemy to use human portage over 600 kilometers rather than over the last 150, would in all probability have slowed down his build-up considerably. Even so, total bombing tonnages went from 834 tons for all of 1949 to 12,800 tons for the last seven months of the Indochina war.

The main mission of the French Far Eastern Air Force was, therefore, entirely adapted to the needs of the ground forces. The same rule applied to the Naval Aviation units stationed in Indochina waters; usually, two aircraft carriers (one, the "Belleau Woods," was on loan from the United States but was entirely French-manned) were on station in Indochina waters with a total complement of four dive-bomber and fighter-bomber squadrons equipped with American "Corsairs," "Hellcats," "Bearcats," and "Helldivers." In addition, the French Navy specialized in coastal surveillance with "Catalina" flying boats and in the grim but essential business of junk-hunting, designed to suppress the important Viet-Minh seaborne supply route along the coast. The French never succeeded in suppressing the junk traffic altogether and neither, according to recent reports, do their South Vietnamese and American successors*.

In terms of tactical organization, all aviation activities in Indochina were subordinated to three regional commands, the *Groupements Aériens Tactiques* (GATAC), or Tactical Air Commands. GATAC South covered all of Cochin-China, Cambodia, and southern Central Viet-Nam; GATAC Center covered the rest of Central Viet-Nam and southern Laos; and GATAC North had jurisdiction over North Viet-Nam and the northern part of Laos. A separate GATAC Laos existed temporarily in 1953-54. Each GATAC, usually commanded by a brigadier, had full tactical control over all aircraft—including those of the Navy— operating in its area, with the exception of the artillery spotter and observation planes which belonged directly to their branch of service.

Coordination between ground forces and the GATAC's was considered very good. Air Force officers were detached to most Mobile Groups as forward air controllers and each year the GATAC's themselves ran several training courses for officers from the ground forces to apprise them of the possibilities—as well as the limitations—of air force support. And those limitations were manifold: the weather in Indochina, even during the dry season, is subject to very sudden and almost unpredictable local changes; during the rainy season (May through September in most areas) days may go by during which flying is almost impossible; and floods may render forward airfields unusable and undermine the concrete foundations of the large rear area airfields.

In addition to the environmental limitations, there was the enemy; an enemy who did not possess a single aircraft but who over the years had acquired a great degree of proficiency in antiaircraft gunnery and in destroying parked aircraft and airbase installations in daring commando raids. The latter finally reached strategic importance during the battle of Dien Bien Phu, when a Viet-Minh commando infiltrated the largest French airbase in North Viet-Nam, Cat-Bi, by crawling for more than a mile

---

*"Smugglers in Junks Supplying Viet-Cong," *The Pacific Stars & Stripes*, Tokyo, July 31, 1962.

through the sewers. Cat-Bi, situated near the coastal city of Haip-hong, was heavily fortified, surrounded by electrified barbed wire and mine-fields and watched even by infra-red devices, in addition to crack troops and watch dogs. By an incredible feat of raw courage and stamina, the Viet-Minh raiders (who would have helplessly drowned in the sewers had there been even light rain that night) emerged directly in the aircraft parking area and at-tached explosive charges to eighteen of the transport planes vitally needed to supply the French garrison in the faraway for-tress. A similar small raid on Hanoi's Gia-Lam airfield also succeeded.

But Dien Bien Phu was to be the finest hour of the aircrews as well as of the 15,094 men who were offered up for sacrifice in the flaming hell below. More than two hundred aircraft* flew 'round-the-clock supply and combat support missions into the valley soon ringed by Communist antiaircraft cannon and machine guns. In view of the north-south orientation of the valley and the prevailing winds, there was usually but *one* approach for the airdropping of supply loads and the approaching planes simply had to run the gauntlet of the Viet-Minh *flak*. The worst part of it was that the obsolete C-47's with their narrow side doors had to make the run *twelve times* in order to drop a load of 2.5 tons, while the "Flying Boxcars" flown by Americans such as Kusak and "Earthquake" McGovern dropped their 6-ton load in one single run—and still got hit. The losses were accordingly high: 48 planes were shot down over the valley, another 14 were destroyed on the ground at Dien Bien Phu, and 167 were damaged through enemy fire.

---

*The total number of airplanes available in Indochina at the time of the Geneva cease-fire was as follows:

Transports:	75	C-47's until March 1954	*Bombers:* 8 "Privateers"
	25	C-47's rec'd March 1954	60 B-26's until May 1954
	24	C-119's (American crews)	30 B-26's rec'd May 1954
	12	Miscellaneous	
			98
	136		*Recon. & Liaison:* 85 Morane, L-5,
Fighter-Bombers:	112	"Hellcat," "Bearcat,"	Siebel, etc.
		etc.	
Helicopters:	5	in action March 1954	
	14	rec'd later	
	19		*Grand Total:* 450 aircraft

Nothing has thus far been said about the incredible strain of that operation on the air and ground crews of the French Far Eastern Air Force and Naval Aviation. At the height of the battle, in April 1954, many crews logged 150 flying hours.* Dozens of pilots collapsed from exhaustion, but simply were doped up and returned to combat, for experienced pilots rapidly became even scarcer than aircraft. When, in the face of possible diplomatic complications, the American civilian air crews and their C-119's were pulled out on April 24 from the Dien Bien Phu run—they were allowed to return to the run on May 1—there remained only fifty French planes capable of flying the long and exhausting mission.

All in all, the French Air Force in Indochina fulfilled its mission as well as could be expected. What it lacked in matériel it more than made up by the knowledge which most of its pilots possessed of the terrain and meteorology of the country they were flying in, and by the relative absence of friction between the ground and air forces staffs. The latter knew that this was first and foremost a ground war and adjusted its own sights accordingly. Yet, there were many voices among the air force personnel who averred that a greater concentration on strategic targets (rear depots, bridges, ordnance plants) of the enemy would have helped the war effort more than a constant "babying" of the ground troops who—in the view of those pilots—finally expected the air force to do what their own artillery or mortars could probably do just as well.

The ground support defenders replied that the Korean war amply proved how ineffectual even the heavy B-29's were against the rudimentary efficiency and invulnerability of a supply system built largely on human carriers and that even a moderate road cut— most bridges in the Viet-Minh zone were mobile and camouflaged when not in use—cost about 70 tons of bombs. And that was far too expensive in terms of aircraft and pilots diverted from direct-support missions. How ineffectual aerial interdiction, at least with non-nuclear weapons, can be in jungle warfare is best evidenced

---

*Gen. L. M. Chassin, *Aviation Indochine*, Paris 1954, p. 215. This is about three times what is considered normal heavy combat flying. Toward the end of the battle, one whole Navy squadron was pulled out at the request of the Medical Service as no longer fit for flying duty.

by the fact that the French Air Force never succeeded in shutting off the Viet-Minh's major road artery, Road 41 [see map, page 67], leading to Dien Bien Phu, no matter how hard it tried. It even lost a long-range "Privateer" in the attempt.

The French never got around, for lack of adequate aircraft, to using helicopters for other than rescue operations, but they used them in Algeria with a vengeance. In fact, no nation today can claim even remotely to have as much combat experience with helicopters as the French acquired in Algeria—although the French, for understandable reasons, keep that fact out of the news. By the time of the Algerian cease-fire in 1962, the French had concentrated no less than *six hundred* helicopters in that country: 380 troop-carrying craft of the H-34 and Vertol-21 type; 25 medium craft of the S-55 and H-19 type, and about 200 light helicopters mainly of the "Alouette" type. In spite of the fact that the barren hills of Algeria made aerial surveillance a great deal easier than the jungle-covered terrain of Viet-Nam, the results of "heliborne" operations were not overly successful. The Algerian nationalists soon learned about the foibles of the lumbering and noisy craft and quickly developed effective techniques for helicopter-baiting and trapping.

There can be little doubt that the experiences learned by the Algerians in anti-helicopter fighting were passed on to the North Vietnamese (and thence to the "Viet-Cong" now fighting in South Viet-Nam) in the course of visits by Algerian Army officers to Hanoi in 1961 and by Viet-Minh officers to Tunisa in April of the same year. The increasing losses of American helicopters in South Viet-Nam during the later part of 1962 clearly show that the Viet-Minh is rapidly learning its lessons.[*]

On the American side, the B-26 and T-28 remained the South Viet-Nam combat "work-horses" until May, 1964, when they were replaced by the less obsolescent A-1 E "Skyraiders" of Korean War fame. They, in turn, may well be replaced later by a "counter-insurgency airplane" specifically designed for such a mission. The U.S. Air Force understandably seeks to maintain a stake in "little

---

[*]*Author's Note*: This was written six months before, in a well-laid "helicopter trap" precisely following the Algerian pattern, 11 U.S. helicopters were shot down and damaged near Vinh Long, South Viet-Nam, on January 1, 1963.

wars" of the future, particularly in view of the growing importance of Army aviation, and new knowledge about the role of air operations in counter-insurgency is constantly being processed at the Air Force's Special Air Warfare Center at Eglin Air Force Base, Florida.

In any case, the possibility of a growing Communist antiair-craft artillery should neither have been as blissfully ignored as it was, nor underrated in such statements as: ". . . jungle rebels are not equipped with ack-ack or interception capability, so that air superiority is practically assured* . . ." For the Viet-Minh had a respectable antiaircraft capability inside South Viet-Nam as early as October, 1953! As French aircraft found out for themselves (ten had been shot down and 244 hit throughout Indochina in 1953), there was a *Trung-Doi Phong Khong* [anti-aircraft platoon] in the Plain of Reeds, armed with two machineguns and one BAR. And in the Mekong delta near Cantho, a *Dai-Doi Phong Khong* [antiaircraft company], armed with a 20 millimeter cannon, four .50 caliber machineguns, and two BAR's, was making life miser-able for low-flying aircraft. Thus, the high losses of helicopters and slow fixed-wing aircraft in Viet-Nam in 1963-64 should have surprised no one and certainly should not lead to a stampede for the use, in Viet-Nam, of high-performance jet aircraft, whose speed would only add to the already-high inaccuracy and unselectiveness of air support. As a highly authoritative American student of revolutionary warfare wrote recently:

> . . . In a form of warfare in which political considerations regularly outweigh the military, air attacks against "suspected enemy groups" are all too likely to be self-defeating. The loss of support brought on by each innocent man or women killed is likely to far outweigh the possible gain of hard-core rebels eliminated.
>
> The speed of even the slowest fixed-wing aircraft is so great that the pilot has little chance of positively identifying an enemy who is not wearing a distinctive uniform, unless the latter obligingly waves a rifle or shoots at him.**

In South Viet-Nam, where the enemy hardly offers conventional

---

*Claude Witze, "USAF Polishes Its New COIN," *Air Force and Space Digest*, June 1962, p. 49.

**James Eliot Cross, *Conflict in the Shadows*. New York: Doubleday & Co., 1963, p. 77.

aerial targets—contrary to North Viet-Nam, where such targets as bridges, dams, plants and sizable cities exist—the use of massive bomb attacks and napalm drops on villages is not only militarily stupid, but it is inhuman and is likely to backfire very badly on the psychological level. To a village which has been occupied by a VC platoon against its will and whose only suffering at the hands of the Communists was the murder of a rather unpopular village chief, "liberation" through massive napalming and attendant losses of innocent inhabitants (not to speak of all property, stored rice, and even farm animals) will be a hollow joke, indeed. The fact that even the heavily-censored Saigon press has recently complained about the "merciless destruction of unharvested rice fields under a column of armored personnel carriers, or the scorched earth of napalm bombing," (*Saigon Post* editorial, January 10, 1964), is an indication of how serious the problem has become. Official reports for 1963 indicate that a total of 23,500 VC had been killed, of whom 7,500 dead (or 37 percent) "were attributed to the fixed-wing tactical air strikes of the Vietnamese Air Force."[*] One might want to ponder the question: How many of those 7,500 were innocent bystanders?

In jungle war, and even more so in a revolutionary war where ideology plays a key role, the air element is unlikely to be able to play a decisive part. In fact, the air element should make it a point to underline its own limitations to the ground commanders, lest they and their troops develop a false sense of over-reliance on air cover, re-supply, and reconnaissance. Many observers have pointed out that in some cases in South Viet-Nam, this already has happened.

Once more, C-47's, "Bearcats," and B-26's are scouring the skies of Viet-Nam in search of the Viet-Minh. It is the same country, the same enemy, the same kind of war. Only the airplane crews have changed.

The Commando Groups

Lai-Chau, August. Two hundred miles behind Communist lines, a small pocket with about two battalions, one of our last toe-holds

---

[*]*The Observer* (MAAG Viet-Nam weekly), March 21, 1964.

upcountry, among the T'ai tribes. Those wonderful T'ai, tall and graceful, frank and hospitable! Their women wear tightly draped black skirts reaching down to the ankles, and blouses with silver clasps; the various tribes are known by the color of the women's blouses as Black T'ai or White T'ai and there is even one group known as "Polka-Dot T'ai."

Lai-Chau was important for several reasons: it controlled the point of confluence of the Nam Na and the Black River and the shortest road from Red China to Laos. It was also the seat of the T'ai Federation headed by an old T'ai chieftain, Déo Van Long. Lastly, it was an important point for the resupply of the long-range commando groups operating behind Communist lines. There was French commando warfare behind Viet-Minh lines, but like much else good during the Indochina war, it was begun too late and, almost until the end of the war, was fought with too little of everything.

But commando warfare was fought since late in 1951, although it did not receive one single mention in the English-language press. For obvious reasons, much will have to remain unsaid for the time being, but those among us who had the privilege of seeing some of the commandos will forever remember them with admiration. Their official designation was *Groupement de Commandos Mixtes Aéroportés* (Composite Airborne Commando Group) known by its French initials of G.C.M.A. until its name was changed in December 1953 to *Groupement Mixte d'Intervention* (G.M.I.) when it received control of all operations behind enemy lines, whether they were airborne or not.

The G.C.M.A.'s were organized on the basis of the experience gathered during World War II by the European *maquis* and by such Allied long-range penetration groups as the British "Chindits" of General Orde Wingate in Burma, and the United States "Marauders" of Brigadier General Frank D. Merrill. However, contrary to the two Allied groups, the G.C.M.A.'s were not meant to return to bases situated behind our own lines but were to remain permanently in enemy territory. Individual men were to be returned via aircraft from secret landing strips if they were sick or wounded or, as often happened, had simply broken down physically or mentally under the strain of that kind of warfare. In other words, the G.C.M.A.'s were not "raider forces," but guerrilla forces; when the

war ended in Indochina, they were also far larger than both the
Chindits or the Marauders ever had been: by mid-1954, there were
15,000 of them, requiring 300 tons of airborne supplies a month.

The core unit of a commando group was usually up to four
hundred strong, each such group being commanded by two or three
French senior NCO's or perhaps by one lieutenant and a few
NCO's. In some cases, even corporals found themselves at the head
of a whole tribe at war with the Viet-Minh.* As is usually the
case in all armies, the commanders of regular units looked askance
at those "bandits" with whom they were supposed to cooperate,
with the result that the recruitment of French cadres for the
G.C.M.A.'s was very difficult.

For an officer to be posted to them meant losing contact with
his parent unit (and chances for promotion and medals) while
some of the sergeants found themselves saddled with tactical and
supply problems usually assigned majors or lieutenant colonels,
but again without the slightest recognition for their special performance. Hence the recruitment of cadres for the G.C.M.A. was
at first based on a wonderful batch of characters and "trouble-
makers" considered too individualistic by their unit commanders
who were glad to get rid of them that way. Let it be said that the
French Army never bothered to give the corporals or sergeants
who commanded whole guerrilla battalions even fictitious officers'
ranks in order to give them "face" with the tribesmen. The latter
obeyed them on affection alone and on the all-important fact that
they proved themselves equal to the task. Those who did not were
not heard from again. Perhaps this *was* the best way to get capable
guerrilla leaders.

The worst part of the G.C.M.A.'s war was the feeling of psychological isolation. The two or three Frenchmen in the group knew
that they were at the mercy of the lone traitor in their unit, the
one disgruntled tribesman who, ten year ago, had been kicked
around in his village by some French NCO drunk with power
and who now saw his time for revenge. Or he may even have been
a member of the dreaded 421st Intelligence Battalion of the Viet-

---

*See René Riessen's book *Jungle Mission*. A French corporal in the G.C.M.A.,
he organized the Hré tribesmen on the southern mountain plateau. He was later
killed in Algeria, doing a similar job with the Special Administrative Sections
(S.A.S.).

Minh forces, a special unit of the Communists whose job it was to gather information among the tribesmen about the operations of the French-led guerrillas. But there also was the fear of the crippling wound, and that perhaps was worse than the fear of death itself. There were operation areas where a wounded man had to be paddled down-river for three days and nights just to reach the nearest airstrip from which he could be evacuated—if there was a plane, if the weather was right, and if the weak radio sets of the groups had managed to make contact with their Headquarters "outside."

Here is one example of such a rescue operation involving. for once, all the modern paraphernalia available. In 1953, an aircraft with equipment for a G.C.M.A. operating 300 miles inside Communist territory crashed in a down draft near Viet-Nam's highest mountain, the 10,000-foot Fan Si Pan. Since the plane had aboard maps showing the location of some of the guerrilla groups and since some of its crew were alive and would no doubt be subjected to torture to reveal the location of the areas they knew about, it was vital for the French High Command to reach the wreck first. A helicopter was available (which, in itself, was a near-miracle) but its range was, of course, insufficient to reach the crash area in a single hop. Also, its slow and lengthy flight would have revealed its objective to ground observers. In a first move, the helicopter was taken apart and loaded on a "Bristol" freighter plane with frontal clam-shell doors. The plane, with luck, made a perfect landing at Lai-Chau, our airhead behind Communist lines. Then. a paratroop commando group was parachuted midway between the crash area and Lai-Chau on a deserted jungle airstrip where it set up a temporary fuel depot and first-aid station.

The whirlybird then made its leisurely way to the midway station. refueled, and went on to the crash area, where the pilot picked up the three survivors and the important documents. The wounded were transferred to "Morane" liaison planes and flown out, while the paratroops kept the airstrip open in the face of information that Communist troops, aware of the unusual air traffic in the area, were converging on the field; the commando group was picked up by the last liaison planes just in the nick of time.

It is obvious that in the majority of cases, the High Command simply could not afford the luxury of diverting a freighter aircraft, three C-47's, one helicopter and a half-dozen liaison planes, plus an airborne surgical team and a "stick" of paratroop commandos, just to rescue three men. The G.C.M.A.'s just had to carry their wounded until they found a suitable airstrip or until the man died —for to let him fall alive into Communist hands would have meant collective suicide for the group.

Another important psychological factor for the French members of the G.C.M.A. (the fear of being wounded being shared equally by both French and natives) was the "endless tunnel" aspect of the whole operation. To train a man for guerrilla work was long and tedious. If he managed to stay alive for more than a year in his assignment, he usually had learned at least one, or even several, mountain dialects perfectly and had physically adapted to the murderous climate and the food and to the way of life in the jungle. The man had become irreplaceable because of his specialized knowledge, and the better he was the more certain he could be that he would be sent out again and again until his luck ran out, his health broke or his mind cracked up. There were no magical "fifty missions" to look forward to, no end to the ordeal in sight beyond the end of the war itself.

For the native tribesmen, the same problem posed itself in different terms: it was obvious that the French were unable to reconquer the highlands in force; thus, the tribesmen's villages were progressively occupied by the Communists who soon set up in each one of them their own network of spies and agents. In a short time they knew whose husband, father or brother fought for the "French reactionaries and their feudal running-dogs." Whole villages were wiped out in reprisal for the aid they had given the G.C.M.A.'s, without the latter being able to offer them any protection, and soon most villages "went neutral," that is, they impartially informed both sides on what the other side was doing. Tribesmen would desert their commando units when their own families were menaced (and who would blame them?); others would refuse to fight in areas which were too far away from their own native habitat; and yet others would refuse to come to the aid of a unit recruited from a tribe with which they usually had bad relations.

In some areas the G.C.M.A. commander would have to marry the daughter of the local chieftain to insure his loyalty and would have to observe dozens of taboos any violation of which would cost him his life and jeopardize his mission, but which would find a poor reception in Hanoi or Saigon as a reason for the postponement of an operation. All this required a practical knowledge of ethnology and anthropology which could not be acquired in colleges and training camps or manuals, the more so as many of the tribes had never been studied and some of them had not even been discovered until a commando group stumbled over them.

It is difficult to imagine life in such a commando group; only a few diaries were kept and many units disappeared never to be heard from again. But I recall one incident involving a group about 60 miles to the south of Lai-Chau. One day, a man staggered into the CP at Lai-Chau; bearded and ragged, he looked like the proverbial "Christ off the cross." The only things that made him recognizable as a soldier were three tiny tarnished chevrons of a *sergent-chef* and his carbine. His eyes shone with a ghastly flicker in his ashen face.

*"Mon Commandant, je viens pour être passé au 'falot',"** he said to Major Leost, the chief of staff for the area ("Sir, I've come in to report for a court-martial"). And then all composure left him. He broke down on his knees, sobbing, and repeating time after time *"J'ai tué mon copain!"* ("I've killed my buddy.")

As the story was pieced together later, the sergeant had been a commando group leader; he had contracted a severe case of malaria during a previous hitch with the G.C.M.A. but had been found "indispensable" and sent back into the jungle. It was during a malaria attack that upon waking up, he saw his French associate cleaning his carbine by the fire and, imagining in his fever that he was a Viet-Minh, he killed him before he could be subdued by the horrified tribesmen. And there he was now, bearing witness against himself, begging for a trial to punish him for a guilt that

---

Falot is French Army slang for a court-martial.

basically was not his but of the system which made men like him "indispensable."

He was returned to Hanoi for treatment and left the G.C.M.A.

There were also the G.C.M.A.'s who, along with the 6th Parachute Battalion, had been offered up for sacrifice to cover the retreat of 1952.

"You should have seen us. Along the route of retreat of the paratroops, the Viets had planted on bamboo pikes the heads of the soldiers they had killed, like so many milestones. Some of the men went berserk from it, others cried hysterically when they recognized the head of somebody they had known; others just swore softly that they'd kill every Vietnamese they'd find as soon as they got to a Vietnamese village."

"In all probability, the Viets had not even killed prisoners to use their heads, but just had cut off the heads from the men who were already dead. It was nothing but an effective piece of psychological warfare."

They *did* burn down the first Vietnamese village they found.

But as in every tragedy, there were the funny incidents which saved most of the men from insanity. There was the case of a Moroccan in a G.C.M.A. who, suffering from a leg wound, had been carried by his buddies for three-and-a-half days to Lai-Chau. Upon his arrival there, he felt that to spend time "outside" in a hospital bed was a pure waste, and thus he proceeded to hobble off to various places of pleasure on one leg and in his underwear.

Unfortunately for him, he met his buddies who had carried him for days on that jungle path and who, seeing him "walking," felt that he had let himself be carried out of sheer laziness. The upshot fell into three separate parts: 1. he was beaten up by his enraged buddies; 2. returned to the hospital with additional injuries; and 3. upon leaving it, was given ten days in the "jug" for malingering and leaving the hospital out of uniform.

Another interesting experience was that of the T'ai tribesmen of the same G.C.M.A. seeing a movie during their stay in Lai-Chau. French Army film units usually preferred showing several short subjects to an audience whose understanding of French was poor rather than one long feature, feeling (correctly) that interest would be better sustained. Many of those short features came from the U.S. Information Service film libraries, and that particular evening they included, of all things, one on a volunteer fire department in a small town in Illinois.

The tribesmen had seen aircraft and jeeps, and even the French Ford sedan which their chieftain Déo Van Long had the French fly in for him (it took him six months of hard work by several hundred coolies to fix a few hundred yards of road upon which to drive it), but they had never seen anything like the hook-and-ladder assemblies shown in the film. Neither had they ever seen *flat* land with no mountains on the horizon, or asphalted and straight roads. The hook-and-latter rig swaying at 60 mph through the Illinois countryside became probably the greatest film success the T'ai hills had ever seen and for days on end, tribesmen would filter in even from the surrounding Communist-held areas to see the "big American car on the straight road."

USIS and an Illinois fire department have many fast friends in some forgotten villages deep in Communist Vietnamese territory to whom America will forever mean nothing else but a hook-and-ladder truck on a paved road.

How effective were the G.C.M.A.'s? Here, opinions are split. Some of the French regulars would say that if the same amount of equipment, tonnage of air transport and flying hours, not to speak of crack noncoms, had been expended on some of the regular units, more tangible results would have been obtained in defending some important positions in various war theaters.

The proponents of the G.C.M.A., on the other hand, could point to the fact that by April 1954, at least ten Viet-Minh regular battalions were engaged in hunting down commando groups behind their own lines, i. e., doing exactly the same thing the French had been forced to do for so many years—guarding depots and communication lines.

For example, the political commissar of Communist Bn. 700 reported to his superiors in the spring of 1953 in a document that was intercepted by a commando group that—

> . . . the French imperialists have succeeded in leaving behind them their agents who continue to be a nuisance to us. At the beginning

they were only a handful but now, the rebel movement against the Democratic Republic of Viet-Nam has increased . . . in speed of movement as well as in numbers. There must be at least two thousand of them now.

This movement begins to worry us seriously. A large part of our forces is pinned down in mopping-up operations against those rebels . . . The reason for the great extension of the rebel movement and why it succeeds in holding out against us stems from the fact that we are not supported by popular opinion.

By the end of 1953, some G.C.M.A. operations began to assume strategic importance. One of their most brilliant operations was a combined attack on the important enemy supply center of Lao-Kay, a city on the Sino-Vietnamese border, connected by a bridge with its sister city of Coc-Leu on the other side of the river. On October 3, six hundred T'ai and Meo tribesmen raided Coc-Leu, supported by a French paratroop platoon which was dropped in directly over the target; the whole operation being reinforced by an intensive bombardment by B-26's. The enemy was taken by surprise and the raiders destroyed important storage depots and killed or wounded about 150 Communists before making a safe getaway into the mountains. The French paratroopers withdrew with them and were handed back to Lai-Chau from one commando group to another.

The fateful battle of Dien Bien Phu was also the supreme test for the G.C.M.A.'s, and opinions as to their relative efficacy vary radically from expert to expert. On the one hand, there are some hard statistical facts: the 5,000 G.C.M.A.'s, operating in northeastern Laos and adjoining northwestern Viet-Nam, consumed about 200 tons of airborne supplies *a month* and tied down 7 Communist battalions in January 1954, 11 in March, 12 in April, and perhaps as many as 14 in May 1954.* The 15,094 men encircled at Dien Bien Phu consumed 200 tons of airborne supplies *per day* and immobilized 28 infantry battalions. In addition to tying down Viet troops, say the G.C.M.A.'s supporters, the French-led guerrillas for all practical purposes reconquered the two Laotian provinces of Phong-Saly and Samneua all by themselves and interdicted the most direct route between Lai-Chau and

---

*Col. Roger Trinquier, *Modern Warfare: A French View of Counterinsurgency*. New York: Praeger, 1963.

Dien Bien Phu throughout the duration of the siege. They also acted as a screen for the French "Condor Force" which sought to break through to Dien Bien Phu (cf. chapter 12), and, after the loss of the fortress, rescued 76 of its men. All this is absolutely true—but it is not the whole story.

The adversaries of the G.C.M.A. concept reply that the expense of highly-specialized officers and noncoms, and of radio sets and special weapons, might well have beefed up several "regular" sectors to the point where they could have resisted rather well to Communist infiltration. But the biggest argument against it is the crucial fact that the G.C.M.A. dismally failed in cutting the extremely vulnerable 800 kilometer-long Communist supply line from Lang-Son to Dien Bien Phu. *That,* so the anti-guerrilla experts say, was the one and only task which the G.C.M.A.'s should have performed at all costs. They never even came near that lifeline, thanks to efficient Viet-Minh counter-measures of which we are to this day blissfully ignorant, to judge from the miserable performance given by anti-Communist forces in South Viet-Nam when it comes to protecting road and rail communications.

In Laos also, American-led Meo tribesmen fought a G.C.M.A.-type war since 1960. Here again, the ardent supporters of special operations will cite the fact that the Meos remained largely undestroyed as proof of the efficacy of the concept, while its detractors will point to the overall fact that the West *lost* Laos as proof that (a) guerrillas are not a strategic weapon; and (b) that guerrilla training is definitely not a substitute for a proper ideological reason for fighting.* I personally tend to agree with the latter view.

The most likely conclusion is that the G.C.M.A.'s were designed for a mission of guerrilla warfare which they fulfilled well, but not for one of raiding against well organized forces, which would have required a level of tactical training and coordination that

---

*In a book that has stirred up much comment in France, Gilles Perrault's *Les Parachutistes,* the author cites damning evidence to show the inefficacy of the paratroops (Crete, Sicily, Normandy, Arnhem, Dien Bien Phu) and asserts that the *real* revolutionary warfare successes stem from mass movements and not from highly specialized military units. That assertion deserves most serious further study.

could not reasonably be expected from primitive tribesmen. On the other hand, anyone who had ever come into contact with the Meo and the T'ai, or the Moi of the southern plateau area, could not help but admire them for their friendliness and steadfastness and also for their fidelity to the French.

The French, like the British in Burma, had treated the minority tribes with more decency than they had ever been treated by the majority population of their own country, thus saving them from the fate of the Plains Indian in America. Asian nationalists will explain this as part of the "imperialistic divide-and-rule" policy, and perhaps it was, but the hard fact remains that, to this very day, a Frenchman is always well received in a tribesman's hut. Schools, vaccinations, a few brick kilns and a bit of human friendship are

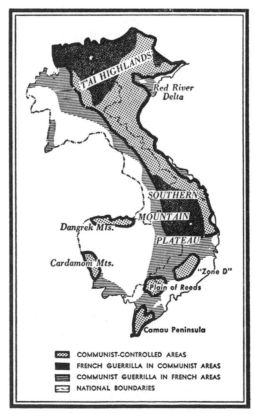

Guerrilla Warfare in Indochina (1953-54).

nothing to apologize for, no matter what their rationales may have been.

The cease-fire of July 1954 also brought an end to G.C.M.A. operations. Frantic efforts were made by the French to broadcast messages to all the groups operating behind Communist lines to fall back to Laos, the 17th parallel, or to the shrinking Haiphong perimeter before the Bamboo Curtain rang down on them for good. But for many, the broadcasts came too late, or the T'ai or Meo could not reconcile themselves to leave their families exposed to the Communist reprisals which now were sure to come. And the Frenchmen who were with them and who could not possibly make their way back across hundreds of miles of enemy territory, stayed with them, to fight with the tribesmen to the end.

This was a fight to the finish, and no quarter was given on either side. One by one, as the last commandos ran out of ammunition, as the last still operating radio sets fell silent, the remnants of the G.C.M.A. died in the hills of North Viet-Nam. There was no "U-2" affair, no fuss: France did not claim the men, and the Communists were content to settle the matter by themselves. French officers recalled with a shudder the last radio message picked up from somewhere in North Viet-Nam nearly two years after the fighting had officially stopped. The voice was a French voice and the message was addressed to the French. It said:

"You sons-of-bitches, help us! Help us! Parachute us at least some ammunition, so that we can die fighting instead of being slaughtered like animals!"

But the cease-fire was in effect and the last French troops left Indochina in April 1956, in compliance with the demands of the Vietnamese nationalists. Yet the few remaining G.C.M.A.'s kept on fighting. No less an authoritative source that the Communists' own weekly *Quan-Doi Nhan-Dan* ("People's Army") of September 3, 1957 reported that from July 1954 to April 1956 their forces in the mountain areas east of the Red River had, "in spite of great difficulties and hardships," killed 183 and captured 300 "enemy soldiers," while inducing the surrender of 4,336 tribesmen and capturing 3,796 weapons. Some of the luckier tribesmen, such as the Muong and Nung who were closer to the French lines, made their way to South Viet-Nam and are now resettled in the southern hills near Dalat, in a setting and climate very close to that of their beloved T'ai country. Others continue to trickle into neighboring Laos, whose own mountain tribes are their close relatives.

By 1959, the struggle was over. The mountaineers were thoroughly purged of all "reactionary" elements and whatever Frenchmen there had been left among them were now dead or captured. Only one Frenchman, Captain C———, who was thoroughly familiar with several mountain dialects, is known to have made his way out of the Communist-occupied zone after a harrowing 500-mile trek through the mountains from tribe to tribe. And thus ended the French experiment of anti-Communist guerrilla warfare in Indochina.

But if there really is somewhere in the Great Beyond a Valhalla where warriors gather, I hope that it will reserve a small niche in a shaded place under a canopy of high trees for the sacrificed tribesmen and their French comrades from the Composite Airborne Commando Groups.

The Foreign Legion

Much has been said about the French Foreign Legion in Indochina, most of which was inaccurate or malicious. One of the widest spread canards was that "the Foreign Legion is doing all the fighting." The fact was that units of the Foreign Legion had been in much of the heaviest fighting but had no exclusive "corner" on it. General de Négrier's stupid and pompous phrase of the Tonkinese campaign of 1884: "Legionnaires, you are here in order to die and I shall send you where one dies," influenced many minds, particularly in Anglo-Saxon countries. The hard statistical fact was that out of a total number of about 40,000 men in the Foreign Legion, there were seldom more than about 20,000 in Indochina —and the French Union Forces counted 278,000 men.

The second canard, spread with equal ardor by American, German and Communist sources, was that "the whole Foreign Legion is German*," with the sub-variant that all those Germans were at least SS generals and other much wanted war criminals. Here, the hard facts were as follows. As a rule, and in order to prevent

---

*In the U.S., a statement to the effect that "80 percent" of the Foreign Legion was German and was doing all the fighting, appeared in *The Commonweal* over the signature of an American general of German origin.

any particular nation from making the Legion into a Praetorian guard, any particular national component is kept at about 25 percent of the total. Even supposing (and this was the case, of course) that the French recruiters, in their eagerness for candidates, would sign up Germans enlisting as Swiss, Austrians, Scandinavians and other nationalities of related ethnic background, it is unlikely that the number of Germans in the Foreign Legion ever exceeded 35 percent. Thus, without making an allowance for losses, rotations, discharges, etc., the maximum number of Germans fighting in Indochina at any one time reached perhaps 7,000 out of 278,000. As to the ex-Nazis, the early arrivals contained a number of them, none of whom were known to be war criminals; French intelligence saw to that.

Since, in view of the rugged Indochinese climate, older men without previous tropical experience constituted more of a liability than an asset, the average age of the Legion enlistees was about 23. At the time of the battle of Dien Bien Phu, any Legionnaire of that age group was, at the worst, in his "Hitler Youth" shorts when the 3d Reich collapsed. As for the principle of using foreign nationals in one's armed forces, it is almost as old as warfare itself; on the contrary, the principle of the single-nationality armed force is quite new and more often than not observed in the breach.

The United States *drafts* foreign residents even in peacetime, (a practice which has given rise to protests by various foreign governments, most recently the Swiss), and the Lodge Act passed by Congress on June 30, 1950, allows up to 12,500 foreign nationals to enlist in the United States Forces, with the one difference that in the French Army non-naturalized foreigners may attain full colonel's rank while in the U.S., they cannot become officers. In recent years, the Foreign Legion had two Swiss regimental commanders, Henri de Corta and Albert de Tscharner (the latter becoming a full colonel in the Swiss Army after retiring from the Legion), and such crowned heads as the King of Denmark and Prince Rainier of Monaco served as officers in the French Army.

Far from being a repository of wanted criminals and mercenaries, the Legion in recent years has been a haven for many displaced persons from Soviet satellite countries for whom the Legion has been a way to a new existence, for any Foreign Legionnaire is entitled to French citizenship upon his discharge. Every wave of political persecution has left its sea-mark on the Legion: Poles persecuted by Czarist Russia prior to World War I, Russian noblemen fleeing the Bolsheviks after 1917 (until 1941 there even was a Tcherkess Cossack cavalry regiment in the French Army in Syria!); then the Jewish refugees from Central Europe fighting against Hitler; followed, ironically enough, by the Nazis and other Germans fleeing the collapse of their home land.* The most recent wave brought in some of the Hungarian freedom fighters of 1956.

In the Legion, no one has a "nationality"—one is a Legionnaire, first and foremost. As the Legion's motto says: *Legio patria nostra* . . . "The Legion is our Fatherland"—and for many it became their grave. A total of 11,710 men and officers of the Foreign Legion died in Indochina from 1945 to 1954.

A unit of the Foreign Legion had to be seen to be believed. When I saw the 3d *Régiment Etranger d'Infanterie* (REI, or Foreign Infantry Regiment) quartered in the fortress-like Spanish monastery at Bac-Ninh, North Viet-Nam, it was still its splendid old self, and not the battered ghost it was after Dien Bien Phu.

A lunch at the officers' mess was a ceremony all of itself, with every detail regulated by century-old ceremonial repeated where-ever there is a Foreign Legion outfit. First, every officer present poured a mouthful of wine into his glass, rose from his chair with the raised glass and repeated in chorus: "To our friends who are in the sands." Then every man drank down the gulp and slammed the glass on the table. That was in memory of the Legion's desert fighting traditions and is called "shaking the sand out of the glass."

Then, called to attention by the senior officer present, they sang the never-to-be-forgotten unnervingly slow marching song of the Foreign Legion, much slower than the normal marching pace since in the desert sands one must take slower but longer strides. It was the song about the blood sausage that was there for

---

*In his book *Histoire de Vichy*, Robert Aron tells the story of the two German Legionnaires sitting together in a French jail in Algiers, one for being a Nazi spy asking to be returned to the then-winning Wehrmacht; the other for being an anti-Nazi, caught by the Vichy authorities in the process of deserting to General de Gaulle.

the Alsatians, the Swiss and the Lorrainers" but not for the Belgians who are *"des tireurs-au-cul"*—shirkers.

After that part of the ceremonial, everyone sat down save the youngest officer who now read the birthdays of the day, congratulated the officers concerned, then read off the day's menu, wished everybody a healthy appetite, and ended the ceremonial by a rousing *"Vive la Legion!"*

The food was about as good as in an excellent Paris restaurant, but the colonel apologized that he had been unable so far to obtain a chef from the Ritz ("the 1st Regiment got the last one who enlisted") but that the Italian chef they had ("from a first-class establishment in Milan; he had beaten up his wife's boyfriend") was really trying his best. A freckle-faced young lieutenant at the lower end of the table turned out to be Pierre Juin, the son of Marshal Juin, the senior officer in the French Army.

As in most army messes the world over, the conversation turned from women to shop talk. One of the battalion commanders spoke of a group of three villages which had been giving him trouble.

"There's no further sense in telling 'em not to trade buffaloes with the Viets and, to top it all, they're very sassy. We get shot at every time we pass by on the highway and I don't feel like losing a good platoon for the sake of mopping up a bunch of mud huts. Let's get the Air Force into this and just wipe 'em off the map."

The operations officer nodded. With his gray eyes and crew cut, he looked very American.

"We'll get *Torricelli* this afternoon and see what they can do (*Torricelli* was the code name for the northern Air Force Headquarters). A flight of B-26's ought to do the job and will get the place properly 'bikinized.' "

Various points of detail were still discussed, but the main point had been agreed upon between the dessert and the coffee. Scratch three villages with their sassy civilian population.

But the Legion fought on and fought well to the bitter end. To be sure, some Legionnaires deserted to the enemy. Ho Chi Minh's adoptive son, Ho Chi Long, was originally such a German deserter, and a few others were repatriated by the enemy to East

"Tiens, voilà du boudin . . ."

FOREIGN LEGION MARCHING SONG
("Here's the Blood Sausage")

I

In Tonking, the immortal Legion
Covered with glory our flag at Tuyen-Quang.
Heroes of Camerone, model brothers
Sleep in peace in your graves.

II

In the course of our faraway campaigns,
Facing fevers, and bullets,
Let us forget, along with our sorrows,
Death, which never forgets us.

Refrain

Here's the blood sausage,
    the blood sausage, the blood sausage,
For the Alsatians, the Swiss, and
    the Lorrainers,
There's none left for the Belgians (bis)
'Cause they're shirkers.

THE VIET-CONG BLUES

[To be sung on a standard "blues" air]

Note: This is the first American military song to come out of the Second Indochina War. It was sung by the Special Forces Team of 1/Lt. John P. Dooley. Courtesy of CBS Radio Network.

I

The Viet-Cong is comin'
They just keep movin' on.
If we don't stop 'em soon,
They gonna' take Saigon.

II

But President Diem
And Madame Nhu
Said: "Special Forces Soldiers,
"No more twisting for you."

III

Got a dirty mess kit
And a hole in my canteen
Met the Viet-Cong yesterday
Got a bullet in my spleen.

IV

Got a special mission
We just train 'em and advise
But if we don't do some shooting
We gonna' have a quick demise.

Refrain

I've got the Viet-Cong Blues
Got bamboo spikes in my tennis shoes.

Germany via Red China and the Soviet Union where they were used for a time to make propaganda against the Indochina war.

The Legion's finest hour came with Dien Bien Phu, where six of its battalions constituted one-third of the garrison*. It fell upon the 3d Battalion of the 13th Foreign Legion Half-Brigade to be the very last unit to go down fighting. Isolated in a strongpoint 2.5 miles south of Dien Bien Phu, it had watched the agony of the fortress, had fired its last heavy artillery ammunition onto the center of the fort itself and then braced itself for the final onslaught.

As the night fell over Dien Bien Phu that Friday evening, May 7, 1954, the men of the 3/13th could see the waves of enemy infantry surge toward them. Methodically they went about their business of destroying all the useless weapons and of caring for their wounded; and in the early dawn, led by their commander, Colonel Lalande, the Legionnaires fixed bayonets in the ghostly light of the parachute flares and—600 against 40,000—walked into death.

Sidi-bel-Abbès, Algeria—Quartier Viénot, Headquarters of the Foreign Legion, May 8, 1954. The voice of Colonel Gardy barely trembled as he read the order of the day.

> . . . We are gathered here to commemorate the heroes who fell in that epic struggle. Let us present the honors to the flags of our units which have disappeared in battle:
> —The 13th Half-Brigade of the Foreign Legion, its regimental service units and its 1st and 3d Battalions;
> —The 1st Battalion, 2d Foreign Legion;
> —The 1st and 2d Foreign Paratroop Battalions;
> —The Mortar Companies of the 3d and 5th Foreign Legion, and the numerous volunteers of other Foreign Legion units dropped into the fortress during the siege . . .

In silent rows, their white kepis and crimson epaulets shining in the sun, the men stood ramrod straight. The bugle's notes

---

*Of the other units, there were two T'ai battalions, one Vietnamese paratroop battalion, four French paratroop battalions, two battalions of Algerians and one of Moroccan infantry, plus French artillery, armor, and service personnel. Yet even General Ridgway, who ought to know better, states in his memoirs that the garrison of Dien Bien Phu was made up "mainly from the mercenaries of the French Foreign Legion."

reverberated from the ochre barracks walls as it played the poignant notes of ". . . *aux Morts.*"

The Foreign Legion had fought its last battle in Indochina.

A last chapter of the Foreign Legion's colorful history in Asia was written, in, of all places, the drab surroundings of an Israeli Navy court-martial in May 1958.

The defendant was a 25-year old man, in the neat white uniform of the Israeli enlisted seaman. Eliahu Itzkovitz was charged with desertion from the Israeli Navy, but his case was not an ordinary one, for he had deserted from a peacetime hitch in Haifa to a twenty-seven months ordeal with the Foreign Legion in Indochina.

Eliahu had grown up in a small town in eastern Rumania when the country threw in its lot with the Nazis at the beginning of World War II. Soon, the Rumanian *Conductorul* (the "Leader") Antonescu began to emulate all the tactics of the Nazis, his own version of the Brownshirts calling itself the "Iron Guard" and practicing mass murder on a large scale. In fact, according to the British writer Edward Crankshaw in his book *Gestapo,* they "offended the Germans on the spot by not troubling to bury their victims; and they offended the R.S.H.A.* by their failure to keep proper records and by their uncontrolled looting."

The Itzkovitz family did not escape the collective fate of the Rumanian Jews. Eliahu and his parents and three brothers were sent to a concentration camp, no better and no worse than most Eastern European camps; one lived a few days to a few weeks and died from a wide variety of causes, mostly beating and shooting. Rumanian camps were not as well equipped as their German models, the "death factories" of Auschwitz and Treblinka with their sophisticated gas chambers. Again, according to Crankshaw, "the Rumanians showed a great aptitude for mass murder and conducted their own massacres in Odessa and elsewhere," and the Itzkovitz family paid its price—within a short time, only Eliahu, the youngest boy, survived.

But he had seen his family die, and he had remembered who

---

*R.S.H.A.—Reichs-Sicherheitshauptamt, the administrative section of the Nazi police in charge of mass exterminations.

killed it. It had been one particular brute, not the coldly efficient SS-type but a Rumanian from a town not too far away from his own home town and who enjoyed his new job. And Eliahu swore that he would kill the man, if it took all his life to do it. More than anything else, it was probably that hatred which kept him alive; he was a skeleton but a living one when the Russians liberated him in 1944. Eliahu then began his patient search from town to town. Of course, Stanescu (or whatever name the brute had assumed in the meantime) had not returned to his home town for good reasons, but Eliahu found his son there and took his first revenge; he stabbed the son with a butcher knife and in 1947, a Rumanian People's Court sentenced him to five years in a reformatory for juveniles.

Eliahu served his time but did not forget. His family's murderer was still at large and he had sworn to kill him. In 1952, he was finally released and given permission by the Communist authorities to emigrate to Israel, where he was drafted into the Israeli army in 1953 and assigned to the paratroops. Training was rigorous in the sun-drenched barracks and stubby fields south of Rehovoth, and thoughts of revenge had become all but a dim memory. There was a new life to be lived here, among the people from all corners of the world who still streamed in and who, from Germans, Poles, Indians, Yemenites or Rumanians, became Israelis. To be sure, Eliahu still met some of his Rumanian friends and talk often rotated back to the "old country," to the war and the horrors of the persecution. Camps and torturers were listed matter-of-factly, like particularly tough schools or demanding teachers, and Stanescu came up quite naturally.

"That s.o.b. made it. He got out in time before the Russians could get him," said a recent arrival, "then he fled to West Germany and tried to register as a D.P. but they got wise to him and before we could report him, he was gone again."

Eliahu's heart beat had stopped for an instant, and when it resumed its normal rhythm, he had shaken off the torpor of peacetime army life. The hunt was on again.

"Do you know where Stanescu went then? Do you have any idea at all?"

"Well—somebody said that he had gone to Offenburg in the French Zone, where they recruit people for the French Foreign Legion, and that he enlisted for service in Indochina. The French are fighting there, you know."

On the next day, Eliahu's mind was made up. He reported to his commanding officer and applied for transfer to the Israeli Navy; he liked the sea, had learned something about it while in Rumania, which borders on the Black Sea, and would be happier aboard ship than as a paratrooper. A few days later, the request was granted and Eliahu was on his way to the small force of Israeli corvettes and destroyers based in Haifa. A few months later, the opportunity he had been waiting for came true; his ship was assigned to go to Italy to pick up equipment.

In Genoa, Seaman Itzkovitz applied for shore leave and simply walked off the ship; took a train to Bordighera and crossed over to Menton, France, without the slightest difficulty. Three days later, Eliahu had signed his enlistment papers in Marseilles and was en route to Sidi-bel-Abbès, Algeria, the headquarters and boot camp of the Foreign Legion, and again three months later, he was aboard the s/s *Pasteur* on his way to Indochina.

Once in the Foreign Legion, Stanescu's trail was not too hard to pick up. While no unit was made up of any single nationality, each unit would have its little groups and informal clans according to language or nation of origin. It took patience, but early in 1954, he had located his quarry in the 3d Foreign Legion Infantry. The last step was the easiest; the Foreign Legion generally did not object if a man requested a transfer in order to be with his friends, and Eliahu's request to be transferred to Stanescu's battalion came through in a perfectly routine fashion. When Eliahu saw Stanescu again after ten years, he felt no particular wave of hatred, as he had somehow expected. After having spent ten years imagining the moment of meeting the killer of his family eye to eye, the materialization of that moment could only be an anti-climax. Stanescu had barely changed; he had perhaps thinned down a bit in the Legion; as for Eliahu, he had been a frightened boy of thirteen and was now a strapping young man, bronzed from his two years of training with the Israeli paratroopers, the Navy and the French Foreign Legion.

There was nothing left to do for Eliahu but to arrange a suitable occasion for the "execution;" for in his eyes the murder of Stanescu would be an execution. Stanescu (his name was, of course, no longer that) had become a corporal, and led his squad competently. The new arrival also turned out to be a competent soldier, a bit taciturn perhaps, but good. In fact, he was perhaps better trained than the run of the mill that came out of "Bel-Abbès" these days. He was a good man to have along on a patrol.

And it was on a patrol that Stanescu met his fate, in one of the last desperate battles along Road 18, between Bac-Ninh and Seven Pagodas. He and Eliahu had gone on a reconnaissance into the bushes on the side of the road, when the Viet-Minh opened fire from one hundred yards away. Both men slumped down into the mud. There was no cause for fear: the rest of the squad was close by on the road and would cover their retreat. Eliahu was a few paces to the side and behind Stanescu.

"Stanescu!" he called out.

Stanescu turned around and stared at Eliahu, and Eliahu continued in Rumanian:

"You are Stanescu, aren't you?"

The man, the chest of his uniform black from the mud in which he had been lying, looked at Eliahu more in surprise than in fear. For all he knew, Eliahu might have been a friend of his son, a kid from the neighborhood back home in Chisinau.

"Yes, but . . ."

"Stanescu," said Eliahu in a perfectly even voice, "I'm one of the Jews from Chisinau," and emptied the clip of his MAT-49 tommy gun into the man's chest. He dragged the body back to the road: a Legionnaire never left a comrade behind.

"Tough luck," said one of the men of the platoon sympathetically. "He was a Rumanian just like you, wasn't he?"

"Yes," said Eliahu, "just like me."

The search had ended and the deed was done. Eliahu was now at peace with himself and the world. He served out his time with the Legion, received his papers certifying that "he had served with Honor and Fidelity" and mustered out in France. There was nothing left for him to do but to go home to Israel. The Israeli

Armed Forces attaché in Paris at first refused to believe the incredible story, but the facts were soon verified with the French authorities and a few weeks later Eliahu was on his way to Israel. At Haifa, two Israeli M.P.'s, perfect copies of their British models with their glistening white canvas belts and pistol holsters, took charge of him and soon the gates of Haifa military prison closed behind him.

The three Israeli Navy judges rose. Seaman Itzkovitz stood stiffly at attention as the presiding judge read out the judgment.

> ". . . and in view of the circumstances of the case, a Court of the State of Israel cannot bring itself to impose a heavy sentence. . . . One year's imprisonment . . ."

But the Legion as a separate corps never recovered its old stature after the Indochina war. Too many of its best men had died there. Beefed up with Hungarian refugees after 1956, it became more and more embroiled in the political by-play of the Algerian war.

Operating side by side in Algeria with French Army draftee units which it considered with cold contempt, it withdrew more and more into itself, developing into a "Praetorian Guard" which obeyed its own officers rather than the French Army as such. The final break came in April 1961, when the elite 1st Foreign Legion Parachute Regiment backed the abortive putsch of General Salan against the French government in Paris. Repression was swift and terrible: the commander of the Foreign Legion, General Gardy— the same who, in 1954, had eulogized the Foreign Legion units annihilated at Dien Bien Phu—was sentenced to death in absentia; dozens of other Legion officers were tried and some executed before firing squads; and the 1st *Régiment Etranger Parachutiste* was disbanded. The Legion paratroopers went into oblivion in proper Legion fashion: as they were carried off from Camp Zéralda in army trucks, the whole camp—thoroughly mined and booby-trapped—collapsed in flame and smoke.

One year later, the Legionnaires grimly went about their business of withdrawing from now-independent Algeria, carefully packing away their hallowed relics and shell-torn battle flags for their move to the Legion's new quarters at Aubagne, near Marseilles on the French Mediterranean coast. The very survival of the Legion was at stake now. Rumor had it that President de Gaulle himself, incensed at the role Legion units and individual members had played in opposing him, desired to disband the whole corps. In any case, gone were the open vistas of the Sahara; the jungle hills of Viet-Nam; the narrow, secretive streets of the Algerian Casbah; and the prestige of a full-dress retreat parade at the Legion's headquarters barracks at Sidi-bel-Abbès.

As of 1964, the Legion slowly adapted to its peacetime role. Independent Madagascar accepted a Legion battalion under its defense agreement with France. Another battalion was to go to the jungles of French Guiana, to hack out roads into the unexplored interior. In Corsica, a Legion battalion and the U.S. Marines from the Sixth Fleet fought a mock war in May, 1963 [no one ever dared announce *who* won]; and the 5th Foreign Legion Regiment was reactivated to go to the French Pacific Islands to participate in the constructio nand protection of France's budding H-Bomb test base.

The twentieth century was catching up with the Foreign Legion.

Sometimes, there occurs an almost irrelevant incident which, in the light of later developments, seems to have been a sign of the gods, a dreamlike warning which, if heeded, could have changed fate—or so it seems.

One such incident occurred to me in October 1953 in Cambodia, at Siem-Réap, not far away from the fabulous temples of Angkor-Wat. I had been in the field with the 5th Cambodian Autonomous Infantry Company and was now in need of transportation back to Phnom-Penh, the capital of Cambodia. Siem-Réap, a quiet and pleasant little place with two hotels catering to the tourist trade and a few French archeologists working around the ruins of Angkor, might as well have been a small garrison town in southern France, such as Avignon or Nîmes.

A few French officers were still around, mainly as advisers to the newly-independent Cambodian Army. Their chores were light; there were no Communists in the area and the handful of obsolescent "Renault" trucks and World War II-type weapons needed a minimum of maintenance and care. An assignment to Siem-Réap was as good a sinecure as could be found in Indochina in October 1953 and the officers made the most of it.

When I went to the Transportation Office that afternoon at 1530, the Cambodian orderly told me apologetically that *"le Lieutenant est allé au mess jouer au tennis avec le Capitaine"* and that they might well stay there for the rest of the afternoon. Since a convoy which I expected to catch was supposed to leave at dawn, I decided to stroll over to the mess in order to get my travel documents signed there.

The Siem-Réap officers' mess was a pleasant and well-kept place; with its wide Cambodian-type verandahs, its parasol-shaded tables and the well-manicured lawns and beautifully red-sanded tennis court, it was an exact replica of all the other colonial officers' messes from Port Said to Singapore, Saigon or even Manila, wherever the white man had set his foot in the course of building his ephemeral empires.

I found the two officers at the tennis court, in gleaming white French square-bottomed shorts (no one in Europe would be caught dead in the ungainly Bermuda pants called "shorts" in the United States), matching Lacoste tennis shirts and knee-long socks. Their skins had lost the unhealthy pallor of the jungle and taken on the handsome bronze of the vacationer engaging in outdoor sports; their wives, seated at a neighboring table, were beautifully groomed and wore deceptively simple (but, oh, so expensive!) cotton summer dresses clearly showing the hand of a Paris designer. Both officers played in the easy style of men who knew each other's game and were bent less on winning than on getting the fun and exercise of it. Three Cambodian servants, clad in impeccable white slacks and shirts, stood respectfully in the shadow of the verandah, awaiting the call of one of the officers or women for a new cool drink.

Since the men were in the midst of a set and I had little else to do, I sat down at a neighboring table after a courteous bow to the ladies and watched the game, gladly enjoying the atmosphere of genteel civility and forgetting for a moment the war. At the next table, the two women kept up the rapid-fire chatter which French women are prone to use when men are present. The two men also kept up a conversation of sorts, interrupted regularly by the "plop-plop" of the tennis ball.

Then emerged from the verandah a soldier in French uniform. His small stature, brown skin and Western-type features showed him to be a Cambodian. He wore the blue field cap with the golden anchor of the *Troupes Coloniales*—the French "Marines"—and the three golden chevrons of a master-sergeant. On his chest above the left breast pocket of his suntan regulation shirt were three rows of multi-colored ribbons: *croix de guerre* with four citations, campaign ribbons with the clasps of France's every colonial campaign since the Moroccan pacification of 1926; the Italian campaign of 1943 and the drive to the Rhine of 1945. In his left hand, he carried several papers crossed diagonally with a tri-colored ribbon; travel orders, like mine, which also awaited the signature of one of the officers.

He remained in the shadow of the verandah's awnings until the officers had interrupted their game and had joined the two women with their drinks, then strode over in a measured military step, came stiffly to attention in a military salute, and handed the orders for himself and his squad to the captain. The captain looked up in surprise, still with a half-smile on his face from the remark he had made previously. His eyes narrowed suddenly as he understood that he was being interrupted. Obviously, he was annoyed but not really furious.

"Sergeant, you can see that I'm busy. Please wait until I have time to deal with your travel orders. Don't worry. You will have them in time for the convoy."

The sergeant stood stiffly at attention, some of his almost white hair glistening in the sun where it peeked from under the cap, his wizened face betraying no emotion whatever.

"*A vos ordres, mon Capitaine.*" A sharp salute, a snappy about face. The incident was closed, the officers had had their drink and now resumed their game.

The sergeant resumed his watch near where the Cambodian messboys were following the game, but this time he had squatted down on his haunches, a favorite Cambodian position of repose which would leave most Europeans with partial paralysis for several hours afterwards. Almost without moving his head, he attentively followed the tennis game, his travel orders still tightly clutched in his left hand.

The sun began to settle behind the trees of the garden and a slight cooling breeze rose from the nearby Lake Tonlé-Sap, Cambodia's inland sea. It was 1700.

All of a sudden, there rose behind the trees, from the nearby French camp, the beautiful bell-clear sounds of a bugle playing "lower the flag"—the signal which, in the French Army, marks the end of the working day as the colors are struck.

Nothing changed at the tennis court; the two officers continued to play their set, the women continued their chatter, and the mess-boys their silent vigil.

Only the old sergeant had moved. He was now standing stiffly at attention, his right hand raised to the cap in the flat-palmed salute of the French Army, facing in the direction from which the bugle tones came; saluting, as per regulations, France's tricolor hidden behind the trees. The rays of the setting sun shone upon the immobile brown figure, catching the gold of the anchor and of the chevrons and of one of the tiny metal stars of his ribbons.

Something very warm welled up in me. I felt like running over to the little Cambodian who had fought all his life for my country, and apologizing to him for my countrymen here who didn't care about him, and for my countrymen in France who didn't even care about *their* countrymen fighting in Indochina . . .

And in one single blinding flash, I *knew* that we were going to lose the war.

11

Death March

WHEN the Indochina war ended on July 20, 1954, the exchange of all prisoners of war held by both parties was part of the cease-fire agreement. Thousands of members of the "Viet-Nam People's Army" (VPA) who, over the past eight years, had been captured by French Union troops, were repatriated. Interned in regular PW camps inspected by the International Red Cross, their physical condition bore eloquent evidence of the adequate treatment they had received while in French Union hands. They were brought to the transfer points in army trucks or river craft.

French Union prisoners returned from VPA captivity on foot, with the exception of the litter cases. The exchange began officially on August 18, 1954 (although by an act of clemency on the part of the VPA High Command, severely wounded French PW's had been released earlier), and soon two factors became clear: there were not going to be as many French returnees as expected, and most of those who returned were walking skeletons in no way different from those who survived Dachau and Buchenwald. In order not to jeopardize the chances of return of certain civilian and military prisoners who might still be in Communist camps, the French Union High Command made a deliberate effort to play down the fate and state of those prisoners who had returned alive to French lines, but a high level group of French military surgeons and medical specialists was called to investigate the exact facts. Those facts which emerged from the painstaking interrogation of thousands of returnees, in addition to those gathered from civilians on the spot and from books published by survivors, give a picture of the Vietnamese Communist attitude towards prisoners of war and military medicine that needs be known in the West, since future complications in the area may compel conflict with the same foe once more under similar conditions.

Since the Indochina war began as an insurrection against the French, the Communist forces at first operated on a hit-and-run basis. Even prior to the outbreak of hostilities they had held several hundred French civilians, including women and children, as hostages. These hostages, along with whatever military prisoners were in their hands in December 1946, were hurried off into the mountains of northwestern Viet-Nam. Needless to say, such a period of fluid operations by irregulars is most dangerous to their prisoners, for the temptation is always present to get rid of these useless consumers who generally slow down operations and pose special security problems. Likewise, the inhospitable climate (temperatures in the uplands drop to freezing in the winter and in the summer the area is acutely malarial) operated its own weeding-out process, particularly on the civilian prisoners. Deliberate killings, however, were not numerous, as the live hostages were considered good for bargaining. Quite a few of them acclimated well and survived their ordeal in surprisingly good condition.

Actual PW camps began to be organized when the ill-fated battles of October 1950 along the Red Chinese border brought the first batch of several thousand prisoners into VPA hands. From 1950 until the end of 1953, all PW's were considered as ordinary prisoners, *regardless of their state of health or their wounds.* French medical officers captured with the troops were sent to Camp No. 1, the officers' camp, almost never being able to administer even first aid to the most urgent cases prior to their separation from their men.

The results of this policy were inevitable, and clearly show up in the wound statistics of the returnees: *not a single PW with injuries of the abdomen, chest or skull survived Communist captivity.* This does not, of course, include those who were lucky enough to be flown directly from the battle field of Dien Bien Phu during the brief local truce arranged for this purpose in May 1954. In most cases, the serious casualties either died on the battle field or within a few days after capture, relieved only by the inexpert medical attention of their own comrades. In the camps themselves, the

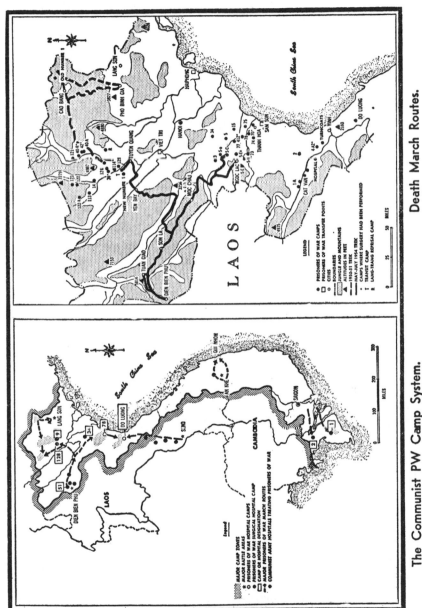

Death March Routes.

The Communist PW Camp System.

VPA maintained an "infirmary," equipped at best with some anti-malaria tablets and a lancet or two, and staffed with a medical attendant of indefinite training.

Occasionally, depending upon the whim of the local VPA commander, some PW's were transported to VPA mobile field hospitals for treatment. But even in those cases, the cure was often worse than the illness, for the PW's, if they survived harrowing portages of hundreds of kilometers on bamboo stretchers, were often left for months without adequate treatment. There are authenticated cases (with photos which would take a fitting place in a museum of horrors) where soldiers were left for eight months with unconsolidated compound fractures, the resulting osteomyelitis being cleaned out without anesthesia. One Foreign Legionnaire marched for 24 days with an arm smashed by machine-gun fire, only to be operated on without antibiotics or anesthesia. An Algerian rifleman, his face smashed by a burp gun burst, walked 30 kilometers with a broken jaw and a gaping hole where his nose had been and was left without surgery from 1952 until his return to the French in 1954. These are but a few and do not include the wounded from Dien Bien Phu.

Only in January 1954 did the VPA begin to set up a few field hospitals near the largest clusters of PW camps, but these were too far apart for the treatment of urgent cases and were equipped for only the lightest surgery. "Hospital Camp" No. 128 was staffed with French medical personnel subordinated to VPA physicians whose state of training in most cases was elementary but who were willing to learn by operating on the prisoners. As one of the French medical officers of Camp 128 pointed out: "We may not have saved many lives by performing surgical operations, but we saved quite a few by preventing our overenthusiastic guardians from performing any."

It is clear that under such conditons, the survival of a serious surgical case would have been a near-miracle. Here again, the statistics are more eloquent than long phrases: out of a total of 10,754 PW's liberated by the VPA, only 612 were active surgical cases. Of the latter, 391 had been captured at Dien Bien Phu and thus had been in Communist hands for less than four months; 718 others also had been surgical cases but their wounds had spontaneously consolidated and their general low state of health required treatment before undertaking remedial surgery. Out of this total of 1330 surgical cases, *only 81* had received any surgery during their captivity; of those, 38 had been operated upon without anesthesia. Only *one* PW is known to have survived an appendectomy while in captivity, and that was performed by a French doctor at Camp 128.

The camps themselves were constructed like the villages surrounding them; they were not identified and their location was never communicated to the French, so that at least in one case a PW camp was razed by the French Air Force, in the belief it was an enemy installation. In certain cases, camp locations were identified by French Union Forces and efforts were made to parachute essential foods, drugs and clothing to the PW's. Such aid was confiscated as "war booty" by the Communists. Camp equipment was nil. Only the officers' camp was provided with a pot large enough to boil the drinking water. All other camps were simply located near streams and the inmates drank the water directly from them. The death rate from water-borne intestinal diseases assumed frightful proportions in certain areas. Camp 5-E counted 201 deaths out of a total of 272 inmates between March and September 1952. Camp 70 lost 120 out of a total of 250 men in July-August 1954. Camp 123 lost 350 men (one-half of its population) between June and December 1953. Camp 114 maintained an average of two deaths a day throughout 1952, and even the officers' camp, with its large complement of French medical officers and its relatively better facilities, showed a mortality rate of 18 percent from 1951 to 1954.

The overall results of this Communist prisoner-of-war policy are clearly apparent in the following table:

Unit type	Missing, 1945-54	Returned, July-Oct. '54	Percent of returnees
French Mainland	6,449	2,587	40.1
North African	6,695	3,369	50.7
Foreign Legion	6,328	2,567	40.6
African	1,748	796	45.6
Vietnamese	15,759	1,435	9.1
Totals	36,979	10,754	Average: 28.5

To this figure must be added a total of 4,744 persons, military and civilian, returned by the VPA between 1945 and 1954 to French Union during "clemency periods." Of the 10,754 PW's returned after the cease-fire, 6,132 required immediate hospitalization. Of these, 61 died within the next three months.

These 61 deaths deserve closer examination, for they reveal clearly that the situation in the PW camps, far from improving as the VPA received more adequate equipment from the Soviet Union and Red China, became actually worse: of the 61, 49 had been captured at Dien Bien Phu and all but 4 had been Communist PW's for *less than four months!* It must also be emphasized that all of them were not surgical cases but simply "walking skeletons"— men who, after 57 days of continuous combat, had simply been marched to death over 500 miles of jungle paths from Dien Bien Phu to the camps of northern and central Viet-Nam under conditions which made the infamous Death March of Bataan look like the proverbial "walk in the sun."

It is still not clear what prompted the VPA High Command to single out the defenders of Dien Bien Phu for especially harsh treatment. Was it merely an unthinking military "snafu"? Was it a militarily logical attempt to remove the maximum number of prisoners from an area where they perhaps could expect rescue by a relief column based in Laos or by an improbable but possible airborne raid? Was it a politically-inspired scheme to influence the French diplomats negotiating in Geneva for a cease-fire? Or was it merely good psychological warfare designed to break down the spirit of the remaining French Union troops fighting on in Indochina? Perhaps all of these motivations played their role in the reasoning of the VPA military and political leaders.

In simple terms, the bulk of these prisoners, about 7,000—with about 1,000 seriously wounded and 3,000 to 4,000 dead left behind on the battle field—faced a trek of between 450 to 530 miles, according to whether they were assigned to the northern or the central Vietnamese camps. These distances they covered over difficult terrain during the rainy season in about 40 days, with an average load of about 35 pounds, many of them carrying litter cases or dragging exhausted comrades.

Even more unfortunate were the PW's being escorted north from the battles in Central Laos and the southern plateau of Viet-Nam. Their officers marched from Laos to Camp No. 1, a distance of 900 kilometers, in 63 days, with the enlisted men covering the 500 kilometers to the camps around Vinh in a record 24 days.

Death rates for these forced marches are not available, but they were considered high by all concerned. Actual executions of those no longer able to march were not too frequent—they were simply left on the path side to die. The Communist escort troops were relayed, none of them following a prisoner group throughout the whole duration of the march. Food given the PW's was cold rice once a day. This diet, to which all but the Vietnamese were unaccustomed, fed to men already exhausted by wounds and by two months of continuous lack of sleep and poor nourishment, seriously affected the health of the column. Dehydration due to continuous dysentery and abnormal perspiration soon made most PW's lose more than one-half their normal weight and probably was responsible for the majority of deaths on the march.

It is also important to note that the various races and nationalities responded differently to both the physical and psychological strains of the ordeal—a fact which also had come to notice in Korea. For obvious reasons, the Africans and Asians withstood the march best, in spite of the fact that the Vietnamese who had fought on the French side were often singled out for particularly harsh treatment. Thus, among the 10,754 liberated PW's, the various groups accounted for the following percentages of hospitalization:

French Mainland 66.7%
Foreign Legion 69.04%
North Africans 60.7%
Africans 24.0%
Vietnamese 24.45%

The especially high casualty rate among the Foreign Legionnaires was attributed to the fact that their predominantly Central European background, with their fair skins and hair, equipped them poorly to withstand the murderous monsoon climate. At the same time, their highly individualistic attitude led them to adopt, in many cases, a "may-the-Devil-take-the-hindmost" view of their fellow Legionnaires although, of course, cases of devotion to weaker friends were not infrequent.

The mainland French were hardly better equipped for the trek, but showed a great amount of cohesion and devotion to their wounded and sick comrades—a quality which the French already had displayed in the Nazi concentration camps of World War II. This cohesion was the stronger as the PW's involved belonged to elite units (commandos, paratroops, etc.) and had succeeded in remaining together as units or parts of units. Wounded and sick were carried along until the camps were reached or until no one was left strong enough to carry them. *"Marche ou crève"* ("March on or croak")—became a byword for the columns as they wound through the steep hills of the T'ai country. In the words of some survivors, "Only the men with strong character, those who had the will to march, to stay in the column, had a chance of survival."

Here, also, hundreds of well-documented cases attest to what this meant in actual practice:

There was the case of Foreign Legionnaire No. 202, of the ill-fated 13th Half-Brigade, wounded both at Dien Bien Phu and later by French bombing on the road between Tuân-Giao and Son-La, who was carried for 500 kilometers through the mountains without a stretcher and whose fractured thigh was immobilized only two months later.

There was Rifleman No. 51, 3d Algerian Infantry, operated on during the battle of Dien Bien Phu for mortar fragments in the liver, who marched for 45 days through the jungle, holding his wound together with his turban.

There was the paratrooper blinded by shell fragments who was half dragged and half carried by his friends for 600 kilometers; the artilleryman with a pierced diaphragm who had to carry 44-pound rice bags; and many of the survivors remember the pathetic image of a man with both legs amputated, abandoned by his comrades and last seen on the road near Tuân-Giao, grimly dragging himself to the transit camp on his hands and the stumps of his thighs.

This was the Death March of the French Union garrison of Dien

Bien Phu, lasting from May to July 1954. It caused more losses than any single battle of the whole Indochina war.

As in Korea, political indoctrination of PW's was standing operating procedure, and, to all appearances, the VPA was better equipped to deal with the various national minorities of the French Union Forces than its North Korean counterpart in dealing with the U.N. nationals. Broadcasts or leaflets directed at French troops were written in French, German, Arabic and even in African dialects. Such materials were prepared by deserters but also, according to published East German sources, by propaganda organizations in various Soviet Bloc nations and by French and Algerian Communists in France.

Every PW camp had its *can-bô* (political cadre) in charge of the "re-education" of the PW's, and the Communists did their utmost to pit one national group against another. For example, the Foreign Legionnaires were told that they were being exploited by the "imperialists" and were offered repatriation to their East European home lands. A few accepted; others were forced to go, and recently there arose the curious case of one such Legionnaire who re-defected from East Berlin to France to serve out his term of enlistment with the Legion. The Algerians and Moroccans were told a story with a different slant, and another propaganda line was presented to the Senegalese.

In order to break down unit morale more rapidly, overseas units were rapidly separated from their French junior officers and NCO's. In fact, the VPA developed an extremely rigid system of racial discrimination in order to sharpen antagonisms. This policy had a measure of success, particularly among the Algerians, but several sources (such as Major Grauwin, the chief medical officer at Dien Bien Phu) mention instances of whole detachments of North African troops who preferred to take in stride the harsh treatment reserved for recalcitrants rather than to turn "progressive."

In certain cases, the political indoctrination began with the wounded themselves. Major Grauwin states that he reached an understanding with the French-trained VPA chief surgeon of the Communist 308th Infantry Division. But one of his colleagues,

Lieutenant Résillot, had the experience of seeing the wounded under his care classified for surgical treatment according to a system of "People's Democratic urgency": ex-prisoners of the French to be treated first, then North African enlisted men, Foreign Legion enlisted men, French enlisted men, and, lastly, French officers. The result was that several patients whose condition required immediate attention died before help could be given them.

In the PW camps, recalcitrant prisoners were subjected to the severest and most humiliating duties. If particularly resistant to Communist indoctrination, they were transferred to Lang-Trang, the feared "Reprisal Camp," which in fact was little else than a death camp. The "re-education" process was an important step in the integration of the PW into the prison camp system, for the "re-educated" prisoner had become a "new man." Violation of camp rules by him were considered a relapse into "reactionary" thinking—a grave fault punishable by death. Claude Goëldhieux, a former PW, described this rationale in the following terms:

> While the Communists considered an evasion prior to political re-education as a benign political mistake, their attitude now changed radically. The escapee now became a deserter, a traitor to the Cause since his eyes had been opened upon the truth. By attempting to escape, he reneged his new-found faith and reaffirmed his former errors. By an individualistic, hence guilty, feeling, he had sabotaged the political action of the mass of prisoners. Thus, he ceased to exist. The sentencing to death was merely a concretization of this non-existence.

The political re-education of prisoners of war is, of course, nothing new. In fact, the United States may perhaps have been the modern innovator of the process. Prisoners, during the Civil War, were indoctrinated to some extent by both sides. Southern forces used units of "galvanized Yankees" (Northern PW's who enlisted in the Southern forces), and the North enlisted Southern prisoners to fight Indians in the Far West. During World War II, "democratization courses" were held in American and British PW camps, and reformed German PW's were promised jobs as interpreters or clerks* in the future occupation administration in Ger-

---

*The French, having seen the Nazis at close range, were under no particular illusion as to the lasting effects of such re-education. The PW's were put to work and, as of 1946, released PW's were allowed to enlist in the Foreign Legion.

many upon their return after VE-Day. On their side, the Nazis recruited 200,000 Russian PW's to serve in the *Wehrmacht,* many of whom proved to be even more savage than the Nazis themselves. In other words, and all pious insistence to the contrary, the soldier in enemy hands has in recent times become a legitimate military target of a new kind. To paraphrase Clausewitz' famous axiom, to defeat the prisoner's mind is to continue the war by other means.

It is another example of the West's slowness in adapting itself to new tactical conditions that Communist indoctrination of PW's in Korea and Indochina took the West by surprise and gave rise to indignant outcries of "foul play." In an article published in a Communist North Vietnamese monthly, *Viet-Nam Advances,* in December 1957, the Communists candidly admitted that to overcome the minds of the PW's was part of the overall struggle. The title of the article simply reads: *"A little-known Aspect of our Resistance War—Our P.O.W.'s."* In the article, one group of French PW's states that:

> Our life in the camp was a practical education . . . Every detail, every rule of life inside the camp was the subject of discussions, criticism and self-criticism.

A French paratroop chaplain, Father Paul Jeandel, who spent three years in Communist camps, has written a book about his experiences which bears the stamp of approval of his Church and which contains some revealing paragraphs on how Communist brainwashing in Viet-Nam affected even strong and trained minds.

> Medieval tortures are nothing in comparison to the atomic-age torture of brainwashing . . . It amputates your soul and grafts another one upon you. Persuasion has taken the place of punishment. The victims must approve and justify in their own eyes the measures which crush them. They must recognize themselves guilty and believe in the crimes which they have not committed . . . I have seen men leave Camp No. 1 who were dead and did not know it, for they had lost their own personality and had become slogan-reciting robots . . . I myself, while not losing my Faith, nearly lost my reason.

The method is that of the drop of water repeated on the stone *ad infinitum,* the evolution of the discussion from the verifiable true fact taken out of context to the unsubstantiated large-scale lie. It may begin with the true statement that the Communist forces, far from being gangs of undisciplined bandits, were a regular force of excellent fighters. This was an obvious fact the captured officer could not deny—and which, often enough, already was a shock to him, for like his comrades-in-arms in Korea, his erstwhile estimate of the enemy was based on what the West had seen of the Chinese Nationalists during the last years of their agony on the mainland.* The next step involved the admission that the Vietnamese non-Communist government was a French puppet—also a fact which could not be denied.

This led to the logical conclusion that it was "unpopular" and, thence, to the apparently logical *sequitur* that the Communist government was "popular," with the political commissar triumphantly repeating: "You see, you've been misled! Your capitalist masters have led you into a war against the popular government of Democratic Viet-Nam." If the brainwashed person refused to accept the apparent logic that the Communist government must be popular if the pro-French government wasn't, and insisted that perhaps both governments were unpopular, then the process would be repeated *ad infinitum* until he saw the light or was dead.

For the recalcitrants, the Viet-Minh had their own subtle methods—apparently subtler than those used by their North Korean and Red Chinese counterparts: all of a sudden, camp discipline would become more rigorous, work hours longer, and the pitifully few drugs available at the camp infirmary non-existent. At first, particularly in those camps where officers or senior NCO's were still present, discipline would be maintained. But soon the die-hards would die or be transferred to the feared Lang-Trang reprisal camp. Often enough, the die-hards themselves would, before dying, exhort their comrades not to be foolish and play the enemy's game by resisting until they all died.

Then, the Viet-Minh would order the prisoners to establish "Peace and Repatriation Committees," with the understanding that those committees would select some prisoners for repatriation

---

*This underestimation of the enemy as a trained fighter ("All you gotta' do is show your face and, pfft, they run . . .") led to some painful surprises. For example, the French High Command had to issue stern orders compelling officers to carry individual weapons in combat besides swagger sticks. And I still recall the paratroop officer who soundly dressed down one of his men who, in jungle combat, had turned his red beret inside out, thus wearing the camouflaged combat lining outside and hiding the revealing bright red. Such an act was considered as "cowardly."

to the "People's Democracies" or to France. Work performance as well as political orthodoxy allegedly were the criteria for repatriation, and many a prisoner, according to official French medical reports, literally worked himself to death in the hope of earning his liberation. A few completely converted French Communists and Foreign Legionnaires were repatriated via Red China and the Soviet Union. Some Eastern European Legionnaires were repatriated to their countries of origin against their own will only to be tried there as "Fascists" by People's Courts*.

But the worst aspect of brainwashing apparently was "criticism and self-criticism" euphemisms for spying upon one's comrades and denouncing one's own sins in public. It did more to break down camp morale than any other single psychological threat. Here again, the beginning was innocent enough; since camp hygiene was essential in order to forestall large-scale epidemics, the Communists would order the prisoners to report any man who violated hygiene rules by, say, urinating near the barracks. Such a violator would then be called to the commissar and confronted with his "crime" which had been obviously reported by someone in his own hut.

"You see," the commissar would say, "your friends have fully understood the meaning of camp solidarity. Now, can you report to me one instance of such lack of solidarity committed by someone else in your hut?" and nine times out of ten, the prisoner would, in turn, report a case of petty larceny or violation of hygiene rules committed by a fellow prisoner. Within a few days, every prisoner would be encased in a cocoon of petty espionage rapidly evolving from benign incidents to actual treason.

In some cases, of course, the very stupidity of the system would be turned against its originators; the prisoners would report hundreds of minutiae which would keep their guardians too busy to pry further along more important political lines. Some prisoners would work out with their colleagues complete dossiers on themselves, all involving such "crimes" as laziness, gluttony, petty

---

*A book published in the Soviet Zone of Germany in 1953, *Légion Etrangère*, by Günter Halle, specifically cites a Soviet aircraft (Ilyushin-12, registration number SSSR-P.1783, aircraft commander Gregory Ivanov, flight engineer Petrov) as having transported such prisoners from Indochina to Eastern Europe. Neither France nor the U. S. raised a protest against such an open violation of the rules of war.

thievery and the like, which would satisfy the less sophisticated brainwashers without really incriminating anyone.

But collective indoctrination—"the raping of the multitudes," as it was called—was, in some ways, even more insidious. "Camp solidarity" became an all-encompassing catchword. A camp was considered to become more "progressive" *en masse.* Hence, each individual breach not only reflected upon the "backslider" himself, but upon the collective conscience of the camp as a whole and resulted in general punishment. The worst act of "individualism," of course, was an attempt to escape, and soon pressures were built up among the prisoners themselves to prevent anyone from escaping for fear of breaking "camp solidarity." As Father Jeandel explains in his book: "Solidarity, which ties every member of a group to his comrades, creates certain obligations towards this group. The Viets knew it and transformed the bonds of solidarity into true shackles of a new type of imprisonment. *Collective conscience prohibits individual evasions. Each individual becomes as much a prisoner of his own comrades as of the Viets.*"

And Father Jeandel, as a priest, was perhaps best able to sum up the experience of indoctrination in one single brief sentence: "The worst wasn't to die, but to see one's soul change."

Like the United States Army in the case of American PW's in Communist hands, the French Union High Command faced the problem of how to deal with returning "progressives," those soldiers who in one way or another had cooperated with their captors. Here, a sharp distinction was made between those who, by their actions, had directly contributed to harm their fellow prisoners or the war effort, and those who merely mouthed Communist slogans in order to avoid undue hardships. It was assumed (wrongly, as it turned out, in the case of the Algerian PW's) that the level of Communist propaganda was so unsophisticated as to cause no harm to general combat morale. On the whole, this has remained true. Communist psychological warfare was, in the long run, *more effective upon civilian morale in France* than upon the combat troops in Indochina.

To the knowledge of this writer, the French Union High Command never adopted a uniform policy with regard to returnees, but dealt with each case on an individual basis. It appears from actual experience that the senior captive officers had let it be known that their subordinates could "go along" with Communist propaganda demands as long as such compliance helped improve the lot of the greatest number of PW's and did not materially harm the war effort. For example, the Communists gave the medical personnel at Dien Bien Phu the opportunity to appeal to Ho Chi Minh's clemency in order to secure the direct evacuation of the most seriously wounded cases by helicopter from the captured battle field to French hospitals. The senior medical officer, Major Grauwin; and his staff, including the lone nurse, Mlle. de Galard-Tarraubes, for days fought the Viet-Minh over every sentence in that clemency appeal; with the political commissar of the 308th Division adding at every point: "Remember, every hour that you refuse to sign, some more of your wounded will die." Which was perfectly true.

Needless to say, Grauwin signed, and the men were saved from absolutely certain death. No one in the High Command felt that Grauwin had not done the right thing, and there is no evidence that other officers faced with similar demands have been penalized by the French Army upon their return.

On the basis of French experience in the anti-Nazi underground (which ran on the perfectly sound assumption that almost everybody would sooner or later talk under torture) the French did not expect their personnel taken prisoner to play the martyr and hero. Prisoner-of-war behavior was expected to conform to two basic tenets: do not hurt your fellow prisoners and do not cause any harm to your comrades-in-arms who are still in the fight. Thus, French Air Force personnel (most likely to fall into enemy hands deep behind enemy lines) was provided with a set of sample answers which would satisfy most PW interrogators and do little harm to the forces in the field. This way the PW's could give the minimum of answers necessary to ensure adequate treatment without feeling that they had "betrayed" their country.

Such answers included: (1) false unit designations, preferably of units which already had been in Indochina and thus could be expected to return; (2) false unit commanders' names (also of men who had previously been there); (3) correct answers as to aircraft types (in any case verifiable by enemy visual observation) but inflated strength figures; (4) congratulate enemy on quality of his camouflage; he might make less efforts to improve it; (5) plead ignorance as to codes, the defense of air bases, construction of new bases; as not being part of flying crews' knowledge; (6) give exact table of French Air Force organization; the enemy knows it in any case and will use that question as test of the veracity of the other answers; etc.

In comparison, the American Fighting Man's Code, created after the bitter experience of the Korean War, seeks to compel each and every individual soldier to live up to extremely high ideals of non-co-operation with the enemy. It is as yet untested to any large extent since only a handful of Americans have fallen into enemy hands since its promulgation. Those who had been held by the Viet-Cong in 1962, had signed statements chastising American policies in Viet-Nam prior to their release. By mid-1964, twenty-four Americans (including a woman doctor) were alive in Viet-Cong hands. The Viet-Cong, in April 1964, made offers to allow them to receive messages and send news via the Cambodian Red Cross. It is likely that, should the United States be involved more extensively in revolutionary wars, prisoner-of-war behavior will in all likelihood be judged by the more flexible French tenets than by the—in my view—unrealistically rigid post-Korean code.

Deserters, of course, were another matter. They, along with the few prisoners (mostly Foreign Legionnaires) who joined the ranks of the Viet-Minh and in some cases fought with them against French troops, are being tried before courts martial. The remarkable aspect in this matter is that, as in the case of some of the American turncoats in Korea, quite a few of them have since 1954 requested their repatriation to France via the International Control Commission in Hanoi, apparently preferring the certitude of a jail sentence at home to "freedom" in Communist North Viet-Nam. The remaining turncoats and their Vietnamese dependents, acquired over the past nine years, returned to France in December 1962, where the worst offenders were sentenced to five years' imprisonment by the French military court at Marseilles. There now remains in North Viet-Nam only a handful of traitors under death sentence in their homeland.

In Indochina, thousands of unmarked graves dot the march routes of the French Union prisoners of war from the China Gates near Lang-Son to the hills of Laos and the swamps of South Viet-Nam, victims of a new era where warfare no longer stops at the barbed wire of the prison compound or respects even the privacy of the prisoner's mind.

12

Why Dien Bien Phu?

THE Indochina war ended July 20, 1954 after a conference at Geneva attended by most major powers, including Communist China and the United States. The conference began May 8, 1954, under the shattering impact of the fall of Dien Bien Phu the day before, and resulted in the loss of all of Viet-Nam north of the 17th Parallel to the Communist government of Ho Chi Minh.

The small kingdom of Laos also had to pay a price for the repeated and successful invasions of its northern domain by the Viet-Minh: two provinces, Phong-Saly and Samneua, were put under the administration of Viet-Minh backed Laotian rebels which had proclaimed themselves *Pathet-Lao*—the "Lao State." After laborious negotiations between the Royal Laotian Government and the Pathet-Lao rebels, the latter agreed to rejoin the national community under certain conditions. An uneasy truce was broken when the rebel forces attacked Laotian government forces in July, 1959, and a third North Vietnamese invasion combined with local Pathet-Lao forces, drove the Laotian forces to the wall.

Therefore, the battle of Dien Bien Phu, the 1959-62 Laos war, and the revolutionary war in South Viet-Nam; deserve closer attention than they have thus far received in this country where even official reports are often couched in terms which make for good journalistic copy but rather poor military-political reporting.* Enough verifiable facts have now become available on an unclassified basis on those three events to allow at least a partial evaluation of developments which, in one case, led to France's defeat in Indochina; in the second, led to a serious setback for the United States; and which, in the third, may yet lead to the loss of all of mainland Southeast Asia to Communist influence.

As the preceding chapters have shown, the Indochina war was not lost through any particular fatal error or through a general collapse of combat morale. As in the Korean war, the non-Communist forces had worked themselves into a tactical corner from which the only exit would have been a considerable broadening of the political and strategic premises on which the war was fought; that is, an attack on the Soviet Russian and Communist Chinese "sanctuaries" behind the actual Communist combatants.

Again as in the Korean war, the number of small errors made was great—and even Dien Bien Phu cost smaller losses in men and matériel than the U. S. X Corps' retreat from the Yalu to Hungnam in November-December 1950. But their cumulative effect on the outcome of the war had farther-reaching consequences than similar errors in Korea, because the French political structure was a great deal shakier than that of the United States (in spite of the fact that the Korean war was far from popular) and because, in comparison to Korea again, the Indochinese war was fought literally on a shoestring. To put it into one single sentence, total French and American expenditures in Indochina until the cease-fire reached roughly *one-half* of the

---

*During 1961, one such previously-classified report went directly to the *Saturday Evening Post*. There was enough cuteness in it to make it palatable even to women readers. Another such report, also released, asserted forcefully that popular support is *not* necessary in revolutionary war. And I recall with a shudder that 1959 report, contributed to SEATO by one of its leading members, which confidently asserted that the Communists had been pushed onto the *defensive* in Southeast Asia and were so hard-pressed that they had given up all thought of armed struggle in favor of "legal struggle" methods! Of such delusions Western defeats are made the world over.

total costs of the Korean war—and while the latter lasted three years, the former lasted almost eight.*

Yet the whole sequence of errors was epitomized in the battle of Dien Bien Phu which, in itself, was not at all typical of the fighting in Indochina. This mainly, no doubt, was because it was better publicized than any other French reverses suffered in that war and because—for the wrongest possible reasons—it had been expected to result in a decisive defeat for the enemy's regular forces. There is available now much documentary material; notably books by France's unfortunate commander-in-chief in Indochina at the time, General Henri Navarre; the then French Premier, Joseph Laniel; and the head of the Commission of Inquiry appointed by the French Government, General Catroux. It is possible to piece together a fairly accurate picture of what *really* brought about the decisions that led to the battle being fought at all, and being fought in the place and with the forces allocated to it.**

All three sources agree on the fact that, initially, *no* showdown battle with the Communist forces had been contemplated for 1953-54; and Navarre adds that, at the most he expected to be able to reach by 1955 a *coup nul*—a tied game—with the enemy. In other words, a situation was foreseen which, eventually, could have led to an Indochinese Panmunjom, but not to a French victory.

One key issue, however, on which Navarre differs with the two other authors, and which is at the heart of the whole tragedy, is that of the reason for defending Dien Bien Phu. As far as Navarre was concerned, the situation was clear: the French Government had made the *political decision*—which was its prerogative and duty—to defend northern Laos (which contains Luang-Prabang, the royal residence, and Vientiane, the administrative capital) from a Communist invasion. This was decided at a meeting of the French National Defense Committee (the French equivalent of the National Security Council in the U. S.) on July

*To lay to rest once and for all the myth of the "American taxpayer financing the French in Indochina": U.S. actual expenditures in Indochina had reached an approximate total of $954 million by July 1954. During 1946-54, the French had spent close to $11 billion of their own funds for the prosecution of the war.

**For other books on Dien Bien Phu, see Bibliography.

24, 1953. The political necessity of defending Laos became even more acute when on October 28, 1953, Laos had signed a mutual defense treaty with France which cemented Laos' membership in the French Union. Since France hoped to sign similar treaties with the neighboring states of Viet-Nam and Cambodia, the French felt that an abandonment of northern Laos would adversely influence such negotiations. Navarre felt in addition that to let the Viet-Minh arrive "in force on the Mekong would be equivalent to opening to it the door to central and southern Indochina*."

Laniel maintains, however, and in this the Commission of Inquiry appears to bear him out, that the instructions given Navarre read that he was, "above everything else, to insure the safety of our Expeditionary Corps." And according to General Catroux, the National Defense Committee, in a directive addressed to Navarre on November 13, 1953 (exactly one week before the landing of the first paratroops at Dien Bien Phu), "invited" the commander-in-chief in Indochina "to adjust his operations to his means."

All three agree on the fact that the French authorities in France were not informed of Navarre's decision to launch "Operation Castor" (the airborne landing at Dien Bien Phu) until six hours *after* the operation had started. Courageously, Navarre affirms in his book (p. 197) that the French Government "did in no way intervene in the conduct of the operations . . . I have always claimed for myself the entire responsibility for the operational decisions leading to the battle of Dien Bien Phu."

His telegram sent to the French Secretary of State for the Associated States at 1615 of November 20, 1953, read in part as follows:

> The veering-off to the north-west of the 316th Division constitutes a serious menace for Lai-Chau and will bring about within a short time the destruction of our guerrilla forces in the highlands. I have,

---

*Letter of General Navarre to the French newspaper *Le Figaro*, of May 25, 1959, in reply to General Catroux' book. The solution of defending Indochina at its narrow waist until troops were available for a definitive push to the north (similar to the withdrawal of U.S. forces in Korea to the 38th parallel after the abortive Yalu campaign) also was advocated at one time by a high U.S. officer then assigned to Indochina, General O'Daniel; and by French General Boyer de la Tour. (cf. the latter's *Martyre de l'Armée Française*, Paris: 1962.)

therefore, decided a thrust upon Dien Bien Phu, which is to be the operations base for the 316th, and whose reoccupation will, furthermore, cover the approaches to Luang-Prabang which, without it, would be in grave danger within a few weeks. The operation began this morning at 1030 by the drop of a first wave of two paratroop battalions . . .

Another vital question in the whole operation is: why Dien Bien Phu at all? Here, Navarre affirms having weighed the pros and cons carefully.

Laos could not be defended by a war of movement. I already have explained in another chapter the reasons why: the nature of the terrain itself and the *lack of adaptation of our forces* [emphasis supplied].

Thus, another method had to be used; that . . . known in modern terms as (the establishment of) "hedgehog" systems or "fortified camps" constituted a mediocre solution but, upon examination, appeared as the only possible one. It would not prevent light enemy detachments from roaming through the countryside, but, leaving in our hands essential points, would prevent an [outright] invasion . . . (p. 191).

Here, the head of the Commission of Inquiry, General Catroux, is harsh with the former commander-in-chief, and most persons acquainted with the area will tend to agree with him.

This was a rather theoretical view of things, based upon insufficient information about the physical conditions prevailing in the area. There are no blocking positions in a country lacking European-type roads and where communications are native paths and waterways . . .

As soon as Dien Bien Phu was faced with important forces, it could neither protect Northern Laos nor exercise a mission of external aggressiveness, of radiating [into the surrounding countryside] or of surveillance. It could only hold the bulk of the enemy and, up to a point, protect Upper Laos from deep enemy penetrations, thus protecting Luang-Prabang, which, in effect, it did (p. 171-172).

In his published reply to Catroux' allegations, Navarre maintains that he would have had to forego any defense of northern Laos, and thus would have jeopardized "my mission of defending the remainder of the Indochinese territory once the enemy's battle force would have reached the Mekong." In strictly military terms, the evacuation of northern Laos would have greatly simplified Navarre's problem of overextended supply lines and forced the enemy to fight close to the French airbases and away from his own supply centers. It is likely that the measure would have had negative consequences upon the loyalty of Laos to the French Union—as it turned out, Laos stayed in it three years and the two other Indochinese states refused to join it anyway—but militarily (and Navarre's contention was entirely based on such considerations) it is hardly likely that the evacuation of northern Laos would have jeopardized the Expeditionary Corps more than the total loss of the garrison of Dien Bien Phu ultimately did.

There remains but to express an appreciation of the conduct of the battle itself once it was joined, and here it appears that Navarre's published explanation might have been more candid. Justifying Dien Bien Phu as the best choice for a "ground-air-base" *(base aéro-terrestre)* in the area, Navarre explains that the valley bottom covered 16 by 9 km, with the commanding heights being at 10 to 12 km from the airfield itself.

> This distance is superior to the useful range of any possible enemy artillery. The artillery would, therefore have to take up positions on the hillsides descending towards the interior of the plain. . . . According to the opinion of the artillerymen, this would be impossible, because the batteries would be in view of the [French] observation posts in the plain either while being put into position or while firing. They would, therefore, be silenced by our counter-battery fire or by our bombers. (p. 195).

As any large-scale map of the area shows, the average elevation of the French-held areas in the center of the plain of Dien Bien Phu was around 350 to 380 meters. The two highest French positions, whose function it was to prevent the enemy from firing directly on the airstrip, were hills Gabrielle (491 meters) and Beatrice (509 meters). Yet, barely 5500 yards from the center of the fortress the enemy held an almost continuous hill line with an average elevation of 1100 meters, preceded by a secondary hill line in the 550-meter altitude range within 2500 yards of the center of Dien Bien Phu! Once hills Gabrielle and Beatrice were lost—and they were lost within twenty-four hours after the actual beginning of the battle—the Communist gunners had a continuous view of all the French positions, and the airfield (upon whose continuous use the success of the battle hinged) became useless within a few days.

Here, obviously, French politicians at home were no longer at fault. The responsibility must necessarily fall upon the three military commanders involved in decreasing order of responsibility: Navarre, the commander-in-chief; Cogny, the northern theater commander, and, finally, Colonel (later Brigadier General) de Castries, the fortress commandant. It must not be forgotten that Dien Bien Phu had been in French hands for almost four full months before the Communists launched their decisive attacks. During those four months, it had been inspected by nearly "everybody that was anybody" in French and American military circles, including Lieutenant General John ("Iron Mike") O'Daniel; and, apparently, had been found to be a sound position.

In fact, two high French sources: Navarre in his book, and French General Pierre Koenig*—hero of the battle of Bir-Hakeim against Rommel's *Afrikakorps* and Minister of Defense in 1954; stated that an *American mission of antiaircraft experts* familiar with the Russian antiaircraft artillery used in Korea had inspected Dien Bien Phu to advise the French and had assured the French that the enemy would be unable to bring his pieces to bear on the airfield.**

In any case, the Americans said, counter-battery fire and judicious choice of drop zones would allow re-supply operations "without excessive losses." And their report added that, "at the very least, night-time resupply operations should remain possible." This joint error in appreciating enemy capabilities in no way exonerates the French northern theater commander, and the head of the Commission of Inquiry flatly lays the fault at his feet. General Catroux asserts that Cogny himself should have inspected the defenses and plans of fire more closely and that, "statutorily," it was his responsibility to instruct de Castries as to where to concentrate his main defensive efforts. Perhaps the gravest accusation raised by Catroux is that the defense rehearsal held at Dien Bien Phu prior to the battle in Cogny's presence was merely a "CPX" —a command post exercise not involving the actual movement

---

*Debates before the French National Assembly, June 9, 1954.

**All this will be discussed in detail in the author's book *Dien Bien Phu,* to be published in 1965 by Lippincott. See also the author's "Dien Bien Phu: A Battle to Remember," in the *New York Times Magazine,* May 3, 1964.

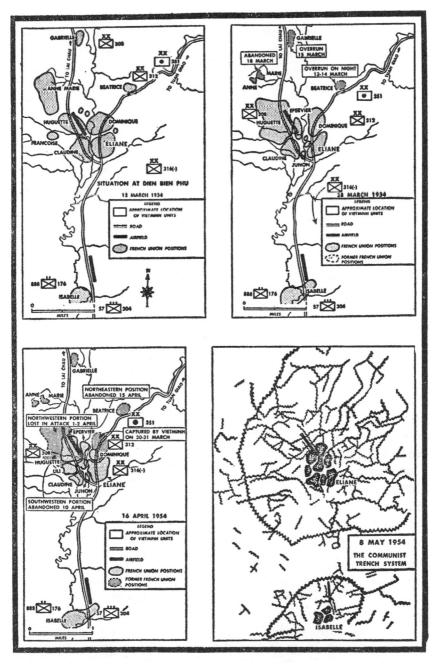

The Agony of Dien Bien Phu.

of troops—which, according to Catroux, failed to show up the obvious planning errors which an actual exercise in the field and with troops would perhaps have clearly pointed out.

Brigadier General de Castries himself, given the intervening years of retrospect, is perhaps the least at fault in the dénouement of the tragedy. An armored cavalryman by service of origin, having commanded one of the famous Mobile Groups in the Red River delta, he was the man of the offensive stabs, of the mobile defense—but neither by training nor character was he particularly suited to hold on doggedly to each terrain feature and to reconquer with grim determination those lost.

First of all, the very layout of Dien Bien Phu into one major fortress and one satellite fortress (Strongpoint Isabelle) 7 kilometers to the south, prevented full concentration of forces and fires. Isabelle by itself absorbed close to three infantry battalions out of a total of twelve, a whole 105mm artillery group, and a tank platoon of M-24's, that is, roughly one-third of the whole defense potential.

Of the eight battalions in Dien Bien Phu itself, three were to be in reserve at the disposal of the fortress commander for eventual counterattacks (along with the remaining seven tanks of the M-24 squadron airlifted into the valley and assembled in the open field by French mechanics) and two battalions were to defend the vital hill strongpoints Gabrielle and Beatrice covering the airfield.

In actual fact, however, the three reserve battalions were immediately assigned defensive sectors along the perimeter and thus were largely unavailable for the counterattack missions to which they initially had been committed. The collapse of the two T'ai mountaineer battalions under concentrated enemy artillery fire further aggravated the situation. Thus, when the Communists, logically enough, began the attack on Dien Bien Phu by a concentrated assault on the two hill strongpoints, both garrisons were practically smothered by the sheer fury of the artillery fire and the masses of enemy infantry resorting once more to the "human-sea" attack. It fell upon the men of the Foreign Legion's famous 13th Half-Brigade to be the first and the last to die in the fortress:

Lieutenant Colonel Gaucher, the commander of the Half-Brigade, was killed in action on March 13; and Colonel Lalande, his successor, was taken prisoner on May 8, 1954, leading the last bayonet charge of the Half-Brigade's 1st Battalion out of strongpoint Isabelle.

The enemy paid a heavy price for Beatrice—in fact, at dawn of March 14, General Giap, the Communist Commander-in-Chief, asked the French for a 4-hour battlefield truce to pick up the mounds of his own dead and wounded covering the shattered remains of Hill Beatrice. Of the 3d Battalion, 13th Half-Brigade, only a few stunned survivors remained, and not one French officer from Beatrice had survived.

Hill Gabrielle's end followed the same pattern. Dien Bien Phu did not possess a single concrete emplacement and the earth, sandbag and log bunkers could not withstand the withering bombardment which now began to fall upon the whole perimeter of the fortress, but particularly on Gabrielle. Here also, both the commander and his deputy were gravely wounded shortly after the beginning of the battle, but the defenders—5th Battalion, 7th Algerian Rifles—fought on in the shambles of their positions. When dawn broke, 4th Company and parts of 2d Company were still clinging to the southern face of the strongpoint. At 0530 March 15, Colonel Langlais, commander of the airborne forces inside the fortress, began to counterattack in the direction of Gabrielle with a weak paratroop battalion withdrawn out of the perimeter and supported by two tank platoons of Captain Hervouet's armored squadron. In spite of the heavy enemy barrage, they succeeded in penetrating into the strongpoint, but the situation there was hopeless; as in the worst days of Verdun in World War I, the intensive enemy bombardment had simply ground the whole top layer of soil into fine sand which no longer lent itself to the digging of bunkers and trenches. All Langlais' paratroopers and the tanks could do was to collect the stunned survivors of Gabrielle and to fall back upon Dien Bien Phu. Giap now controlled the commanding heights. The battle of Dien Bien Phu already was lost.

The basic fact which emerged from the new situation was simple in its starkness: the enemy's artillery proved largely impervious to the French counterbattery fire and to aerial strafing or bombing. Again General Navarre provides the answer to the obvious question.

> All around our positions, the enemy had created a network of camouflaged paths which permitted the [unhindered] transport of ammunition . . . to the vicinity of the batteries.

> We knew that a large number of artillery and AA gun emplacements had been prepared, but their camouflage had been so perfect that only a small number of them had been located prior to the beginning of the attacks.

> Under the influence of [Communist] Chinese advisers, the Viet-Minh command had used processes quite different from the classical methods. The artillery had been dug in by single pieces. The guns had been brought forward dismantled, carried by men, to emplacements where they had direct observation of their targets. They were installed in shell-proof dugouts, and fired point blank from portholes or were pulled out by their crews and pulled back as soon as our counterbattery fire began. Each piece or group of pieces was covered by massed antiaircraft artillery put into position and camouflaged in the same manner as the guns. This way of using the artillery and AA guns was possible only with the "human ant hill" at the disposal of the Viet-Minh and was to make shambles of all the estimates of our own artillerymen. It was the major surprise of the battle (p. 218-219).

On March 16, 1954, the artillerymen in Dien Bien Phu knew that their two groups of 105mm howitzers and their lone battery of 155mm (which had been intended to be the "final argument" in the expected counterbattery duel with the enemy) were not only hopelessly outnumbered* but that they were also outgunned.

The enemy's gun emplacements had been dug in on the slopes facing them almost without disturbing the cover of bushes and foliage, thus hiding the flashes of the guns and spreading the smoke to a vague pall without precise points of origin. In order to strafe those emplacements, the Air Force's fighter-bombers had to fly directly into the axis of the guns and of their attending antiaircraft guns and machine guns, with heavy losses in planes and pilots. Wet foliage (for this was the rainy season) proved al-

---

*Communist artillery included at the outset one regiment each of 105's and 75's, eighty 37mm Russian antiaircraft guns and one hundred .50 cal. antiaircraft machine guns, increased during the battle by two additional groups of 105's and several *Katyusha* (multi-tube rocket launcher) batteries, also of Soviet origin.

most impervious to napalm, and the combination of wet leaves and napalm created dense smoke which further camouflaged enemy infantry movements to the French gunners. Concentrating air action on one-by-one bombing of the gun emplacements would have required an air force which was beyond the means of the French and for which the Indochina theater had no suitable airfields.*

The French had made a fatal error and the artillerymen were the first to recognize and acknowledge it. Colonel Piroth, commander of the artillery at Dien Bien Phu, committed suicide that night.

On March 18, the 3d T'ai Battalion, defending the northern sector of strongpoint Anne-Marie covering the approaches to the airfield, broke under the sheer terror engendered in the minds of those simple mountaineers by the continuous bombardment. Anne-Marie North had to be abandoned. The airfield was now in full view of the enemy gunners. The last plane to land at Dien Bien Phu was ambulance aircraft No. 434 of Transport Squadron "Béarn." It landed at Dien Bien Phu at 0345 of March 28, 1954, loaded twenty-five casualties aboard and taxied to the end of the runway when the starboard engine developed an oil leak. The plane returned to the "taxistand" and unloaded its wounded. Repairs had to be delayed until the early dawn since lights could no longer be used near the airfield.

At 1100, No. 434 was ready, and the wounded who had spent the night in slit trenches near the airfield were again carried out on the apron. The Viet-Minh artillery chose that moment to hack the ambulance plane to pieces. The aircraft's crew, which remained in Dien Bien Phu to the end, included a French nurse, Mlle. Geneviève de Galard-Tarraubes.

But not only in the field of artillery techniques had the French (and their American advisers, apparently) underestimated the

---

*A massive American air raid on the enemy artillery around Dien Bien Phu (French code name: "Operation Vulture") had at one time been considered, but was abandoned in view of possible political consequences, and also on the ground of objections raised by General Matthew B. Ridgway as to the military implications of such an action. See his book *Soldier*, New York 1956, pp. 274-278. Ridgway felt that the cost of an American victory would have been "as great as, or greater than, that we paid in Korea." One may well wonder if General Ridgway still is of this opinion in 1964.

enemy. Another important error was made in underestimating the enemy's siege techniques. Far from relying on firepower alone, the Communists had made a veritable fetish out of the digging of approach trenches; followed by the brutal pounding of concentrated artillery fire for several hours, ending in the blowing up of the remaining wire obstacles with bangalores. The first waves of Communist shock troops (many of them following their own barrage so closely that they would die under their own shells) then materialized almost out of nowhere from trenches which had been driven to within ten yards of the French forward positions.

All this was pure, orthodox, 18-century siege technique, and the only remedy against it was of equal vintage—the sortie, the disorganization of the enemy's siege system by powerful infantry counterattacks designed to give the fortress ampler "breathing-space." De Castries desperately tried to stave off death from strangulation. As long as the available manpower and the sparse ammunition allowed it,* French tanks and infantry delivered attacks outside the perimeter but never were they able to reach the strength necessary to dislocate the enemy's tightening net or to regain terrain outside the shrinking perimeter of the fortress itself.

Basically, three errors were committed at Dien Bien Phu, each at a different command echelon:

(1) the choice of fighting such a decisive battle so far from all major French centers of strength;

(2) the capital error in the underestimation of the enemy's capabilities; and

(3) the positioning of forces within the fortress itself. This latter point includes the already-mentioned fact that a large part of Dien Bien Phu's artillery was positioned at strongpoint Isabelle, seven kilometers to the south, with the result that it could not effectively intervene in the battle for Hills Gabrielle, Beatrice or Anne-Marie.

There remained two other solutions to the siege of Dien Bien Phu—the breakout of the garrison or the breakthrough of an

---

*The fortress began the battle with about six days of ammunition on hand and nearly ran out of it on the second day of battle. Afterwards, resupply operations permitted only the most careful expenditure of ammunition.

outside relief column. The breakout (mainly for the garrison of Isabelle) was dubbed, fittingly enough, "Albatross," and the breakthrough to Dien Bien Phu was given the code name of "Condor." We already have seen how "Albatross" ended. "Condor," in order to face 40,000 enemy troops, would have required a troop strength which was unavailable in Indochina, and, had it been available, would have been unable to cross the roadless jungle of northern Laos without extensive and lengthy preparations. After winding itself for weeks on end through empty villages and impenetrable jungles, the understrength "Condor" force, under Colonel Boucher de Crèvecoeur, had reached a point 40 miles from Dien Bien Phu when it fell. All it could do was to serve as a rescue buoy for the seventy-odd men who succeeded in breaking out of the doomed fortress.

The supposition has often been raised that the fatal flaw in the preparation of the French for the battle of Dien Bien Phu lay in faulty intelligence. Recent research on that point shows that this was not the case. In fact, as early as November 28, 1953 (that is, eight days after the initial French airborne landing), the French *Deuxième Bureau* provided the High Command with an estimated enemy strength figure of twenty-nine infantry battalions. That estimate overstated reality by only one battalion.

On December 27, 1953, French Air Force intelligence, basing its estimate on aerial photography of the Viet-Minh's camouflaged positions with ultra-sensitive film, estimated that the enemy's potential strength would be about 49,000 men, including 33,000 combatants. Those figures were within 10 percent of reality. While the enemy could spring on the French some unpleasant tactical surprises—for example, the multi-tube Russian rocket launchers which intervened in the battle during its last days were certainly not part of what French intelligence had "programmed"—the worst errors made were simply those of an outrageous overestimation of one's own worth (a national flaw of which my countrymen seem to be afflicted since before Julius Caesar's campaigns in Gaul, which, incidentally, culminated in a Gallic Dien Bien Phu at a fortress called Alesia) and an underestimation of the enemy's innate capabilities as a fighter, artilleryman, and supply carrier.

According to information recently made public by former President Eisenhower, American estimates of the situation in Indochina were as unjustifiedly optimistic or uncognizant of the realities on the terrain in 1953-54 as they were of the rapidly deteriorating situation in South Viet-Nam in 1957-64. Thus, in February, 1954, when General Navarre and his staff already knew that, in case of a head-on clash with the Communist main battle force, Dien Bien Phu would be doomed, President Eisenhower wired to Secretary of State John Foster Dulles who was then in Europe that "General O'Daniel's most recent report is more encouraging than [that] given to you through French sources."*

And when the battle turned into utter disaster and the problem of the breakthrough arose, President Eisenhower was notified of a plan devised by General O'Daniel which provided—of all things —for "an attack from Hanoi to Dien Bien Phu by armored groups and mechanized infantry elements." Obviously, General O'Daniel must have been totally unaware of the high cost in blood and armor of the battle for Hoa-Binh (40 miles from the Red River delta); let alone of a 200-mile "dash" through totally roadless jungle in the face of at least three Communist divisions (the 320th and 324th plus five independent regiments) readily available outside of the Communist five-division siege ring around the doomed fortress! Without direct enemy interference and with a maximum of engineering personnel and equipment available, it took the United States Army about *eighteen* months to build the Ledo Road in Burma (112 miles long): One can readily guess how long the French engineers would have taken to build a road twice that length across terrain just as savage as that of Burma—and under direct enemy attack. Yet, even in 1963, President Eisenhower still wondered in his memoirs why the O'Daniel plan for saving Dien Bien Phu "was considered but never attempted by the French High Command." (p. 351) The reason for it was quite simply that it was probably the most wildly implausible plan ever made for that kind of situation. Such a plan had not even worked in September, 1944, in the open plains of Western Europe, when British and American armor failed to complete a 60-mile dash to hack out the British 1st Airborne Division (reinforced) from

---

*Dwight D. Eisenhower, *Mandate for a Change*. New York: Doubleday & Co., 1963, p. 344.

Arnhem airhead in Holland; or when Hitler's Fourth Panzer Army tried to break through to Stalingrad in December, 1942, across the South Russian steppe. In the jungles of Indochina, it would have been plain suicide and would have totally destroyed the French Union Forces in a few weeks, without bringing the slightest respite for Dien Bien Phu.

But the French planners, even without O'Daniel's help, had made other important miscalculations.

The hampering effect of the monsoon on the enemy's motor transport (he immediately switched to use of more human carriers) was hopefully taken into account, but the even worse effect of the same monsoon on our own air transport (not replaceable by humans) just as readily discounted. Thus, as the battle reached Verdun-type intensity on March 31, 1954, the fortress ran completely out of hand grenades and 81mm mortar shells and subsequent resupply operations never succeeded in replenishing the depleted stocks. Between the weather and enemy antiaircraft artillery, victualing the doomed fortress became an unending martyrdom for both suppliers and supplied. There was the black day of April 15, when three C-119 "Flying Boxcars" dumped 19 tons of 105mm howitzer and 120mm heavy mortar ammunition into enemy lines. The enemy, amply supplied in American artillery, re-used the shells immediately. A few days later, two French fighters strafed their own positions in the shrinking fortress; and supply levels, estimated at 200 tons per day, often dropped to 90 tons and, on some particularly bad days, to nothing.

What the battle did not provide in material achievements, it amply made up in human (or rather inhuman) heroism. Lest one forgets—and one easily does—*one-third* of the garrison was Vietnamese when the battle opened in March 1954. Another 25 percent were Foreign Legionnaires, 22 percent were mainland Frenchmen, and 20 percent were African (mostly Moroccans). In the course of the battle, five more paratroop battalions —one Vietnamese, one Foreign Legionnaire and the other three mainland French—and three complete Airborne Surgical Detachments were parachuted into the flaming hell of the valley, bringing the share of mainland Frenchmen in the garrison up to 35 percent. Special mention should be made of the 1,530 volunteers who jumped into Dien Bien Phu as individual replacements for specialists (radiomen, gunners, etc.) who had become casualties. Of those men, 680 had *never* jumped from an airplane,* and again, there were almost eight hundred Vietnamese among those who were dropped into the fortress. The last group of 94 volunteers was dropped in at 0520 on May 6—one day before the fortress fell. This perhaps was the best answer to those who, to this day, like to dismiss the French-trained Vietnamese forces as mere "mercenaries." For what Dien Bien Phu had to offer one day before its fall, there just was not enough money around to make it worth the fight.

It is not impossible that one of the causes of the relatively low combativity of the present-day South Vietnamese troops can be traced to the fact that their seniors who fought with (but not *for*) the French at Dien Bien Phu, had been depicted to them for eight years as "valets and mercenaries of the colonialists"—just as the Communists did in their own propaganda—while, for example, the Indian, Pakistani, or Moroccan national armies look back with great pride upon the traditions of military valor which their fighting men acquired while dying for Britain or France, from Flanders' fields to Monte Cassino or Stuttgart. That pride in past achievements is alive in their uniforms and insignia (often unchanged from colonial days), in the battle streamers of their unit flags, and in the traditions of their regiments.

At least the Communist Viet-Minh forces can look back upon twenty years (as of 1964) of successful achievements, including several major military victories over a powerful enemy. As I could see for myself during a long visit to the North Vietnamese Army Museum in Hanoi, that tradition is being kept alive and made into the veritable "mystique" necessary to build up esprit de corps. The South Vietnamese Army, on the other hand, was deliberately made to turn its back on eighty years of military association with France, in the course of which Vietnamese performed heroically as air aces, won the Legion of Honor at

---

*One noteworthy fact emerged out of the drop of non-qualified jumpers: their drop casualties were no higher than those of the paratroop regulars, which tends to confirm the view of those who hold that a parachute is merely a means of delivery but not a way of fighting.

Verdun, and valiantly served on battlefields of three continents.*
Its traditions begin with the birth of the Vietnamese Republic
in 1955, and its only visible tie to its earlier military past is the
red béret of the paratroops. That, unfortunately, is not enough
to instill esprit de corps into a whole army, and the price for that
error is now being paid throughout South Viet-Nam. Money can
provide helicopters; it cannot provide fighting spirit.

It would be a measure of consolation if one at least could say
that Dien Bien Phu had not been fought in vain and that the
thousands who suffered and died there or on the death march
to the Communist prison camps had in some measure influenced
the fate of the Indochina war. The harsh fact is that their sacrifice
delayed, but did not prevent, the collapse of the French position
in the key Red River delta. Hopelessly infiltrated by 80,000 Communist guerrillas and by four regular regiments, the daily opening
of the Hanoi-Haiphong lifeline had degenerated into a series of
melées involving complete mobile groups. On the southern Plateau, G.M. 100 was on the way to its own agony, and in the plains
of South Viet-Nam, a call-up of 100,000 Vietnamese to the colors
of their own armed forces yielded some 9,000 men, most of them
unfit for combat duty.

The cease-fire negotiated at Geneva on July 20, 1954, all pious
cries of "sell-out" notwithstanding, was, like that of Panmunjom
one year earlier, the best obtainable under the circumstances.

---

*There is perhaps no better example of the Vietnamese fighting spirit than
former emperor Duy-Tan, removed from the Vietnamese throne by the French
during World War I for his anti-colonial activities. Having opposed the French
all his life, he nevertheless felt that the only way Viet-Nam could become independent was to show France that its men could fight. In World War II, he enlisted
in the Foreign Legion, rose to the rank of major under the name of Vinh-San,
became one of General de Gaulle's early associates, and the only Vietnamese to
bear the coveted title and medal of "Companion of the Order of French Liberation." He was killed in an air crash in late 1945.

13

The Loss Of Laos

I N RETROSPECT, the three-year old Laotian conflict which was temporarily resolved by the neutralization of Laos on July 23, 1962 under a coalition government, was probably one of the most avoidable conflicts on record, and one that was beyond a doubt one of the most misreported in recent American history. While it is pointless here to go into the political details of the story,* it can be safely said that a good part of the American setback in the area was due to a hopelessly over-optimistic estimate of the fighting ability of the Royal Laotian Army—*not* by the Pentagon, apparently (at least not in the first stages of the affair), but by the political planners in Washington. In fact, the Pentagon refused until 1958 to even set a "force level" for Laotian forces to be supported by U.S. aid on the perfectly sound assumption that their stand against a determined Communist attack would be at best uncertain. It was finally persuaded to do so on political grounds.

A part of the blame for the sad state of the Laotian Army must inescapably fall on the French training mission which had a training monopoly in Laos until late 1958 but had not helped the Laotian Army to adapt itself to the realities of its own chaotic terrain and communications. The French reply to that accusation

---

*For examples of attempts to tell the public how misled it was in Laos, see William J. Lederer (Capt., USN, Ret.), *A Nation of Sheep,* or this writer's "The Laos Tangle," in *International Journal,* Toronto, May 1961.

was that, as advisers in an independent country, it was hard to make the Laotians do something they were reluctant to do (i.e., field training), and, after three years of similarly frustrating experiences, the U.S. military advisers who succeeded the French between 1959 and 1962,* tended largely to agree with them. Heavily overpaid ($32 a month per soldier) in relation to the country's civilian pay scales (a gross per-capita income of about $100 a year); composed on one hand of Volunteer Battalions (BV's) which cannot be used outside of their areas of recruitment, and on the other of regular battalions which are somewhat more flexible, the Royal Laotian Army was structurally ill suited to come to grips with a fluid guerrilla force.

It did have its own guerrilla groups, inherited in good part from the French GCMA's, but they were miserably underpaid for the considerable risks they had to assume. Their families lived in villages where the Communists could carry out reprisal raids while the families of the regular forces lived in the large cities of the plains.

The result of this situation was that, in the "Laos war" of 1959, the Laotian forces were at a considerable disadvantage in relation to the rebel groups. But here again, as in the case of many events in Asia, it is necessary first to eliminate some of the misinformation spread about the matter by incredibly sloppy press reporting for the sake of pure sensationalism. It can be said that, with the laudable exception of the *Wall Street Journal,* the *St. Louis Post-Dispatch,* and *Time,* the American press gave a completely distorted picture of what happened in Laos in the summer of 1959, with the *Washington Post* and the *New York Times* being among the worst offenders.

Basically, the Laos rebellion of 1959 stemmed from the fact that native pro-Communist forces led by Prince Souphanouvong, refused to abide by an agreement made between them and the Royal Lao Government. That agreement provided for the integration of two ex-rebel battalions (commonly known as *"Pathet-Lao"* units) into the Lao Army. When integration was to take place in May 1959, the Pathet-Lao demanded a larger number

---

*By virtue of the Geneva neutralization agreements of July 1962, the U.S. military and the Communist "advisers" had to evacuate Laos within 75 days, leaving again the French as the only military training personnel in Laos, for a maximum period of five years.

of officers' positions than was warranted for two battalions; and while the Lao Government interpreted the agreement to mean that the rebel soldiers would be integrated on an individual basis, the Pathet-Lao demanded that the two battalions remain intact as a cohesive force—a demand that was clearly unacceptable to the Government as it would have constituted a grave danger to the security of the armed forces.

On May 11, 1959, the integration ceremonies were slated to be held for one of the rebel battalions stationed on the wide open *Plaine des Jarres* (Plain of the Urns) military camp, and for the

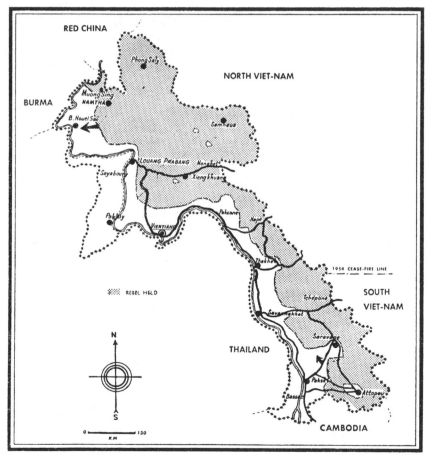

The War in Laos, 1959-1964.

other battalion stationed at Xieng-Ngoeun, near the royal capital of Luang-Prabang. Both units refused to participate in the ceremonies, and the Royal Lao Army began to surround the rebel unit at the Plaine des Jarres with the equivalent of five loyal army battalions. The rebel battalion was understrength and counted perhaps 420 combatants in addition to a certain number of women and children. Its armament included two machine guns, four 81 mm mortars, and twenty BAR's.

After several days of negotiations, the rebel commander agreed to the integration of his troops for the morning of May 19. That night, a heavy rain fell on the Plaine des Jarres, soaking to the skin the five Lao battalions surrounding the barracks of the Pathet-Lao, but the rising sun soon began to disperse the light fog which had lain over the camp.

In the Pathet-Lao barracks, not a soul stirred. A lone "Peugeot" panel truck, the only vehicle the Pathet-Lao had acquired since leaving the jungle in 1957, stood near the barracks on its flat tires; the uniforms provided by the Lao Army to the rebels for the integration ceremony had remained in the barracks in neat stacks and bundles. Only the broad-cleated French jungle shoes, the famous "Pataugas," had been thoroughly sabotaged by machete incisions made in their soles. A few dead dogs lay around the compound, killed by the departing rebels so that they would not give away the movement of the column. The 2d Pathet-Lao Battalion had left the camp and filtered with women and children through a cordon of five infantry battalions on a wide open plain without being detected.

Within less than a week, and in spite of almost immediate pursuit by infantry units and even by airborne elements parachuted across their path, the Pathet-Lao had disappeared again into the forest near the border of Communist North Viet-Nam. The 1st Battalion at Xieng Ngeun at first failed to make its getaway and accepted integration, swearing an oath of loyalty to the Lao Government. When most senior Loatian officials and foreign diplomats were in nearby Luang-Prabang on August 8, 1959, to celebrate the marriage of a princess of the Royal House, about two hundred officers and men of that rebel battalion also took to the hills in the direction of North Viet-Nam, overpowering and destroying the small Lao Army garrisons in its path. The Laotian rebellion of 1959 had begun in earnest.

Basically, the pattern of Pathet-Lao attacks followed to the letter that of Viet-Minh forces against the French, with both sides fighting exactly true to previous patterns and with the same results. The fighting fell into three periods:

1. From July 18 to July 31, with main emphasis upon a rebel thrust deep into Samneua Province, seeking to cut it off from the rest of Laos.

2. From August 1 to August 29, a period of generalized insecurity with emphasis upon pin prick attacks throughout almost every province of the country.

3. From August 30 to September 15, resumption of heavy localized attacks against Lao Army posts in Samneua, with thrusts along the traditional invasion route towards Luang-Prabang and Vientiane.

Press dispatches bore such news as "Viet-Minh troops advanced to within 13 miles of Samneua city" (UPI), and even the staid British agency Reuters headlined on September 3 that "the Royal Laotian Army was today preparing to defend the capital of Vientiane"; while on September 5, an editorial of the *Washington Post*, citing the "splendid examples of alert, on-the spot reporting" of its columnist Joseph Alsop, spoke of a "full-scale, artillery-backed invasion from Communist North Viet-Nam." All this was just so much nonsense.

In his column of September 3, 1959, speaking of the attacks against the Laotian posts along the Nam River, Alsop averred that the Lao commanding general was informed of the fall of the river line posts by a pilot's word and by villagers, one of whom had a "severe leg wound. They had walked in (to Samneua) from Muong Hêt and Xieng Khô, 61 and 70 kilometers respectively." In another of his dispatches, he spoke of "125-millimeter" cannon, probably meaning 105mm, which were also mentioned in other reports.

The hard facts were that (a) the Laotian Army command in Samneua *did* know what went on in the border posts since it had radio communications with them; (b) a villager with a severe leg wound does not cover 45 miles in two days of march in the Laotian jungle; and (c) the maximum effective range of a 105 being around 10,000 yards, the Viet-Minh artillery would have been hard put to fire at Xieng-Khô, 14 kilometers and two hill ranges away from North Viet-Nam. But the myth, once created, proved extremely hard to kill.

Two weeks later, the letdown began. Even the *New York Times* reporter in Laos, who, until then, had swallowed whole every press release circulating in Vientiane, noted on September 13 that "briefings have noticeably played down the activities of North Viet-Nam in the conflict. This led some observers to believe that Laotian political tacticians were creating a background that would soften the blow if the [United Nations] observer report on intervention by North Viet-Nam was negative." Indeed, the Security Council report of November 5, 1959, did fail to substantiate the theory of a Communist outside invasion of Laos.

On September 22, 1959, the Laotian Government, according to AP, "avoided accusing North Viet-Nam of aggression in documents put before the special United Nations fact-finding committee," and the same agency reported that Sam Teu, which allegedly had been the scene of "five days of fierce fighting, was practically unscarred." Richard Dudman, from the *St. Louis Post-Dispatch*, visited Sam Teu then and found the battle scene reduced to the following proportions: from 600 attackers to about 200; from 300 defenders to 30 (with another 110 in the surrounding hills), and from an hour-long barrage by 330 mortar shells to a few unidentifiable holes, with no evidence of destroyed buildings or trenches. In addition, the fort had not been taken, but its garrison had withdrawn to the hills at night and had peacefully reoccupied it in the morning.

The same veil of uncertainty covered the problem of Communist prisoners. Had there been any, and if so, were they North Vietnamese taken on Lao territory in combat? When the facts were known (and in the meantime, there had been an interesting "numbers game" beginning with about fifty, then thirty, then seventeen, twelve, seven and, finally, two prisoners), the Lao Government preferred to base its case on other evidence.

It remained for the authoritative military commentator Hanson W. Baldwin to sum up the situation in the following terms:

> It would be a thankless military task, indeed, to use Laos as a base from which to conquer the rest of Southeast Asia . . . The Laotian Communist rebels have provided most or all of the few aggressors.* There is no hard evidence of participation by regular North Vietnamese or (Red) Chinese soldiers.

There is, of course, not the slightest doubt that certainly North Viet-Nam and perhaps even Red China, gave military and political support to the Laotian rebellion. But their aid was in no way as overt as originally suggested in the alarming reports spread around the world by American press media, some of which went so far in their affirmations as to accuse almost anyone who doubted their stories as being either a blind fool or "soft" on Communism. Joseph Alsop's "Open Letter" to Henry Luce, the publisher of *Time* and *Life* (both of which refused to be stampeded by their less hard-headed colleagues) is a prime example of this attitude.

It would be at least a small matter of comfort to be able to report that the West had learned its lesson from the invasion scare of 1959, but this was not to be. Late in 1960, a few days after the pro-American government of Prince Boun Oum had eliminated the neutralist administration of Prince Souvanna Phouma, a new Communist "invasion" of Laos was reported. The Laotian government, with as little (if not less) information to go on than the year before, reported to the world at large on December 31, 1960, that "seven battalions of North Vietnamese troops" had invaded the little country.

While the British and French—whose sources of information in Laos already had proved more reliable the year before—awaited more hard facts to go on, Washington took up the cudgels in full, both officially and in the press. In a somber column, Mr. Joseph Alsop spoke of the "yawning drain" which Laos was likely to be engulfed in; compared the 1954 Geneva settlement to the Munich

---

*Here also, a wild "numbers game" ensued, in which the original six hundred fifty Pathet-Lao combatants, no doubt reinforced by about several hundred tribesmen, became up to 11,000 invaders. None of the operations mounted by the rebels required at any time a concentration of more than two or three companies. Psychological warfare and sound jungle tactics did the rest.

sell-out of 1938; and called our Canadian allies who had staunchly defended the Western viewpoint in the international cease-fire commission (the other members being India and Poland), "approximately neutral."

The Russians, to be sure, immediately supplied the Pathet-Lao forces with arms and ammunition—mostly *American*, from Indochina war stocks, since the rebels could always count on capturing supplies from the Lao troops. On the pro-American side, the Lao forces were supplied with light combat aircraft (half of which were shot down or otherwise lost after two months of operations), as if strafing invisible targets in the jungle was to be more effective in 1961 than it was in 1954. After seven years of laboriously ignoring the mountain tribes, frantic efforts now were made to organize Meo tribesmen along G.C.M.A. lines in order to saddle the Pathet-Lao with a guerrilla problem of their own.

What happened next will have to go down as one of the most botched military operations in recent history. Captain Kong-Lê, the young American-trained paratroop officer who headed the Laotian troops faithful to neutralist premier Prince Souvanna Phouma, methodically withdrew northward, after a withering bombardment of the capital city of Vientiane by Right-wing forces of Prince Boun Oum and General Phoumi Nosavan, which did little else but make a shambles of the city and kill about one thousand civilians (not 600, as reported). A concentration of 125 howitzer shells fell into the French Military Mission's compound, where 170 French women and children, along with six hundred Laotian civilians, had taken refuge; killing 52 Laotians and wounding 69 Laotians and Frenchmen.*

But undefeated Kong-Lê, taking with him not only his own paratroop battalion but also the bulk of the male students of the Vientiane *Lycée*, reached Vang-Vieng, midway between Vientiane and Luang-Prabang at the entrance of the key road to the Plaine des Jarres. On New Year's Day 1961, that vital area fell into his hands almost without a shot. General Phoumi, backed by American instructors and equipment, announced a "general offensive" against the Plaine, with its three airfields, and which now had

---

*Personal on-the-spot investigation by the author, July 1962.

become the funnel for a vast Soviet airlift of equipment and North Vietnamese instructors. That Right-wing offensive, launched on January 7, failed miserably, in spite of the fact that at that time the Pathet-Lao's forces barely exceeded 15,000 men and Kong-Lê's units hardly numbered 3,000; while Phoumi could muster upward of 60,000 men. A more limited offensive against the Sala Phou Khoun-Vang Vieng crossroads ended in a Pathet-Lao—Kong-Lê counteroffensive which, on April 24, 1961, completely routed the Right-wing forces who abandoned their American advisers (a captain and three sergeants) in enemy hands. On May 2, 1961, fourteen nations, including Russia and the United States, met at Geneva to hammer out exactly what the United States had sought so strenuously to avoid: a neutral coalition government including Communist members in key posts.

It took another full year to get the various Laotian factions to agree to such a government, and in the meantime both the Right wing and its opponents sought to improve their military posture. American Special Forces groups and more equipment poured into the country, but the Right-wing Laotian troops—totally deprived of any cause they considered worth fighting for—simply never developed any real fighting ability, regardless of how hard their American instructors tried. A new limited offensive, launched in January 1962 by Mobile Groups 12 and 14 against Pathet-Lao positions near Nhommarat and Mahaxay in Khammouane Province (see end paper map), ended in total discomfiture of the Right-wing forces (and again in the abandonment of their American instructors, who returned to their own lines a week later). The neutralists and Pathet-Lao answered on May 6 by an offensive of their own against the northern position of Nam-Tha, a Dien Bien Phu-like valley bottom in which General Phoumi, against urgent American advice, had concentrated about 5,300 regulars and almost 1,700 of his own militia forces.

After a brief fire fight, in which one of Phoumi's elite paratroop battalions was badly mauled and threw a panic into the whole vast body of troops, the entire garrison simply took to its collective heels. This time, however, the American advisers were forewarned and had been picked up in time by helicopters; the latter, incidentally, also took with them Lao Army General Bounleuth, the northern commander-in-chief, who had thrown away his rank insignia and disguised himself as a private.

What followed then was an exact replica of the previous "cry wolf" periods of the Laotian crisis. In spite of the fact that U.S. Colonel Edwin Elder, the commander of the Nam-Tha MAAG detachment, immediately warned with the coolness of the professional soldier that there was "no evidence to show that Chinese or [North] Vietnamese had participated in the attack," the Laotians—and much of the U.S. press, and official Washington with them—immediately clamored that they were again faced with a large-scale "foreign invasion." As on previous occasions, such talk merely increased the demoralization of the Laotian troops; they covered the 60-odd miles between Nam-Tha and Thailand in an astounding 48 hours and infected the unattacked border garrison of Ban Houei Sai with their own panic. Ban Houei Sai was announced as having fallen into Communist hands at 0300 on May 11, 1962, *while in actual fact no organized enemy unit was within thirty miles of the town!* Yet, in response to that "threat," American, British, Australian, and New Zealand troops began to arrive in neighboring Thailand. The only casualties in Ban Houei Sai were those Laotian soldiers who drowned in the Mekong as they tried to cross it into Thailand, or who were injured as they were trying to burn vehicles and ammunition dumps in the city itself. Soon, the American MAAG detachment, some hardy Western journalists, and Norris Smith, a USIS official from Vientiane; were the only "defenders" of the deserted town, while across the river in Thailand, the bedraggled Laotian soldiers were partly disarmed and then airlifted off to southern Laos for "rest and recuperation" after their foot-racing ordeal.

All that, if nothing else, brought the stalled negotiations into swing again. General Phoumi Nosavan clearly saw that his dispirited troops, regardless of how numerous and well-armed they were, were no match for the fanatic Pathet-Lao and Kong-Lê forces. On June 12, 1962, he and Prince Boun Oum traveled the hard road to the enemy headquarters at the Plaine des Jarres and agreed to a coalition regime. Five weeks later, the neutralization of Laos was an accomplished fact, with Red Prince Souphannouvong's Pathet-Lao detachments appearing in Vientiane

in their ill-fitting North Vietnamese fatigues with Russian automatic rifles, while Prince Souvanna Phouma's neutralist troops
sported brand-new French paratroop uniforms and Russian
tommyguns, as well as a thirty-vehicle regiment of Soviet-built
tanks and armored cars.

The Laotian "troika" proved politically and militarily shaky
from the beginning. The right-wing forces, still the most numerous
with about 50,000 men under arms as against 8,000 neutralists
and close to 20,000 Pathet-Lao, still were hoping for outside
support for a "third round" with the Communists. And the latter
were using "salami tactics"—i.e., taking the enemy slice-by-slice
—in dealing both with the right wing and with their own neutralist
allies of yesterday. General Kong-Lê's positions on the vital Plaine
des Jarres were gradually whittled down to a precarious toehold
by a succession of small-scale attacks. Other attacks in the Central
Laotian "corridor" covering the Ho Chi Minh Trail, notably a
limited offensive in direction of Thakhek in January, 1964, again
brought Communist forces dangerously near to the vital Mekong
valley, as did a subsequent attack toward Paksane in May.

Political tensions in Vientiane brought the departure of Pathet-
Lao elements from that city in September, 1963. From then on,
an eventual resumption of severe military clashes was to be expected, and both sides prepared for it. Right-wing military forces
continued to behave as dispiritedly as in the past: On February 27,
1964, a right-wing battalion "lost" the important Phou Khé ridge
east of the Plaine des Jarres to what was alleged to be—as usual—
"vastly superior North Vietnamese-supported" enemy forces. A
counterthrust by Kong-Lê's neutralist forces on March 1 showed
no evidence of the presence of such forces. On the other hand,
the Meo tribesmen of Colonel (later General) Vang Pao, organized along GCMA lines by American Special Forces and supplied even after the 1962 cease-fire by a special-mission "airline,"
fought well and gave the Pathet-Lao a few rear-area security problems of its own. But here again, I fear, an essentially correct method
was used to solve the wrong problem: As any good ethnic map of
Indochina shows, the Meo only occupy the mountaintops. It is
the White and Black T'ai who occupy the vital midlands, often to
within a few miles of the Mekong valley and also deep into Com-

munist North Viet-Nam and even Red Chinese Yunnan. A resistance movement built on the Meo can essentially be only *defensive* since the Meo tribesmen would sooner or later run head-on into T'ai tribes; whereas a resistance or guerrilla movement built on the T'ai (as was done by the GCMA) could well have become the source of an offensive tribal ground swell which might well have changed the complexion of the whole Laos and Viet-Nam problem in the long run.

As the situation worsened in South Viet-Nam, a tendency apparently developed both in Saigon and among right-wing Laotian elements to think that joint planning in the counter-insurgency field might improve the situation on both sides of the common border. There probably also was a feeling that a Communist reaction against *both* countries might bring about large-scale American help to what would be in effect an Indochina War at 1953 level, with a single front running from Ban Houei Sai to north of Hué —as proposed then by General O'Daniel. On March 15, 1964, secret talks took place between General Phoumi and General Nguyên Khanh, the revolutionary premier of South Viet-Nam. On April 19, a right-wing coup took place in Vientiane, in the course of which two Laotian generals, Kouprasith Abbhay and Siho Lapouthancoul, took power and in fact sequestrated Laotian prime minister Souvanna Phouma despite strong American, British, French, and even Russian, pressures to release him. When he was finally allowed to resume power (but under the aegis of the right-wing generals), Prince Souvanna Phouma's role as a coalition premier was shakier than ever and he was put on notice by the Pathet-Lao on April 24, that it would not accept a Vientiane government dominated by the right-wing junta.

Apparently undeterred by Western and Russian warnings that further junta pressure on Souvanna Phouma would only increase the Pathet-Lao's aggressiveness and support by Hanoi and Peking, the Laotian right wing compelled Phouma to accept a merger between the neutralist and right-wing forces. The new Laotian General Staff, set up as a result of that merger, gave nine jobs to the right-wing forces against one totally unimportant post (that of Assistant Inspector General) to neutralist General Amkha Souk-havong. It remains to be seen whether the Pathet-Lao offensive which followed, and which swept the now merged right-wing and neutralist forces off the Plaine des Jarres, was a deliberate act of aggression or a direct reaction to the right-wing coup in Vientiane. In any case, Laos again seemed to be headed toward the kind of "polarization" into Right and Left which had gotten it into deep trouble twice before. The fact that General Kong-Lê's forces—particularly his Russian armor, which grimly held on to the western rim of the Plaine until it ran out of ammunition—again fought well and are now mostly fighting against the Pathet-Lao rather than with them as in 1961-62, is perhaps the one bright glimmer in the whole sorry mess. But that factor alone is unlikely to keep Laos from foundering once more, either on the battlefield or at the conference table.

Many explanations have been given for the incredibly poor performance of the Phoumi forces, of which the most often-heard is that, as Buddhists, they are hesitant to take human life. That, of course, is plain nonsense. Most higher religions forbid the taking of life as a matter of principle, but that has never stopped nations from fighting wars. The Thai, Cambodians, and Burmese likewise are Buddhists (and so are a good many Nepalese Ghurkas and the Tibetans), but that has not stopped them from fighting murderous wars if it was in their interest to do so. The Buddhist Kong-Lê forces and many of the Pathet-Lao who were Buddhists, also gave a good account of themselves.

Here again, it had been forgotten that the main ingredient in revolutionary war is *revolution*. And "our" Laotians simply had nothing to be revolutionary about.

14

The Second Indochina War

I N SOUTH Viet-Nam, methods of subversion even more sophisticated than those used in Laos have led to results which may, in the long run, be even more disastrous for the West than what happened in the little mountain kingdom. Relative peaceableness of the Communists in the years 1954-56 was mistaken for weakness. A Vietnamese Government release handed to all visitors in 1957, citing alleged Communist losses or surrenders since the cease-fire, ended with the following phrase: "From this we can see that the Viet-Minh authorities have disintegrated and have been rendered powerless." And in April 1959, no less than a senior military adviser to the Vietnamese Government would report to a U.S. Congressional Committee that the Viet-Minh guerrillas ". . . were gradually nibbled away until they ceased to be a major menace to the Government."

Unmindful of the bloody lessons of the Indochina war, the new South Vietnamese Army was trained to be a field force ready to face its North Vietnamese rivals in the kind of set-piece battle they had refused to the French for eight long years: mobile groups were merged into light divisions, light divisions into full-sized field divisions, and the latter topped off by full-fledged army corps. The valuable *Dinassaut* were largely disbanded since the French had invented them and there was no equivalent in American

manuals, and were soon followed into oblivion by the commando
forces. No attempt whatever was made to reconstitute anything
approaching the G.C.M.A.'s until 1962.

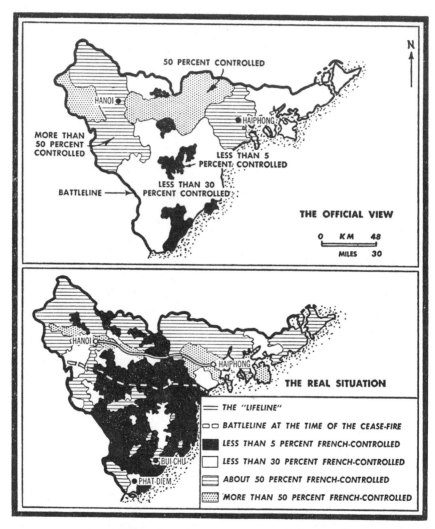

Revolutionary Warfare in North Viet-Nam, 1953.

(The upper map was based on military intelligence information; the lower
map on administrative information, showing absence of civilian control over
villages and towns inside the French battle line. A similar situation prevails in
South Viet-Nam since 1961.)

But the Communists once more refused to do things by the book of Western rules. Sometime late in 1957, they began a new terror offensive directed almost entirely against the village mayors and administrators who, in a rural country, are the backbone of the government. In 1958, the American ambassador to South Viet-Nam reported that such killings took place at the rate of twenty-five a month. On May 5, 1961, Secretary of State Dean Rusk mentioned a figure of 3,000 small officials killed in Viet-Nam during 1960, while in his message of May 24, 1961, President Kennedy gave a figure of 4,000 killed in the same period. Also early in 1960, Communist guerrillas who had infiltrated in South Viet-Nam felt strong enough to attack regular Vietnamese Army posts, such as the one at Trang-Sup, where a whole Vietnamese battalion was destroyed and all its equipment fell into rebel hands. And, as a few years ago under the French, heavy Vietnamese units set out in a clatter of armor and a roar of trucks to chase after small black-clad figures stealthily operating in small groups —and found nothing.

The regular forces, bogged down with their heavy equipment, were used time and time again for anti-guerrilla missions for which they were neither trained nor psychologically suited. On October 21, 1960—almost duplicating the destruction of Mobile Group 100 six years earlier—a thousand Communist crack troops infiltrated the Kontum area and crushed a string of Vietnamese army posts in a battle which lasted until November 8. Finally, on November 11, 1960, three Vietnamese paratroop battalions—the elite force of the American-trained army—rebelled and marched on President Ngo Dinh Diem's palace in Saigon, claiming that his government had failed to make a sufficiently determined effort in its fight against the Communists. Although the paratroopers were subdued the next day by armored forces which had remained loyal, the hard fact remains that the paratroopers' revolt had been one of frustration—the frustration of crack troops being misused for a mission which they cannot possibly expect to accomplish successfully.

Combating the Insurgency

Throughout the first half of 1961, the situation in South Viet-Nam simply went from bad to worse. A special study mission, sent to Viet-Nam to make recommendations on suitable reform, came forth with little else but some minor military improvements and an eighteen-month "counter-insurgency plan" which was out-run by events by the time it left the mimeograph machine. It was the study mission in October 1961 of General Maxwell D. Taylor, Chairman of the Joint Chiefs of Staff in 1962, which, after a brief stay in Viet-Nam, came forth with wide-ranging recommendations for political, military, and economic reforms; of which, according to Brigadier General S. L. A. ["Slam"] Marshall, the noted military writer, less than "one-fourth . . . was bought by the Administration."*

The creation of a U.S. Military Assistance Command, Viet-Nam (USMACV) under General Paul D. Harkins on February 9, 1962, marked the opening date of America's direct involvement in the new Indochina war. Although the word "adviser" is care-fully added to the name of every American operating in the country, it soon acquired the quotation marks usually reserved for assertions no one takes quite seriously any longer. Since 1961 Americans die in Viet-Nam, and in American uniforms. And they die fighting.

On April 6, 1962, agreement was reached with the South Viet-namese government for the gradual implementation of two ambi-tious pacification plans: "Sunrise" and "Delta." They involved the gradual extrication from Communist control of the civilian population through the creation of "Strategic Hamlets" defended by militia forces. Following the successful British pattern applied in Malaya, the removal of guerrilla control over the population would eventually deprive it of the civilian environment upon which the guerrilla, according to Mao Tse-tung, must depend in order to survive. By the end of 1963 it had failed badly.**

That "grand design" ran into military and political trouble al-most from the start as the Diem regime was totally unwilling to proceed with the political and economic reforms that were ab-solutely essential to the success of the program, and as Strategic

---

*Brig. Gen. Marshall, " 'Pedee' Harkins' New Problem," *Bangkok World,* March 8, 1962.

**For a more thorough examination of counterinsurgency failures in Viet-Nam, see Fall, B., *The Two Viet-Nams: A Political and Military History.* (3d rev. ed.) New York: Praeger, 1964.

Hamlets were placed as spearheads into areas that were totally under Communist control. Under pressure from Saigon to "produce results," local district officials proclaimed hamlet completion figures totally out of line with reality and, as earlier under French rule, the foreign experts tended to fall into line with the officially expressed optimism, until it became clear after the fall of the Diem regime on November 2, 1963, that a bare twenty per cent of the total of about 8,000 hamlets was truly viable and likely to be defended in case of a VC attack.

One of the contributing factors to this erroneous appraisal was the superficial resemblance of the Vietnamese hamlet program with what the British had done in Malaya. In Malaya, a total of 423,000 Chinese "squatters" had to be removed into 410 villages, to deprive the 8,000 Chinese guerrillas of the bulk of the civilian environment they could count upon. In South Viet-Nam, in order to be successful, the plan would have to involve anywhere between 12,000 to as much as 17,000 hamlets and a total of perhaps eight million people. In addition, Malaya was cut off from any Communist "active sanctuary," whereas South Viet-Nam's border with Laos, a 300-kilometer-long maze of jungle valleys, is almost hopelessly uncontrollable. Even the short cease-fire line with North Viet-Nam along the 17th parallel is more or less a sieve, as was shown in the Department of State's *White Book on North Vietnamese Aggression,* published in December 1961. Cambodia provides no haven for Communist infiltrators, in spite of Vietnamese accusations to the contrary. However, occasional passages of guerrillas in the boundary areas of the country where it abuts on Laos and Viet-Nam are, of course, impossible to jugulate entirely.

Not that total jugulation of the South Vietnamese border area would by now guarantee eventual victory any more than the successful closing of the Algero-Tunisian border brought French victory in the Algerian war: the hard fact is that, save for a few specialized antiaircraft and antitank weapons and cadre personnel not exceeding perhaps 3,000 to 4,000 a year or less, the VC operation inside South Viet-Nam has become self-sustaining. In fact, the worst guerrilla areas are not even abutting on any of Viet-Nam's foreign borders. And while the complete closing of the South Vietnamese border to infiltrators certainly remains a worthwhile objective, to achieve it along 700 miles of jungle-covered mountains and swamp would just about absorb the totality of South Viet-Nam's 1964 forces of 250,000 regulars and 250,000 paramilitary troops of various kinds. That should be made clear before undue official optimism in high places—the bane, thus far, of all reporting on Viet-Nam—again produces a situation from which there can be no exit but a general feeling of mutual re-crimination and letdown.

As the counterinsurgency "grand design" in Viet-Nam stands in 1964, the Hamlet program—their title was redesigned to "New-Life Hamlets" after Diem's fall—was retracted to more sensible proportions and more emphasis is being given to militarily clearing and holding a given area before entrusting its protection to the lightly-armed village militia.

The latter part of the "grand design" in Viet-Nam would in-volve the gradual clearing of whole key areas in which the popula-tion had been regrouped into Strategic Hamlets; while highly mobile anti-guerrilla forces seek out the enemy hard-core units and destroy them. In a final phase, now hardly expected to come about before the late 1960's, the remaining hostile guerrillas will either be pushed back across the border or sealed off to starve and die out in the most inaccessible parts of the Vietnamese jungle. That, at least, is the theory. The reality, as will be seen, is some-what different.

The Enemy

On the enemy side the situation is somewhat simpler. First of all, the objectives of the struggle, both immediate and long-range, are clear—in the immediate future, whatever is left of countryside authority of the Saigon government must be under-mined and the Strategic Village plan at least challenged in key areas. As a long-range objective, Viet-Nam must be reunified under the authority of Ho Chi Minh, although an intermediate situation of a neutral Viet-Nam may prove acceptable for a period of years. To carry out this program, the Communists have several political and military tools at their disposal: militarily, they can count upon limited outside support, but not to the extent which would give the United States a valid pretext to carry the war to North Viet-Nam proper. Hanoi has worked hard for ten years to build up an industrial plant of some dimensions; it does

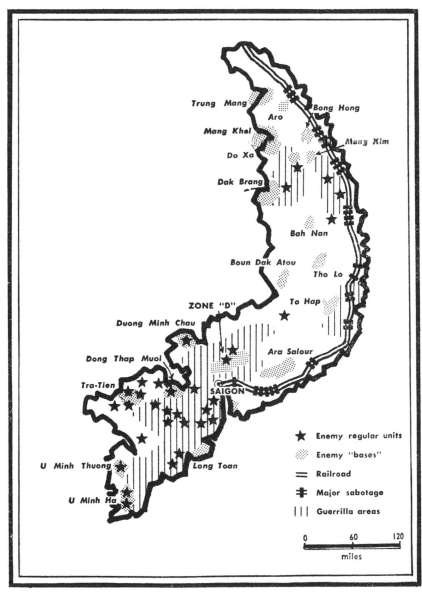

Communist Operations 1962-1964.

not wish to see it knocked out in a series of even conventional saturation raids.

Politically, the Communist bloc will do everything in its power to help the South Vietnamese insurgents through pressure of all kinds, and to build up the stature of the "Southern National Liberation Front" whose directing committee could well blossom out into a "Liberation Government" when the time might be considered ripe.

The military forces of the Liberation Front, like those of the Viet-Minh, fall into three categories: the local militia, levied only for a particular mission but returning to its farming job afterwards; the regional units, which operate within their home province and act as screens for the regulars; and, finally, the *chu-luc* [main force] battalions of locally-raised or infiltrated regulars, who can be counted upon to carry out most of the major operations. Those regular battalions are usually numbered from 502 upward, the highest known number being, thus far, 634. Some of the regular units carry a particular name drawn from the history of Viet-Nam or its revolutionary past. The companies of those regular battalions are numbered in the 200 series. As of mid-1964, only four regiments—the famous 108th and 803d which destroyed G.M. 100; the 120th; and the 126th, another mountaineer unit—have been fully identified as operating south of the 17th parallel.

The overall command of the Liberation Front military forces —on our side they are being referred to as *Viet-Cong,* a disparaging term for "Vietnamese Communists"—lies with two zone commanders, one for the southern part of South Viet-Nam and the other for the hill areas and Central Viet-Nam south of the 17th parallel. Their operations in turn are coordinated by a "Committee for Supervision of the South" located north of the 17th parallel. Ostensibly, however, political control of the southern insurgency lies with the Executive Committee of the Liberation Front, headed by Nguyên Huu Tho, a left-wing lawyer from Saigon. The Committee, though dominated by Communist elements, also contains non-Communists. The flag of the Liberation Front is composed of horizontal bars of sky-blue (top) and red (bottom), with a five-pointed yellow star at its center.

Contrary to what we usually like to believe, political orthodoxy does not exclude tactical flexibility. In fact, very often it favors it. This is a lesson that is being learned by anti-Communist forces in Viet-Nam, and learned the hard way. The enemy never forgets that its fight is first and foremost *political* rather than *military*. It has not forgotten the basic reason for fighting a war, which is to bring the enemy to a point where one can impose one's will upon him—whether by brute force or psychological persuasion.

The insurgents in South Viet-Nam make an intelligent use of a mixture of both methods: Vietnamese village chiefs, youth leaders, school teachers, notables, and other administrative or social leaders of the population are killed or cowed; and American or South Vietnamese units are engaged when victory is almost certain, and always with maximum propaganda effect. The capture of American Special Forces men has already been used for such purposes, and their release even more so. Two of them, after being held prisoner for weeks within a few miles of a Vietnamese Army unit, were released as an "act of clemency" on Communist Labor Day, May 1, 1962. American medical missionaries, abducted from the well-protected Ban Mé Thuot area, were not recovered, in spite of intense search activities. The bombing of American installations in Saigon is also a significant part of the psychological campaign to destroy the belief in the ability of the Vietnamese-American forces to protect their own rear areas and the people who entrust their defense to them.

Another key target is South Vietnamese communications. For years prior to the spreading of the South Vietnamese insurgency to its present proportions, I have lectured on the extreme likelihood that the road and rail lifelines along the Vietnamese seashore would become almost useless in case of a full-fledged guerrilla war.* That fear became full reality during the first half of 1962. No less than nineteen trains were partly or completely destroyed—in one gigantic ambush ninety miles from Saigon on June 5, 1962, two supply trains were destroyed and looted, while the armored troop train that escorted them simply pulled out—

---

*According to a first-hand report by Howard Sochurek, "Slow Train Through Viet-Nam's War," in *National Geographic*, September 1964, "since 1961 . . . 128 locomotives have been damaged," and of 23 new diesel locomotives given last year to Viet-Nam by U.S. aid, twelve were wrecked four months later.

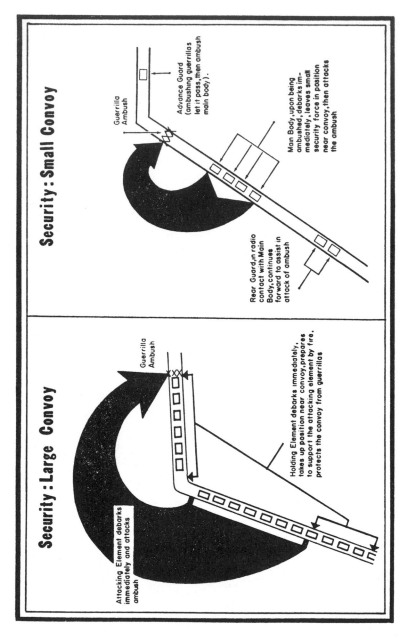

Convoy Ambush in Theory . . . .

and rail bridge or rail line cuts average about one every thirty-six hours. All major roads are under attack, and even armored convoys are subject to daylight ambushes, often within less than thirty miles from Saigon. Night traffic, both road and rail, is at a standstill.

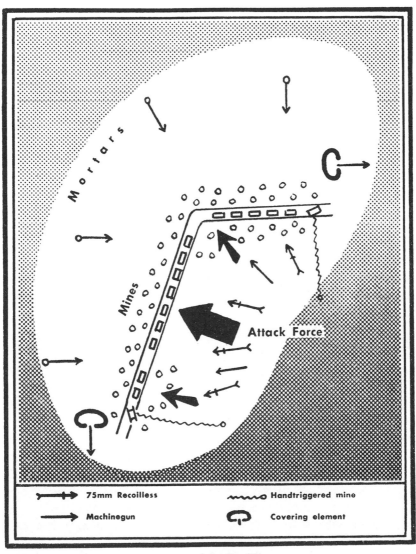

. . . and in Reality.

Americans still have to learn from the French that the latter lost during the Indochina war over 500 armored vehicles, 398 of which (almost two armored divisions!) were destroyed by enemy action between 1952 and 1954. The most important aspect of that part of the war was that *eighty-four* percent of those vehicles were lost through mines and booby-traps and only a handful through conventional antitank weapons. Present operations in South Viet-Nam confirm that Viet-Minh have lost none of their fearsome ability to lay traps for motorized convoys. Many an ambush in recent months differed only in size from that which destroyed G.M. 100 in 1954. Otherwise, the errors of the friendly forces and the tactics of the enemy were entirely the same.

How limited our own imagination in this field is, is nowhere better illustrated than in the two accompanying diagrams, extracted from a *prize-winning* article on counter-guerrilla operations.*

The two charts assume that the enemy would (a) always block the convoy from the front; and (b) leave the flanks of the ambush area both unattacked and, above all, *unmined* and *untrapped*. Both assumptions, as this book has amply shown, are perfect nonsense. (See the chart marked ". . . and in Reality.") In Viet-Nam, the usual "ritual" is to blow up the lead vehicle through a teleguided mine, so as to block the progress of the rest of the convoy, and do the same to the rearguard, so as to block all retreat. The ambush then usually develops along a stretch of road whose sides and ditches have been thoroughly mined or provided with caltraps; and the whole ambush area is well covered by enemy mortars, recoilless artillery, and machine guns. In most cases, secondary ambushes are laid for the rescue elements likely to come up from either the rear or ahead.

That schoolbook view of Communist ambushes—and apparently ignoring or forgetting the bloody lessons learned by the French from similar ambushes—still can lead American advisers and their Vietnamese charges into disastrous situations. Thus two American officers, Captain Walter P. McCarthy and First Lieutenant William F. Train, III, were killed in a well-laid

---

*The diagrams originate from a highly respected American military magazine published in 1962, which shall remain nameless.

Communist ambush a bare 22 miles north of Saigon on June 16, 1962. The guerrillas had prepared their ambush at 0700 without any of the villagers who had seen them betraying them to nearby government forces. The ambush, which took place within earshot of Ben Cat army post, proceeded entirely according to the pattern shown in the above map titled ". . . And in Reality." A civilian truck which happened to precede the convoy closely, was blown up on a hand-triggered land mine, thus blocking the path of the two lead armored cars of the convoy which were promptly riddled with 57mm recoilless rifle shells. The two American officers riding in an open jeep behind the armored cars never had a chance. Of the 28 men in the seven-vehicle convoy, one man survived. Reinforcements set out immediately from Ben Cat and were promptly blocked by felled trees across their paths, which had to be gingerly removed one by one, lest they be mined. They reached the convoy, stripped of its equipment, three hours later. A helicopter-borne pursuit force left Saigon airport at 1500 (e.g., about eight hours *after* the ambush had taken place). It found, of course, no trace of the ambushers.

Captain Don J. York was to die on July 14, 1962 in a *three mile long* ambush 40 miles north of Saigon, in which the 19-vehicle convoy in which he rode and which was manned by elite paratroopers, was badly mauled. The lead mine got York and his jeep, while other mines and recoilless rifle fire soon disabled the rest of the convoy. The 280 paratroops lost about thirty dead and at least twice as many wounded but a go-for-broke drop of two additional paratroop companies saved the rest from annihilation. Here also the Communists evaporated. Obviously,* the old tactics which brought about the demise of gallant G.M. 100 and of officers such as McCarthy, Train, and York, are badly in need of revision. As of 1964, they certainly had not been.

---

*David Halberstam, a highly respected American observer, wrote in the *New York Times Magazine* of November 4, 1962, that some of the American military in Viet-Nam tended "to be overly critical and almost patronizing about the earlier French effort here, and it would probably behoove them to remember . . . that the French were not exactly naïve in the war . . . and that it has yet to be proved that the present effort is really combating the enemy where he lives any more than the French effort did."

There is some evidence that some of the earlier experiences of the French are now being given a certain amount of attention among American specialists in the guerrilla warfare field.

What, in reality, might pay off is the *interspersion,* within the convoy, of armored elements unlikely to be destroyed simultaneously (as was the case of the armored platoon of G.M. 100, traveling in a group), and their counterattack against one of the flanks of the ambush in combination with part of the convoy's infantry, in the hope of rolling up one of the enemy's pincers— providing that such armor will last long enough to do so before being destroyed by mines. Air cover, up to a point, still seems the best answer, but even so, to fight one's way out of a well-laid Viet-Minh ambush is as grim an affair in 1964 as it was in 1952.

Examples of other such errors unfortunately abound and should have been totally avoidable if only some attention had been paid to French experiences in Indochina and Algeria. On January 7, 1962, for example, a Viet-Minh unit attacked the Civil Guard post of Binh-Phu at midnight. At 0330, the post was overrun, with the enemy killing or capturing 23 men, along with an important booty of two machine guns, 16 individual weapons, and two radio transmitters. The local South Vietnamese sector commander ordered a counter-sweep by two American-trained Ranger units supported by motorized (!) elements of the Civil Guard.

The Viet-Minh commander, at least, had read his own book of rules and had set up a counter-ambush at about 1,500 yards from the destroyed post, into which the rescue forces promptly fell, the more so as the Rangers, instead of "sweeping" on foot, had decided to ride along with the Civil Guards in order to gain time. They lost, according to their own report (which may have been optimistic) four dead and ten wounded.*

A somewhat different occurrence showing up yet another misconception took place on March 4, 1962 at Bo-Tuc, 135 kilometers north of Saigon, where an ARVN post of about half a company was to protect an agricultural development center of

---

*Republic of Viet-Nam, State Secretariat of the Presidency, Communiqué of January 10, 1962. That nothing had apparently been learned in the following two years was clearly shown when on May 15, 1964, two Vietnamese Ranger companies with an American officer walked into a VC ambush "baited" by a simultaneous attack against five small posts along Provincial Road 16 near Tan-Uyên, 25 miles north of Saigon. The two companies suffered over 100 casualties, including the American officer. Similar disasters on an even larger scale were to take place later.

about one hundred farm houses. Attacked at 2245, the soldiers withdrew into their fort while abandoning the village and its helpless population to the Viet-Minh. At noon of March 5, ARVN paratroops, dropped in a clearing around nearby Road 4, reached Bo-Tuc, whose assailants already had been strafed by AD-6's, but the Viet-Minh already had retreated into the shelter of the nearby forests.

Since the ARVN post had held—it had lost 18 dead and 12 wounded—and the enemy abandoned several weapons on the battlefield, the affair was hailed as a "success."* What was conveniently overlooked was that the soldiers had saved their own skins but had left the village to be completely burned down by the enemy! Psychologically, the enemy had scored the vital point that the ARVN could not defend the civilian population entrusted to it but would look to its own safety first. That point had been openly made in the Saigon press during an earlier Viet attack on the provincial seat of Phuoc Thanh (40 km north of Saigon) in which the defending Ranger unit took to the woods and left the enemy in control of the city long enough to execute "traitors" and capture important supplies.

In another fairly typical operation, reminiscent of the "Street Without Joy," South Vietnamese Civil Guard and Militia forces, supported by 105mm howitzers and patrol boats, cornered part of a regular Viet battalion on March 28, 1962. The South Vietnamese force of two battalions and four companies encircled the Communist force on Thanh Tan Island in the Mekong delta 35 miles south of Saigon (see map) on the evening of the previous day.

At 0400 of March 28, the southern wing of the encircling force established itself along the *rach* [river inlet] Cai-Cam, while another force crossed over from Ham Luong and landed at the northern tip of Thanh Tan. After an initial violent clash with the encircling force, the Viet-Minh unit at first attempted a breakthrough across the Cai-Cam opposite the village of Thanh-Ngai, which was stopped by friendly artillery. By 1100, the last remaining *Bao-An* [Civil Guard] and militia reserves from Truc-Giang

---

**Journal d' Extrême-Orient*, Saigon, March 7, 1962; and *Times*, March 16, 1962.

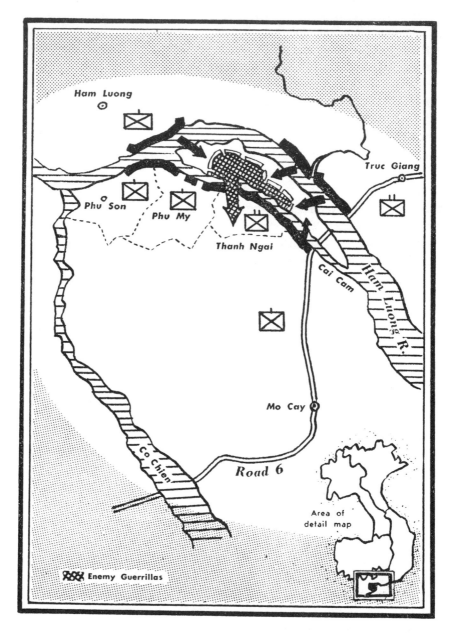

Escape from Thanh Tan Island, March 28, 1962.

were ferried across the Ham Luong river to the eastern shore of Thanh Tan, and the mop-up began in earnest.

Just as the South Vietnamese forces thought that they had completed the encirclement, the Viet-Minh once more concentrated its forces and fell upon the Civil Guards who had crossed over from Thanh-Ngai and who progressed through the open rice field without protection from their own artillery. In a matter of minutes, the line was broken through and the bulk of the enemy force escaped into Mo-Cay Island, leaving behind a total of only twenty dead and fourteen prisoners.

Almost exactly two years later, on April 9, 1964, the VC attacked the district seat of Mo-Cay (20,000 inhabitants) itself, again with true and tried methods: It first attacked an outpost 8 kilometers from town and held by 15 Civil Guards, who promptly clamored for help. An ARVN battalion was dispatched from Mo-Cay to its rescue and was promptly ambushed from three sides 5 kilometers from town. While the battalion was thus occupied, a VC battalion-size force attacked Mo-Cay itself. Its weakened garrison fortunately held on long enough to receive helicopter-borne reinforcements in the afternoon. The VC made a deliberate withdrawal since they had lost the benefit of surprise, after shooting down two helicopters and one escorting fixed-wing aircraft. The South Vietnamese lost 24 dead, 23 wounded and 13 missing. Communist losses were unknown.

In yet another form of tried and true guerrilla tactics, the Viet-Minh occupied the district headquarters town of Thanh Tri, 12 miles from the Soc Trang U.S. Marine helicopter base, on June 4, 1962, killing fifteen Civil Guards and three civilians, capturing fifteen militiamen; and taking with them a booty of two mortars, five machine guns, ten rifles, fifteen carbines, several miscellaneous weapons and four two-way radios, using a force of less than one hundred men.

First staging diversionary attacks against an outpost four miles from town, they succeeded in luring the bulk of the district's Civil Guard company to come to the rescue of the attacked outpost. As the *Bao-An* rushed away, the Viet-Minh methodically cut all approach roads and blocked the canals in the area by sinking sampans across them. The town was overrun so fast that its weakened garrison never knew what hit it. By the time the first Marine helicopters lumbered into sight at high noon, the enemy had vanished into the nearby swamps and forests—prisoners, wounded, booty, and all.

That particular gambit has in fact become the one habitually used against the Strategic Villages: in a given area, several of them are being simultaneously aroused by a few bursts of BAR fire, which promptly results in wild radio calls for help (an extensive program of equipping all the villages with $500 two-way radio sets has been underway since 1961), while the one village which was left alone all of a sudden is swamped by mortar fire and screaming hordes of enemy infantry. Indeed, while the defenses of the Strategic Villages and Hamlets, with their bristling bamboo pikes and earth bunkers, may look impressive to news photographers, their ability to withstand kerosene-laden "Molotov cocktails" is nil and the weaker among these villages have become a convenient place for the enemy to find a first-aid chest, some weapons, and—above all—a two-way radio set.

Capture of a sizable number of these radio sets has resulted in the establishment of veritable Communist antiaircraft defense radio networks around the American air bases in South Viet-Nam, thus depriving the aircraft of much of their ability to strike without warning. The American counterploy to this Communist gambit was the use, as of late July 1962, of "roving" helicopter-borne forces. Troop-laden helicopters would simply take off from their bases in groups and await the call of a spotter aircraft which would point out to them a target of opportunity upon which the "heliborne" force would swoop down. The method restored some effect of surprise to the helicopters but also makes them more vulnerable to enemy light antiaircraft weapons, whose gunners are becoming more efficient in aiming at moving aircraft. That was also the experience of the very large French heliborne forces used in Algeria; once the charm of the novelty had worn off on the Moslem guerrillas, they proved quite adept at shooting down the lumbering craft.

In fact, one of the U.S. Army's most experienced specialists in helicopter warfare, Brig. Gen. Carl I. Hutton (Retired), expressed the same view on the eventually diminishing returns of the helicopter combat tactics, on the basis of the French Algerian experience. The French, General Hutton says,

> were able to demonstrate statistically that it resulted in killing more guerrillas than any other system they had tried. Nevertheless it was bound to fail and I am afraid that the Viet-Nam effort may also fail . . .
>
> Because the helicopter is inherently so effective, these tactics do result in local successes. They fail strategically, however, because they leave the initiative to the guerrillas. They permit the guerrillas to choose the place and time of fighting and they allow entrapment situations.*

As the struggle in South Viet-Nam grew increasingly bitter during 1963 and 1964, VC operations grew in size and ferocity. While in September, 1963, an American general assigned to Viet-Nam referred to only "hard-core companies" in an official briefing (see Appendix III), open attacks against fixed ARVN positions by full VC battalions became commonplace by mid-1963, and the military situation worsened to an appreciable degree long before the Buddhist crisis erupted in May, 1963, or Diem was toppled from power. In effect, the highest weekly incident count reported by the Pentagon prior to January, 1964, was 1,021 incidents during *Têt* (lunar New Year) of February, 1963, i.e., four months before the Buddhist outbreaks. This point needs to be made, and made clearly before a new mythology becomes accredited which blames the military setbacks of 1963-64 *not* upon the military and civilian bunglers who are responsible for them, but on the Buddhist monks or the American press corps in Saigon.

The hard and brutal fact is that, for a variety of reasons which can be as coldly analyzed as the French defeats described earlier in this book, the strictly military aspect of the Vietnamese insurgency was being as rapidly lost in 1961-62 as its socio-political aspects were. It is the highly-respected chief of the Tokyo bureau of *The New York Times*, Robert Trumbull, who in his recently-published work *The Scrutable East*, makes a point which needed

---

*The New York Times, September 21, 1963. The creation of the roving "Eagle flight" tactics has attempted to remedy the situation, but with uncertain success and at the price of exposing the fragile craft to increasingly accurate ground fire.

saying much earlier and still might do some good even at this late date:

> We are told now that the war [in Viet-Nam] was being lost in 1961, but the Washington version at the time was quite different. The conclusion has to be that someone, somewhere along the line, was guilty of gross incompetence or of lying.*

Facing the Facts

This problem of having to live with and face up to unpleasant facts is probably one of the most difficult which threatens the peace of mind of the contemporary politician, military planner, or historical analyst. Of the three, the last at least has the advantage of being uninvolved in the process of everyday operational responsibility—with the result, of course, that the other two categories may well accuse him of "Monday-morning-quarterbacking." This does not relieve the serious-minded journalist and, above all, the historical analyst (who does not face the deadline pressure of the newsman), of the serious responsibility of recording the facts as they stand. This is particularly important in so embroiled a situation as South Viet-Nam since 1960, where the perspective for analysis-in-depth is, for obvious reasons, still lacking.

As will be seen in the forthcoming paragraphs, even a simple recital of the bare facts and of statements made in itself tells a deeply impressive story, whose lesson surely will not be lost to the attentive reader.

> *January 2, 1963:* At the village of Ap-Bac near My-Tho in the Mekong Delta, 200 VC soldiers hold their ground against 2,000 ARVN troops supported by helicopters, fixed-wing aircraft, and M-113 amphibious personnel carriers; shoot up 5 helicopters, kill 3 Americans, and break out.
> *January 30:* Admiral Harry D. Felt, Commander-in-Chief, Pacific, states in Washington that the "South Vietnamese should achieve victory in three years." Admiral Felt defines victory "as the situation wherein the South Vietnamese control 90 percent of the rural population." He added that Saigon then controlled 51 percent.
> *March 5:* "This is the key year, 1963," General Paul D. Harkins said in Saigon, in winding up a "mostly optimistic appraisal of the war's course" in South Viet-Nam, in which he affirmed that the "South Vietnamese armed forces have now attained the experience, training,

---

The Scrutable East. New York: David McKay, 1964, p, 249.

and necessary equipment required for victory." (*Washington Post*, March 6, 1963.)

May 8: Protesting Buddhists, angered by cancellation of Buddha's Birthday ceremonies, are fired at by ARVN armor at Hué. Eight are killed.

July 25: Boun Enau Special Forces training camp for mountain tribal guerrillas is overrun.

July 26: Rang-Rang airstrip inside "Zone D" is evacuated by ARVN.

August 14: A total of 21 regular VC battalions is now reportedly operating in the Mekong Delta. This is about twice the strength of the previous year and outnumbers the unit strength fielded by the two ARVN divisions stationed in the same area.

August 28: "There has been no evidence of any increase in the number of Viet Cong units in the [Mekong] delta even though we expected there would be because our strategy is to sweep them steadily southward and finally corner them . . . the delta area under our control is increasing, not spectacularly, but steadily." (Marguerite Higgins, quoting a senior MAC-V officer, in the *New York Herald Tribune* of that date.)

September 12: General Harkins states that one "can categorically say we're winning the war in the Mekong delta."

September 13: "Confidential reports from high American authorities in Saigon say that the war can be won in nine months. They say that the border with North Viet-Nam has been 95 percent closed and that the task of sealing the border with Cambodia is proceeding. The Viet-Cong guerrillas are being starved out." (Marquis Childs, in the *Washington Post*, of that date.)

September 22: The ARVN 9th Division moves into the Mekong Delta.

September 25: ". . . despite variations in the quality from province to province, there is no doubt that the gamble has paid off. This spring, therefore, this war was being won. It can still be won . . ." (Joseph Alsop, *Washington Post*, of that date.)

October 2: "Secretary McNamara and General Taylor reported their judgment that the major part of the United States military task [in Viet-Nam] can be completed by the end of 1965 . . ."

"They reported that by the end of this year, the U.S. program for training Vietnamese should have progressed to the point where 1,000 U.S. military personnel assigned to South Viet-Nam can be withdrawn . . ." (White House statement, of that date.)

October 4: Madame Ngo Dinh Nhu refuses to comment on rumors that her husband had negotiated with the Viet-Cong. (She was to admit such negotiations in statements made in February, 1964.)

October 19: Violent engagement in Chuong Thien province. The ARVN loses 43 dead, 100 wounded. There are 13 U.S. wounded and 14 aircraft hit by enemy fire.

November 1: "Victory, in the sense it would apply to this kind of war," is "just months away and the reduction of American advisers can begin any time now," says General Harkins.

Maj. Gen. C. J. Timmes, Chief of MAAG Viet-Nam, states that "our job here was to train an army for the Government of Viet-Nam. I feel we have completed that part. The Vietnamese armed forces are just as professional as you can get. . . . like the American soldier, they're loyal to their government." (*The Pacific Stars and Stripes* [U.S. Armed Forces in the Far East], of that date.)

November 2: After a rebellion begun on November 1, at 1 p.m., the Vietnamese armed forces, led by their military leaders, overthrow Ngo Dinh Diem. The latter and his brother Nhu are murdered at about 10 a.m. General Duong Van Minh becomes Chief of State; former vice-president Nguyên Ngoc Tho becomes prime minister.

November 24: 300 VC attack Hiep-Hoa Special Forces training camp 20 miles from Saigon, held by 200 Vietnamese and 12 Americans. After 40 minutes, 37 Vietnamese are dead, 4 Americans made prisoner; 300 weapons and 20,000 rounds of ammunition are lost.

December 1: American troops are being returned to the U.S. under October 2 plan.

December 17: VC blow up gasoline supplies at Camau airfield. (Nha-Trang airfield was infiltrated on September 23; 2 C-47's were blown up.)

December 23: A VC dump with 7 tons of ammunition falls into ARVN hands at Tan-Hiep.

January 17, 1964: A joint Vietnamese-American survey of the Strategic Hamlet program shows gross flaws, less than 20 percent of villages as viable. General Khanh was to say in April that VC controlled close to 7 million (about 57 percent) of South Viet-Nam's rural population. Such provinces as Kien-Hoa in the Mekong Delta were 70 percent VC-held. In Long-An 20 out of 219 hamlets were functioning.

January 17-19: Attack against VC's Thanh-Phu Island stronghold in Mekong Delta. Two helicopters with U.S. crews destroyed; one British colonel killed. VC battalion breaks out against encirclement force of 2,500 marines, paratroops and rangers, supported by 27 helicopters and landing craft.

January 27: Secretary McNamara testifies before the House Armed Services Committee:

"Viet-Cong activities were already increasing in September [1963] and continued to increase at an accelerated rate in October and November, particularly in the Delta area. And I must report that they have made considerable progress since the [November 1] coup."

January 30: General Nguyên Khanh overthrows the Duong Van Minh regime and becomes Vietnamese premier. He promises to maintain South Viet-Nam in the fight against Communism.

February 4: At Hau-My, near Cantho (Mekong Delta), a post is overrun. There are 32 ARVN casualties; among other weapons, two 81mm mortars are lost to the VC.

February 7: The ARVN post of Thoi-Lat is overrun. The rescue column is ambushed in the classical pattern: there are 32 dead, 20 wounded, 38 missing; 104 weapons and 3 radio sets lost. On the same day a VC attack against Ben-Can (Tayninh) causes 114 casualties.

February 18: Secretary McNamara testifies before Congress that the "bulk" of the U.S. forces in Viet-Nam can still be expected to leave by 1965.

February 27: VC Battalion 514 breaks out of an encirclement at Long-Dinh (Mekong Delta).

March 5: In a press conference at the Pentagon, Secretary McNamara states:

"We saw no reason, and the Government of South Viet-Nam saw no reason, why our military police units should remain in South Viet-Nam to do a job that the South Vietnamese had been trained to perform and were entirely competent to perform and, therefore, we withdrew them." (See entry below for May 5.)

March 17: President Johnson decides to send more personnel to Viet-Nam.

March 26: In a major policy speech, Secretary McNamara announces that an additional $50 million would be requested for Viet-Nam, and that the war there might not be finished "in the first thousand days of the Johnson administration."

April 9: The police training center and fort of Go-Den, 15 miles from Saigon, is overrun. Of the 98 trainees and instructors, 26 are dead, 34 wounded, and 37 missing. All their weapons are captured. The attacker is VC Battalion 361.

April 11: Severe attack on Mo-Cay.

April 12-20: The battle for Kien-Long (Chuong Thien province, west of Mekong). Kien-Long is overrun, the district chief and family murdered. For the first time in the Second Indochina War, the VC operates simultaneously with three battalions, holds its own against aircraft in broad daylight and makes its withdrawal in good order. VC casualties: 175 dead and 1 captured. ARVN casualties: 55 dead, 175 wounded, 17 missing. Overall Viet-Nam losses for the week: 200 dead, 660 wounded, and 140 missing for the ARVN; 1 dead, 26 wounded for the U.S. advisers.

April 25: VC Battalion 514 is defeated at Binh-Chanh (Mekong Delta).

April 27: VC regular strength is now estimated at 45 battalions.

April 28: 5,000 ARVN troops break into the Mang-Xim and Do-Xa VC strongholds in the Plateau area. Do-Xa was the headquarters of Brig. Gen. Nguyên Don, VC commander for Central Viet-Nam. He and his covering force break out, but supply dumps are captured, including

145 small arms, 9 submachineguns, 1 mortar, 132 lbs. of TNT. On the ARVN side, 4 helicopters and one AD-6 are shot down, 18 other helicopters hit.

May 2: Communist terrorists damage the escort carrier *USNS Card* with a limpet charge attached to its hull while it was moored in Saigon. The *Card* was raised eventually.

May 5: An American military police company is being returned to Viet-Nam in view of ARVN's apparent inability to maintain security of U.S. installations.

May 8: Charges are made in the U.S. that U.S. aircraft in Viet-Nam are inadequate.

May 14: 75 "Skyraiders" (A-1E) are to be delivered to Viet-Nam. The number is later raised to 100.

May 15: The U.S. Military Assistance Advisory Group, Viet-Nam (MAAG-VN), is absorbed by Military Assistance Command, Viet-Nam (MAC-V).

May 18: The White House requests an additional $125 million for economic and military aid to Viet-Nam.

May 19: The office of the U.S. Military Attaché to South Viet-Nam closes. MAC-V thus absorbs all U.S. military obligations in South Viet-Nam.

May 20: General Nguyên Khanh launches the *"Bac Tien"* (March to the North) movement.

June 1: Conference in Honolulu of senior American officials concerned with the Viet-Nam problem.

June 20: General Paul D. Harkins retires as Commanding General, MAC-V. He states that "we're gradually winning back control" and that 12 out of 43 Vietnamese provinces are "pacified." General William C. Westmoreland becomes the new commander, MAC-V. He states that he will not let the monsoon season slow down counterinsurgency operations.

June 21: Viet-Cong forces overrun Suoi-Da Special Forces camp, north of Saigon. Three Americans, 60 Vietnamese missing. Armament lost.

June 24: General Maxwell D. Taylor appointed as American ambassador to Viet-Nam.

June 27: A Viet-Cong battalion is mauled at Bau Cot, 60 miles NW of Saigon.

June 29: A New Zealand military engineer detachment under Lt. Col. William T. Foley arrives in South Viet-Nam.

June 30: A Special Forces "Strike Company" is wiped out by the VC in Darlac Province.

July 2: An ARVN supply convoy is wiped out on Road 19.

July 4: Plei Krong Special Forces camp is overrun.

July 6 Nam Dong Special Forces camp is attacked.

July 9: Plei Jrirang Special Forces camp is attacked.

July 12: A large ARVN relief force is lured into an ambush in Chuong-Thien Province: 111 casualties, 109 weapons lost.

July 20: General Khanh pledges to "march north" once more. This view is not endorsed by the U.S.

July 22: The air commodore of the VNAF announces that Vietnamese "combat units" operate inside North Viet-Nam.

July 26: "Events of the last few weeks indicate that the Viet-Cong guerrillas have lost the initiative in their war of subversion in South Viet-Nam and that a final decision may be expected in the next six to 12 months." (The *Los Angeles Times*).

July 28: An additional 5,000 U.S. troops will be sent to South Viet-Nam, raising total U.S. Forces there to 21,500. The official ARVN casualty rate rises to 950 per week (or close to 50,000 a year).

July 29: General Khanh asserts the right of South Viet-Nam to strike back at North Viet-Nam.

July 30-31: A South Vietnamese naval force strikes at the North Vietnamese radar and naval installations at Hon Mé and Hon Ngu Islands. Units of the U.S. 7th Fleet were not informed of the strike (*Washington Post*, August 8, 1964).

August 1: The VC overrun a post at Vinh-Loc, 4 miles from Saigon.

August 2: The U.S. Navy destroyer "Maddox," on patrol in the Gulf of Tonkin, is pursued by North Vietnamese PT-(patrol torpedo) Boats 30 miles off the North Vietnamese coast. The PT-Boats are driven off by gunfire and air attacks from the carrier "Ticonderoga."

August 3: President Lyndon B. Johnson orders U.S. naval forces to destroy attackers in any future incident.

August 4: Destroyers "Maddox" and "C. Turner Joy" report at 2152 hours (9:52 p.m.) that they are under "continuous torpedo attack." Two North Vietnamese PT-Boats reported sunk.

August 5: U.S. Navy aircraft attack five North Vietnamese ground targets supporting the PT-Boats in 64 sorties; report destruction of an oil storage depot and 25 PT-Boats.

August 7: Secretary of Defense Robert S. McNamara denies that U.S. ships in the Gulf of Tonkin were providing "cover" for South Vietnamese naval craft operating against North Vietnamese targets.

August 11: U.S. aerial reconnaissance shows small numbers of Chinese Communist jet aircraft on North Vietnamese airfields.

August 12: A major combined operation involving 96 helicopters, 1,000 heliborne troops and 4,000 ground troops in Binh Duong Province north of Saigon fails to make contact after VC gunfire drives heliborne troops off planned landing zone.

August 17-18: Battle of Hoa-My and Hiep-Hung. An ARVN battalion suffers severe losses in a classical relief force ambush. Heavy VC casualties are subsequently denied by MAC-V.

August 20: Another ARVN battalion is destroyed near Ben-Tré upon returning from a fruitless sweep. Four U.S. advisers are killed with the unit.

August 25: The military regime of General Khanh falls temporarily, is restored September 3.

September 7: "[General] Taylor, Here to See [President] Johnson, Sees Political Lull in Viet-Nam" *(Washington Star).*

September 13: Elements of the ARVN IVth Corps mutiny and seize Saigon. Mutiny collapses next day.

September 18: Another encounter between U.S. destroyers and NVN PT-Boats in the Tonkin Gulf.

September 20: Rhadé tribesmen from the Special Forces mutiny and demand autonomy for the Plateau area. Mutiny is quelled by U.S. advisers on September 28.

By mid-1964, the war in South Viet-Nam—though involving by and large smaller units on both sides than the French Indochina War did—reached a pitch of violence and bloodiness which largely equals that of the earlier hostilities. ARVN losses for 1963 alone ran to 21,000, and losses for the first seven months of 1964 were 13,120; exceeding known Communist losses for the first time. Civilian losses also run commensurably high, probably exceeding the quarter-million mark in 1964.

And thus, the Second Indochina War goes on—from action to counteraction; from new devices which fail (such as "defoliation" of forests and fields with chemicals) to older devices which work (small river craft and sea-going junk forces); from Vietnamese and French casualties in 1946-1954 to Vietnamese and American casualties as of 1961. In South Viet-Nam, the West is still battling an ideology with technology, and the successful end of that Revolutionary War is neither near nor is its outcome certain.

15

The Future of
Revolutionary War

M UCH has been written in the United States in recent months
about "guerrilla" and "counter-guerrilla," "insurgency"
and "counter-insurgency," "internal war" and "political
warfare," "limited war" and even "sub-limited war;" to be fought by
Rangers, Scouts, Raiders, "Jungle Jims," MATA's and even plain
conventional Special Forces. The very proliferation of names and
organizations—the above list is by no means comprehensive and
every military and civilian branch of the government is likely to
make its own contribution to it at any time—reminds one of the
usual habit of doctors to invent disease names that are the more
euphonious as there is less known about the disease.

Not one of the names shown in the previous paragraph comes
close, however, to combining the military *and* political aspects of
the wars that are being dealt within one single term. All but one
of them deal with the military aspect alone, while "political warfare" deals with its political aspects but gives no hint of its military
dimensions. "Psychological warfare" goes even one step further
backward in concentrating on method alone, without giving any
hint as to its purpose. So does the expression "brushfire war,"
which only hints at smallness and suddenness but also leaves the
key element of purpose in the shadow.

The only expression which, to my mind, combines both method and purpose in one comprehensive and uncomplicated term is "Revolutionary Warfare." First used in its present sense by Mao Tse-tung in 1936,* it was picked up by the French officers who were captured by the Viet-Minh after 1949 and who, upon their return, made it a part of France's military terminology. It the United States, the term "revolutionary war" never quite caught on; and the only American writer who ever made a book-long study of it did not even attempt to define the term.** In France also, the development of a Revolutionary Warfare (RW, henceforth) doctrine, met with a great deal of resistance. General de Gaulle, in his inimitable icy style, allegedly smothered a junior officer who attempted to speak to him about Revolutionary Warfare with the pithy remark: "I know of two types of warfare: mobile warfare and positional warfare. I have never heard of revolutionary warfare."

Yet, before the Algerian war had ended with the independence of that country on July 2, 1962, de Gaulle was to hear a great deal about RW and precisely from those officers who had become engrossed with it during the Indochina war.

It was in France also that the subject finally became one of serious academic study and was taken out of the hands of the improvisers and sloganeers. Thus, a professor at the French Army War College, Colonel Gabriel Bonnet, wrote in 1958 the first history of RW throughout the ages,† in which he gave it its basic definition. Revolutionary Warfare, says Colonel Bonnet, consists in the *application of irregular warfare methods to the propagation of an ideology or political system.* Other definitions along similar lines were given by other French officers who had to deal with the problem. Dealing both with purpose and method, Colonels Trinquier and Lacheroy asserted that revolutionary warfare aimed at

---

*Mao Tse-tung, *Strategic Problems of China's Revolutionary War*. First English edition. Peking 1954: Foreign Languages Press.

**Tanham, George K., *Communist Revolutionary Warfare: The Viet-Minh in Indochina*. New York 1961: Praeger.

†Cf. Bibliography.

... the overthrowing of the government established in a given country and its replacement by another regime . . . thanks to the active participation of the population, conquered physically and morally by simultaneously destructive and constructive processes, according to precisely-developed techniques. *

All this differs radically from the American emphasis on *guerrilla techniques* alone and the almost total discounting of the primacy of the political factor in revolutionary warfare operations. There is no better example of this almost fatal "blind spot" than the flat assertion made on June 28, 1961, by Dr. Walt W. Rostow, Chairman of the Department of State's Policy Planning Council, before a graduating class of the U. S. Army Special Warfare School at Fort Bragg to the effect that the need of a popular government or a popular cause in order to win a revolutionary war is, "at best," a "half-truth." The overwhelming weight of the evidence appears, unfortunately, to be on the other side. It can, in fact, be postulated that *NO* revolutionary war can be won without at least a measure of popular support!

Let no one be foolish enough to bring up here the example of the Soviet partisans fighting heroically against the Germans "for Stalin." First, Stalin was intelligent enough to dub the war a "Great Patriotic War" in defense of the "Russian Fatherland" (not Marxism-Leninism); and second, the Nazis were criminally stupid enough to treat the Russian people so badly that, in comparison, Stalin's tyranny at least had the slim advantage of being homegrown. In the past, many other dictatorial regimes have (often to their own surprise) found their people rise to "their" defense against a *foreign* invader. Here again, what the people were defending was their citizenship (not the oppressive regime) against alien domination. It is in a civil war—and this is what the Second Indochina War, both in Laos and Viet-Nam, essentially is—that the distinction between dictatorship and democracy, or, on a more elementary level, between the competing "qualities" of government, becomes vital.

---

*Col. Roger Trinquier, *op. cit.;* and Col. Lacheroy (ed.), in special issue on RW by *Revue Militaire d' Information*, Paris, February-March 1957, p. 8.

This, thus far, seems to have been clearly understood only too rarely as the American public (and the military specialist as well) is being drowned by what the well-known military expert Hanson W. Baldwin calls "the muddy verbosity and the pompous profundity that are beginning to mask the whole subject of counterinsurgency and guerrilla war."* Of late, too many amateur counter-insurgency cooks have had their hands at stirring the revolutionary warfare broth, concentrating on tactics that are not new and often erroneous; or on gadgets that are expensive to produce and usually more trouble than they are worth. But very few people seem to have the courage to point to the ultimate shortcomings of any wholly military solution to the guerrilla problem, or to stress the potential boomerang effect of phony reforms or *ersatz* ideologies.

As Peter Paret and John W. Shy correctly point out in their slim volume on *Guerrillas in the 1960's,*

> . . . The current assumption that the popular mind, especially in illiterate, unsophisticated societies, can be manipulated at will is false. Unlike machine-gun bolts, ideologies are not easily interchangeable...
> Thus the tasks of counterguerrilla warfare are as much political as military—or even more so; the two continually interact. As with the guerrillas themselves, political considerations may often have to override military considerations if permanent success is to be achieved.

The Viet-Minh realized this in full, and their best theoretician —so completely ignored in the United States that his name does not even figure in any of the RW bibliographies which have sprung up—Truong Chinh ["Long March"], the former secretary general of the Vietnamese Communist Party and present president of the North Vietnamese legislature, stated as early as 1947 in his book *La Résistance vaincra* [The Resistance Will Win]:

> I. *Politics and military action.* These two questions are closely related: "War is a continuation of politics." (Marx) . . . Military action is a measure by which politics are execu.ed . . .
> . . . [there are] those who have a tendency only to rely on military

---

New York Times, November 11, 1962.

action . . . They tend to believe that everything can be settled by armed force; they do not apply political mobilization, are unwilling to give explanations and to convince people; . . . fighting spiritedly, they neglect political work; they do not . . . act in such a way that the army and the people can wholeheartedly help one another . . .

Once more, the enemy has been kind enough to give us the recipe of his victory. He also has shown us that he has time and time again applied that very principle with signal success. No one can in all honesty blame General Vo Nguyên Giap and Truong Chinh for our own illiteracy in the field of Revolutionary Warfare or for our own doctrinaire blindness to military developments in North Viet-Nam, simply because they do not happen to be as spectacular as a new missile or they suffer from insufficient advertising.

Thus, in the absence of an encompassing philosophical reason to defend what we profess to believe in—there was a time when we believed in the "Four Freedoms" and found that belief a sufficiently encompassing reason to defeat Hitler—we must have recourse to technical gadgets such as helicopters and plant-killing chemicals in order to defeat Revolutionary Warfare forces which numerically are vastly inferior. This hard fact must be hammered in until it is constantly on the mind of those who have to contend with RW: Why is it that we must use top-notch elite forces, the cream of the crop of American, British, French, or Australian commando and special warfare schools; armed with the very best that advanced technology can provide; to defeat Viet-Minh, Algerians, or Malay "CT's" [Chinese Terrorists], almost none of whom can lay claim to similar expert training and only in the rarest of cases to equality in fire power?

The answer is very simple: It takes all the technical proficiency our system can provide to make up for the woeful lack of popular support and political savvy of most of the regimes that the West has thus far sought to prop up. The Americans who are now fighting in South Viet-Nam have come to appreciate this fact out of first-hand experience.

Speaking of the Communist guerrillas the South Vietnamese 7th Division had to face, its American adviser, Lieutenant Colonel Frank B. Clay—son of General Clay, the "Hero of Berlin"—

said: "They have the same spirit as the Crusaders and Saracen soldiers who established the medieval empires—all fired up for a cause."

And this explains why the difference between "guerrilla warfare" and "revolutionary warfare" is so important: just about anybody can start a "little war" (which is what the Spanish word *guerrilla* literally means), even a New York street gang. Almost anybody can raid somebody else's territory, even American territory, as Pancho Villa did in 1916 or the Nazi saboteurs in 1942. No dictator has ever been totally safe from an assassin's bullet. But all this has only rarely produced the kind of revolutionary ground swell which simply swept away the existing system of government.

Conversely, once such a revolutionary movement exists, whether fanned from the outside or created out of internal pressures alone, it is difficult to suppress with the help of military specialists alone—particularly foreign specialists. And those anti-insurrectional systems which eventually prevailed over the revolutionaries simply did so by accepting large parts of the program advocated by the latter: in Malaya, Britain granted the independence which the CT's said they stood for, and the succeeding Malay regime granted the socio-economic reform measures the Communists had made part of their program. In the Philippines, Magsaysay defeated the Huks not solely on the strength of new military tactics (there were none) but on that of his implemented social reforms which took the wind out of the Huks' propaganda sails. As his most intimate American adviser, Major General Edward G. Lansdale, was to say in 1962:

> . . . the Huks had analyzed the people's grievances and made the righting of these wrongs into their slogans. And the change came when Ramon Magsaysay became Defense Minister. He was from the people, loved and trusted them. He and the army set about making the constitution a living document for the people. As they did so, they and the people emerged on the same side of the fight. The Huks lost support and had to go on the defensive.*

---

*"Guerrilla Warfare," in *Newsweek*, February 12, 1962. In *Foreign Affairs* of October 1964, General Lansdale also made a strong plea opposing the use of heavy weapons against village targets in Viet-Nam.

That, in a nutshell, is what makes the difference between defeat and victory in Revolutionary War: the people and the army must "emerge on the same side of the fight." It had worked in the Philippines and Malaya. In South Viet-Nam, that essential condition did not yet exist as of early 1963.

And that is why it is so important to understand that guerrilla warfare is nothing but a tactical appendage of a far vaster political contest and that, no matter how expertly it is fought by competent and dedicated professionals, it cannot possibly make up for the absence of a political rationale. A dead Special Forces sergeant is not spontaneously replaced by his own social environment. A dead revolutionary usually is.

Active Sanctuary

Still, special geopolitical conditions may bring about a situation particularly favorable to the sustenance of a revolutionary war. Probably the most important such condition is the existence of what—for want of a better term—I call an *active sanctuary*.

An active sanctuary is a territory contiguous to a rebellious area which, though ostensibly not involved in the conflict, provides the rebel side with shelter, training facilities, equipment, and—if it can get away with it—troops.

The active sanctuary came into being as a result of the "Cold war," for the simple reason that the nations providing such services to a rebellion could always count upon one (or even both) of the two super-powers to protect them from the direct reprisals that would have been their fate at almost any other moment of history. Here, the examples abound; besides Korea and Indochina and their Red Chinese sanctuary, there is the the example of the Tunisian sanctuary for the Algerian rebels, in which various states and territories of Africa could openly proclaim on January 29, 1960 that they would set up volunteer forces based in Tunisia to help the rebels fight the French in neighboring Algeria, knowing full well that the French would probably not dare to invade tiny Tunisia. In the single case since World War II when two Western nations, Britain and France, attempted to rebel against the unwritten law of the sanctity of the harasser by landing in Egypt, they found both Russia and the United States in unison to bring them—not Egypt—to heel.

The Soviet Union fully recognized the importance of the active sanctuary problem when she notified Norway, Turkey, Pakistan and Japan after the U-2 "spy plane" affair that she intended to bombard with guided missiles any foreign bases from whence "aggressive acts" would be committed against her. The West has yet to find the intestinal fortitude to apply the same principle to Communist activities in the same field.

In brutal fact, the success or failure of *all* rebellions since World War II depended entirely on whether the active sanctuary was willing and able to perform its expected role. The long-forgotten Greek Communist rebellion held its own as long as Tito's Yugoslavia was on good terms with Stalin. Communist terrorism in Malaya began to wither only when Thailand finally decided to police its border more effectively and granted the Malayo-British forces the right of hot pursuit in a fairly deep zone along the Thai-Malayan border. Egypt's *fedayeen* ("Self-sacrificers") wreaked havoc in Israel's border settlements for eight years until Israel's 27th Armored Brigade made hash of their base areas in the Gaza Strip in 1956. They have not been heard from since.

The heroic youths who died in Berlin in June 1953 and in Budapest in November 1956 died uselessly and hopelessly because of the very fact that they lacked such a sanctuary. And they lacked such a sanctuary because until now the West has always shied away from using such tactics on its mighty opponent, or, worse yet, has been *cowed* by him into not using them.

Not that suitable targets are lacking on the other side; a small bit of help would have gone a long way in Tibet and other areas of Southwest China; some bazookas ("privately donated," of course) to the Hungarian rebels could have made the Russians look fairly silly in front of the United Nations since prolonged rebel resistance would probably have permitted presentation of the rebel case in front of that body. Support for the independence of the twenty-five million Moslems of Soviet Central Asia (colonized by the Russians far more brutally than Algeria ever was by the French) with suitable Kazakh, Kirghiz or Turkmen delegations to various "anti-colonial congresses," would pay off more handsomely than long tirades about "massive reprisal." As long as the problem of the active sanctuary is not solved politically as well as militarily, the West might as well settle down to a long losing streak of "brushfire wars."

Yet, guerrilla forces are not invincible. A guerrilla force's logistical requirements may be simpler than that of a large regular force, but it has some rock-bottom needs which must be filled through outside support, or it dies.* Conversely, the abundance of such logistical support to a regular force opposing guerrillas does not necessarily grant it a sure-fire chance of victory over the lightly-armed partisans. Neither do more sophisticated weapons automatically insure superiority. As one French officer put it aptly: *"Non-sophistication does not preclude fire power."* The Viet-Minh proved the veracity of this axiom time and again.

In Indochina, furthermore, the Communists could rely upon a long historical tradition of protracted conflicts with overwhelmingly strong adversaries. Viet-Nam fought with China for close to 1,500 years (of which she was occupied by the Chinese for 1,000 years), and even fought the feared Mongols, being one of the few nations to have defeated them on the field of battle, in 1278. Marshal Tran Hung Dao, then the leader of the Vietnamese forces and a sort of Far Eastern Clausewitz in his own right, defined his tactics in words which might well have been used by his Communist compatriot Giap seven centuries later:

> The enemy must fight his battles far from his home base for a long time . . . We must further weaken him by drawing him into protracted campaigns. Once his initial dash is broken, it will be easier to destroy him.

Speaking of the Indochina war, French Air Force General Chassin, one of the former commanders of the French Far Eastern Air Force and a long-time student of Mao's tactics, states in his work on French air operations in Indochina:

> In fact, one could ask the question whether—by depriving them of an air force and by allotting them miserly amounts of artillery, heavy weapons and ammunition—the masters of the Communist world did not want to force the (Viet-Minh) to discover and practice warfare methods which are capable of stalemating the most modern Western armaments short of mass destruction weapons.**

---

*The Cuban fiasco of April 1961 is ample proof of this.
***Aviation Indochine*, Paris 1953.

In this, the Soviets seem to have fully succeeded, and the senior Communist leaders, Ho Chi Minh himself and Prime Minister Pham Van Dong, both of whom I was able to interview during my stay in Hanoi in 1962, expressed a tranquil confidence in the ability of the guerrillas in South Viet-Nam to hold their own almost indefinitely, practicing the art of revolutionary war. They of course denied that North Viet-Nam was being used as an active sanctuary to support Liberation Front operations, but the special report presented by the Indian and Canadian members of the International Control Commission (ICC) for Viet-Nam on June 2, 1962, states that

> . . . there is evidence to show that the PAVN [People's Army of Viet-Nam] has allowed the Zone in the North to be used for inciting, encouraging and supporting hostile activities in the Zone in the South, aimed at the overthrow of the Administration in the South . . . in violation of Articles 19, 24 and 27 of the Agreement on the Cessation of Hostilities in Viet-Nam.

It has often been suggested (Colonel Trinquier, in his previously-cited book, is an ardent advocate of the method) that the best answer to a revolutionary war waged from an active sanctuary is the counter-infiltration of that sanctuary itself. There is beyond a doubt merit to the thought, and the fact that the Meos turned out to be the only reliable anti-Communist fighters in Laos seems to confirm the theory—even if it must be admitted in all fairness that the Meos were in fact much more interested in saving their opium trade rather than the Phoumi regime in Vientiane. Infiltrations by South Vietnamese intelligence groups into North Viet-Nam have been reported in the North Vietnamese press, and trials took place against such infiltrators. They have thus far been less than successful.

But here again, the element of real popular support is vital. The French were never able to infiltrate RW elements into Tunisia in order to disturb the Algerian Liberation Army build-up there; and the one lone attempt of the French Secret Army Organization to set up a *maquis* in a hill area outside of the French-populated urban zones of Oran and Algiers, failed miserably. On the contrary, Secret Army terrorism in those same urban zones where it could count upon the active and passive complicity of the French population, did succeed in establishing for a time virtual control over perhaps two million people in the face of both French government and Algerian Moslem opposition. The fact that the Algerian Liberation Movement finally negotiated with the French extremists showed not only the strength of the extremist RW organization but also the realism of the Algerian Moslems who, as RW fighters themselves, knew the fearsome capabilities of the process and felt that the concessions asked for were relatively cheap in the face of the frightful cost of a Congo-like civil war in the country. In that narrow sense, it can be said that the Secret Army had proved at least as effective as the Algerian nationalists in supporting certain political demands by military action. From the point of view of international morality, it can only be hoped that the process will not find too many adepts in other countries.

It is absolutely true that, as Dr. W. W. Rostow asserts, "a guerrilla war mounted from outside a . . . nation is a crude act of international vandalism," and that it is somewhat difficult to accept "the outcome of a guerrilla war, mounted from outside a nation, as tantamount to a free election." What Dr. Rostow omits to say is that it has *always* been the West who has been craven enough to accept the outcome of guerrilla wars as "tantamount to a free election" because of its refusal to deal forthrightly with the problem of the active sanctuary, no matter how brazen the latter has been. The Soviet bloc, on the other hand, has always been careful to adhere to Dr. Rostow's precept, as witnessed in East Berlin (1953), Budapest (1956), and Tibet (1961). But in any case, the operative clause of "outside support" does not hold; a revolutionary war may enjoy widespread popular support and *still* receive considerable outside aid; or, conversely, may be genuinely indigenous and thoroughly unpopular. If Dr. Rostow's distinction had existed in 1776, La Fayette's and Rochambeau's help to George Washington and his rebellious colonists would have been "an act of international vandalism" but the independence movement in the thirteen colonies was nonetheless genuine, even if France provided a trans-Atlantic "active sanctuary" for the Americans. Conversely, a Latin American or Middle Eastern military *putsch* is not a revolutionary movement, though it may be entirely concocted by a junta of rebellious officers with no alien connections.

"International vandalism" in the form of Revolutionary War is going to be with us for a long time to come. We might as well reconcile ourselves to its existence, quit inventing new names and slogans for it, and settle down to study its rules, so that we might be in a better position the next time when we have to face its grim realities.

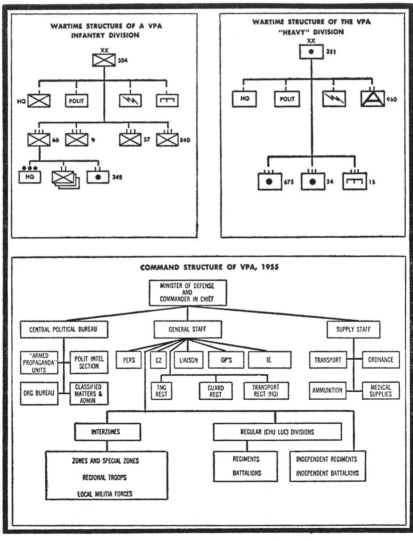

Vietnamese Communist Army Organization.

The Lesson

If nothing else, the ignominious defeat in Laos* and the bottomless pit the South Vietnamese insurgency has become for the time being, are ample proof that the Viet-Minh and its allies throughout the Indochinese peninsula have lost nothing of their fearsome ability to fight and win a prolonged jungle and swamp war against superior forces slow to throw away the traditional "book."

The rule which was painted in large letters in the halls of the French guerrilla warfare school in North Viet-Nam and which appeared every month on the first page of its monthly magazine: "Remember—the enemy is *not* fighting this war as per French Army regulations,"** will have to be remembered a great deal oftener than it has thus far. The fact that the word "French" will now have to be replaced by "American" makes the lesson only the more urgent for the United States.

If nothing else, the continuing insecurity in Laos and South Viet-Nam proves that in five years of uneasy peace, the Viet-Minh forces and their Laotian satellites had lost none of their ability to fight and win a jungle and swamp war against superior forces fighting such a war according to the traditional "book." Considering the less than startling results of such Western methods in nearly all areas of the world where they have come face to face with the new Revolutionary Warfare of the Communists, all branches of the armed forces of the United States and her allies should begin to study and teach the theory and practice of such warfare.

The Indochina war has shown that serious studies are almost totally lacking in such fields as modern river warfare and the

---

*Lest any reader take exception to the word "defeat" as applied to the Laos situation which obtained after the neutrality agreements of July 23, 1962, let it simply be remembered that the original American objective in Laos was to make it part of the Free World defense system in the Southeast Asian area, and that $400 million were spent trying to bring this about. Measured against intent and expenditure, what developed is a defeat, all double talk to the contrary notwithstanding.

**Before any interested reader starts swamping the French Army with requests for back copies of the guerrilla warfare magazine, let me warn him that it is unavailable for love or money. It was discontinued in the early 1950's and not even the Historical Services in Paris have a full set of it.

use of rivers as vital supply lines in countries where the road and rail net is destroyed or inadequate; that swamp-going units cannot be improvised with hit-and-miss equipment and their tactics developed at the last moment on a trial-and-error basis; that aerial reconnaissance and ground support must adopt an entirely new set of rules when confronted with enemy and friendly units dispersed under an unbroken canopy of high trees. In other words, *Revolutionary Warfare cannot be left to happy improvisation any more than can nuclear warfare.*

There is little else left to be said about the men who fought and died in that horrible mess, except to record what they achieved politically. Self-styled specialists and professional anti-colonialists assert today that the Viet-Minh Communists would never have won control over even North Viet-Nam, had the French granted "real independence" to the three Indochinese states in 1945. This is, of course, an extremely tempting theory. Its only trouble is that it omits one single hard fact: the Communist government of Ho Chi Minh was in full control of the country's administration as of VJ-day. Until the French returned to Hanoi in March 1946, it used its unhindered control to liquidate hundreds of Vietnamese anti-Communist nationalists likely to get in the way. For the French to grant independence to such a government would have, without the slightest doubt, resulted in a solidly Communist Vietnamese state at the latest by the time the Chinese Reds occupied the areas bordering on Viet-Nam in December 1949.

It is also likely that, within a few years thereafter, the weak kingdoms of Cambodia and Laos would have had to resume their historical rôle as buffers and satellites of their stronger Vietnamese neighbor, thus bringing about domination of the whole Indochinese peninsula by Communist forces.

Whether this was intended by the French or not, the Indochina war for a time bought freedom for about twenty-one million people out of thirty-eight million, and for about 223,000 square miles of land out of 285,000.

And this is perhaps as good an epitaph as any for the men who had to walk down the joyless and hopeless road that was the Indochina War until 1954; and for the Americans who now have to follow their footsteps.

Appendix I

GLOSSARY OF ABBREVIATIONS

Note: French abbreviations in most cases carry periods between the capital letters, while American abbreviations do not. For the sake of simplicity, periods have been omitted here in all cases.

ARVN (VN) Army of Viet-Nam.

BAR (US) Browning Automatic Rifle.

BM (Fr) *Bataillon de Marche,* or in some cases, *Bataillon Montagnard.*

BMC (Fr) *Bordel Mobile de Campagne.*

BMI (Fr) *Bataillon de Marche Indochinois.*

BV (Fr) *Bataillon de Volontaires,* Laotian Army static units.

CAT (US) Civil Air Transport, Taiwan-based American-owned private airline.

CIDG (VN) Civilian irregular defense groups.

CP (US) Command Post.

DNA (Fr) *Division Navale d'Assaut,* also referred to as *Dinassaut—* French tactical naval units for river warfare.

DZ (US) Drop Zone, term also used by French Army.

FOM (Fr) *France d'Outre-Mer,* Overseas French territories from 1945 to 1958. FOM food rations were tropical-type rations.

FUF (Fr) *Forces de l'Union Francaise,* (US) French Union Forces —collective term for French forces in Indochina, including native forces under French command.

GAP (Fr) *Groupement Aéroporté,* airborne regimental combat team.

GATAC (Fr) *Groupement Aérien Tactique,* French Air Force Tactical Group. Staff unit responsible for one of Indochina's five air commands: Cambodia, Laos, South, Central and North Viet-Nam.

GCMA (Fr) *Groupement de Commandos Mixtes Aéroportés* [The French word "Mixte," in military parlance, may stand for "Joint, Miscellaneous, Provisional, Composite," etc.], Composite Airborne Commando Group. Transformed in December 1953 into GMI.

383

GM	(Fr)	*Groupement Mobile*, mobile regimental combat team. Some armored groups existed, known as *Groupement Blindés* (GB).
GMI	(Fr)	*Groupement Mixte d'Intervention*, Composite Intervention Group. Administrative headquarters for French-native raider and guerrilla groups operating behind Communist lines.
GVN	(VN)	Government of Viet-Nam.

LCM, LCT, LST, LSSL, LVT   US Navy designations for landing vessels of various types.

MAAG	(US)	Military Assistance Advisory Group.
MAC-V	(US)	Military Assistance Command, Viet-Nam.
MLR	(US)	Main Line of Resistance.
NVN	(VN)	Navy of Viet-Nam.
PFAT	(Fr)	*Personnel Féminin de l'Armée de Terre*, Female personnel of the French Ground Forces, equivalent of the US WAC's.
PIM	(Fr)	*Prisonniers-Internés Militaires*, Military and civilian prisoners of the French forces.
PK	(Fr)	*Poste kilomètrique*, Military post designated by number of kilometers from a fixed point of reference, e.g., PK 22.
PW	(US)	Prisoner of War.
REI	(Fr)	*Régiment Etranger d'Infanterie*, Foreign Legion Infantry Regiment.
RW		Revolutionary Warfare.
RICM	(Fr)	*Régiment d'Infanterie Coloniale du Maroc.*
RVNAF	(VN)	Republic of Viet-Nam Armed Forces.
SKZ	(VN)	*Sung Khong Giat* [last word pronounced "Ziat"], Vietnamese Communist term for recoilless rifle.
TDKQ	(VN)	*Tieu-Doan Kinh-Quan*, Vietnamese Nationalist commando battalions.
VC	(VN)	Viet-Cong: Communist South Vietnamese forces.
VNAF	(VN)	Viet-Nam Air Force.
VPA	(US)	Viet-Nam People's Army, official designation of Vietnamese Communist forces.

Appendix II

COMPARISON BETWEEN FRENCH AND U. S. LOSSES

FRENCH AND AMERICAN LOSSES, INDOCHINA AND KOREA

	French Union Forces	(Indochina States)	Total Losses	U. S. Forces Korea
Dead or missing	75,867	18,714	94,581	29,166
Wounded	65,125	13,002	78,127	105,785
Total Casualties	140,992	31,716	172,708	134,951

FRENCH AND AMERICAN LOSSES (KILLED ONLY) SINCE 1914

Period	U.S.A.		France
1914-18	130,000		1,894,000
1939-45	325,464		580,000 [a]
1950-53	29,166	1946-54	75,867 [c]
1961-64	225 [b]	1954-62	18,800 [d]
Totals	484,855		2,568,667

a. See table on following page.
b. Laos and South Viet-Nam.
c. Does not include French losses in Korea.
d. Algeria.

385

FRENCH LOSSES DURING WORLD WAR II

Battle of France (1939-40)	92,000
Free France (1940-45)	58,000
French Underground	24,000
P. W.'s in Germany	43,000
Executed as hostages	30,000
Killed in concentration camps	200,000
Civilians killed by Allied bombing	66,000
Civilians killed by German and Allied ground operations .	67,000
	580,000
Alsatians drafted into German Army and killed in action .	38,000
French pro-Nazi collaborators killed by Underground ...	40,000
Grand total	658,000

Appendix III

REPORT ON VIET-NAM

[Note: The following report on the situation in Viet-Nam was presented to the annual meeting of the Association of the U.S. Army in Washington on October 23, 1963 (i.e., eight days before the overthrow of the Diem regime by the Vietnamese Army), by Brigadier General Frank A. Osmanski, J-4 of MAC-V at the time. The text is as introduced in the *Congressional Record* of November 6, 1963, with the exception of about twenty words referring to a short film. I have added footnotes where I felt that the text needed amplification or contained what, in my view, constitutes factual errors.—B.B.F.]

This report on Vietnam will be neither profound nor prophetic but the optimism it will reflect sincerely is genuinely that of General Harkins, whose greetings I am charged to bring to this conference.

General Collins has explained the strategic importance of the Republic of Vietnam.

I shall report on the military situation there, under four headings: "Terrain, Weather, and Enemy"; "Friendly Forces"; "Counter-Insurgency Strategy and Tactics"; and "Results to Date."

TERRAIN, WEATHER, AND ENEMY

The Republic of Vietnam comprises three terrain regions: the central highlands, the central lowlands, and the Mekong Delta. The highlands are virgin country with tropical rain and bamboo forests and a broad grassy plateau at their center; inhabited by mountain migratory tribesmen; with a climate conducive to tea, coffee, and a little rice. The lowlands are a generally dry coastal plain with sand dune growths; a sedentary agrarian people; and insufficient rice for lack of water. The delta has bountiful rice paddies, a coastline of mangrove swamps, a central plain of reeds, and a maze of canals; is peopled by scattered[1] rice-farmers and fishermen; and its heavy seasonal rainfall causes annual flooding. The nature of the counter-insurgency is vastly different in each of these regions.

The weather in the Republic of Vietnam is hot and humid, with two distinct seasons, wet and dry, which vary by region in response principally

---

[1] One could hardly call the heavily-populated Mekong Delta population "scattered." The Delta contains 50 percent of the total population of South Viet-Nam.

to two monsoons annually. Rainfall and sunshine are alternately intense, temperatures average 80° Fahrenheit, and there are about 10 typhoons a year and frequent high winds.

The enemy is the Vietcong, the VC, meaning Vietnamese Communist, for which cadres and arms caches were left behind[2] when Ho Chi Minh ostensibly led his followers north in 1954. VC forces are of three strata: hardcore, guerrillas, and porters. Hard-core companies[3] are outfitted in khaki twill with steel or bamboo helmets and carry modern United States or bloc-country arms. Guerrillas wear the standard dress of the Vietnamese peasant, black cotton or satin pajamas, and carry obsolescent French or self-manufactured weapons. Porters wear as little as a loincloth and are unarmed. VC nonexplosive weapons include caltrops, spike-traps, poisoned darts, and even enraged water buffaloes. In a sense their physical endurance, patience, and ingenuity are also VC weapons, for they have been known to live in dark tunnels for weeks, to remain underwater for long periods by breathing through hollow reeds, and to lie in ambush for as long as 48 hours. The VC wage their war from their ancestral strongholds in the U Minh Ha Forest, Plaine des Joncs, war zones C and D, and the Do Xa area; and from trackless provinces which they dominate, myriad small hidden bases, deep caves and long tunnels, and other safe havens. VC-initiated incidents are of four types; propaganda, terrorism, sabotage, and armed attacks. Their logistic support is from five sources: levy on the peasantry, import from other countries, capture from Government of Vietnam (GVN) forces, local purchase, and self-production.

FRIENDLY FORCES

The Republic of Vietnam Armed Forces (RVNAF) consist of a regular army, air force, and navy (including a marine corps) and three paramilitary forces: the civil guard, self-defense corps, and special forces. In addition there are the civilian irregular defense groups (CIDG), including hamlet militia, mountain scouts, border surveillance units, and trail watchers; and then such semiautonomous but gun-bearing patriotic organizations as the Republican Youth, Catholic Youth, and Women's Solidarity Movement. Assisting and advising these are the U.S. Military Assistance Command of about 14,000 and a small Australian Army Training Team.[4] Collaterally

---

[2] There are also infiltrators from the North, as shown in the ICC report quoted in chapter 15; 1964 U.S. estimates speak of about 3,000-4,000 infiltrators a year.

[3] There existed full-fledged hard-core VC *regiments* (about 2,500 men each) as early as May, 1961. To speak of "companies" only is to downgrade enemy strength or organizational ability. Furthermore, VC forces do not come in the three strata cited but in hard-core units, regional units, and local militia. There are in addition porter units and *Dich-Van* political-administrative units.

[4] There also existed in Viet-Nam since 1962 a British Military Advisory Mission under R. K. G. Thompson, particularly concerned with the Strategic Hamlets. A British colonel was killed flying in a U.S. helicopter in 1964. A small New Zealand force arrived later in 1964.

the civilian field agencies of the GVN ministries, the U.S. Operations Mission and the U.S. Information Service contribute to the civil aspects of the counterinsurgency. In gross numbers the military, paramilitary, and police forces of the counter-insurgency out-number the VC about 5 to 1.[5]

STRATEGY AND TACTICS

The strategy of the counter-insurgency is three-pronged: the strategic hamlet program, field operations, and psychological operations and civic action.

These three methods intermingle. In essence, the strategy is to win battles and to win people.

The strategic hamlet program is the Republic of Vietnam's national program to physically and ideologically separate the people from the VC and to win their support and confidence by providing them security, democratic government, and social and economic development. The program consists of (1) clear and hold operations, (2) province rehabilitation, and (3) portions of the CIDG program.

Clear and hold operations clear the VC from, and deny them, a specified area intended as the site of a strategic hamlet.

Province rehabilitation executes Province-prepared and nationally approved civil-military plans providing financial and supply support for the establishment of strategic hamlets.

Those portions of the CIDG program associated with the strategic hamlet program are designed to develop home-defense units for strategic hamlets.

Strategic hamlets, originally conceived as a defense against VC attack, now have become a means for effecting political, economic, and social progress. The Government of Vietnam has recognized this development and considers that the strategic hamlet is primarily the point of impact of a political and social revolution which will serve as a foundation for economic progress.

Field operations are directed variously at securing sites for strategic hamlets, destroying the VC logistic structure, killing or capturing VC's, or gaining or regaining control of Government of Vietnam territory. They are of three basic types:

(1) Clear and hold operations, executed in direct support of the strategic hamlet program, with the mission to clear an area of, and deny it to, the VC during the construction phase of a strategic hamlet.

(2) Fix and destroy operations, based on specific intelligence, with the mission to contact and destroy VC forces or installations; and

(3) Search and clear operations, with the mission to destroy or clear

---

[5] That proportion is correct. It has not substantially changed in four years of build-up on both sides. A 10-to-1 ratio is usually required to defeat an insurgent force. (Cf. the speech made by the Chairman of the State Department's Policy Planning Council before the Special Warfare School, Ft. Bragg, on June 28, 1961.)

VC from an area of suspected activity. In addition, reconnaissance, security, and search and rescue operations and ambushes are conducted.

Psychological operations and civic action each consist of two related programs. Psychological operations are aimed, first, at supporting the strategic hamlet program by rationalizing the need for rural citizens to move to, or at least to organize into, a more secure locality and by providing them the incentive toward self-development for political, social, and economic improvement. The other aspect of psychological operations is directed at the softer strata of the VC, to whom radio and loudspeaker broadcasts and airdropped or artillery-fired leaflets are aimed, primarily to induce them to avail themselves of chieu hoi, the "open arms" or "welcome home" amnesty program.

Civic action is aimed at improving the socio-economic welfare, political integration, and personal security of the citizenry through Federal [sic] support, education, and self-help. Its two basic programs are civic action proper and medical civic action. Civic action proper advises, trains, and assists hamlet inhabitants in setting up local government and trains both the hamlet administrators and citizenry in building and establishing physical facilities such as marketplaces, schools, dispensaries, information centers, chapels, pagodas, and water supply points and in formulating and administrating programs of self-help and scientific improvement in education, agriculture, stockraising, and disease control. Medical civic action trains local nurses and directly treats local people. To date almost 600,000 treatments have been given by medical civic action teams at an average cost of $1 each. Coordinated with the supporting U.S. military medical civic action program are the USOM medical projects as well as Medico, CARE and Hope.

The tactical principles and techniques which are proving successful in the counter-insurgency are essentially those, especially of small-unit tactics, which have been taught in U.S. service schools for years. The tactical problem remains to find, fix, and destroy the enemy. Of prime importance in the tactical operations of the counterinsurgency is the heliborne strike.

RESULTS

The military events of this past year in the Republic of Vietnam have contributed substantially both to the development of improved counter-insurgency techniques and toward ultimate victory for the Republic of Vietnam.[6]

In order that its training advice to the Republic of Vietnam AF may be effective and timely, MAAG-Vietnam publishes a series of "Lessons Learned," [7] which are the after-action distillate from both the extollable and deplorable experiences of actual combat. In the main they reiterate and reemphasize the timetested fundamentals taught in current U.S. military

---

[6] For an opposite view on developments of that period, see Secretary of Defense McNamara's statements January-March, 1964.

[7] This publication is unavailable to the public.

doctrine at our service schools. With content particularly derived from counterinsurgency experience in Republic of Vietnam are lessons learned about U.S. Army helicopter operations, M-113 operations, Vietcong ambushes, organization and employment of artillery, province rehabilitation operations, psy war and civic action, the limitations of paramilitary forces such as the CG, SDC, and hamlet militia, and guidelines to U.S. advisors with Allied forces.

MAAG-Vietnam also has published and keeps current a manual on the "Tactics and Techniques of Counter-Insurgency Operations," which is excellent.[†]

Under the Commander, U.S. Military Assistance Command Vietnam (Comusmacv) there is a Joint Operations Evaluation Group, Vietnam (JOEG-V), whose director has two functions: first, to represent the U.S. Advanced Research Projects Agency (ARPA) in the combined U.S.-RVN Combat Development and Test Center-Vietnam (CDTC-V); and, second, to evaluate from the U.S. joint viewpoint the results of tests conducted by CDTC-V and the two U.S. service test agencies in RVN: the U.S. Army Concept Team in Vietnam (ACTIV) and the U.S. Air Force Test Unit (AFTU). The more significant of their tests of equipment and tactics are the following:

In May of this year test was completed of a version of the C-123 aircraft, modified to shorten landings. This aircraft demonstrated improved capabilities to carry heavy loads into short fields.

Another test project completed by the Air Force, in which the Army was interested, was that of the U-10B helio-courier plane. Its report recommended that further tests and evaluation be conducted to select an aircraft better suited to perform the counter-insurgency mission.

The AR-15 Armalite rifle is still being tested in the Republic of Vietnam. Prospects for its wider use are favorable.

Motor convoys in RVN are frequently subjected to costly ambushes, in some of which U.S. advisors have been killed. These ambushes are extremely short in duration and characterized by murderous fire from VC automatic weapons. Countermeasures are being developed to enable troops to survive the withering fire of these ambushes and to launch a superior barrage of area fire in return. New techniques for moving and escorting convoys are being explored and new weapons systems are being developed.

Communications are often a problem in RVN because the terrain or atmospheric conditions tend to limit the range and performance of standard radio sets. A new family of radio antennas, which can be fabricated locally and used with the standard radio sets already issued, is being developed to overcome this problem.

The U.S. Air Force Test Unit is also in the process of testing a tactical

---

[†] This publication is unavailable to the public.

air positioning system (TAPS) and a tactical air control system (TACS), the results from which are still pending.

The ACTIV test program so far has been concerned with four general areas of operation: Army aircraft, armored personnel carriers, Army engineering know-how, and Army communications and electronics equipment.

In the field of Army aviation, there have been significant evaluations of the operation of armed helicopters, Mohawks, and Caribous. It has been found that these aircraft substantially enhance the operational capabilities of the ground forces and that they can survive in a counter-insurgency environment, that indeed the losses have been remarkably low when measured against sorties and hours flown or missions successfully accomplished.

Perhaps the most interesting test conducted to date has been that of the armed helicopter. ComUSMACV has on numerous occasions paid tribute to the outstanding accomplishments of Army and Marine helicopter units, both armed and transport, in support of the counterinsurgency.

The testing of the Mohawk in target acquisition continues in the southern part of Vietnam, following the completion of initial tests in a surveillance role in the north. The tests have demonstrated that a limited number of Mohawk aircraft, decentralized and placed under the control of the division, are compatible with ground operations and that this aircraft is well suited for the accomplishment of the full range of counterinsurgency reconnaissance missions, excepting those requiring large area coverage.

Caribous, as used in RVN for tactical transport of troops and materiel, have proved to be exceptionally versatile because of their capability to take off and land on short, unimproved runways without damaging them. At present the Caribous in the Republic of Vietnam are assigned to the southeast Asia airlift system but so far some of them have invariably been further allocated to the direct support of the U.S. senior corps advisors. These Caribous are proving to be effective in both the forward area transport and centralized airlift roles.

In the field of armored personnel carrier utilization, both M-113's and M-114's were tested. M-113's are used in Republic of Vietnam both for their intended purposes and in the role of tanks, which is feasible because the Vietcong lack armor and antitank weapons. However, numerous modifications have had to be made to transform the M-113 into a more suitable counterinsurgency fighting vehicle. To protect machine guns mounted on it, the M-113 has been modified with a gun shield and cupola. The M-113 has performed well, particularly in the flat rice paddies of the Mekong Delta, where its cross-country mobility was hampered only by the many canals. To overcome this obstacle, several techniques have been developed, among them brush fill, block and tackle, capstan and anchor, aluminum balk bridging, and push bars. On the other hand, the M-114, although present in Republic of Vietnam, has not been employed nearly so extensively as the M-113. As a first generation vehicle, several changes will be required before it will achieve full operational compatibility with the M-113, a third generation vehicle.

Among the most productive of ACTIV's evaluations has been the test of U.S. Army engineer teams, called engineer control and advisory detachments (ECAD's), which have been introduced to provide engineering assistance and direction for small construction projects of benefit to the rural population. Materials for the ECAD's projects were supplied by ACTIV, USOM, and the local government at minimal cost and labor was provided by local civilians. During the 120-day period of the test, 2 ECAD's supervised the construction of 96 projects ranging from simple pigsties to a 200-foot bridge. It has been concluded from their activities, as well as from the activities of the parallel U.S. Navy Seabee training advisory teams (STATS), that small, well-trained engineering teams can successfully implement civic action aspects of counter-insurgency operations.

In the area of communications and electronics, ACTIV has been engaged in confirming the suitability of current communications doctrine and developing new concepts, techniques, and hardware for use in counter-insurgency operations, such as a new heliborne command post utilizing the UH-1B helicopter equipped with additional radio equipment, a heliborne public address set for psychological operations, a new navigation system for Army helicopters, and the introduction of high frequency single-sideband radios into Army aircraft.

Now, a note about U.S. Army helicopter maintenance, which plagued all Army personnel for the first 6 months after the introduction of the CH-21's into the Republic of Vietnam.[8] The maintenance problems which have arisen have been concerned essentially with defective rotor blades, engines, and control cables in the CH-21's and, more recently, with drag-struts and magneto assembly arms in the CV-2B's and main mast bearings in the UH-1B's. These problems have all been solved so that, whereas a year ago the CH-21's were operating at about 50 percent average availability for about 25 hours average flying each per month, the present averages for all U.S. Army aircraft in the Republic of Vietnam are 70 percent and 50 hours, with twice the original numbers of aircraft now on hand.

About a year ago it was discerned that all programs necessary to the winning of the counter-insurgency would by spring 1963 be either completed or in process definitely toward satisfactory completion.[9] The MAAG advisory detachments had in the preceding year expanded manifold, had extended down to battalion level, and were being effective in advising, persuading, and assisting the RVNAF toward victory. The combat intelligence network was complete and tied together with adequate communications.

---

[8] There was no mention of trouble with various fixed-wing aircraft types, although personnel then in Viet-Nam was openly complaining about them even then, and earlier.

[9] That estimate is pretty typical of the highly overoptimistic view of counter-insurgency timetables then held in Saigon.

Additional U.S. aviation units and MAP-provided armored personnel carriers had enhanced the mobility of the RVNAF. Adequate sealift and airlift systems would soon be established and operating on a combined basis for the movements support of operations. The formal training of the RVNAF was well underway, oriented on such subjects as security, shooting, small unit tactics, and lessons learned from recent operations. The program to resettle the Montagnards and train them into hamlet militia, strike forces, trail watchers, and scout detachments was in full swing. U.S. Special Forces detachments had been introduced in significant numbers and Vietnamese Special Forces were being developed. The CIDG forces were being trained. Modern battle equipment was in country. The strategic hamlet program had been formalized and was beginning to be put on a planned basis with programed support. It all asked to be used in a concerted effort to beat the VC.

The national campaign plan was conceived to concert that effort. All ministries of the Government of Vietnam, branches of the Republic of Vietnam AF, and allied supporting agencies were cooperatively and co-ordinately to intensify their actions to help defeat the Vietcong. Significant progress can now be reported.

The intensity of operations mesaured in terms of the percentage of available forces on the average engaged in daily combat, has been rising steadily, to the point where it is now about 2½ times what it was a year ago.

In the last months Republic of Vietnam AF operations of battalion or larger size have at times doubled in number over what they had been when the NCP [10] was initiated and small-unit actions have increased by 50 percent. On the other hand, Vietcong-initiated actions have remained essentially unchanged in numbers. Republic of Vietnam-initiated operations outnumber Vietcong-initiated incidents about 10 to 1.

Secret bases of the Vietcong which had not been entered by other than the Vietcong in 14 years have since been reconnoitered, invaded, and fought through with signal success.[11]

Vietcong casualties have been considerably higher than those of the Republic of Vietnam AF, with an overall favorable ratio of about 4 to 1 for killed in action and 3 to 2 overall.[12]

Losses of weapons have averaged close to even on both sides.[13] While

[10] National Campaign Plan.
[11] This refers to the stab into "Zone D," which, by the time the report was made, already had been withdrawn.
[12] It takes a 10-to-1 "kill ratio" or better to make a dent into an insurgent force. In fact, VC forces have been increasing their strength steadily since 1961. For the first half of 1964, the loss ratio for the first time reached a dangerous 1-to-1 figure.
[13] Even by official reports (overoptimistic because ARVN units, whenever possible, attempt to under-report weapons losses), 1963 weapons losses ran at 2.5-to-1 in favor of the VC. And while ARVN weapon losses can indeed be replaced more readily from US stocks, the qualitative improvement which captured US automatic small arms makes to VC ordnance is noteworthy and worrisome.

admittedly, the weapons being lost to the Vietcong are better quality than the crude home-made ones being captured from them, the loss of any weapon by the Vietcong is more nearly disastrous to them than is the loss of even a fine weapon to the Republic of Vietnam AF because of the great disparity in supporting logistic systems.

Whereas the volume of Vietcong antiaircraft fire seems to be increasing and the quality of VC antiaircraft weapons may be improving, it is still limited principally to .30 caliber rifles and only a few machineguns.

The Vietcong are limited logistically for food and medicines in the highlands and for weapons everywhere; and they are gradually losing the support of the people as sources of funds, intelligence, and recruits.[14]

Defectors from the Vietcong are surrendering themselves at a rate twice what it was a year ago. On the other hand, the rate of Republic of Vietnam AF desertions has steadily decreased.[15] Moreover, villagers are now more readily disclosing information of the Vietcong to the Republic of Vietnam AF and the provincial administrators.

The Chieu Hoi [16] program is swelling with returnees who wish to forswear and repent their misadventures into communism.

While infiltration of Vietcong personnel and material is known to take place, the exact volume and trend are still imponderables. Nevertheless, large groups and quantities are not involved, the infiltration of cadres is dropping significantly, and smuggling is the biggest problem.[17]

The strategic hamlet program has progressed from 40 percent of hamlets completed and 45 percent of population included as of January 1, 1963, to a present position of about 75 percent completion both as to construction and population included, with another about 15 percent currently under construction. Although the program will soon be completed, much still remains to be done to bring some of the earlier hamlet construction and organization up to more recently established standards.[18]

Most significantly of all, the Government of Vietnam gained in the year between July 1962 and July 1963 some 6 percent in effective control of the rural population whereas the Vietcong during the same period lost 10

_____

[14] For an opposite view, see Secretary McNamara's statements of 1964. Officially it was conceded that the population effectively controlled by the VNG dropped from 51 per cent in January 1963 to 34 per cent in the spring of 1964.

[15] As of mid-1964, the opposite is true.

[16] "Open Arms" surrender program. A total of 12.067 persons surrendered during the first year of its operation, to February 18, 1964, including women. The low number of weapons returned (less than 1 to 100 returnees) seems to indicate that many returnees are non-hard-core personnel and often simply peasants caught in a VC-controlled area.

[17] This contradicts high-level official statements as to danger of North Vietnamese infiltration and urgent necessity to create effective border controls.

[18] Large-scale difficulties with the Hamlet program had been known to specialists for more than a year. They were openly admitted in December, 1963.

percent. (The apparent discrepancy of 4 percent is a gain in the neutral or undecided category, wherein the population have switched at least from being Vietcong-oriented to being neutral, in effect a further gain for the Government of Vietnam.)[19]

The Government of Vietnam gain in area control is less spectacular, only 1 percent in the past year; in fact, in a sense, it is overshadowed by a Vietcong statistical gain of 5 percent in the neutral or previously uncontrolled areas. In simple terms, this signifies that the Government of Vietnam has gained in the populated areas—that is, has won people—whereas the Vietcong have extended their control over relatively uninhabited areas—that is, has gained control of empty territory.[20]

The security of road movement is a cogent index to gains by the Government of Vietnam. Many roads which a year ago were death traps by ambush are now traveled regularly by unescorted or lightly escorted Republic of Vietnam AF military convoys.

The railroad, too, is now more fully used. Whereas until September 1962 all night traffic had been suspended for fear of attack from ambush, trains now run 24 hours every day.[21]

There are economic indicators also of Government of Vietnam gain in the past year; rice is again available for export and its price is stable.[22]

Finally, despite some recent distraction caused by the Buddhist and student demonstrations and the rumors of coups, the attitude of the Government of Vietnam and of its public servants is definitely in the vein to solve, in this order of priority, its dominant problems of communism, disunity, and underdevelopment.[23]

There have, of course, been costs for this progress, some of them serious. Whereas strategic hamlets are being built at an average cost of only about $5 per person accommodated, there are more than 1,000 Vietnamese casualties monthly; and U.S. casualties in personnel and aircraft have not been insignificant:

For the 21 months between January 1, 1962, and October 15, 1963, there were 63 U.S. killed, 348 U.S. wounded, and 5 U.S. missing; and

---

[19] See Note 14.

[20] The Mekong Delta is one of the most densely-inhabited areas of Viet-Nam, and one of the richest. The statement made was not supported by fact when it was made, nor was it correct by mid-1964.

[21] Heavily-escorted trains run on certain stretches, but at an incident rate of at least 3 a week. Civilian road traffic is largely subject to paying "taxes" levied by the VC.

[22] The rice exported in 1963 (300,000 tons as against 1.5 million tons in peacetime) had largely paid "taxes" to the VC. In addition the US imports close to $30 million of various foods to Viet-Nam which should normally be a food surplus area.

[23] The "distraction" of Buddhism was to end eight days later in the murder of Ngo Dinh Diem. Two previous attempts at murdering Diem also came from the Vietnamese armed forces.

for the 9 months between January 1963 and October 1963, while many U.S. aircraft were shot down or crashed, not all were lost.

Finally, what of the prospect for ultimate victory? In January 1963, Admiral Felt, CINCPAC, predicted here in Washington that the counterinsurgency in RVN would be won "within 3 years." General Harkins is on record as saying he considers that a "realistic target date" but "believes we can do even better." More recently, Secretary McNamara and General Taylor reported to President Kennedy "their judgment that the major part of the U.S. military task (in the republic of Vietnam) can be completed by the end of 1965." General Don, Acting Chief of the Joint General Staff of the Vietnamese Armed Forces, declared just 2 weeks ago that victory will be achieved in the war aganist the Vietcong in 1964. These stand as the authoritative predictions.[24]

The remaining battles will be fought most savagely in the delta, the traditional stronghold of the Vietcong,[25] where they are most numerous and deeply entrenched, where strategic hamlets are the most difficult to build and the program for building them got off to a late and sporadic start,[26] and where counterinsurgency operations are the most strenuous and the death throes of the Vietcong will be most violent. It is there that the toughest fighting and the fiercest Vietcong reactions are still in prospect before final victory will be won.

[24] For changed views on those predictions, see previous chaper.
[25] Significantly, the Mekong Delta had *never* been a "traditional" VC stronghold. "Zone D" is north of Saigon in the jungle, and Camau Peninsula is far beyond the Mekong. During the earlier Indochina War, the Buddhist sect forces and the Catholic militiamen of Ben-Trê held the Communist thrust in fairly effective check. It is a measure of the unawareness of the situation which prevailed in Saigon that the Mekong Delta was allowed to deteriorate to the extent it did.
[26] The Strategic Hamlet program's "Operation Delta" in fact started in the Mekong area.

Appendix IV

A MILITARY BIBLIOGRAPHY OF INDOCHINA

Note: This is not a general bibliography on Indochina but one which concentrates entirely on books or articles dealing with the military situation from 1945 to 1964. There exist several English-language bibliographies which can be consulted for more general readings.

1. Strategy and General Background

Bonnet, Gabriel (Col.), *Les guerres insurrectionnelles et révolutionnaires.* Paris: Payot, 1958. (New psychological warfare concepts based upon experience in Indochina.)

Catroux (Gen.), *Deux actes du drame indochinois.* Paris: Plon, 1959. (Evaluation of military tactics by former head of French Inquiry Commission.)

Dinfreville, Jacques (pseud.), *L'opération Indochine.* Paris: Editions Inter-Nationales, 1953. (View on overall strategy by senior officer.)

Lancaster, Donald, *The Emancipation of Indochina.* New York: Oxford University Press, 1961. (Best English-language book on Indochina, 1940-1955.)

Laniel, Joseph, *Le drame indochinois.* Paris: Plon, 1957. (Reply to General Navarre's book by French Premier at time of battle of Dien Bien Phu.)

Marchand, Jean (Gen.) *L'Indochine en guerre.* Paris. Pouzet et Cie, 1955. (Most comprehensive military history of Indochina from 1870 to 1954.)

Navarre, Henri (Gen.), *Agonie de l'Indochine.* Paris: Plon, 1956. (Book by the last wartime French commander-in-chief, showing decisions which led to defeat.)

Paret, Peter, and John W. Shy, *Guerrillas in the 1960's.* New York: Praeger, 1962. (Brief but good statement of guerrilla theories.)

Perrault, Gilles, *Les parachutistes,* Paris: Editions du Seuil, 1961. (Study on the socio-psychological aspects of the use of elite forces.)

Prosser, Lamar McFadden (Maj.), "The Bloody Lessons of Indochina," *The Army Combat Forces Journal.* Washington, June 1955.

Trinquier, Roger (Col.), *Modern Warfare: A French View of Counter-insurgency.* New York: Praeger, 1964. ("Modern War," to the author, means "Revolutionary War.")

2. Land Warfare

Ainley, Henry, *In order to die.* London: Burke, 1955. (Combat experiences of an Englishman serving with the Foreign Legion in Cambodia.)

Baldwin, Hanson W., "A Hell of a Place to Have to Fight in." New York: *Life*, March 31, 1961. (Evaluation of terrain and battle conditions in Indochina.)

Bauer, Hans E., *Verkaufte Jahre.* W. Germany: C. Bertelsmann Verlag, 1957. (Combat experiences of a German serving with the Foreign Legion in Tonking and North Africa.)

Boyer de la Tour (Gen.) Pierre, *De l'Indochine à l'Algérie—Martyre de l'Armée Française.* Paris: Les Presses du Mail, 1962. (Memoirs of former French commander-in-chief, South Indochina; contains complete reprint of French counter-insurgency regulations applied in South Viet-Nam.)

Dejean, Maurice, "The Meaning of Dien Bien Phu," *United States Naval Institute Proceedings.* Annapolis, July 1954. (Views on military situation in Indochina after Dien Bien Phu, by the then French High Commissioner to Indochina.)

Durdin, Tillman, "Life and Death on Hill 135," *The New York Times Sunday Magazine.* February 28, 1954.

d'Excideuil, Henry, *Rizières sanglantes.* Paris: Peyronnet, 1954. (Notes in the form of a novel of a captain commanding native commando groups.)

Ely, Paul (Gen.). *L'Indochine dans la tourmente.* Paris: Plon, 1964. (Memoirs of the last French commander-in-chief in Indochina, particularly valuable on America's role in the battle of Dien Bien Phu.)

Fall, Bernard B., "The Navarre Plan," *Military Review.* Fort Leavenworth, December 1956.

Graham, Andrew (Lt. Col.), *Interval in Indochina.* London: St. Martin's Press, 1956. (Notes by former British military attaché.)

Grauwin, Paul (Maj.), *Seulement médecin.* Paris: France-Empire, 1956. (Notes of French medical officer stationed in Indochina for more than ten years.)

Indochine—Sud-Est Asiatique. Monthly magazine, Saigon 1950-1954. (One of the best single sources on various types of combat operations.)

Jeandel Paul (Rev.), *Soutane noire—Béret rouge.* Paris: Editions de la Pensée Moderne, 1957. (Experiences of a chaplain in a paratroop battalion captured by the enemy.)

de Pirey, Philippe, *Opération Gâchis.* Paris: La Table Ronde, 1954. (A soldier tells about the "mess" *(gâchis)* and "snafus" attending the Indochina war.)

Larteguy, Jean. *The Centurions.* New York: 1962. (Novelized but accurate account of psychological impact of Indochina war on French Army.)

Rénald, Jean, *L'enfer de Dien Bien Phu*. Paris: Flammarion, 1954. (A hasty but not too inaccurate report on North Viet-Nam during the last battles by a reporter who was on the spot.)

Riessen, René, *Le silence du ciel*. Paris: Editions de la Pensée Moderne, 1956. (Paratroop commando operations as seen by a junior non-commissioned officer.)

Roy, Jules (Col.), *La bataille dans la rizière*. Paris: Gallimard, 1953. (Battle impressions of a senior air force officer who was in Indochina as an observer and who was also familiar with the war in Korea.)

——————, *La bataille de Dien Bien Phu*. Paris: Julliard, 1963. (Account of the battle of Dien Bien Phu based on interviews with some of its participants but without access to the documentation dealing with the battle.)

Tauriac, Michel, *Le Trou*. Paris: La Table Ronde, 1955. (Novel about armored car platoon in South Viet-Nam.)

3. Revolutionary Warfare

Black, Edwin F. (Col.), "The Problem of Counter-Insurgency." *U. S. Naval Proceedings*, October 1962.

Cross, James Eliot, *Conflict in the Shadows: The Nature and Politics of Guerrilla War*. New York: Doubleday & Co., 1963. (Excellent and straightforward, "let-the-chips-fall-where-they-may" analysis of RW problems.)

Fall, Bernard B., *Communist Subversion in the SEATO Area*. Bangkok: Southeast Asia Treaty Organization, 1960. (Analysis of Communist operations in Malaya, Thailand, Laos, and South Viet-Nam in 1959-60.) Not publicly available.

——————, *The Two Viet-Nams: A Political and Military History* (Revised ed.) New York: Praeger, 1964. (Deals in part with "Insurgency: Facts and Myths.")

Galula, David (Maj.), *Counter-insurgency Warfare: Theory and Practice*. New York: Praeger, 1964. (The "how-to" book in the field—and the best of them all.)

Georges, Marcel, *Mon ami Sinh*. Paris: Editions France-Empire, 1963. (Account of the leader of a GCMA force infiltrated in a Communist rear area. He eventually lost a hand and a leg when he fell on a booby-trap laid on his path.)

Favre, Claude-Pierre (Lt.), *La loi des partisans*. Paris: France-Empire, 1964. (Interesting and brief account of French officer's attempt at "converting" a Viet-Minh political officer. The attempts fails.)

Lacheroy (Col.), ed., "La guerre révolutionnaire," special issue of the *Revue Militaire d'Information*, Paris: March-April, 1957. (A key study of the whole revolutionary problem.)

Leroy, Jean (Col.), *Un homme dans la rizière*. Paris: Editions de Paris, 1955. (Experiences of a Eurasian who, through his intimate knowledge of the area, suceeded in winning over a whole province to the anti-Communist side.)

Marchand, Jean (Gen.), *Dans la jungle "Moi."* Paris: Peyronnet, 1951. (Experiences by the former commanding general of the most inaccessible jungle areas of Indochina.)

Riessen, René, *Jungle Mission*. New York: Crowell, 1957. (The best book written about jungle warfare in Indochina as fought by the French long-range penetration groups. Covers the same area as Marchand's book, but six years later and as seen by the small unit leader on the spot.)

Rolland, Pierre, *Contre-Guérilla*. Paris: Louvois, 1956. (A French captain carries out some sucessful anti-guerrilla operations in Cambodia, devising his own methods as he goes along.)

Tregaskis, Richard, *Viet-Nam Diary*. New York: Holt, Rinehart, Winston, 1963. (Journalist's account of U.S. participation in South Viet-Nam; overoptimistic and overdrawn.)

Truong, Chinh, *Primer for Revolt: The Communist Takeover in Viet-Nam*. New York: Praeger, 1963. (By far the best Communist Vietnamese study on Viet-Nam's own revolutionary war problem.)

4. Aerial Warfare

André, Valérie (Capt.), *Ici, ventilateur!* Paris: Calmann-Levy, 1954. (A woman M.D. helicopter pilot tells of her experiences in combat rescue work in Indochina.)

Bourdens, Henri, *Camionneur des nuées*. Paris: France-Empire, 1957. (An extremely lucid account of the importance of civilian pilots in logistical support work by one of the best pilots involved in such operations.)

Chassin, L. M. (Gen.), *Aviation Indochine*. Paris: Amiot-Dumont, 1954. (A former commander-in-chief of the French Far Eastern Air Force Command gives a highly readable account of air operations, their possibilities and limitations.)

Friang, Brigitte. *Les Fleurs du Ciel*. Paris: Laffont, 1955. (Recital of airborne operations by girl reporter.)

5. Naval Warfare

Brossard, (Cdr.) M.de, *Dinassaut*. Paris: Editions France-Empire, 1952. (Excellent account of northern river operations by former commander of 1st Naval Assault Division. Out of print.)

Julien-Binard, Louis (Cdr.), "Souvenirs de Nam-Dinh, Mars 1954," *La Revue Maritime*. Paris, December 1956. (Well-documented river operation by the commander of *Dinassaut* No. 3.)

Kilian, Robert, *Fusiliers-Marins d'Indochine*. Paris 1948. (Early account of some Marine-type landing operations.)

Mauclére, Jean, *Marins dans les arroyos*. Paris: Peyronnet, 1951. (Very vivid account of small-vessel operations on South Vietnamese rivers.)

Mordal, Jacques, *Marine Indochine*. Paris: Amiot-Dumont, 1953. (Good account of French naval operations in the Indochina theater. Shows belated emphasis on river operations in support of land movements.)

6. The Enemy

(*) denotes a Communist source.

Anonymous, *Les premiers jours de notre combat*. Hanoi (Communist North Viet-Nam): Foreign Languages Publishing House, 1958. (Short stories by members of Communist forces on their experiences during the Indochina war. Some are very detailed and revealing.) (*)

Black, Edwin F. (Col.), "Master Plan for Conquest in Viet-Nam," *Military Review*, June 1963. (Good and concise statement on Communist overall strategy in Viet-Nam.)

Burchett, Wilfred, *The Furtive War: The United States in Viet-Nam and Laos*. New York: International Publishers: 1963. (The insurgency in South Viet-Nam, as seen by the other side. The author, an Australian, was inside South Viet-Nam with VC forces. See also his articles published in the Spring of 1964 in the *National Guardian*.) (*)

Courtade, Pierre, *La Rivière Noire*. Paris: Les Editeurs Français Réunis, 1953. (A novelized account, based on Communist sources, of the battle for the Black River, by a French Communist.) (*)

Department of State, *A Threat to the Peace: North Viet-Nam's Effort to Conquer South Viet-Nam* (2 vols.), Washington: Government Printing Office, 1961. (Documents on current North Vietnamese subversion, including PW interrogation reports.)

Deuxième Bureau de l'Etat-Major des F.T.N.V., *Règlement d'infanterie viet-minh: Le bataillon et la compagnie d'infanterie dans l'attaque d'une position fortifiée*. (Book, translated by French Intelligence, of Viet-Minh regulations concerning the attack of French fortified positions. Unclassified.)

Fall, Bernard B., *The Viet-Minh Regime*. New York: Institute of Pacific Relations, 1956. (Contains several chapters on Communist guerrilla warfare and logistics.)

——————, "Indochina—The Last Year of the War: Communist Organization and Tactics," *Military Review*. Fort Leavenworth, October 1956.

——————, *Le Viet-Minh—1945-1960*. Paris: A. Colin, 1960. (Contains updated chapters on Viet-Minh forces, their organization and logistics.)

Goeldhieux, Claude, *Quinze mois prisonnier chez les Viets*. Paris: Julliard, 1953. (Very lucid account by ex-prisoner of Viet-Minh PW treatment, brain-washing, etc.)

Grauwin, Paul, *Doctor at Dien Bien Phu*. New York: John Day, 1955. (Experiences of the chief surgeon of the fortress during the siege and while a Communist prisoner.)

Halle, Günter, *Légion Etrangère*. East Berlin: Verlag Volk und Welt, 1952. (Very detailed account by German Foreign Legionnaire who joined Communists after capture. Typical of at least a half-dozen other such books by German ex-PW's.) (*)

Karnow, Stanley, "This is Our Enemy." *Saturday Evening Post*, August 8, 1964. (Good account of VC structure and operations.)

Ngo Van Chieu, *Journal d'un combattant Viet-Minh*. Paris: Editions du Seuil, 1955. (Combat operations from 1946 to 1951 as seen by Communist officer.) (*)

Nguyên Kien, *Le Sud-Vietnam depuis Dien Bien Phu*. Paris: Maspero, 1963. (Communist Vietnamese view of South Viet-Nam.) (*)

Nguyên Van Thong, *et al*, *Return to Dien Bien Phu and other stories*, Hanoi: Foreign Languages Publishing House, 1961. (Short stories by VPA soldiers about their experiences during the first Indochina war.) (*)

Pagniez, Yvonne, *Le Viet-Minh et la guerre psychologique*. Paris: La Colombe, 1955. (Brief account of Viet-Minh infiltration techniques by a Swiss journalist.)

Tanham, George K., *Communist Revolutionary Warfare: The Viet-Minh in Indochina*, New York: Praeger, Inc., 1961. (Uneven study of Viet-Minh revolutionary warfare.)

Vo Nguyên Giap (Gen.), *L'Armée Populaire de Libération du Viet-Nam*. North Viet-Nam: Foreign Languages Publishing House, 1952. (General report by Communist commander-in-chief.) (*)

—————————, *Dien Bien Phu*. Hanoi: Foreign Languages Publishing House, 1959. (Excellent brief acount of the battle of Dien Bien Phu by the Communist commander-in-chief. Only English-language account of the enemy side of the operation.)

—————————, *People's War, People's Army*, New York: Praeger, 1962. (Much overrated compendium of articles, including Dien Bien Phu brochure. Far less useful than Truong Chinh.) (*)

INDEX

Indochina and Viet-Nam are omitted or incomplete because they recur throughout the book. (Note. Geographic names are italicized.)